# The Commonwealth, South Africa and Apartheid

This book explores the role of the modern Commonwealth in the international campaign against *apartheid* in South Africa. Spanning the period of South Africa's *apartheid* state, from its foundation in 1948 until its ending in April 1994, the author demonstrates that, after the 1960 Sharpeville massacre and South Africa's subsequent exclusion from the Commonwealth, the organisation was able to become both "pathfinder and interlocutor" on the road to South Africa's freedom. As well as South Africa's ejection from the Commonwealth, *apartheid's* increasing isolation was sustained by the Commonwealth's pioneering work in boycotting *apartheid* sport, as well as campaigning to stop arms sales. It also played an important role in internationalising economic and financial sanctions, credited by some as the final nail in *apartheid's* coffin, and was able to make an important and distinctive contribution to the transition to democracy. At the same time, critical debates within the Commonwealth about racial and political equality transformed the association from a docile, post-imperial organisation, led by the UK and in its own interests, to a modern, multiracial 'North-South' forum for reconciling global difference and overcoming the legacies of colonialism. This comprehensive and authoritative account of the Commonwealth's engagement with *apartheid* South Africa is intended for all those who study and research the modern Commonwealth, its structure and influence, and for those with a general interest in contemporary post-war history.

**Stuart Mole** was for sixteen years a senior officer of the Commonwealth Secretariat as the organisation's campaign reached its climax. He was the Special Assistant to Shridath 'Sonny' Ramphal (the second Commonwealth Secretary-General) and Director and Head of the Office of Chief Emeka Anyaoku (the third Secretary-General). He visited South Africa and the neighbouring states many times as part of the Commonwealth's campaign. He has just completed seven years of doctoral research into the subject area, culminating in the award, in December 2020, of a History PhD from the University of Exeter. His research, which in some respects has changed his own perceptions, has involved consulting hitherto unseen or neglected archives in the UK and South Africa.

# The Commonwealth, South Africa and Apartheid
Race, Conflict and Reconciliation

**Stuart Mole**

LONDON AND NEW YORK

First published 2023
by Routledge
4 Park Square, Milton Park, Abingdon, Oxon OX14 4RN

and by Routledge
605 Third Avenue, New York, NY 10158

*Routledge is an imprint of the Taylor & Francis Group, an informa business*

© 2023 Stuart Mole

The right of Stuart Mole to be identified as author of this work has been asserted in accordance with sections 77 and 78 of the Copyright, Designs and Patents Act 1988.

All rights reserved. No part of this book may be reprinted or reproduced or utilised in any form or by any electronic, mechanical, or other means, now known or hereafter invented, including photocopying and recording, or in any information storage or retrieval system, without permission in writing from the publishers.

*Trademark notice*: Product or corporate names may be trademarks or registered trademarks, and are used only for identification and explanation without intent to infringe.

*British Library Cataloguing-in-Publication Data*
A catalogue record for this book is available from the British Library

ISBN: 978-1-032-07746-8 (hbk)
ISBN: 978-1-032-07747-5 (pbk)
ISBN: 978-1-003-20861-7 (ebk)

DOI: 10.4324/9781003208617

Typeset in Times New Roman
by Apex CoVantage, LLC

# Contents

|  |  |
|---|---|
| *List of Figures* | *viii* |
| *Notes and Abbreviations* | *x* |
| *Acknowledgements* | *xiii* |
| *Prologue* | *xiv* |

**1  Introduction – Whose History?**  1

  *1 Examining* Apartheid *and the Commonwealth 1*
  *2 Evidence and Archives 4*
  *3 The Commonwealth 10*
  *4* Apartheid *and South Africa 12*

**2  The Decline of the 'Imperial' Commonwealth**  18

  *1 Introduction 18*
  *2 The Post-war Commonwealth 19*
  *3 The 1949 London Agreement 24*
  *4 Conclusion 27*

**3  Afrikaner Nationalism and the Rise of *Apartheid***  31

  *1 Introduction 31*
  *2 Smuts and the United Nations 31*
  *3 The Royal Tour and the 1948 Elections 33*
  *4 Smuts, Segregation and* Apartheid *36*
  *5 Resisting* Apartheid *39*
  *6 Britain, South Africa and a Changing Commonwealth 42*
  *7 Conclusion 43*

**4  Sharpeville and South Africa's Commonwealth Exit**  48

  *1 Introduction 48*
  *2 Sharpeville, the Referendum and the Republic 51*

*3 South Africa's Commonwealth Exit: The Aftermath 60*
*4 Conclusion 65*

**5 The Rhodesian Rebellion, Arms to South Africa and the 'New' Commonwealth**   72

*1 Creating a New Commonwealth 72*
*2 The UK Turns to Europe 75*
*3 The Commonwealth Secretariat 77*
*4 The Rhodesian Rebellion 80*
*5 Arms to South Africa 85*

**6 Boycotting *Apartheid* in Sport**   94

*1 Introduction 94*
*2 South Africa, Sport and Race 95*
*3 The Commonwealth,* Apartheid *Sport and the Gleneagles Agreement 99*
*4 Conclusion 106*

**7 Implementing Gleneagles and Problems of Implementation: from New Zealand to Moscow**   112

*1 Introduction 112*
*2 Challenges to Gleneagles 112*
*3 Conclusion 126*

**8 Zimbabwe's Birth – Thatcher's Triumph?**   132

*1 Introduction 132*
*2 The Lusaka CHOGM 1979 133*
*3 The Lancaster House Agreement 138*
*4 Zimbabwe's Birth 141*
*5 The Fifth Brigade, Matabeleland and the* Gukurahundi *143*
*6 Conclusion 145*

**9 Mission to South Africa – Negotiating with *Apartheid***   150

*1 Introduction 150*
*2 After Zimbabwe: The Commonwealth, the UK and Southern Africa 153*
*3 The 1985 Nassau Summit: Sanctions and a Divided Commonwealth 157*
*4 The Negotiation Initiative – The Eminent Persons Group Is Born 158*

    5 *Deploying Diversity and Securing Access 161*
    6 *Mission to South Africa 164*
    7 *Mandela and Dialogue: The "Possible Negotiating Concept" 165*
    8 *The Breakdown: The EPG Leaves 171*
    9 *The EPG and South Africa's Negotiated Solution 172*
  10 *Conclusion 173*

**10 The Sanctions Campaign and 'Endgame'**     180

    1 *Introduction 180*
    2 *The EPG's Report – And a Change of Direction 182*
    3 *The London Review Meeting 185*
    4 *Internationalising Sanctions 187*
    5 *Conclusion 191*

**11 Ending *Apartheid* – A Troubled Transition**     195

    1 *Introduction 195*
    2 *Overcoming a Divided Commonwealth 197*
    3 *South Africa and the 'New' Commonwealth 201*
    4 *Combatting Violence 207*
    5 *The National Peacekeeping Force 216*
    6 *Conclusion 218*

**12 The 'Freedom Elections' and *Apartheid's* End**     225

    1 *Introduction 225*
    2 *Violence and the Election 226*
    3 *The Freedom Elections 229*
    4 *South Africa and Commonwealth Membership 231*
    5 *Conclusion 235*

**13 The Commonwealth Without a Cause? *Apartheid* and After**     240

    *Conclusion 240*

    *Appendix*     *254*
    *Index*     *257*

# Figures

| | | |
|---|---|---|
| 1.1 | "Africa – Freedom in Our Lifetime," 1960 | 2 |
| 1.2 | Africans demonstrate against the pass laws, 1960 | 13 |
| 2.1 | Prime Minister of India Jawaharlal Nehru arrives at Marlborough House, London (1962), accompanied by Morarji Desai, Finance Minister, and M.C. Chagla, Indian High Commissioner to the UK | 22 |
| 2.2 | King George VI meets Commonwealth leaders, 1949 | 26 |
| 3.1 | Princess Elizabeth prepares to deliver a radio broadcast on her twenty-first birthday, Cape Town, 1947 | 34 |
| 3.2 | Protestors gather outside the Johannesburg Drill Hall as the Treason Trial begins, 1956 | 41 |
| 4.1 | Harold Macmillan welcomes Archbishop Makarios of Cyprus to the Commonwealth, 1960 | 55 |
| 4.2 | Nelson Mandela on a visit to London, 1962 | 62 |
| 5.1 | Queen Elizabeth II with Commonwealth leaders, Commonwealth Prime Ministers' Meeting, London 1962 | 73 |
| 5.2 | Arnold Smith (L.) meeting Commonwealth law officers, London, 1966 | 79 |
| 5.3 | Lee Kuan Yew, Prime Minister of Singapore, in discussion with the British Prime Minister, Ted Heath, Singapore, 1971 | 87 |
| 6.1 | UK Prime Minister Harold Wilson and Mrs Mary Wilson welcome India's Minister for External Affairs, Sardar Swaran Singh, Commonwealth Prime Ministers' Conference 1966 | 101 |
| 6.2 | Commonwealth leaders, hosted by UK Prime Minister Jim Callaghan, at their Gleneagles Retreat, 1977 | 107 |
| 7.1 | Children protesting in defiance of the security forces | 123 |
| 8.1 | President Kenneth Kaunda, Ziaur Rahman, President of Bangladesh, and Mrs Margaret Thatcher (with Lord Carrington) at the opening session of the 1979 Lusaka CHOGM | 136 |
| 8.2 | Simon Muzenda, Robert Mugabe and Joshua Nkomo of the Patriotic Front at the Lancaster House Constitutional talks, London, 1979 | 139 |

| | | |
|---|---|---|
| 8.3 | Commonwealth election observers meet a white voter, Rhodesia/Zimbabwe, 1980 | 141 |
| 9.1 | The Commonwealth Eminent Persons Group with Shridath Ramphal, Marlborough House, 1986 | 162 |
| 9.2 | John Malecela and his EPG colleagues meet Winnie Mandela, 1986 | 168 |
| 10.1 | Archbishop Desmond Tutu | 181 |
| 10.2 | The EPG in session | 182 |
| 10.3 | The CHOGM Review meeting, Marlborough House, August 1986 | 186 |
| 11.1 | Nelson Mandela and F.W. de Klerk exchange greetings | 196 |
| 11.2 | Welcome to CODESA, 1992 | 206 |
| 11.3 | ANC march against violence in Natal, Johannesburg, July 1990 | 207 |
| 11.4 | Observed by Dr Moses Anafu of COMSA, Inkosi Mhlabunzima Wellington Hlengwa successfully appeals for an end to hostilities and the safe return of ANC refugees, Commonwealth-sponsored community meeting in Umbumbulu, KwaZulu/Natal, 1992 | 214 |
| 12.1 | Nelson Mandela and Chief Anyaoku at Marlborough House, 1993 | 228 |
| 12.2 | Black and white voters queue in South Africa's first democratic elections, 1994 | 230 |
| 13.1 | The Queen, the Prince of Wales, Chief Emeka Anyaoku, Mrs Bunmi Anyaoku and Thabo Mbeki, Deputy President of South Africa, at a Marlborough House reception to mark South Africa's return to Commonwealth membership, 1994 | 249 |

# Notes and Abbreviations

**Terminology**

As regards terminology, it is necessary to explain the use of several terms. Firstly, references to 'Britain' and the 'British' Government are descriptions which today would be regarded as both inexact and politically insensitive. However, it was not until 1999 that, at the suggestion of the Commonwealth Secretariat, the UK government ceased to use 'Britain' and 'British' as its national description in Commonwealth documents and meetings and, as in other international fora, became known as 'the United Kingdom/UK'. Thus, for the duration of this study, the former description was used. Given that quoted sources often reflect this, the old and modern appellations have been used interchangeably.

Secondly, a similar issue arises with the use of the term 'non-white'. At first sight, this may also appear archaic and imprecise. However, it is a description which, in the context of *apartheid*, is widely used in the period, both within South Africa and internationally. It captures the binary nature of the *apartheid* system, being one of white supremacy which excluded from economic and political power all other 'non-white' groups. 'Non-white' is therefore a collective description covering Black Africans, Cape Coloureds, Indians and other 'non-white' racial categories defined by the Population Registration Act (1950). After all, this was a cornerstone of *apartheid*. Nevertheless, where it is more accurate to use a specific description, this has been used in preference to the generic term.

**Abbreviations**

| | | |
|---|---|---|
| AAM | – | Anti-*Apartheid* Movement |
| ANC | – | African National Congress |
| AWB | – | Afrikaner Weerstandsbeweging |
| AZAPO | – | Azanian People's Organisation |
| CFMSA | – | Commonwealth Committee of Foreign Ministers on Southern Africa |
| CHOGM | – | Commonwealth Heads of Government Meeting |

| | | |
|---|---|---|
| CMAG | – | Commonwealth Ministerial Action Group |
| CODESA | – | Convention for a Democratic South Africa |
| COG | – | Commonwealth Observer Group |
| COMSEC | – | Commonwealth Secretariat |
| COMGEP | – | Commonwealth Group of Eminent Persons to South Africa |
| COMSA | – | Commonwealth Observer Mission to South Africa |
| COSATU | – | Congress of South African Trade Unions |
| CP | – | Conservative Party (South Africa) |
| CPAG | – | Commonwealth Peacekeeping Assistance Group (South Africa) |
| CRO | – | Commonwealth Relations Office |
| DP | – | Democratic Party |
| EC/EEC | – | European Community/European Economic Community |
| ECOMSA | – | European Community Observer Mission in South Africa |
| EPG | – | Eminent Persons Group (sometimes COMGEP) |
| EU | – | European Union |
| FCO | – | Foreign and Commonwealth Office |
| FF | – | Freedom Front |
| FLS | – | Frontline States |
| HART | – | Halt All Racial Tours |
| IFP | – | Inkatha Freedom Party |
| MCC | – | Marylebone Cricket Club |
| MK | – | Umkhonto We Sizwe |
| NAM | – | Non-Aligned Movement |
| NIS | – | National Intelligence Service (South Africa) |
| NP | – | National Party |
| NPKF | – | National Peacekeeping Force |
| OAU | – | Organisation of African Unity |
| OAU-OMSA | – | OAU Observer Mission in South Africa |
| PAC | – | Pan-Africanist Congress of Azania |
| PF | – | Patriotic Front (of Zimbabwe) |
| PS | – | Permanent Secretary/Private Secretary |
| PUS | – | Permanent Under-Secretary |
| SACP | – | South African Communist Party |
| SADC | – | Southern African Development Community |
| SADCC | – | Southern African Development Coordination Conference |
| SADF | – | South African Defence Force |
| SDU | – | Self-Defence Unit |
| STST | – | Stop the Seventy Tour |
| TEC | – | Transitional Executive Council |
| TRC | – | Truth and Reconciliation Commission |
| UDF | – | United Democratic Front |
| UDI | – | Unilateral Declaration of Independence |
| UNGA | – | United Nations General Assembly |

| | | |
|---|---|---|
| UNOMSA | – | United Nations Observer Mission in South Africa |
| UNSC | – | United Nations Security Council |
| ZANU | – | Zimbabwe African National Union |
| ZANLA | – | Zimbabwe African National Liberation Army |
| ZAPU | – | Zimbabwe African People's Union |
| ZIPRA | – | Zimbabwe People's Revolutionary Army |

# Acknowledgements

Too often the Commonwealth has been seen, and judged, through the eyes of outsiders. While this may be inevitable, I felt it was important for the Commonwealth to tell its own story about confronting racism in Southern Africa, particularly *apartheid*, because no full history of this yet exists. And yet it was a struggle that went to the heart of the Commonwealth's commitment to racial equality. It defined, and it changed the organisation even as it helped end the *apartheid* system. In so doing, it fundamentally altered the association's relationship with the former imperial power, the UK.

In that respect, I have greatly benefitted from the advice and insights of Commonwealth friends and former colleagues and from academics and scholars working in this field. Both Kamalesh Sharma and Patricia Scotland, as Commonwealth Secretaries-General, have in turn allowed me to consult Commonwealth archives not at that time available to the public.

Material forming much of Chapter 11 and a small part of Chapter 12 has been previously included in an article of which I was the sole author titled "Bloody Commonwealth Peacemongers: The Role of the Commonwealth in South Africa's Transition from *Apartheid*" in *Commonwealth & Comparative Politics* (2020), 60:1, 1–26. Permission for this material to be reused in my book has been given by the publisher, the Taylor & Francis Group, and I am most grateful.

Similarly, a paragraph of the Prologue draws upon material I authored which was published on the website of *The Round Table: The Commonwealth Journal of International Affairs* titled "Exploring Commonwealth Myths" (29 May 2018). Though no copyright was assigned in this case, I am also grateful to *The Round Table* for agreeing to the reuse of this material.

Many images in this book have been readily provided by the Commonwealth Secretariat, and two have come from the Margaret Ballinger Collection at the University of Cape Town, all thankfully without charge. A final image was provided by the Royal Collection Trust.

Finally, I want to thank my immediate family, Helen and Caitie (as well as Alex and Sam) for bearing the brunt of my work's impact on our lives together. They have endured many monologues on its contents and watched the book's lengthy gestation and birth with great patience. It is a story I have long wanted to tell – and, through their support, they, and many others, have helped me realise that ambition.

Stuart Mole

# Prologue

This book is a work of history, a detailed examination of how issues of race, particularly in Southern Africa, shaped the modern Commonwealth and gave the new association enduring purpose. In particular, it draws on new evidence and insights to illustrate and assess the importance of the Commonwealth's campaign against *apartheid* in South Africa. Yet it does not seek to contain in another age the issues and tensions which sometimes drove racial conflict and which were ultimately resolved by reconciliation – in South Africa and in the wider Commonwealth. If, as E.H. Carr has said, history is "an unending dialogue between the present and the past," recent years have provided their own memories of past battles and are worth recalling for the lessons that can still be learnt.[1]

In April 2018, there was unaccustomed media coverage of the Commonwealth. At the beginning of the month, the XXI Commonwealth Games opened on Australia's Gold Coast. There were equal tallies of medals won by male and female athletes, and the integration of able and para-athletes was striking, forming "a rich and highly watchable schedule."[2] Though far from being a global competition, world records at the Commonwealth Games tumbled. Unusually, politics intruded with English diving Olympian, Tom Daley, urging changes to the archaic and oppressive laws which deny equal rights on LBGT issues in many Commonwealth countries. It was a timely reminder that discrimination comes in many forms.

A few days after the Games' closing ceremony, the biennial Commonwealth Heads of Government Meeting (CHOGM) convened in London (the first such summit in the UK for over twenty years). The high turnout of Heads of Government was less an indicator of the organisation's contemporary vitality and more a sign that the Queen's offer of Buckingham Palace and Windsor Castle for significant parts of the summit had proved particularly attractive to Commonwealth leaders and their spouses.

The summit was also sprinkled with other royal celebrity, most notably Prince Harry and his new wife, the American actor and writer, Meghan Markle. The couple's engagement, in November 2017, had been particularly welcomed in the Commonwealth where Markle's mixed race identity chimed well with an organisation composed of many multiracial and cosmopolitan societies. Both played an active role in events prior to, and during, the London CHOGM. Prince Harry was given the role of Commonwealth Youth Ambassador, and Markle later accepted the patronage of a number of Commonwealth organisations, notably the Association of Commonwealth Universities. Their fairy-tale wedding at St George's Chapel, Windsor, in May 2018, and their new status as the Duke and Duchess of Sussex were widely interpreted as evidence of a British royal family open to change and at ease with the African American cultural aspects included in the wedding ceremony. Not all approved, however, and the author and academic, Kehinde Andrews, wrote: "Hailing a Black royal as a sign of supposedly 'modern' Britain is in fact symbolic violence, part of a discourse designed to legitimise continued racial oppression by masking it."[3]

If the 2018 CHOGM was unusual in its use of royal venues, it was also exceptional in having the question of the future headship of the association placed squarely on its agenda by the current incumbent, Queen Elizabeth II. Speaking at the opening ceremony of the summit, in the crimson and gold splendour of Buckingham Palace's ballroom, the Queen referred to her "pleasure and honour" in serving the Commonwealth since being appointed by Heads of Government in 1952, following the death of her father, George VI. But in recognition that the post is not hereditary but remains in the hands of Commonwealth leaders, she continued: "It is my sincere wish that the Commonwealth will continue to offer stability and continuity for future generations and will decide that one day the Prince of Wales should carry on the important work started by my father in 1949."[4] Conscious that, given her age and health, the Queen no longer travels abroad and is unlikely to attend another Commonwealth summit in person, Heads of Government later in the meeting put on record their gratitude for the "duty and commitment" the Queen had shown to the Commonwealth in the seven decades she had been Head and agreed without equivocation that "the next Head of the Commonwealth shall be His Royal Highness, Prince Charles."[5]

Less prominent in the media coverage was mention of the leaders' policy discussions, which included areas where it was felt that the Commonwealth could make a specific contribution, like climate change and a 'blue charter' for oceans; trade, investment and connectivity; and cybersecurity.[6] Reports were also received from two of the four separate forums, held in the wings of the summit, which were representative gatherings, respectively, of women, young people, business and civil society. This public manifestation of the contemporary Commonwealth, however, provided an incomplete picture of an organisation still troubled by some of the shadows and tensions of its past.

One of the enduring images of Danny Boyle's widely acclaimed Opening Ceremony of the 2012 London Olympics was the large model of the *M.V. Empire Windrush* which entered the Olympic Stadium with its two funnels belching smoke and, walking alongside, hundreds of volunteers depicting its West Indian passengers, arriving in the drab surroundings of post-war Britain with hope and expectation. "Windrush" has been held up as the symbol of post-war Commonwealth immigration, though, as David Olusoga has pointed out, this has served to obscure the generations of Black citizens who since the Roman invasion have lived in various parts of the UK.[7] Nevertheless, it sustained the image of a multicultural and tolerant UK, constructed to a significant extent by decades of immigration from various parts of the Commonwealth.

However, in 2017, 'Windrush' conjured up an entirely different meaning as a shocking scandal emerged. Hundreds of Commonwealth citizens, long settled in the UK, many of whom had arrived from the Caribbean with the 'Windrush' generation of 1948–1973 (and some on the *Empire Windrush* itself) were wrongly labelled illegal immigrants, denied their rights, detained and even deported. While all had arrived with full British citizenship (or had subsequently been born in the UK), after many decades few still retained the documentation to prove their right to remain in the UK. The problem was made worse by the UK Border Agency which in 2009 took the decision to destroy the landing cards of many of these Commonwealth citizens.[8] There was widespread public anger that, in the words of the Joint Council for the Welfare of Immigrants: "so many Black Britons had had their lives devastated by Britain's deeply flawed and discriminatory immigration system."[9] The scandal quickly spread internationally and "substantially overshadowed" the preparations for the 2018 London CHOGM with its pronounced royal character. Mindful of their capacity for influence at such a time, Caribbean High Commissioners in London met together a week before the meeting and called on the UK government to change its approach. After initially refusing to discuss the issue, the British Prime Minister, Theresa May, met Caribbean leaders in an attempt to defuse the crisis. In the view of Ruth Craggs, the Summit therefore "provided a platform through which the UK government was forced to engage with the issue at the highest level."[10] The Home Secretary, Amber Rudd, apologised for the 'appalling' treatment of Windrush citizens, promised to 'right the wrongs' and introduced a compensation scheme for victims. She later resigned for 'unintentionally' misleading MPs about the government's 'hostile environment' policy. However, in November 2021, the Home Affairs Select Committee found the compensation scheme in disarray with only 5.8% of those believed to be eligible for compensation having received payment and twenty-three people having died before compensation payments could be made. The MPs declared that "instead of providing a remedy, for many people the Windrush Compensation Scheme has actually compounded the injustices faced as a result of the Windrush scandal."[11]

Many felt that the 2016 referendum vote on Britain's continuing membership of the European Union (EU), coupled with the surge in racially motivated violence that followed the Brexit vote, was given impetus by "a divisive approach to race, religion and migration." In making this analysis, John Burnett asks rhetorically: "[I]f a hostile environment is embedded politically, why should we be surprised when it takes root culturally?"[12] Of course, many who voted for the UK to leave the EU would deny that issues of immigration and race influenced their decision. While the leaders of the Commonwealth's fifty-three member countries sent out a unanimous message of support for the UK remaining in the EU, Sue Onslow commented that the 900,000 or so Commonwealth citizens entitled to vote in the referendum "were by no means a monolithic bloc supporting the Remain camp."[13]

The Commonwealth was further troubled by the loss of its newest royal celebrities. In January 2020, the Duke and Duchess of Sussex announced that they were stepping back from their royal duties and would "transition into the new working model." This would involve becoming members of the Royal Family "with financial independence," though their commitment to the Queen remained "resolute" and "unwavering." Part of this new model involved a commitment to "Strengthening the Commonwealth" both through pursuing their various Commonwealth roles and in their overseas tours.[14]

However, it quickly became clear that the aspiration of a continuing royal role, coupled with financial independence and residence outside the UK, had not been agreed with Buckingham Palace and that there would be considerable difficulties in reconciling the two ambitions. In 2021, amid deteriorating relations with other family members, the Duke and Duchess of Sussex gave an explosive interview with the US broadcaster (and friend of the couple), Oprah Winfrey. In the interview, Meghan spoke about how she had contemplated suicide while in the UK and had been discouraged from seeking professional help; that the "question of race had also infused her relationship with the royal family," affecting attitudes to the treatment of their son, Archie; and how Harry felt "really let down" by his father, Prince Charles, and cut off financially.[15] The Duke and Duchess of Sussex's allegations of racism had included that "an unnamed member of the royal family had been worried about how dark their son Archie's skin tone might be before he was born."[16] Harry's brother, William, responded forcefully that the Royal Family "is very much not racist."[17] Public opinion rapidly polarised. A YouGov poll showed positive opinion of Prince Harry falling by nearly 10% in the UK (and of Meghan by a lesser amount); however, there was far greater sympathy for the Sussexes in the United States and internationally.[18]

In the Commonwealth, Harry and Meghan's interview came at a time when some of the old antagonisms between the British Government and a serving Commonwealth Secretary-General had bubbled to the surface. Having hosted the 2018

CHOGM, the British Prime Minister occupied one of the three key leadership positions in the organisation, namely that of 'Chairperson-in-office'. The Secretary-General Baroness Patricia Scotland – the first woman to occupy the post – had been born in Dominica, to Caribbean parents, but had moved with her family to the UK at the age of 2. Qualifying as a barrister, she had then gone on to a successful career in Labour politics, being created a life peer, serving in various ministerial positions in the Labour government of Tony Blair and, under Gordon Brown, becoming the first woman to be appointed Attorney-General. She was therefore from a quite different political stable to that of the new chairperson, the instinctive populist (and leader of the Brexit cause) Boris Johnson. The British Government, during Scotland's first four-year term, came to question her record and competence and, together with some other member governments, argued that she should not be given a second (and final) four-year term. Scotland's supporters argued that this was little more than an attempt by the former imperial power "to prevent the re-election of the first black woman head of the organisation."[19]

With the global Covid-19 pandemic preventing Commonwealth leaders from meeting to resolve the issue of Scotland's tenure, the allegations of racism against the Royal Family and against the British Government over the handling of the Windrush scandal caused added alarm. In the Caribbean, it seemed that both issues "had fuelled demands in former Caribbean colonies to drop the Queen as their head of state."[20] It was no coincidence that Rev. Guy Hewitt, then High Commissioner for Barbados in London, and who played a leading part in mobilising Caribbean diplomatic pressure on the UK government, had also been a prominent voice foreshadowing the transition of Barbados from a Commonwealth Realm to republican status.[21] More recently, Prince William and his wife, Kate Middleton, the Duke and Duchess of Cambridge, toured the three Caribbean realms of Belize, Jamaica and the Bahamas on behalf of the Queen to express her gratitude for their loyal support over the course of her reign. While the royal couple were warmly received personally, there were a series of reminders that the relationship between the Head of State and the three countries concerned might be in question. There were some protests and several PR blunders. "Times have changed," remarked the BBC's Royal Correspondent, Johnny Dymond, continuing: "The Royal Family have in the past been pretty good at changing with them." But "Not on this tour," he concluded.[22]

The issues that swirled around the 2018 CHOGM had echoes of some of the challenges that had consumed the Commonwealth in the seven decades since the Second World War. An inescapable underlying theme – and one which came to define the organisation – was race: where did the Commonwealth stand on the question of racial justice? That fundamental question was posed in many forms. As decolonisation brought freedom and self-determination in the former empire, what place was there in the Commonwealth for its new citizens, alongside those of the old Dominions? Would the relationship be one of equality or would the Commonwealth become a two-tier organisation, if not formally then certainly in practice? More specifically, if there was formal political and racial equality between member nations, did the benefits and habits of cooperation and consultation extend equally, and how could this be ensured? If the 'new' Commonwealth was still led and controlled by the British Government, how would it be apparent that the association operated in the interests of all with shared objectives, rather than in the national interests of the former imperial power? What new structures, processes and programmes would be necessary to transform the organisation to one genuinely answerable to all its members, regardless of size and wealth? In addressing the dominant issue of racism in Southern Africa, more particularly in Rhodesia and in *apartheid* South Africa, was the British Government and its extensive ties to white rule in the region part of the problem – or a prominent position of leverage which could help find an equitable solution? Should conflict with British interests and policies be pushed to the point of rupture, or was the new Commonwealth condemned to remain locked in the UK's symbiotic embrace if it wanted an avenue to global influence?

Of course, racial justice is far from being the sole purpose of the organisation. Sonny Ramphal, the second Commonwealth Secretary-General, saw the association as "a co-mingling of humanity in all its variety." He continued: "What we have to offer the world is a special capacity for communication across the lines of geography and race and wealth – a facility by which a quarter of the world's states may enlarge understanding and advance cooperation."[23] Even so, the Commonwealth's ability to act as such a global forum continues to depend on trust and on equity in establishing a connection, and a channel of communication, between all members. Emeka Anyaoku, in reflecting on his time as Ramphal's successor in the office of Secretary-General, has spoken of the major crises that threatened the continuing cohesion of the Commonwealth. These challenges, he argues, were "fuelled by debates among its members over situations in which the issue of racism and racial discrimination were the underlying factors."[24]

Following the end of the Second World War, the old imperial framework which had given the 'Empire and Commonwealth' its unity was being dismantled or transformed. The indivisibility of an Imperial Crown, as an essential requirement of Commonwealth membership, gave way to the looser symbolism of a headship of the organisation, embracing both republics and monarchies. The underlying mythology of a common 'English' identity and citizenship, offered by the mother country to its colonial subjects, came to be increasingly tested as Commonwealth immigrants experienced the realities of life in the metropole. Without the benefit of a founding charter, it was left to an emerging and modern Commonwealth to lay down the bedrock of its new unity, based on their shared values. After nearly seventy years, those values were finally codified in the adoption by Heads of Government of the Commonwealth Charter.[25] The various elements of that charter, accumulated over time, could be found in the various declarations, statements and agreements of Commonwealth leaders. However, McIntyre points out that leaders were not consciously seeking to construct a charter or constitution – they were reacting to specific circumstances, often of crisis, and the need to agree 'guiding norms'.[26] Given its colonial antecedents, it is therefore unsurprising that the most immediate and enduring test for the Commonwealth should have been its commitment to political and racial equality. This, Anyaoku argues, made the Commonwealth "the first global organisation to have its rhetoric and actions driven

xx  *Prologue*

by the principle of racial equality." It is the Commonwealth's long journey out of empire and racial segregation and, as a changed organisation, its pursuit of racial justice which is therefore the central theme of this study of racism, conflict and reconciliation.

**Notes**

1. Edward Hallett Carr, *What Is History?* (London: Vintage Books, 1967).
2. Carly Earl, "'Share the dream' – the Games that celebrated disability sports." *The Guardian*, 15 April 2018. Theguardian.com/sport/2018/apr/16/share-the-dream-the-games-that-celebrated-disability-sports, Accessed 7 April 2022.
3. Kehinde Andrews, "The post-racial princess: Delusions of racial progress and intersectional failures" *Women's Studies International Forum*, 84: 102432 (2021), 2.
4. Laura Smith-Spark, "Britain's Queen hopes Prince Charles will 'one day' lead Commonwealth," *CNN* 19 April 2018. htpps://edition.cnn.com/2018/04/19/europe/queen-prince-charles-commonwealth-meeting-intl/index.html, Accessed 8 April 2022
5. The Leaders' Statement, "Commonwealth Heads of Government Meeting 2018," *London* 20 April 2018. www.chogm2018.org.uk/sites/default/files/CHOGM%202018%20 Leaders%20Statement.pdf, Accessed 8 April 2022.
6. Commonwealth Secretariat, CHOGM Communique 2018 "Towards a common future" https://thecommonwealth.org/chogm/2018, Accessed 9 April 2022.
7. David Olusoga, *Black and British: A Forgotten History* (London: Macmillan, 2016), 523–524.
8. Russell Taylor, "Impact of 'Hostile Environment' Policy Debate on 14 June 2018," House of Lords Library Briefing, 11 June 2018, 22. https://lordslibrary.parliament.uk/research-briefings/lln-2018-0064/Accessed 9 April 2022.
9. Website, "Windrush scandal explained," The Joint Council for the Welfare of Immigrants. Https://www.jcwi.org.uk/windrush-scandal-explained, Accessed 22 February 2022.
10. Ruth Craggs, "The 2018 Commonwealth heads of government meeting, the Windrush scandal and the legacies of empire," *The Round Table: The Commonwealth Journal of International Affairs*, 107:3 (2018), 361–2.
11. Committees, "Compensation scheme failures have compounded injustices faced by Windrush generation – Committee finds," *Home Affairs Select Committee*, 24 November 2021. www.committeesparliament.uk/committee/83/home-affairs-committee/news/159118/compensation-scheme-failures-have-compounded-injustices-faced-by-Windrush-generation/, Accessed 22 February 2022.
12. John Burnett, "Racial violence and the Brexit state," *Race & Class*, 58:4, (2017), 86.
13. Sue Onslow, "What Brexit means for the Commonwealth," *Commonwealth Opinion*, Institute of Commonwealth Studies, 7 July 2016. Https://commonwealth-opinion.blogs.sas.uk/2016/what-brexit-means-for-the-commonwealth/, Accessed 21 February 2022.
14. Website, "Serving the monarchy" and "strengthening the Commonwealth" *The Official Website of the Duke & Duchess of Sussex*. https://sussexroyal.com/monarchy/, Accessed 23 February 2022.
15. Sarah Lyall and Tariro Mzezewa, "What we learned from Meghan and Harry's interview" *The New York Times*, 8 March 2021. Https://www.nytimes.com/2021/03/08/world/europe/recap-of-harry-meghan-oprah-interview.html, Accessed 23 February 2022.
16. Valentine Low, "Sussexes feel free after doing Oprah interview" *The Times*, 11 March 2021, 2.
17. News Report, "Prince William: Royal Family is 'very much not racist" *BBC News*, 11 March 2021. www.bbc.co.uk/news/av/uk-56359393, Accessed 23 February 2022.
18. Connor Ibbetson, "The proportion of the public thinking positively of Prince Harry is down 10pts" *YouGov*, 3 September 2021. Https://yougov.co.uk/topics/politics/

articles-reports/2021/09/03/public-opinion-continues-fall-narry-and-meghan, Accessed 23 February 2022.
19. David Brown, "Fight to oust Head of Commonwealth" *The Times*, 2 September 2021.
20. Greg Wilford & Jane Flanagan, "Racism claim fuels unease in Commonwealth nation" *The Times*, 11 March, 2021.
21. Barbados became a republic, after fifty-five years of independence, on 30 November 2021.
22. Jonny Dymond, "Prince William and Kate: The PR missteps that overshadowed a royal tour," *BBC News* 25 March 2022. www.bbc.co.uk/news/uk-60870417, Accessed 9 April 2022.
23. Shridath Ramphal, *Glimpses of a Global Life* (Hertford, UK: Hansib, 2014), 251.
24. Emeka Anyaoku, *The Inside Story of the Modern Commonwealth* (London, Ibadan and Nairobi: Evans Brothers Ltd, 2004), 205.
25. Commonwealth Secretariat, *The Commonwealth Charter* (London: The Stationary Office, 2013). https://assets.publishing.service.gov.uk/government/uploads/system/uploads/attachment_data/file/136337/Cm_8572.pdf, Accessed 15 April 2022.
26. W. David McIntyre, *A Guide to the Contemporary Commonwealth* (Basingstoke and New York: Palgrave, 2001), 86.

**References**

Commonwealth Secretariat, *The Commonwealth Charter* (London: The Stationary Office, 2013).
David Olusoga, *Black and British: A Forgotten History* (London: Macmillan, 2016).
Edward Hallett Carr, *What is History?* (London: Vintage Books, 1967).
Emeka Anyaoku, *The Inside Story of the Modern Commonwealth* (London, Ibadan, Nairobi: Evans Brothers Ltd, 2004).
Shridath Ramphal, *Glimpses of a Global Life* (Hertford: Hansib, 2014), 251.
W. David McIntyre, *A Guide to the Contemporary Commonwealth* (Basingstoke, New York: Palgrave, 2001).

# 1 Introduction – Whose History?

## 1 Examining *Apartheid* and the Commonwealth

The starting point for this book is the genesis and growth of the Commonwealth in its modern form, following the adoption of the London Declaration in 1949.[1] By chance, this followed, a year earlier, the election in South Africa of the Afrikaner Nationalist government of Daniel Malan which was to begin the construction of the *apartheid* state. South Africa was at that point a Dominion within the British Commonwealth (under the Statute of Westminster 1931) and had fought alongside the UK and other Commonwealth nations in two world wars. Nevertheless, racial discrimination and segregation had long been a feature of the Union, and this had created public tension between South Africa and India over the treatment of citizens of Indian descent, even before India had gained her independence. The divisive issues of race and identity were to increase in importance as the character of the Commonwealth altered with the accession to membership of many post-colonial states from Africa, Asia, the Caribbean and the Pacific, and following the acrimonious exit of South Africa from the association.[2] As the period unfolded, opposition to racism in Southern Africa, and specifically to *apartheid*, became the leitmotif of the Commonwealth's evolution and at the heart of its claim to be a multiracial and modern international organisation.[3] But how distinctive and significant was the Commonwealth's contribution to the international campaign against *apartheid* alongside other international and regional organisations, such as the United Nations, the Organisation of African Unity (OAU) or the Frontline States (FLS)? Was its often-difficult relationship with the UK government during that time a measure of how far its independence of action was compromised by Britain's deep economic, political, cultural and security links with South Africa?[4] Or did the uniqueness of the Commonwealth's ties to the former imperial power create a capacity for special influence? Where the Commonwealth operated with genuine independence distinct from and often in opposition to the UK, were its actions substantive and far reaching – or symbolic and self-serving?

Answering these questions will involve examining how the Commonwealth's actions were perceived at the time, both within South Africa, by all shades of opinion, and externally, by international organisations, national governments and independent commentators and academics. It will also be necessary to consider how the

*Figure 1.1* "Africa – Freedom in Our Lifetime," 1960. Margaret Ballinger Papers, Special Collections. University of Cape Town.

Commonwealth operated as a distinct diplomatic entity and ask whether existing theories of diplomacy, with their emphasis on state actors alone, provide an adequate framework for assessing the role of international organisations such as the Commonwealth in addressing multifaceted international issues. As well as looking at diplomatic methods, it is also important to examine the link to, and significance of, a shared set of ideas driving the new Commonwealth leadership (the Secretary-General and Heads of Government) as well as the part played by mass protest and civil society action within individual Commonwealth countries, and the influence that these had on the UK and other Commonwealth governments. Lastly, and drawing examples across the period, it will be important to test the Commonwealth's specific claim to have a comparative advantage in the field of mediation and conflict resolution.

The Commonwealth's assertion that it conducted a sustained, principled and significant crusade against *apartheid* in all the years of the racial ideology's existence goes to the heart of Commonwealth mythology. It is held up, as the current Commonwealth Secretary-General has put it, as "our collective refusal to turn a blind eye to *apartheid*."[5] One of the great figures of the Commonwealth's anti-*apartheid* struggle, the second Secretary-General, Shridath Ramphal, put it thus: "For the entire Commonwealth there remained a duty as part of humanity, and in furtherance of Commonwealth values, to remove the stain of *apartheid* from human society."[6] However, that prolonged engagement by the Commonwealth with racism in Southern Africa also created historical legacies which, arguably, had their own considerable effect on the relevance and purposes of the contemporary Commonwealth.

In all this, understanding of the Commonwealth and *apartheid* has been clouded by two myths. These are, firstly, that the Commonwealth was a fierce opponent of *apartheid* from the system's inception, in 1948, until its ending in 1994. In reality, it was only after the 1960 Sharpeville massacre, the formation of an independent Secretariat and the appointment of the first Commonwealth Secretary-General, that opposition to racism in Southern Africa, and specifically to *apartheid*, assumed substance and coherence. The second myth, constructed in part in opposition to the first, was that the Commonwealth's actions against *apartheid* throughout the period were variable and insignificant, being "at best very marginal."[7] The evidence of archival and other material relating to the main areas of Commonwealth activity offers a more balanced and positive assessment than this familiar trope.

In exploring the collective contribution of the Commonwealth to the international campaign against *apartheid*, and in assessing the extent to which its role was unique in character and demonstrated measurable impact, there are a number of different milestones worthy of recognition. The first is South Africa's departure from the Commonwealth in 1961 and the beginnings of *apartheid's* journey into international isolation. The second is the development of the sporting boycott and the adoption of the Gleneagles Agreement on sport and *apartheid* in 1977. The third is the mission to South Africa of the Commonwealth Eminent Persons Group (EPG) in 1986 and how this impacted both on the sanctions campaign and on the prospects for a negotiated internal settlement. The fourth deals with the Commonwealth's role in international assistance to South Africa's transition out of *apartheid* between 1991 and 1994. Each of these served to highlight a range of Commonwealth strategies. These were negotiation, diplomacy, mediation and conflict resolution, humanitarian and other assistance, and collective international pressure to secure economic, sporting and other sanctions. In each case, the Commonwealth considers its actions to have been important and, in most instances, there is a demonstrable degree of international recognition of the Commonwealth's collective role, as expressed in the private and public comments of relevant actors.

At the same time, none of these interventions took place in isolation from the development of the Commonwealth's own shared norms, as well as how those principles were impacted more widely, and the organisation's growing perception that these were challenged by the enduring institutional racism of *apartheid*. In this respect, a useful starting point would be to consider how scholars have assessed the engagement of the United Nations with *apartheid* since it first began to address South Africa's racial policies on 8 December 1946. The UN General Assembly's (UNGA's) votes on South Africa's treatment of its Indian population and on the status of the mandated territory of South-West Africa predated the introduction of *apartheid* from 1948 but not the racial laws, customs and attitudes which provided the *apartheid* state with its substantial foundations. In considering most of that forty-seven-year period, Stultz suggests that "no subject has been more enduring before the world body than *apartheid*."[8] The uniqueness of the United Nations'

4  *Introduction – Whose History?*

anti-*apartheid* regime must surely lie in the quality and evolving nature of the international body's actions. Stultz's approach is to draw upon the work of Donnelly in asking what constitutes an international human rights 'regime', acting upon certain international norms, which may themselves be evolving.[9] For Donnelly, a regime's decision-making can move through four distinct categories: declaratory, promotional, implementing and enforcement, and Stultz applies this to the United Nations' actions on *apartheid*.[10]

In many ways, the Commonwealth's own relationship with *apartheid* served to influence, as well as reflect, key developments at the United Nations. Prominent Commonwealth figures were actively involved in the development of the United Nations in its early years.[11] Jan Smuts of South Africa, and Sir Charles Webster of the UK, together with the Australian Herbert Evatt, were instrumental in the drafting of the Preamble to the UN Charter, Smuts's segregationist views notwithstanding.[12] A few years later, John Peters Humphrey of Canada provided the first draft of the Universal Declaration of Human Rights, though his role is sometimes overlooked as the 'forgotten framer'.[13] Evatt, by then President of the UNGA, helped secure the Declaration's adoption and proclamation. Even so, until 1965 a British-led Commonwealth avoided attempts to agree collective human rights' norms within its ranks. However, with the creation of an independent Secretariat and with the growth of a broader membership, this attitude changed. Thereafter, the 1971 Singapore Declaration, the 1977 Gleneagles Agreement and the 1991 Harare Declaration were all significant in creating a wider impact at the United Nations and elsewhere and influencing international norms. As a result, Stultz's application of Donnelly's framework to the United Nations can also be helpful when applied to the Commonwealth. The development of the Commonwealth's 'human rights regime' over the four decades of the period is therefore a constant feature.

## 2  Evidence and Archives

What is the evidence underpinning the arguments presented in this book? Firstly, an extensive range of relevant Commonwealth material has been examined, including shared Commonwealth records, personal testimonies and oral histories, private correspondence and memoirs and secondary literature. Secondly, archival material in Commonwealth member countries, particularly the UK and South Africa, as well as other states involved in the anti-*apartheid* campaign, has been interrogated, as well as political comment, writing and analysis. Thirdly, the perspective of other international organisations, particularly the United Nations, as well as relevant regional organisations, academics and analysts and civil society participants has been considered and referenced.

The primary archival base is the Commonwealth Secretariat archive at Marlborough House. This intergovernmental archive is an essential locus of evidence and differs from national, colonial and governmental archives in several important ways. Unlike the national archives of member countries which are established and governed by domestic legislation, the Commonwealth archive is international, containing the shared Commonwealth records of all member countries. Its status is recognised in the British legislation which established the Commonwealth Secretariat as an international organisation domiciled in the UK. In setting out its privileges and immunities, the Commonwealth Secretariat Act (1966) declared: "[T]he Commonwealth Secretariat shall have the like inviolability of premises, official archives and communications as is accorded by law in respect of the premises, official archives and communications of a sending state."[14] The regulations and conventions governing the archive, and arrangements for its proper care, are the responsibility of Commonwealth governments collectively and these were only developed in the 1990s as the Secretariat approached its thirtieth anniversary. Not only did the Commonwealth have to decide if it wished to adopt the widespread use of the thirty-year rule, after which time eligible records would become public, but, in deciding to do so, it resolved the dilemma that otherwise some of its shared records might be made publicly available elsewhere by the member countries concerned under their own national legislation.[15]

Another difference between national archives and the Commonwealth archive lies in the differing attitudes to political accountability. In national systems there is often strong continuity and vitality evident in the civil service. Civil servants answer to their political masters, but political power can be remarkably transient. Commonwealth Secretaries-General, on the other hand, have been used to a much longer shelf life. Smith and Anyaoku served for ten years each and Ramphal for fifteen. Only more recently has the length of incumbency begun to shorten.[16] As a result, the Secretariat is much more focused on the dominant and generally enduring figure of the Secretary-General.

External influences are also processed differently. In the case of, say, the UK foreign service policy positions and advice are peppered with the regular reports and intelligence supplied by ambassadors and missions abroad. This material is invariably filtered through British diplomats on the ground, with all the benefits and pitfalls that may come from those judgements and perspectives. The Secretariat, on the other hand, is keenly aware that it must be an assiduous and impartial facilitator of Commonwealth consultation. It does not have a network of missions or offices in member countries, and its interface is with Commonwealth High Commissions in London or points of contact within Commonwealth capitals.

What implications does this have for historical research? The Commonwealth archive, little over 50 years old, is largely the product of a cautious mindset. The Secretariat, though based in the UK and disproportionately influenced by it, has usually had around thirty Commonwealth nationalities among its staff. This diversity, whatever its merits, tends to induce a sense of hierarchy and defensiveness in its internal exchanges, as well as in its dealings with member governments. While ostensibly committed to open and transparent governance, Gilbert suggests that there is a contrary attitude in the Secretariat that the "essentially private 'family' character of the Commonwealth association can only be preserved if things said, and recorded, in the unique atmosphere of the 'bosom of the family' are kept within that assembly."[17] It is unusual for annotations on draft letters or documents to be anything like as frank and open as is the case with publicly available UK records. Missions are invariably conducted in 'discreet and non-public' ways, and the Secretary-General may prompt a President or Prime Minister to appear as the initiator of action, rather than him- or herself, in order to generate a more effective outcome.[18] This fiction may be maintained after the event in whatever accounts appear in the public sphere. Ramphal's close aide, Moni Malhoutra, observing the Secretary-General's diplomatic method during the 1979 Lancaster House talks, remarked: "He was like a spider at the centre of a web."[19]

At the same time, the multilateral nature of policy exchanges retained and processed by the Secretariat inevitably provides a breadth of perspective not normally present in national archives. This is particularly so in terms of the Secretary-General's correspondence and meetings with individual Heads of Government, as well as the records of collective Commonwealth meetings, particularly the CHOGM and its Heads-Only Retreat. This material reveals the complex network of relationships that exist among the Commonwealth's leadership. That relationship goes to the heart of the argument, central to this thesis, that at its best the Commonwealth can generate a distinctive multilateral diplomatic dynamic in addressing and resolving controversial issues. A multilateral archive is also a useful corrective to the predominant frame of national histories, with the Commonwealth archive offering a perspective that sometimes is against the grain of official government histories. Catherine Hall, as a British historian, is one of those who have become convinced that "in order to understand the specificity of national formation, we have to look outside it."[20] This 'transnational thinking' disturbs national histories and, while marking 'positive presence and content', also helps reveal 'negative and excluded parts'.

Other Commonwealth and institutional archives have also been consulted, including the Royal Commonwealth Society (RCS) Collections at Cambridge University Library, the Institute of Commonwealth Studies collections at the University of London, and the Anti-*Apartheid* and African collections in the Bodleian Library at Oxford. These archives illuminate the relationship of various Commonwealth bodies and other civil society organisations, notably the Anti-*Apartheid* Movement (AAM), to the official Commonwealth, as well as the role of key individuals at various critical points in the Commonwealth's development. The RCS, based at that time in Northumberland Avenue in central London, was a notable gathering point for South African exiles and visitors from across the Commonwealth. Its programme of meetings in the basement auditorium of the Society provided many leaders and advocates of national independence with a public platform in the UK. Oliver Tambo, Thabo Mbeki and Aziz Pahad used the club and early contacts were made with Lynda Chalker, at that time a junior Foreign Office Minister. Her covert meetings with Tambo became more formalised in 1986, even though the official policy of the UK was that it would not talk to 'terrorists'.[21] Given this history of contact, it is little surprise that the RCS should have been the venue for Mandela's first press conference in the UK on his release from prison.[22] Similarly, the Institute of Commonwealth Studies was able to provide its own support to South African exiles and the anti-*apartheid* cause. After Albie Sachs had survived assassination in Maputo in 1988 and had recovered from his extensive injuries, he was provided with a desk, office and living support to work on a post-*apartheid* constitution for

South Africa.²³ He would later become one of the most celebrated members of South Africa's new Constitutional Court.

There is an abundance of memoirs and biographies of Commonwealth leaders in this period which offer insights into their relationships with each other and with the organisation.²⁴ It is also particularly useful to have the speeches, correspondence and memoirs of each of the Commonwealth Secretaries-General, most specifically Arnold Smith, Sir Shridath ('Sonny') Ramphal and Chief Emeka Anyaoku. How useful are these kinds of memoirs as opposed to speeches and correspondence? Rather like official communiques, declarations or minutes, a high degree of caution is necessary in analysing their content. By the 1960s, it would be extremely unusual to find a Commonwealth leader or Secretary-General with either the appetite or the time to prepare their own speeches (on the highly personalised Churchillian model). But, to a greater or lesser extent, substantial figures would work with a team of writers and advisers and, at the editorial stage in particular, would put their own stamp on the speech, perhaps with some specific rhetorical flourishes. The same would be true of official (as opposed to private) correspondence. This, too, might be subject to an extensive drafting process before arriving at a settled view, not just of the principal but of his or her organisation also. What will sometimes be available to the researcher will be the various drafts, pieces of advice and marginal annotations which led to the adoption of an agreed text.

Memoirs are individual and exclusive in their perspective. It is difficult to imagine that any are not, to a major extent, self-serving and therefore lacking in self-criticism. At the same time, how the authors deal with key challenges, or say they did, and what individuals, issues and events are glossed over or left out entirely can tell the reader a great deal. Certainly, the greater the number of memoirs and autobiographies, the more the opportunity to refine areas of contestation, as well as to absorb the fresh perspectives and new sources of information they may bring. All have their limitations but better that many flourish, rather than allowing the single, egotistical narrative of a former president, Prime Minister or public servant to dominate public memory.

As far as the national archives of Commonwealth countries are concerned, the National Archives at Kew, London, contain a rich store of British primary sources (and Commonwealth records up until 1965). Margaret Thatcher's private archive, opened in 2003, is widely available online (with the original documents held at Churchill College, Cambridge, and at Kew). The work of the Margaret Thatcher Archive Trust in digitising material up to and beyond the end of her premiership has been very useful in providing a counterpoint to Commonwealth records and biographies. Other national archives of member countries have been consulted online, including Library and Archives Canada and the National Archives of Australia. The United Nations' online archives have also been an invaluable source, given the interplay between the United Nations and the Commonwealth on many different levels.

An archival perspective from South Africa has also been essential. However, there are several specific difficulties about researching the *apartheid* era in South Africa. Firstly, with *apartheid's* end in sight, it is now known that the regime went to very considerable lengths to expunge all evidence of its crimes. In 1992, President de Klerk authorised the destruction by the National Intelligence Agency of 44 tonnes of incriminating material.[25] This was incinerated at night at a location outside Pretoria. Huge amounts of other sensitive records have also disappeared in what Verne Harris has called a "large-scale and systematic sanitisation of official memory."[26] Secondly, whether in part because of the deliberate destruction of official records or for other reasons, there is very little material relevant to the Commonwealth in the South African National Archives in Pretoria after the country's exit from the Commonwealth in 1961. There are discrete collections which should be accessible, such as Nelson Mandela's prison records originally held by the Department of Correctional Services. However, in practice, a formal freedom of information (FOI) request may be necessary.

Considerable amounts of more recent official material are stored at the Department of International Relations and Cooperation, also in Pretoria. This can only be accessed by approaching the archivist with an FOI request. That said, the not-for-profit organisation Open Secrets has in recent years used fifty FOI requests to access recently de-classified papers in eight South African Government departments, with some success. Nevertheless, Van Vuuren reflects that "access to most public records remains a challenge in democratic South Africa."[27]

As Verne Harris has argued, *apartheid* created "a formidable memory resource." He explains: "By their silences and their narratives of power, their constructions of experience, *apartheid's* memory institutions legitimised *apartheid* rule."[28] He continues: "A vast, simmering memory of resistance and struggle was forced away into informal spaces and the deeper reaches of the underground." Harris points out that record destruction not only affected official documents but also included material confiscated by the state from opposition and other non-state groups and then destroyed, as well as material obliterated in government bombings and raids.[29] Yet documents, diaries, photographs and political literature survived often in private hands. In the latter stages of *apartheid* as well as after 1994, a significant amount of material was deposited at collecting institutions, notably various South African universities. This includes the special collections at the William Cullen Library, University of Witwatersrand, and at the Jagger Library, University of Cape Town. There have also been initiatives like the South African History Archive (SAHA), now based in the old women's jail on Constitution Hill in Johannesburg. This independent archive was established in the 1980s on the initiative of the United Democratic Front (UDF), the Congress of South African Trade Unions (COSATU) and the African National Congress (ANC), although it is now non-aligned politically. Apart from its archival collections, SAHA aims to encourage use of South Africa's FOI laws to access histories which might have been lost or hidden. The genesis and focus of the archive at the Nelson Mandela Foundation in Johannesburg was rather different, but it is today a well-resourced facility, which, inter alia, offers insights into Mandela's relationship with the Commonwealth, both prior to and after his release from prison.

This range of archive material is clear evidence of South Africa's deeply contested and fragmented history. Baines points out that post-conflict societies "are often characterised by contestation over the ownership and meaning of the past" in what he describes as "memory wars."³⁰ This is a further special feature of research into *apartheid* in South Africa. The breadth of archival material reveals something of the spectrum of perspectives evident in the country's public memory. But it also offers an insight into another important continuum which stretches from the international to the domestic and to society's grassroots. As well as the private papers and diaries of some of the key figures involved, the records of a variety of non-governmental organisations and material from community campaigns (on, say, non-segregated sport or violent clashes in Crossroads township or conflict resolution in KwaZulu-Natal) have provided fascinating insights into 'bottom-up' accounts of events which are more often portrayed and understood 'top down'.

Even so, the proclamation of public history can have a more deliberate purpose. Baines recounts how President Zuma used the commemoration of the twentieth anniversary of the battle of Cuito Cuanavale to claim that Umkhonto We Sizwe's (MK's) cadres had taken part in what the president characterised as the Cuban victory over the *apartheid* army. This myth of MK involvement, which was unsupported by any evidence, was an example, according to Baines, of "memorialisation as a means to frame and shape the narrative of the armed struggle."³¹

There are other narratives which compete to fill the gaps in South Africa's social memory, including 'struggle' art, literature and theatre, as well as museums, monuments and memorial sites. The District Six Museum eloquently tells the story of a vibrant and variegated dockside community in Cape Town ripped apart and destroyed by forced removals under the Group Areas Act. The Robben Island Museum, the Voortrekker Monument, Liliesleaf Farm, the *Apartheid* Museum in Johannesburg and St George's Cathedral in Cape Town are all part of a tapestry of remembrance. Often in contrast, there are also surprising confluences in "South Africa's negotiation of the past."³² These 'alternative' archives have played a legitimate part in illuminating important aspects of South Africa's history and occasionally providing fragmented and faint reflections of its Commonwealth connections.

What all archives have in common is the inevitably selective way in which documents and records are deposited, classified and catalogued. The Commonwealth Secretariat's archive tells the reader much about the nature of the organisation – how it is led, its varied staff, its sometimes-conflicting priorities, its value system, its sense of duty and mission. The archive also illustrates how the organisation is embedded in a mesh of pan-Commonwealth relationships that ostensibly dictate its existence but are also its source of sustenance and energy. In that respect its archival characteristics are predictable. At the same time, the Secretariat archives offer a discreet and inevitably partial qualification and muffled response to the public narratives created by national member governments. In many cases, this may remain unexplored and therefore of little consequence: in the case of South Africa and *apartheid*, uncovering that material opens up an important new dimension of understanding. Like its national and international counterparts, the Commonwealth archive is in some measure self-serving. However, taken together with other archival sources, and with biography and oral history, it achieves its potency, even in its absences, gaps and silences.

However formidable and ordered the archive is, it is never just a grouping of papers because, suggests Bernard, "the human subject and the bodily remnant (the traces left behind of a life lived) are ever discernible."[33] Even in the most extreme of circumstances, such as the act of record destruction or criminal concealment, there is room to discern the human subject. President Nixon intended his notorious tapes to be a further instrument of his control, not damning evidence in his impeachment. When the British Colonial Office sought to destroy evidence of torture and abuse in Kenya, Uganda or Malaya, it did not expect some local colonial officers tasked with this duty to decide that some archives, including 'dirty' material, should be saved and repatriated to the UK because of their value to future historians.[34] As the Stasi moved to destroy its vast store of records on East Germany's citizens, it did not anticipate a huge popular protest to surround its headquarters, frustrate its plans and thereafter expose the truth of its totalitarian repression. Harris comments that there is 'poetic justice' in the way that the records of the *apartheid* state have sometimes been used to expose human rights violations and support the claims of those seeking restitution and justice.[35]

This common vulnerability in potentially the most impenetrable and shuttered archive is a cause for hope. Stoler concludes that colonial archives need to be read 'with' the archival grain, rather than against it, looking for "its regularities, for its logic of recall, for its densities and distributions, for its consistencies of misinformation, omission, and mistake – along the archival grain."[36] In this respect, context is all important, as is an appreciation of the influence of the appraiser of the material who, as Harris points out, creates archival value, particularly in what Harris describes as a transformational discourse.[37] This study will probe the reasons for the Commonwealth's apparent absence from South Africa's metanarrative of resistance and liberation and, in so doing, will emphasise the importance of the sub- or even counter-narrative which may be uncovered across the 'total' archive.

## 3   The Commonwealth

There are a variety of accounts of the Commonwealth's role in the international struggle against *apartheid*. Given the importance of the issue to Commonwealth mythology and the proportion of the Commonwealth Secretariat's human and financial resources spent on combatting racism in Southern Africa over the years, compared with other programme priorities, it is unsurprising that four former Commonwealth Secretaries-General have written about their experiences and recollections in some detail. Arnold Smith's account is largely confined to the Rhodesian crisis, though he also refers to the controversies in 1970–1971 about the UK's wish to resume arm sales to *apartheid* South Africa.[38] Shridath Ramphal and Emeka Anyaoku, in their collected speeches as well as their memoirs, give special prominence to racism, South Africa and *apartheid*.[39] Don McKinnon offers a more limited perspective, largely from the vantage point of being New Zealand's Foreign Minister (and Deputy Prime Minister) during the 1990s.[40] The Commonwealth Secretariat's own publication, released at the height of the sanctions campaign and well before *apartheid's* end, inevitably provides an incomplete and rather propagandist perspective.⁴¹ Much more useful are the biennial reports of the Commonwealth Secretary-General.⁴² Although the practice of issuing biennial reports has been disrupted in recent years, the reports between 1966 and 1995 are rich in detail. A number of general books about the Commonwealth covering the period of study (McIntyre, Mayall) include analysis of the Commonwealth's engagement with *apartheid*.⁴³

What should be the most authoritative external source for assessing the role of the Commonwealth during this period is South Africa's official history of the *apartheid* struggle, produced through the South African Democracy Education Trust at the behest of President Thabo Mbeki. Volume 3, which focuses on international solidarity, declares on its opening page: "It must be emphasised from the outset that not all countries, organisations and movements could be covered in detail in this volume. Those chosen have a special significance."⁴⁴ There is no chapter or section on the Commonwealth, though some Commonwealth countries are covered individually.⁴⁵ Chapters are also devoted to the part played by various other countries in the international campaign against *apartheid*. These include Austria, Belgium, France, the Federal Republic of Germany, the German Democratic Republic, Italy, Switzerland, Spain, Portugal and Greece, alongside more prominent contributors such as Cuba. While there are numerous references in the volume to the Commonwealth, these are scattered and often lacking in context. There are also several glaring omissions such as any reference to the 1986 mission to South Africa of the Commonwealth EPG. This fragmented approach is in contrast to the volume's introduction, which states: "The most significant international organisations that supported the anti-*apartheid* struggle were the United Nations and its agencies; the Organisation for African Unity (OAU); the Non-Aligned Movement (NAM) **and the Commonwealth**" (my emphasis).⁴⁶

Audie Klotz has included the Commonwealth in her examination of three multilateral organisations (the others are the United Nations and the OAU) and their part in the anti-*apartheid* cause.⁴⁷ Her purpose is to place the multilateral pursuit of moral principles – in this case, opposition to *apartheid* – in contrast with the conventional theory that the foreign policies of sovereign nations are wholly driven by national interests. In the case of the Commonwealth, she analyses developments in the association leading to the break with *apartheid* South Africa in 1961 and then considers the Rhodesian rebellion and the emergence of a collective Commonwealth policy on the issue, independent of the British Government. Her study concentrates on the Commonwealth's adoption of various multilateral economic and financial sanctions on South Africa after 1985, in opposition to the UK. Her contention is that, in the case of *apartheid*, the advocacy of the moral norm of racial equality played a central role "in defining identity and interest" and creating "globalised concern over domestic discrimination," overriding strategic and economic interests.⁴⁸ She concludes that "the evolution of Commonwealth policies offers an example of successful multilateral sanctions."⁴⁹

The reality may be more nuanced and will be explored in depth in the third case study, which addresses Commonwealth sanctions. Nevertheless, Klotz raises an important question, as does her focus on multilateralism as a distinct and effective form of international diplomacy. Kotz's study of the Commonwealth and *apartheid* is not comprehensive, even though it is a rare example of serious analysis of the phenomenon. Much more widespread is the perception that the Commonwealth contribution was sporadic, of limited value or of no value at all. This last perspective is exemplified by Geoffrey Wandesforde-Smith who applauds the laying bare of "the myth that the Commonwealth has accomplished much of enduring significance since the end of the Second World War."[50] Even contesting that prevailing viewpoint is suspect, argues Murphy, because "it tends to be [only] supporters who feel that it is actually worthy of study."[51]

This volume aims to fill a substantial gap in current knowledge by telling the full story of the Commonwealth's battle for racial justice in Southern Africa – in helping end white settler rule in Rhodesia, as well as contributing to the end of *apartheid* in South Africa.

## 4  *Apartheid* and South Africa

There is an abundance of literature and other material on South Africa and the origins and development of the *apartheid* state. This includes histories of British colonialism and its rivalry with Dutch settlers, as well as clashes with other migrant and indigenous peoples, and the emergence of the Afrikaner identity in the form of the republics, and the conflict which became the Boer War.[52] Later colonial history, and the formation of the Union in 1908, led to a recurring imperative to achieve the unity of English and Afrikaner whites, through 'white fusion', and this had its repeated reiteration in the *apartheid* era. Afrikaner thinking and identity, and the emergence of the concept of *apartheid*, owed much to the turmoil of the mid-war and post-war years.[53] This included influences sympathetic to National Socialism.[54] The triumph of Afrikaner nationalists at the 1948 elections and the creation of *apartheid* are sometimes characterised in opposition to a post-imperial liberal concept of enlarging freedom for all races, but this idealised view is not supported by the firmly segregationist views and actions of the defeated Jan Smuts and many of his parliamentary colleagues, who were unable to comprehend the menace posed by *apartheid*.[55] The history of the marginalised non-whites – of Black African, Indian and Coloured peoples – and their struggle against *apartheid* has only more recently achieved the recognition it deserves. Even so, William Worger warns that too often "Africans as historical actors are presented primarily as victims," rather than having made a contribution to their own history.[56] Alongside the settler and 'liberal' interpretations of South Africa's history have been radical economic and social analyses, including those built on Marxist theory, which point to the development of 'racialised capitalism' and its adaptation to the *apartheid* era.[57]

The growth of internal resistance to the *apartheid* regime in the 1970s and 1980s and the public recognition of those who suffered under *apartheid* (and some of those prepared to atone for their wrongdoing) through the Truth and Reconciliation Commission (TRC) process have led to a new emphasis on 'struggle' literature. As well as offering a 'bottom-up' (as opposed to 'top-down') perspective this new literature has facilitated far greater attention to those whose stories have previously not been heard, particularly women and young people.[58]

*Figure 1.2* Africans demonstrate against the pass laws, 1960. Margaret Ballinger Papers, University of Cape Town.

Lastly, the recognition in 1961 by the United Nations that *apartheid* was a *sui generis* system of racial oppression which exceptionally necessitated action by the international community, overriding any impediments to intervention under the UN Charter, also stimulated the growth of a global AAM. The part played by international protest, boycott and sanctions, military or other support to the liberation and democratic forces (and assistance in facilitating negotiations) also has a rich literature. As Rob Skinner argues, "It was in the intersections between networks of anti-*apartheid* and rights activists, state institutions and international organisations, from the Commonwealth to the United Nations, that a language of human rights would be formed."[59]

The integration of these various narratives, however, is deeply contested. Twenty-five years after the end of *apartheid*, South Africa is "set apart from most other nations by the intensity of its embrace of a future through the re-negotiating of its past."[60] In the eyes of Cuthbertson, South Africa is "imprisoned by its historiography."[61] In a post-conflict society like South Africa, Gary Baines suggests that the propagation of irreconcilable views of the past "has fuelled 'memory wars' in which self-appointed custodians contest the meaning of history."[62] Saul Dubow contends that the recent past is not yet properly historical and that therefore "impulses to remember and to forget exist in tension with each other."[63] The marking in 2016 of the fortieth anniversary of the 1976 Soweto Student revolt was characterised by attempts to claim or apportion 'ownership'.[64] Much in the way of evidence has been lost or fragmented, and decades of censorship have affected what little public information is available.⁶⁵ Even so, Harris denies that what archives that remain are a quiet retreat for a few scholars and others. They are, on the contrary "a crucible of human experience, a battleground for meaning and significance, a babel of stories, a place and a space of ever-shifting power-plays."⁶⁶ Coombs asks how new national histories might engage "larger structural narratives and material conditions and individual lived experiences."⁶⁷

This is not only a question of competing and unresolved narratives but also about the impact of these historical legacies on present-day South Africa. Teresa Barnes points to the 'applied history' which contributes to policy-making.⁶⁸ Baines highlights some of the foundational myths "that legitimates ANC rule."⁶⁹ Ellis also analyses how the ANC has learnt "to live by certain historical myths."⁷⁰ Van Vuuren argues that *apartheid* South Africa's corruption, its economic crime and its secretive international networks cast a long shadow over present-day South Africa.⁷¹ In such a national environment, it is hardly surprising if the Commonwealth's place in South Africa's history is either automatically set within a British and colonial historical context or, in its more modern form, poorly remembered or discarded.

**Notes**

1 Commonwealth Secretariat, *The Commonwealth at the Summit (Vol.1): Communiques of Commonwealth Heads of Government Meetings 1944–1986* (London: Commonwealth Secretariat, 1987), 29.
2 Arnold Smith with Clyde Sanger, *Stitches in Time: The Commonwealth in World Politics* (London: Andre Deutsch, 1981), 154.
3 Krishnan Srinivasan, "Principles and practice: Human rights, the Harare Declaration and the Commonwealth Ministerial Action Group (CMAG)," In *The Contemporary Commonwealth: An Assessment 1965–2009*, ed. James Mayall (London and New York: Routledge, Taylor & Francis Group, 2010), 67.
4 Ronald Hyam and Peter Henshaw, *The Lion and the Springbok: Britain and South Africa since the Boer War* (Cambridge: Cambridge University Press, 2003), 139–143.
5 Patricia Scotland, "OPINION: Racism seeks to drive us apart but there are rays of hope." 8 June 2020. Thomson Reuters Foundation News, Accessed 4 August 2020, www.news.trust.org/item/20200608160407-704ug/.
6 Shridath Ramphal, *Glimpses of a Global Life* (Hertford, UK: Hansib Publications Limited, 2014), 404.
7 Chris Saunders, "Britain, the Commonwealth, and the Question of the Release of Nelson Mandela in the 1980s," *The Round Table: The Commonwealth Journal of International Affairs* 106: 6 (2017): 659.
8 Newell Stultz, "Evolution of the United Nations Anti-*Apartheid* Regime," *Human Rights Quarterly* 3:1 (1991): 1.
9 Jack Donnelly, "International Human Rights: A Regime Analysis," *International Organisation* 40:3 (1986): 599–642.
10 Stultz, "Evolution of the United Nations Anti-*Apartheid* Regime," 2.
11 "Partnership and policy," *The Round Table: A Quarterly Review of the Politics of the British Commonwealth* 37:145 (1946): 3–7.
12 Peter Marshall, "Smuts and the Preamble to the UN Charter," *The Round Table: The Commonwealth Journal of International Affairs*, 90:358 (2001): 57–59.
13 Mary Ann Glendon, "John P. Humphrey and the Drafting of the Universal Declaration of Human Rights," *Journal of the History of International Law* 2:2 (2000): 250.

14 *The Commonwealth Secretariat Act (1966)*, Part 1 of schedule (2), Legislation.gov.uk, Accessed 3 March 2017, www.legislation.gov.uk/ukpga/1966/10. The legislation was enacted on 10 March 1966 but was deemed to have come into operation on 1 July 1965 when the Secretariat was established.
15 Jay Gilbert, "The Commonwealth Secretariat and its documentary heritage," *The Round Table; The Commonwealth Journal of International Affairs* 92: 372 (2003): 663.
16 Since 2000, the Secretary-General's term of office has been four years with the possibility of a second and final term, providing no other candidates successfully contest the extension.
17 Gilbert, "The Commonwealth Secretariat and its documentary heritage," 662.
18 The Commonwealth Group of Eminent Persons, *Mission to South Africa: The Commonwealth Report* (Harmondsworth, UK: Penguin Books, 1986), 21.
19 Richard Bourne (ed.), *Shridath Ramphal: The Commonwealth and the World* (London & Hertfordshire: Hansib, 2008), 19.
20 Catherine Hall, *Civilising Subjects – Metropole and Colony in the English Imagination 1830–1867* (Cambridge: Polity, 2002), 9–10.
21 "In Britain, Foreign Office Minister Lynda Chalker meets Oliver Tambo, president of the ANC," 24 June 1986, *South African History Online*, Accessed 10 October 2019, www.sahistory.org.za/dated-event/Britain-foreign-office-minister-lynda-chalker-meets-olivertanbo-president-anc/.
22 Verity Sharp, "Nelson Mandela and the Commonwealth," blog posted on 6 December 2013, Accessed 5 May 2018, https://thercs.org/new-and-blogs/blogs/nelson-mandela-and-the-commonwealth/.
23 Albie Sachs recounted his experiences as a visiting fellow of the ICS at a seventieth anniversary conference in Senate House on Monday, 25 March 2019.
24 Smith, *Stiches in Time*; Ramphal, *Glimpses of a Global Life;* Emeka Anyaoku, *The Inside Story of the Modern Commonwealth* (London: Evans Brothers Ltd, 2004).
25 Hennie van Vuuren, *Apartheid, Guns and Money: A Tale of Profit* (London: Hurst & Co. 2018), 1.
26 Verne Harris, "The archival sliver: Power, memory and archives in South Africa," *Archival Science* 2: 1–2 (2002): 65.
27 Van Vuuren, *Apartheid, Guns and Money*, 20.
28 Harris, "The archival sliver," 69.
29 Ibid, 70.
30 Gary Baines, "Legacies of South Africa's *apartheid* wars," *Oxford Research Encyclopaedia of African History*, published online: 25 February 2019, Accessed 29 September 2019, https://doi.org/10.1093/acrefore/9780190277734.013.452.
31 Baines, "Legacies of South Africa's *apartheid* wars," 11.
32 Harris, "The archival sliver," 85.
33 Bernard, "Unpacking the archive," 97.
34 Shohei Sato, "Operation legacy: Britain's destruction and concealment of colonial records worldwide," *The Journal of Imperial and Commonwealth History* 45:4 (2017): 708.
35 Harris, "The archival sliver," 79.
36 Stoler, "Colonial archives," 100.
37 Harris, "The archival sliver," 83.
38 Smith, *Stitches in Time*, 204–220.
39 Shridath Ramphal, *One World to Share: Selected Speeches of the Commonwealth Secretary-General 1975–1978* (London: Century Hutchinson, 1979); Ron Sanders (ed.), *Inseparable Humanity: An Anthology of Reflections of Shridath Ramphal* (London, Hansib Publications Ltd, 1988); Emeka Anyaoku, *The Missing Headlines: Selected Speeches* (Liverpool: Liverpool University Press, 1997), 143–184.
40 Don McKinnon, *In the Ring: A Commonwealth Memoir* (London: Elliott and Thompson Ltd, 2013).

16  Introduction – Whose History?

41 Commonwealth Secretariat, *Racism in Southern Africa: The Commonwealth Stand* (London: Commonwealth Secretariat, 1987).
42 Copies of the Secretary-General's biennial reports to Commonwealth Heads of Government from 1966 are held at the Commonwealth library and archives in Marlborough House, London.
43 Mayall, *The Contemporary Commonwealth*, 210–223; McIntyre, *Guide to the Contemporary Commonwealth*, 38–43.
44 Gregory Houston, "Introduction," *The Road to Democracy in South Africa: International Solidarity* (Vol.3) (Pretoria: South Africa Democracy Education Trust, University of South Africa, 2008), 1–40.
45 These are Canada, Australia, New Zealand and India.
46 Houston, *The Road to Democracy*, 1–40.
47 Audie Klotz, *Norms in International Relations: The Struggle Against Apartheid* (New York: Cornell University Press, 2010), 55–72.
48 Klotz, *Norms in International Relations*, 9.
49 Ibid, 71.
50 Wandesforde-Smith, "Taking the measure of the Commonwealth," 1.
51 Philip Murphy, *The Empire's New Clothes: The Myth of the Commonwealth* (London: Hurst & Co, 2018), x.
52 Thomas Pakenham, *The Boer War* (London-NY-Sydney-Toronto: Weidenfeld & Nicholson Ltd, 1979).
53 D.W. Kruger, *The Making of a Nation: A History of the Union of South Africa 1910–1961* (Johannesburg-London: Macmillan, 1969), 189–192, 226.
54 Alex Hepple, *Political Leaders of the Twentieth Century: Verwoerd* (England: Harmondsworth, 1967), 88–97.
55 Saul Dubow, *Apartheid 1948–1994* (Oxford: Oxford University Press, 2014), 31.
56 William Worger, "Combining the history and historiography of South Africa," *The Journal of African History* 44:1 (2003): 154.
57 Among the best known is Harold Wolpe, "Capitalism and cheap labour-power in South Africa: From Segregation to *Apartheid*," *Economy and Society* 1:4 (1972): 425–456.
58 This includes Cherryl Walker, *Women and Resistance in South Africa* (New York: Monthly Review Press, 1982); Colin Bundy, "Street sociology and pavement politics: Aspects of youth and student resistance in Cape Town, 1985," *Journal of Southern African Studies* 13:3 (1987): 303–330.
59 Robert Skinner, "The dynamics of anti-*apartheid*: international solidarity, human rights and decolonisation," In *Britain, France and the Decolonisation of Africa: Future Imperfect?* ed. Andrew Smith & Chris Jeppesen (London: UCL Press, 2017), 119.
60 Harris, "The archival sliver," 82
61 Greg Cuthbertson (Emeritus Professor, UNISA), in conversation with the author, June 21 2016, Pretoria.
62 Baines, "Legacies of South Africa's *apartheid* wars," 10.
63 Dubow, *Apartheid*, 2.
64 The author's impressions of contemporary media coverage, Johannesburg, June 2016.
65 Stephen Ellis, *External Mission: The ANC in Exile, 1960–1990* (London: Hurst & Co., 2014), 310.
66 Ibid., 85.
67 Annie Coombes, *Visual Culture and Public Memory in a Democratic South Africa* (Durham and London: Duke University Press, 2003), 10.
68 Teresa Barnes, "The state of academic historiography in South Africa," *Journal of African History* 48:3 (2007): 508.
69 Baines, "Legacies of South Africa's *apartheid* wars," 11.
70 Ellis, *External Mission*, 308.
71 Van Vuuren, *Apartheid, Guns and Money*, 489.

## References

Alex Hepple, *Political Leaders of the Twentieth Century: Verwoerd* (England: Harmondsworth, 1967).
Annie Coombes, *Visual Culture and Public Memory in a Democratic South Africa* (Durham and London: Duke University Press, 2003).
Anyaoku, *The Inside Story*, Op.Cit.
Arnold Smith with Clyde Sanger, *Stitches in Time: The Commonwealth in World Politics* (London: Andre Deutsch, 1981).
Audie Klotz, *Norms in International Relations: The Struggle against Apartheid* (New York: Cornell University Press, 2010).
Catherine Hall, *Civilising Subjects – Metropole and Colony in the English Imagination 1830–1867* (Cambridge: Polity, 2002).
Commonwealth Secretariat, *Racism in Southern Africa: The Commonwealth Stand* (London: Commonwealth Secretariat, 1987).
Commonwealth Secretariat, *The Commonwealth at the Summit (Vol.1): Communiques of Commonwealth Heads of Government Meetings 1944–1986* (London: Commonwealth Secretariat, 1987).
Don McKinnon, *In the Ring: A Commonwealth Memoir* (London: Elliott, Thompson Ltd, 2013).
D.W. Kruger, *The Making of a Nation: A History of the Union of South Africa 1910–1961* (Johannesburg-London: Macmillan, 1969).
Emeka Anyaoku, *The Missing Headlines: Selected Speeches* (Liverpool: Liverpool University Press, 1997).
Hennie van Vuuren, *Apartheid, Guns and Money: A Tale of Profit* (London: Hurst & Co, 2018).
James Mayall (ed.), *The Contemporary Commonwealth: An Assessment 1965–2009* (London, New York: Routledge, 2010).
McIntyre, *Guide to the Contemporary Commonwealth*, Op.Cit.
Philip Murphy, *The Empire's New Clothes: The Myth of the Commonwealth* (London: Hurst & Co, 2018).
Ramphal, *Glimpses of a Global Life*, Op. cit.
Richard Bourne (ed.), *Shridath Ramphal: The Commonwealth and the World* (London, Hertfordshire: Hansib, 2008).
Ronald Hyam and Peter Henshaw, *The Lion and the Springbok: Britain and South Africa Since the Boer War* (Cambridge: Cambridge University Press, 2003).
Ron Sanders (ed.), *Inseparable Humanity: An Anthology of Reflections of Shridath Ramphal* (London, Hansib Publications Ltd, 1988).
Saul Dubow, *Apartheid 1948–1994* (Oxford: Oxford University Press, 2014).
Shridath Ramphal, *One World to Share: Selected Speeches of the Commonwealth Secretary-General 1975–1978* (London: Century Hutchinson, 1979).
Sifiso Ndlovu (ed.), *The Road to Democracy in South Africa: International Solidarity (Vol.3)*, (Pretoria: South Africa Democracy Education Trust, University of South Africa, 2008).
Stephen Ellis, *External Mission: The ANC in Exile, 1960–1990* (London: Hurst & Co., 2014).
The Commonwealth Group of Eminent Persons, *Mission to South Africa: The Commonwealth Report* (Harmondsworth: Penguin Books, 1986).
Thomas Pakenham, *The Boer War* (London, Sydney and Toronto: Weidenfeld & Nicholson Ltd, 1979).

# 2 The Decline of the 'Imperial' Commonwealth

## 1 Introduction

In May 1944, as the allied forces prepared for 'Operation Neptune' and the invasion of Nazi-occupied France, Commonwealth Prime Ministers met in London. In addition to the British Prime Minister, Winston Churchill (who was in the chair), those also present were John Curtin of Australia; W.L. Mackenzie King of Canada; Peter Fraser of New Zealand; and Field Marshal Jan Smuts of the Union of South Africa. Ireland was not represented, being neutral in the conflict and because, with the adoption of the 1937 constitution, many in Ireland considered that they were no longer part of the British Commonwealth.[1] British India, with 3.4 million personnel under arms, had as its spokesman General Sir Hari Singh, the Maharaja of Jammu and Kashmir. Sir Godfrey Huggins, the Prime Minister of Southern Rhodesia, was also present at Churchill's invitation (notwithstanding the territory's status as a self-governing British colony).

The purpose of the meeting was to endorse the conclusions of the Moscow Declaration, laying out the war aims of the allies. The mood was upbeat. The five Prime Ministers signed a declaration which proclaimed: "Though hard and bitter battles lie ahead, we now see before us . . . the sure presage of our future victory."[2] Their declaration concluded with the following stirring words:

> We rejoice in our inheritance of loyalties and ideals, and proclaim our sense of kinship to one another. . . . We believe that when victory is won and peace returns, this same free association, this inherent unity of purpose, will make us able to do further service to mankind.[3]

Yet, as Kumarasingham points out, "the pre-1947 Commonwealth was unabashedly an imperial organisation concerned with defence obligations, (and) with an overarching Crown acting as the formal constitutional denominator."[4] Although the Dominions were self-governing within a free association of nations, they shared with the UK both common values and a rich historical experience. All had achieved statehood and their present form as a result of mass, white migration from the British Isles (though also from other European nations) to the 'new' world. These British white settler nations had sustained a formidable military alliance through two world wars. Although Vimy Ridge and Gallipoli had fired a growing sense of national identity and an increasing desire to direct their own destinies, the Dominions, almost without exception, also wanted to retain an overt connection to their British rootstock. This kinship sprang from a largely common, and certainly unmistakeably white, source – notwithstanding the indigenous peoples that the nation-builders had encountered and largely supressed in the course of their mission. Only in the case of the Union of South Africa was the reality rather different. There, the overriding preoccupation of its leaders had been with divisions and tensions between the white Afrikaans and white English communities, exacerbated by bitter memories of conflict and conquest. In truth, South Africa was no 'white' Dominion since most of its citizens were 'natives' and non-whites – Black Africans, Indians and those of mixed race, otherwise known as 'Coloureds'.

None of this was generally apparent outside South Africa in the aftermath of an exhausting global conflict. Indeed, South Africa's Prime Minister and war leader, Field Marshal Jan Christian Smuts, felt that the British Commonwealth had much to offer a post-conflict world and a nascent United Nations. "Elements of the future world government . . . are already in operation in our Commonwealth of nations," he declared. It was, he argued, "the only successful experiment in international government,"[5] echoing Zimmern, Gilbert Murray and others who had seen the Commonwealth as 'a world experiment'.[6]

## 2   The Post-war Commonwealth

Barely a year after the end of hostilities in Europe and nine months since his own ejection from office as Prime Minister, Winston Churchill used a visit to Fulton, Missouri, in the United States to warn of the dangers of a new conflict. Speaking alongside President Harry Truman, who had introduced him, Churchill declared: "From Stettin in the Baltic to Trieste in the Adriatic, an iron curtain has descended across the Continent."[7] Humanity, so recently emerged from a devastating global conflict, must be protected from the "two giant marauders, war and tyranny," he argued. While this should be achieved through the United Nations and respecting its Charter, "neither the sure prevention of war, nor the continuous rise of the world organisation will be gained without . . . the fraternal association of the English-speaking peoples," Churchill affirmed.[8] Such an alliance was not, in his view, at variance with the need for overriding loyalty to the United Nations. Rather, it was, he argued, the means by which the world organisation would achieve its full stature and authority. The "sinews of peace" (the title of Churchill's Fulton speech) comprised a good understanding of the Soviet Union under the auspices of the United Nations, which in turn would be underpinned by the combined strength and security of the English-speaking world.

Commonwealth countries played a significant part in the United Nations' early beginnings. *The Round Table* commented:

What is important for British readers to consider is the markedly polyphonic contribution to the concert of nations which has been offered during 1946, not so much by the United Kingdom as by the members of the British Commonwealth. Both in the United Nations Organisations and in the Peace Conference of Paris the present year has seen the emergence of the British Dominions to unprecedented prominence on the stage of world affairs.[9]

That positive view was later echoed by John Holmes, the Director-General of the Canadian Institute of International Affairs. "The UN and the Commonwealth are the two institutions which have profoundly affected the history of the world since 1945," he argued.[10] In his view, the Commonwealth, as a group, proved an active force during the first decade of the United Nations. Firstly, there was an unofficial agreement at San Francisco that one of the six non-permanent seats on the Security Council should go to a Commonwealth member country (other than the UK). When the Security Council was expanded in the 1960s and a geographic basis established for the rotating membership, the Commonwealth continued to be well represented. As Ingram has argued, "[t]he Commonwealth voice in the Council, therefore, in practice has not diminished; if anything, it has increased."[11] Secondly, there was also a provision for there to be a Commonwealth Vice-President of the General Assembly (a practice that lasted until the early 1960s). Thirdly, while it did not claim to be an organised caucus, Commonwealth countries met as a group, and discussed the developing agenda, without necessarily arriving at common positions. It was thus perceived as a presence in the United Nations working for good. As Lord Greenhill, the former Head of the British Diplomatic Service, put it, the Commonwealth can be "the leaven in the lump."[12]

In the eyes of some (at any rate, before the intractable problems of the Rhodesian rebellion began to intrude) Britain also offered a model for how the de-colonisation might be achieved. In the view of Holmes: "As an institution, the Commonwealth set the pattern of the UN's concept of colonial development and a model, imperfect but tangible, of interracial community."[13] Iain Macleod, who became British Colonial Secretary in 1959, had much earlier set out the Doctrine of Lesser Risk: that it was dangerous for the de-colonisation process to go too fast – but still more dangerous for it to go too slow. As his biographer, Nigel Fisher, put it, "[w]e could have postponed independence, but only by the rule of the gun and at the risk of bloodshed. As it was, we devolved power too quickly but with goodwill."[14] In the immediate post-war years, an exhausted and bankrupt Britain, in Palestine, Kenya and India, had had a taste for just how costly and painful attempting to hold back nationalist forces might be, let alone in circumstances, such as in Palestine, where the incompatibility of the UK's promises and commitments in various quarters made a peaceful resolution well-nigh impossible. The British Foreign Secretary, Ernie Bevin, whose reputation was damaged by his handling of the Palestine issue, later declared that it "all goes back to the 1917 dishonesty of inconsistent promises to the two sides."[15] The bombing of the King David's Hotel in Jerusalem (the administrative and military headquarters of the British mandate) on 22 July 1946 by the Irgun, with the loss of ninety-one lives (mainly local Arabs), and with forty-six injured, had a profound impact. It encouraged the UK in the belief that the Mandate was 'unworkable' and that the search for a solution should be entrusted to the United Nations. The withdrawal of British forces quickly followed. There was a diminishing appetite for holding down imperial possessions by force of arms.

As it was, the British public's growing sense of unease about the imperial role was considerably aggravated by the 1959 Hola scandal during the Mau Mau insurgency in Kenya.[16] At the Hola detention camp, eleven Mau Mau prisoners had been beaten to death and many dozens more left with serious injuries. However, it was only in 2011, with the 'discovery' of a large cache of secret colonial files at Hanslope Park, near London, that the full scale of systematic colonial violence was laid bare. The files on Kenya documented "graphic accounts of torture, rape, and murder," as well as of extrajudicial hangings.[17] This led the British Foreign Secretary, William Hague, to admit to parliament in June 2013 that "Kenyans were subject to torture and ill-treatment," prompting the government's "sincere regret."[18] The British Government also agreed to pay nearly £20 m in costs and compensation to over 5,000 Kenyan victims of the colonial administration.[19] The 'migrated files', unearthed largely due to the tenacity and skill of David Anderson, revealed similar stories in Cyprus, Malaya and elsewhere. For Murphy, "at the heart of this bloody aspect of imperialism was a vacuum of legitimacy" which troubled many, including within the colonial system.[20]

The viability of an expanded 'imperial' Commonwealth, blending old Dominions with new, also faced profound challenges in the post-war years. Firstly, the 1947 Indo-Pakistan conflict, over the allegiance of the princely state of Jammu and Kashmir, confirmed the view that the concept of the Commonwealth as a military or defensive alliance was increasingly problematic. A report of a Cabinet Committee, circulated in advance of a meeting of the British Cabinet on 28 October 1948, highlighted the issue: "In matters of defence, it is our hope that in war the self-governing members of the Commonwealth will usually be found fighting together on the same side and never be found fighting on opposite sides."[21] The report, in acknowledging the reality of Ireland's wartime neutrality, continued: "In recent months we have faced the possibility – hitherto regarded as even more unthinkable – of war between two members of the Commonwealth."[22] A Commonwealth relationship in defence terms could not therefore be defined in ways which would be generally acceptable, the report concluded. Indeed, Jammu and Kashmir was to be the cockpit for three further wars between Pakistan and India.

Secondly, the war in Kashmir tested the notion that the Dominions of the British Commonwealth were "united by common allegiance to the Crown."[23] Ever since the passing of the Statute of Westminster, the divisibility of the Crown had been conceded with the British monarch given different legal expression in each of the Dominions. The conflict between the two new Dominions of Pakistan and India was therefore also a case of King George VI being at war with himself. This acute dilemma did not escape the attention of General Sir Douglas Gracey, the British Commander-in-Chief of the Pakistan Army. He refused the order of Muhammad Al-Jinnah (then Pakistan's Governor-General) to send troops into Kashmir on the grounds that Indian and Pakistan forces had taken an Oath of

*Figure 2.1* Prime Minister of India Jawaharlal Nehru arrives at Marlborough House, London (1962), accompanied by Morarji Desai, Finance Minister, and M.C. Chagla, Indian High Commissioner to the UK.

Allegiance to King George VI, and that therefore conflict between the two was not possible. However, Gracey's former Commander-in-Chief, Lord Mountbatten, by then Governor-General of India, had no such inhibitions in authorising the despatch of Indian forces once Jammu and Kashmir's new constitutional status in India had been proclaimed.

Thirdly, India was embarking on the adoption of a new constitution which would make the country a sovereign, democratic republic. This was at variance with the Statute of Westminster which stated that "the Crown is the symbol of the free association of the Members of the British Commonwealth of Nations" and that the Dominions were united by a common allegiance to the British Crown. Despite this requirement, Nehru wanted India to remain in the Commonwealth as a republic.[24] Some wondered why India would wish to retain its membership. As Mansergh put it:

> Certainly, the fact that South Africa, as a member of the Commonwealth, enforced racial segregation as a matter of political principle by itself, seemed to many leading Congressmen in 1947 why India should secede once the transitional advantages of membership had been reaped.[25]

It was a question which Jawaharlal Nehru was later to address directly in a debate, on 16 May 1949, in the Indian Constituent Assembly. He was asked: "How can you join a Commonwealth in which there is racial discrimination and there are other things happening to which we object?" He admitted that this was a fair and troubling question. But he explained: "When we have an alliance with a nation or group of nations, it does not mean that we accept their other policies. It does not mean that we commit ourselves in any way to something that they may do."[26]

In the course of 1948, the UK government grappled with how the Commonwealth might reconcile allegiance to the Crown with republican status. It was clear that, with the Berlin blockade by the Soviet Union precipitating the first crisis of the cold war, the UK was anxious not to lose India and Pakistan from the Commonwealth. "If . . . India and Pakistan should feel compelled to withdraw from the Commonwealth, its prestige and influence in the world would be seriously impaired," declared a note from the Cabinet Secretary, Sir Norman Brook. He continued: "And, internally, the effect might be, not to reinforce the cohesion of the remaining members of the Commonwealth, but to encourage the forces already working in the direction of separation and disintegration."[27] Did the answer lie in creating a "Commonwealth of British and Associated Nations"? The advantages of such a scheme, in the eyes of the Committee on Commonwealth Relations, were that it would not tamper with the basic requirement of common allegiance to the Crown; it would retain the 'British' prefix to the Commonwealth, for those linked by 'sentiment and emotion', and it might bring a wider grouping of nations into some kind of association with Britain and the Dominions. On the other hand, the Committee were troubled by the fact that

> a refusal to contemplate some alternative form of association other than that devised in the interests of a group of British communities is incompatible with the aims of our Colonial policy, which holds out to peoples who are largely non-European the ultimate goal of self-government within the Commonwealth.[28]

It was difficult to see how a two-tiered system would work in practice, and there was concern that some 'British' Dominions (such as South Africa or even Canada) might prefer 'associated' status rather than remaining in the inner circle (and thereby weakening the core). There were, in any case, difficulties in offering the outer circle of associated states any material benefits not otherwise available to foreign states. There was the issue of Commonwealth consultation, long understood to be a defining feature of the association. However, the UK (responsible for the organisation's administration) already consulted only when and with whom it chose to and feared greater definition. "The United Kingdom Government would still find it necessary to exercise discretion in deciding the basis of consultation with other Commonwealth countries."[29] Even more alarming was the thought that a new association would have to be held together by some sort of defining charter, including a provision for the expulsion of those who abused its provisions (something which was finally achieved with the signing of the Commonwealth Charter by the Queen in 2013).[30]

With no clear alternative strategy, the Cabinet were left tinkering with a redefinition of 'common allegiance' to the Crown. This conclusion was reinforced by consultations with Canada, Australia and New Zealand. While all were ready to revisit the nature of the Commonwealth relationship,

> they were uneasy about the possible consequences for the Commonwealth of having admitted to full membership three Asiatic countries whose peoples do not share the common heritage and sentiment which are the strongest of the bonds uniting the older members of the Commonwealth.

New Zealand's Prime Minister, Peter Fraser, who had enthusiastically welcomed India as an independent Commonwealth dominion in 1947, was now alarmed by these latest developments. Kumarasingham describes him as fearful of losing "a Commonwealth moored in defence ties and Crown collegiality to the bicephalous monster of Indian neutrality and republicanism."[31]

Nevertheless, leaders of the 'old' Commonwealth did not want to see these countries follow Burma in seceding from the association and agreed that "no effort should be spared to retain India, Pakistan and Ceylon within the Commonwealth . . . (and) . . . some constitutional anomalies would be a small price to pay" for their continuing involvement. Even so, whatever concessions these might be, they should "in no circumstances be allowed to impair or disturb the existing relations between the 'central' members of the Commonwealth (the United Kingdom, Canada, Australia and New Zealand)."[32] Perhaps the 'two-tier' Commonwealth was alive and well after all.

## 3  The 1949 London Agreement

The 1948 Commonwealth Prime Ministers' Meeting, hosted by the British Prime Minister, Clement Attlee, in No. 10 Downing Street, saw the attendance for the first time of the Prime Ministers of India, Pakistan and Ceylon. The meeting's final communiqué remarked that "[t]heir presence symbolised the extension of the bounds of democratic freedom which reflects the spirit and steadfast purpose of the Commonwealth." It continued: "This blending of the West and the East in a lofty task of building a lasting peace on the foundations of freedom, justice and economic prosperity provides a new hope for harassed mankind."[33] Even so, pressure was mounting for some kind of solution to India's looming republicanism, and Clement Attlee reported to his Cabinet: "During the past two weeks I and some of my colleagues have been discussing with Pandit Nehru the possibility of devising some satisfactory constitutional link, preferably through the Crown, which would be acceptable to public opinion in India."[34]

This was the task of the 1949 Commonwealth Prime Ministers' Meeting, gathered in London once more, barely six months from their last conference. Even so, it was clear that Nehru was the lynchpin in arriving at any solution. Referring to discussions in advance of the meeting, Nehru said:

> I am afraid I am a bad bargainer. I am not used to the ways of the market place.... I think it is far better to gain the goodwill of the other party, to come to a decision in friendship and goodwill, than to gain a word here or there at the cost of ill-will. So I approached the problem in this spirit.[35]

Despite this, it was clear that any solution involving a limitation on India's national sovereignty, however notional, would be unacceptable. This scotched the hope of the UK and various Dominions that India might accept the King's jurisdiction in its external relations.[36] But some recognition of the Crown as a symbol of unity and therefore as 'head' of the organisation had been mooted for some time.[37] That said, the British Cabinet appreciated the dangers of elevating the Crown into an obstacle, rather than an opportunity. Cabinet members recognised that

> although the Crown had been the bond of unity in the Commonwealth, it would be a disservice to the Crown if Commonwealth Ministers allowed a position to develop in which the Crown was made to appear a stumbling-block to the continued cohesion of the Commonwealth.[38]

The eventual decision, which was unanimous, built upon the wording of common allegiance and free association contained in the Statute of Westminster but with a twist.

> The Government of India have, however, declared and affirmed India's desire to continue her full membership of the Commonwealth of Nations and her acceptance of The King as the symbol of the free association of its independent member nations and as such Head of the Commonwealth.[39]

In emphasising the King's symbolic role, the formulation appeared to deflect any suggestion that the arrangement impinged on India's national sovereignty. Afterwards, Nehru explained to the Indian Parliament:

We would not deny that cooperation simply because in the past we had to fight and thus carry this trail of our past *karma* along with us. We had to wash out that past with all its evil . . . the fact that we have begun this new type of association with a touch of healing will be good for us and good for them and, I think, good for the world.[40]

Of course, the arrangement was framed as a response to India's request alone, and this immediately prompted a hostile reaction in large parts of Pakistan where many felt they had been 'outmanoeuvred' and that Pakistan should forthwith declare herself an Islamic Republic.[41] However, the notion that the agreement was 'not a precedent' was clearly unrealistic. As Sir Peter Marshall, a former Commonwealth Deputy Secretary-General put it, the use of any such disclaimer was "normally a sign that its disregard is accepted as inevitable."[42]

The seeds of a new association had indeed been sown: the unspoken notion of 'British' rootstock as an essential pre-condition for 'central' members had been abandoned and with it the 'British' pre-fix to the now preferred title "Commonwealth of Nations." The terminology of 'Dominions' began to be supplanted by the more neutral term, 'Commonwealth member countries'. Neither republicanism nor

*Figure 2.2* King George VI meets Commonwealth leaders. Buckingham Palace, 1949. Commonwealth Secretariat.

race would now be impediments to the growth of this new Commonwealth – though its Prime Ministers had not begun to consider the implications of what had been started in the adoption of the London Declaration. Many thought it an ingenious solution, and the agreement was widely welcomed in the UK as it was in Australia, Canada, New Zealand, South Africa, India, and Ceylon. Others were more fearful of a formula that, legally, has been described as "pragmatic nonsense."[43] Robert Menzies, the former Australian Prime Minister, told an Empire Day rally in Melbourne that the formula reduced the status of the Crown from "pulsing reality to a heartless lawyer's document." He felt Commonwealth Prime Ministers "had thrown away all the elements which made the British Commonwealth of Nations a united people."[44] This was echoed by those in the 'old' Dominions who deplored the loss of the 'British' prefix.

## 4  Conclusion

Was the adoption of the London Declaration therefore the start of the modern Commonwealth, as many have claimed? In the eyes of the Commonwealth Secretariat, the 1949 Declaration was when "the modern Commonwealth was born," with the agreement's formulation providing the "crucible" for its emerging character.[45] Marshall agrees that the practice of dating the Commonwealth from 1949 has become widespread.[46] Craft alights upon the concluding sentence of the Declaration which speaks of "free and equal members of the Commonwealth of Nations, freely cooperating in the pursuit of peace, liberty and progress."[47] Craft sees this as evidence of the organisation's "norm and values-based institutional character" and sees 'peace, liberty and progress' as the three enduring areas of its "principle mandate."[48] It was, he argues, a "simple, modest statement of the Commonwealth's raison d'être."[49] This is a tempting but illusory approach. Firstly, the British Government explicitly rejected the idea that the declaration covering membership should include any statement of shared principles. In stressing the loose and informal nature of the Commonwealth, the Cabinet Secretary counselled that it would be "inexpedient to confront the self-governing members of the Commonwealth with a formal definition of the principles of their association."[50] By the same token, there could be no provision for expulsion.[51] This general approach had the concurrence of the 'central' members of the Commonwealth.[52] Secondly, many recognised that the less definition, the better. To the extent that Commonwealth cooperation should be built about the practice of consultation, military cooperation or mutual aid, complexities and anomalies abounded and were better left unstated and unresolved. As a result, McIntyre contends that "a de facto 'two-tier' system of consultation emerged, especially in defence matters."[53] Thirdly, several Commonwealth figures were involved in drafting the Preamble to the UN Charter, most notably Jan Smuts. Coming into force in October 1945, the preamble spoke of "saving succeeding generations from the scourge of war" and the need to maintain international peace and security; it set out its faith in fundamental human rights, including "equal rights of men and women, and of nations large and small," and agreed to promote the "social progress and better standards of life in larger freedom," by creating international machinery for the "economic and social advancement of all peoples."[54] Coming nearly four years later, the Commonwealth's reference to 'peace, liberty and progress' could scarcely be considered a plausible elaboration of the global agreement in the UN Charter, much less the foundational document of an entirely new international organisation. The London Declaration was not therefore the start of a new Commonwealth, but it did ensure that the death of the old 'imperial' Commonwealth would only be a matter of time.

Another key component in the disintegration of the old order was *apartheid* South Africa and the presence in London of its new Prime Minister, Dr Daniel Malan. In a statement to the House of Assembly on his return, Malan said that the loss of India to the Commonwealth would have been harmful to trade and to the anti-Communist cause. He was in favour of the agreement providing there was "no meddling in any way with (the) freedom and independence of the various members of the Commonwealth."[55] In a taste of what was to come, he added: "My opinion has always been . . . that the greatest unity will be obtained in the case of South Africa, too, when we become a Republic."[56] Field Marshal Jan Smuts, the once Commonwealth colossus and now Leader of the Opposition, voiced his disquiet. It was "a leap in the dark" and reduced the Crown to a vague symbol. He thought grave risks had been taken in agreeing the Declaration.[57]

**Notes**

1 While the British Government took the view that Section 3 of Ireland's 1936 External Relations Act maintained a clear constitutional link with the British Crown, and therefore the Commonwealth, Irish political leaders expressed a different perspective. This is captured by an exchange between Viscount Jowitt, British Lord Chancellor, and Sean McBride, Ireland's Minister of External Affairs, at a Commonwealth meeting at the Palais de Chaillot, Paris, 16 November 1948, and contained in a Memorandum by the Lord Chancellor and the Secretary of State for Commonwealth Relations on Eire's future relations with the Commonwealth. TNA, C.P. (48) 272, B.
2 Commonwealth Secretariat, *The Commonwealth at the Summit (Vol.1)*, 13.
3 Ibid., 14.
4 Harshan Kumarasingham, "The 'new commonwealth': A New Zealand perspective on India joining the commonwealth," *The Round Table: The Commonwealth Journal of International Affairs* 95:385 (2006): 443.
5 Mark Mazower, *No Enchanted Palace*, (Princeton: Princeton University Press, 2008), 37.
6 Ibid., 85.
7 Winston Churchill, "Sinews of peace," Speech at Westminster College, Fulton MO, 5 March 1946, Accessed 19 June 2019, htpps://www.nationalchurchillmuseum.org/sinews-of-peace-iron-curtain-speech.html.
8 Ibid.
9 "Partnership and policy," *The Round Table: A Quarterly Review of the Politics of the British Commonwealth*, 37:145 (1946), 3.
10 John Holmes, "The Commonwealth and the UN," In *A Decade of the Commonwealth 1955–1964*, ed. W.B. Hamilton, Kenneth Robinson and C.D.W. Goodwin (Durham, N.C: Duke University Press, 1966), 16.
11 Derek Ingram, *The Commonwealth at Work* (Oxford: Pergamon Press, 1969), 33.
12 Ibid., 32.

13 Holmes, "The Commonwealth and the UN," 16.
14 Nigel Fisher, *Iain Macleod* (London: Andre Deutsch, 1977), 143.
15 Cabinet Secretary's Notebook, Meeting of the British Cabinet, 12 January 1949, TNA CAB 195/7.
16 Susan Williams, *Colour Bar: The Triumph of Seretse Khama and His Nation* (London: Allen Lane, 2006), 309.
17 Caroline Elkins, "Looking beyond Mau Mau: Archiving violence in the Era of decolonization," *American Historical Review* 120:3 (2015): 854.
18 Ibid., 856.
19 Press Association, "UK to compensate Kenya's Mau Mau torture victims," *The Guardian*, 6 June 2013, www.theguardian.com/world/2013/jun/06/uk-compensate-kenya-mau-mau-torture, Accessed 27 April 2022.
20 Murphy, *The Myth of the Commonwealth*, 107.
21 Third Report: "Commonwealth relationship," by Norman Brook, Presented to Cabinet, 21 May 1948, TNA, CAB/129/30.
22 Ibid., Annex 1, 1.
23 Preamble, Statute of Westminster (1931), Accessed 5 May 2020, www.legislation.gov.uk/ukpg/1931/4/pdfs/ukpga_19310004-en.pdf,1.
24 Clement Attlee, Memorandum to Cabinet on "The Commonwealth relationship," 26 October 1948, TNA, CAB/129/30, 2.
25 Nicholas Mansergh, *The Commonwealth Experience (Vol.2), From British to Multiracial Commonwealth* (London: Palgrave Macmillan, 1982), 146.
26 Memorandum by the Secretary of State for Commonwealth Relations, "The Commonwealth relationship," 16 June 1949, TNA, CAB/129/35, 15–16.
27 Fourth Report, "Commonwealth relationship," by Norman Brook, presented to Cabinet, 21 July 1948, TNA, CAB/129/30, Annex II, 4.
28 Ibid., 9.
29 Ibid., 11.
30 The Commonwealth Charter, setting out the core values of the association, including democracy, human rights and the rule of law, was adopted on 19 December 2012 and signed by Queen Elizabeth II, as Head of the Commonwealth, on 11 March 2013 (Commonwealth Day). Formal provision for the suspension or expulsion of a member country, for serious and persistent violation of the Commonwealth's fundamental principles, was contained in the Millbrook Commonwealth Action Programme of 1995.
31 Kumarasingham, "A New Zealand perspective on India joining the Commonwealth," 443.
32 Report by Cabinet Secretary on consultations with Canada, Australia and New Zealand, in "Commonwealth relationship," 14 September 1948, TNA, CR (48) 5, 13.
33 Commonwealth Secretariat, *The Commonwealth at the Summit (Vol.1)*, 26.
34 Memorandum by the Prime Minister, "Commonwealth relationship," 26 October 1948, TNA, CP (48) 244, 2.
35 Speech by Pandit Nehru in the Indian Constituent Assembly, 16 May 1949, in Brook, "The Commonwealth relationship," TNA, CAB/129/35, 17.
36 Brook, "Commonwealth relationship: Draft principles," 14 September 1948, TNA, CAB/129/30, 17.
37 Brook, "Commonwealth relationship" (Third Report), 5.
38 Conclusions of Cabinet, 3 March 1949, TNA, CAB 128/15.
39 Commonwealth Secretariat, *The Commonwealth at the Summit (Vol.1)*, 29.
40 *Hindustan Times* (17 May 1949), 18, Hindustantimes.com/topic/archive.
41 Brook, "The Commonwealth relationship," TNA, CAB/129/35, 7.
42 Peter Marshall, "The Commonwealth at 60," *The Round Table: The Commonwealth Journal of International Affairs* 98:404 (2009): 536.
43 Geoffrey Marshall, *Constitutional Conventions: The Rules and Forms of Political Accountability* (Oxford: Clarendon Press, 1984), 170.

44 Memorandum by Secretary of State for Commonwealth Relations, "Reactions to the 1949 Commonwealth Declaration," presented to Cabinet on 16 June 1949, TNA, CAB 129/35.
45 Commonwealth Secretariat, "Commonwealth celebrates 60th anniversary," 2009, Accessed 7 May 2020, www.thecommonwealth.org/history-if-the-commonwealth/commonwealth-celebrates-60th-anniversary.
46 Marshall, "The Commonwealth at 60," 536.
47 Commonwealth Secretariat, *The Commonwealth at the Summit (Vol.1)*, 29.
48 Hugh Craft, "Between the idea and the reality," PhD Thesis (Australian National University, 2008) 102.
49 Hugh Craft (former Australian diplomat), interview with the author, 3 August 2018, London.
50 Brook, "Commonwealth relationship," Third Report, 4.
51 Brook, Fourth Report, 11.
52 Brook, "Commonwealth relationship: Consultations with Canada, Australia and New Zealand," 14 September 1948, TNA, CAB 129/30, 14.
53 W. David McIntyre, "Canada and the creation of the Commonwealth Secretariat, 1965," *International Journal*, 53:4 (1998): 754.
54 Preamble to the United Nations' Charter, October 1945, Accessed 9 May 2020, https://www.un.org/en/sections/un-charter/preamble.
55 "Reactions to the 1949 Commonwealth Declaration," 8.
56 Ibid., 12.
57 Ibid., 4.

## References

Commonwealth Secretariat, *The Commonwealth at the Summit (Vol.1)*, (London: Commonwealth Secretariat, 1987).
Derek Ingram, *The Commonwealth at Work* (Oxford: Pergamon Press, 1969).
Geoffrey Marshall, *Constitutional Conventions: The Rules and Forms of Political Accountability* (Oxford: Clarendon Press, 1984).
Hugh Craft, "Between the Idea and the Reality," PhD Thesis (Australian National University, 2008).
Mark Mazower, *No Enchanted Palace* (USA: Princeton University Press, 2008).
Nicholas Mansergh, *The Commonwealth Experience (Vol.2): From British to multiracial Commonwealth* (London: Palgrave Macmillan, 1982).
Nigel Fisher, *Iain Macleod* (London: Andre Deutsch, 1977).
Philip Murphy, *The Myth of the Commonwealth,* (Op.Cit.)
Susan Williams, *Colour Bar: The triumph of Seretse Khama and his Nation* (London: Allen Lane, 2006).
W.B. Hamilton, Kenneth Robinson and C.D.W. Goodwin (eds.), *A Decade of the Commonwealth 1955–1964* (Durham, N.C: Duke University Press, 1966).

# 3 Afrikaner Nationalism and the Rise of *Apartheid*

## 1 Introduction

At the end of the Second World War, the reputation of Field Marshal Jan Christian Smuts, South Africa's Prime Minister and a member of the Imperial War Cabinet, could not have been higher, whether at home or abroad. He had confounded his Nationalist opponents and, on 6 September 1939, had brought South Africa into the war against Germany. After the shock of the fall of Tobruk (with the surrender of a substantial proportion of South Africa's fighting strength), he had steadied the recovery and helped deliver the great Allied victory at El-Alamein. He had gained a resounding electoral victory in South Africa in 1943, winning a large parliamentary majority. As peace approached, he and other Allied leaders looked forward to "a World Organisation to maintain peace and security . . . endowed with the necessary power and authority to prevent aggression and violence."[1] After final victory, Smuts led the South African delegation to San Francisco and witnessed the birth of the United Nations, having helped draft the preamble to the UN Charter. South Africa's "grand old man" had shown "inspired leadership," enthused *The Round Table*.[2] Indeed, it added that "by international consent [he] belongs to the world as much as to South Africa."[3] Yet he was soon to receive a rude awakening at the hands of the UNGA. He had some inkling of what was to come once he had arrived in New York, telling Jan Hofmeyr, his faithful lieutenant:

> There is a growing, widespread opinion adverse to us. South Africans are getting into ill-odour, owing to the colour bar and wrong native publicity. . . . I fear our going will not be good (and) I see a worsening atmosphere.[4]

## 2 Smuts and the United Nations

UNGA's opening session, held in its temporary home at Lake Success in New York State, delivered a rebuff to South Africa on two counts. Firstly, it rejected a bid by Smuts for the incorporation of the mandated territory of South-West Africa into the Union of South Africa. The Union had administered the former German colony under a mandate granted in 1919 by the victorious powers through the Treaty of Versailles. In arguing for incorporation, Smuts cited a unanimous resolution of the

10.4324/9781003208617-3

territory's Legislative Assembly (a wholly European body) and by 'an informal referendum of the natives' which he argued showed a majority in favour.[5] UNGA rejected that view,

> considering that the African inhabitants of South West Africa have not yet secured political autonomy or reached a stage of political development enabling them to express a considered opinion which the Assembly could recognise on such an important question as incorporation of their territory.[6]

Accordingly, UNGA declined the request and instead invited South Africa to propose a trusteeship agreement within the UN system.

Secondly, a not-yet-independent India had reacted to South Africa's passing of the Indian Act by tabling a resolution in the Steering Committee.[7] *The Round Table* agreed that the law, "whatever its merits or faults, discriminates against Indians on grounds of race."[8] Despite protests from Smuts that this was interference in South Africa's domestic affairs and therefore not permitted under Article 2(7) of the Charter, a stronger resolution was eventually carried by the General Assembly by thirty-two votes to fifteen, with seven abstentions. This initiative, led by Vijaya Lakshmi Pandit, Nehru's sister, was accompanied by India's severing of trade and diplomatic links with the Union. It was, comments Vineet Thakur, "a spectacular diplomatic performance" which outwitted the South African delegation.[9] It also led to some sharp exchanges between the Indian and British delegations. The UK, at that stage still India's colonial ruler, felt that an important point of principle about the Charter was at stake, which as a permanent member of the Security Council necessitated its support for South Africa. India, expecting at least neutrality, was aghast at Britain's "double-dealing."[10] In any case, India argued that, under international law, it could legitimately claim to speak for South Africa's Indian citizens because citizenship rights had been denied to them.[11] It was an early sign of what was to come, even before the formal advent of *apartheid*.

Indeed, the United Nations became the arena for expressing the tensions and disagreements between Commonwealth members over South Africa, rather than in the formal councils of the Commonwealth. In the ten votes on South Africa and *apartheid* in the General Assembly between 1946 and 1960, the UK and Australia consistently supported South Africa, as did Canada and New Zealand (though to a lesser degree).[12] India, Pakistan and Ceylon were equally consistent in taking the opposite view. The UK also failed to support Security Council resolution 134 (1960) condemning South Africa in the wake of the Sharpeville massacre. It was not until the following year that, for the first time, the British Government voted for a UN resolution condemning *apartheid*.[13]

In addition to the UK's protestations that the UN Charter required the principle of non-interference, the British may have also been influenced by the prevailing Commonwealth convention that members refrain from criticising their colleagues. This was both to respect the norms of collegiality and also because such a step risked provoking retaliation in kind (a feature which was to become more pronounced in years to come). India was certainly wary of providing Pakistan with any opportunity to raise the issue of Kashmir. More importantly, India knew it could at least win votes on the floor of the General Assembly while, at that time, any similar move in the Commonwealth would have been clearly futile, as well as procedurally invalid. Indeed, as late as 1957 (with Ghana attending for the first time) the Commonwealth Prime Ministers' Meeting of that year declared that it was "[n]ot their function . . . to record agreed decisions or formal resolutions."[14] Attempts by Ghana to raise the issue of South-West Africa the following year were firmly rebuffed, and consequently the Commonwealth's newest member supported a legal challenge by African countries at the International Court of Justice.[15] Indeed, in the nine Commonwealth summit meetings held since the end of the Second World War, between 1945 and 1957, no mention is made of South Africa, *apartheid* or racial discrimination, even though these meetings recorded wide-ranging discussions, including on non-Commonwealth countries such as Indo-China, Korea, Japan, Israel, the United States of America and Germany. The Commonwealth's silence on *apartheid* was no more than the unity of the graveyard. It certainly did not suggest an organisation in the forefront of the anti-*apartheid* struggle.

## 3   The Royal Tour and the 1948 Elections

If Smuts had been humiliated at the United Nations, he hoped that within South Africa his reputation, and that of his United Party (UP), would be lifted by the 1947 Royal tour. Without the alchemy of "the crown's charisma," Smuts, the British Government and the royal family feared that South Africa might be lost to the Commonwealth.[16] Leaving behind a UK in the grip of a bitterly cold winter, King George VI and Queen Elizabeth, accompanied by the two young princesses, Elizabeth and Margaret, arrived in Cape Town at the end of February. This was only the second visit by a British sovereign to a self-governing member of the Commonwealth.[17] As well as opening the South African Parliament in Cape Town, the King and his family travelled ten thousand miles in two months, across South Africa and beyond, at the height of a baking hot summer. In addition to visiting the self-governing colony of Southern Rhodesia, the party also went to the Protectorate of Northern Rhodesia and to the High Commission territories (Basutoland, the Bechuanaland Protectorate and Swaziland). During the visit, Princess Elizabeth celebrated her twenty-first birthday and delivered a memorable broadcast to the Empire and Commonwealth from Cape Town. In it, she made her 'solemn act of dedication' in which she pledged: "I declare before you all that my whole life, whether it be long or short, shall be devoted to your service and the service of our great imperial family to which we all belong."[18]

The royal visit attracted large and friendly crowds, at a multiplicity of events, even if it was "soaked in segregation."[19] It appeared unaffected by a call for a boycott by the Natal Indian Congress (the body founded by Mahatma Gandhi) in protest against discriminatory government legislation and by the more restrained disengagement from key events by Afrikaner Nationalist politicians. In the latter respect, the King made his homage to a number of potent Afrikaner symbols, moving one commentator to argue, rather optimistically, that the monarch was

*Figure 3.1* Princess Elizabeth prepares to deliver a radio broadcast on her twenty-first birthday, Cape Town, 1947. Royal Collection Trust.

aligning himself with a movement "on which the future greatness of the South African Union most clearly depends . . . that may eventually fuse the cultures of the two white races into a wider culture that will be beyond race, though not beyond nationality."[20] Black Africans, by and large, resisted the call for a boycott with the traditional notion that monarchy stood above the failings of governments having a powerful appeal. Sapire contends that "the royal family's graciousness, apparent colour-blindness and genuine interest in Africans" were contrasted with the rigid etiquette of South African society.[21] Demonstrations of loyalty by Africans also signified "a powerful rejection of the *herrenvolk* mentality associated with the Afrikaner nationalist movement."[22]

Smuts was reported to be in his element and "everywhere."[23] However, whatever the royal visit did for the monarchy and the reputation of South Africa's future Queen (or the chimera of white 'fusion'), its success had no appreciable impact in lifting the popularity of Smuts's UP. Indeed, there were increasing indications of political change among the white electorate, leading a commentator to observe: "The political tide in the Union is certainly flowing at present against the Government of General Smuts and the United Party."[24] Assessing the prospects for the elections, *The Economist* asked why Smuts, over a range of issues such as the United Nations, native or Indian policy, often seemed equivocal:

> He is too much an international statesman not to realise how the tide is flowing in a world which is shortly to see an independent India. But his political acumen is too great for him to risk his leadership of his country by taking too pronounced a liberal line which would drive many of his Afrikaner supporters into the Nationalist camp.[25]

As the general election approached, many predicted that the UP would slip from the commanding heights of its wartime victory of 1943. Even so, few expected this to result in a victory for the Nationalists. "There is a widely held opinion that General Smuts will be successful," predicted *The Round Table* a month before polling.[26] The overriding message of the Reunited National Party (HNP), led by Dr D.F. Malan, was a racial appeal on the question of 'native policy'. "*Swart gevaar*" ('the black peril') could only be contained by implementing the doctrine of *apartheid* ('apartness' or separation).[27] Nelson Mandela was then a young lawyer who, of course, as a Black African had no vote. But he followed the course of the campaign with a deep and troubled interest. *Apartheid*, he recognised, was

> a new term but an old idea . . . it represented the codification in one oppressive system of all the laws and regulations that had kept Africans in an inferior position to whites for centuries. What had been more or less *de facto* was to become relentlessly *de jure*.

He continued: "The often haphazard segregation of the past three hundred years was to be consolidated into a monolithic system that was diabolical in detail, inescapable in its reach and overwhelming in its power."[28]

The HNP's naked appeal to prejudice and fear had the desired result. To the shock of Jan Smuts and the UP, the HNP emerged as decisive winners, gaining twenty-seven seats. Together, the HNP and the Afrikaner Party had seventy-nine seats and an overall majority over the seventy-four won by the UP and their Labour allies. More startling so, this parliamentary majority was won on a clear minority of votes cast, such were the vagaries of the First-Past-The-Post electoral system.

Smuts's popular vote of 524,230 was 11% more than the 401,834 votes gained by Dr Malan. The UP and its allies had piled up pluralities in well-populated urban seats while the Afrikaner parties had won more sparsely habited rural constituencies. This was not a cruel twist of fate but rather a culpable failure of Smuts and the UP to put in place a fresh delimitation of constituency boundaries prior to the election. This failure to take "the most elementary political precautions" was estimated to have cost Smuts around twenty seats and certain victory.[29] Damaged by incumbency and the privations of war, and unable to counter the strident racial message of the nationalists, the UP suffered the ultimate humiliation of the loss of Smuts's Standerton seat to a nationalist newcomer. "It was a tremendous blow to his self-esteem from which he never recovered. He was utterly crushed in spirit," writes Kruger. "In 1943 he had been placed on the highest pinnacle of political power, and a brief five years later he had been pulled down from the heights he loved to climb."[30] A broken man, Smuts died barely a year later at Doornkloof, having lost his brilliant and liberal colleague, Jan Hofmeyr, six months earlier. For Mandela, the election result was also a shock. "I was stunned and dismayed," he wrote: "but Oliver (Tambo) took a more considered line. 'I like this', he said. 'I like this'. I could not imagine why. He explained, 'Now we will know exactly who our enemies are and where we stand'."[31] Allister Sparks put it another way, describing the result of the 1948 elections as "the moment when South Africa parted company with the world."[32]

The incoming Nationalist government began the dynamic introduction of the policy of 'separate development', namely *apartheid*. Steadily, the residual rights of non-whites were removed. They were disenfranchised, including with the abolition of the Coloured roll and, some years later, the removal of the Native Representative Council and the limited right of Black Africans to vote for four white parliamentary representatives. The Group Areas Act enforced geographic separation, reserving to whites the best land and restricting the movement of Blacks through the pass laws. Mixed marriages and sexual relations across the races were forbidden, and a system of racial classification established. Eventually, segregation was carried into all walks of life, including education and employment (though some of the churches resisted the division of their congregations and ministry).

## 4 Smuts, Segregation and *Apartheid*

To what extent can the foundation of the apartheid state be laid at the door of Smuts and his promotion of earlier segregationist policies? Was *apartheid* an inevitable manifestation of late colonialism or an aberrant, and abhorrent, mutation on a body politic otherwise naturally evolving into a more rational form, driven by economic growth and rising prosperity? To what extent were the beginnings of the *apartheid* state rejected by the UK and by the Commonwealth more widely? Can 1949 therefore plausibly be regarded as the start of the Commonwealth's life-affirming crusade against *apartheid*?

The notion that the authoritarian, *apartheid* state was wholly an Afrikaner ideological construct provided some whites with the shelter of what is sometimes called 'the English alibi'. The basis of the alibi was as follows: While there had certainly been a 'colour bar' operating throughout the British Empire, which had separated colonists from native people, this was a near universal reflection of the times among the European powers. In any event, the situation in South Africa was compounded by the awkward relationship of the descendants of Dutch settlement on the Cape, the Afrikaners, with white settlers of English origin who supported the British Empire (the Cape colony was ceded to Britain by the Netherlands in 1814). Although British policies in the Cape colony had reflected an 'enlightened' approach to other race groups (allowing non-whites to qualify for the franchise and stand for elected office), this had been strongly resisted by the Afrikaners. Conflict between the two white populations broke out in the First and Second Boer Wars, concluding, after heroic Boer resistance and brutal British suppression of its population, with victory by the imperial power. This was sealed by the Peace of Vereeniging (1902). Thereafter, and in the creation of the Union of South Africa in 1910, every effort was made to secure both a single state (as opposed to a federation) and the unity of the two white populations. No one better exemplified the conflicting pressures of trying to achieve reconciliation and unity between these two than Smuts. Coming from Afrikaner farming stock, he shared the Boers' pain of a 'century of wrong'.[33] As a young man, he joined the Boer cause and rode with the commandos, showing daring, skill and courage. But he also persuaded the Boer generals to accept peace at Vereeniging (a treaty he himself helped draft) because he feared that the alternative would be "the destruction of the Afrikaner people."[34] Thereafter, Marks considers him "the architect of South African unification" through the 1910 constitution.[35] Sauer, a liberal Cape colony MP and Minister, and like-minded colleagues had tried to entrench a non-racial franchise into the constitution of the new Union. When this was rejected, he sought to extend the Cape-qualified franchise to the whole of the Union. This would have seen the gradual enfranchisement of other races, including Black Africans, as they became 'civilised'. This too failed, and only with difficulty was this arrangement retained for the Cape alone. Crucially, it was the intervention of Smuts that blocked the extension of the Black franchise outside the Cape.[36] His lifelong quest for the fusion of the two white 'races' was, as Dubow put it, "the language of common South Africanism, sufficiently capacious to unite Boers and British, not least in opposition to blacks."[37] As Sir Alfred Milner, then British High Commissioner for South Africa, said in 1897:

> I personally could win over the Dutch in the Cape colony and indeed in all of the South African dominions in my term of office . . . without offending the English. . . . You only have to sacrifice the "n****r" absolutely and the game is easy.[38]

When eventually the moment came for the Bill to be presented to the British Parliament to ratify the Union, there was no attempt to reopen the question of the non-white franchise. On this, Herbert Asquith, the UK's Liberal Prime Minister, expressed regret, but the combined will of the colonial parliaments of South Africa was allowed to prevail.

Both before the First World War and between the wars, the political rights of non-whites in all parts of the Union were not advanced but were further reduced. The 1913 Natives Land Act removed from Black Africans the right to own land in 90% of the country reserved for whites and was a cornerstone of *apartheid*, only repealed in 1990. The Natives (Urban Areas) Act 1923 extended the requirement to carry passes to all those Black Africans working in 'white' urban areas. Politically, the Representation of Natives Act 1936 removed the right of non-whites in Cape province to qualify for the common roll. Instead, a Native Representation Council was established (only to be later abolished). This therefore was the "framework of the segregationist state" to which Smuts contributed much.[39]

Nevertheless, proponents of 'the alibi' argue that, in the changed conditions of the aftermath of the Second World War, a more enlightened policy was beginning to develop under Smuts (despite his being a lifelong segregationist committed to the 'paramountcy' of the whites). The first signs of this, it is argued, came in a speech by Smuts in advance of the 1943 elections. In it, he declared that "isolation has gone and segregation has fallen on evil days, too."[40] Many have seen these remarks as political expediency, quickly forgotten. But some detected a change away, not from political segregation but, to a trusteeship based on 'welfarism', with major government interventions "to address the education, health and housing conditions of the African people."[41] The Prime Minister now seemed to favour the relaxation of restrictions on Black Africans recommended by the Fagan Commission.[42] This had proposed that the existing laws which forced migrant Black labour to live on native reserves be relaxed. It argued for a stable African workforce in the urban areas, both to respond to the needs of business and to stimulate consumer demand. Smuts accepted "the reality of permanent African urbanisation" and was increasingly sceptical of policies which kept Black Africans on rural 'tribal' reserves.[43] While showing little sign of responding to the political grievances then being expressed both through the Native Representative Council (the only representation, albeit indirect, that Black Africans possessed within the white democratic structures) and directly through the ANC, the Transvaal Indian Congress and other bodies, Smuts encouraged substantial increases in Black welfare, wages and working conditions in the period.[44] Many felt that rising prosperity and increased demand for Black labour, with greater skills, would in time make rigid racial segregation outdated and counterproductive.

This approach put Smuts at increasing odds with the HNP which wanted to intensify and formalise segregation into the *apartheid* system. For their part, the HNP responded with the Sauer Commission which arrived at diametrically opposite conclusions to Judge Fagan. The influx of Black Africans into the towns and cities demanded a policy of 'total *apartheid*'. Racially segregated trading zones needed to be created to prevent white businesses being undermined by competition from cheap Black labour. Separation in all aspects of life became the guiding vision, even if the immediate practicalities still made the use of African labour in the urban areas a necessity. "The cornerstone of the Nationalist doctrine of *apartheid*," declared Dr Nicolaas Diederichs, a Nationalist MP and later ceremonial State President, is that we are here dealing not merely with a group . . . but that we are dealing with two population groups and races that differ from each other radically, peoples and races who on account of their fundamental differences and natural limits must be kept apart from each other to the advantage of both.[45]

Was Smuts 'the founding father' of *apartheid*? Smuts was undoubtedly imbued by a racism that was at times 'visceral'.[46] Hofmeyr despaired of his leader's equivocation leading up to the 1948 election and by some of his unreconstructed campaign speeches. But Smuts made Hofmeyr his deputy and heir apparent and defended him in the face of Nationalist demands that "Hofmeyr must be destroyed."[47] Smuts's casual racism and refusal to address the enormity of 'the native question' were inexcusable and diminished his reputation, but this did not make him an advocate for the *apartheid* idea, which he "adamantly and vociferously opposed."[48]

*Apartheid* was not inevitable and, as Dubow has argued, it was "only one of several competing visions of the future."[49] Muthien is clear that "*apartheid* is not simply an extension of old racial practices but represents a distinctive form of racial domination."[50] With Wolpe, she recognises 'historic discontinuities and differentiated continuities'. In any case, although Hyam describes the new regime as a 'seismic' change, the full articulation of *apartheid* took many years. In this respect, Deborah Posel sees a series of distinct phases as the system intensified, opposition fell away, and formal separation and oppression covered all aspects of life.

## 5 Resisting *Apartheid*

While it is understandable to regard the 1948 elections as the 'turning point', the 'English alibi' would be more plausible if the UP had not been so equivocal in the face of *apartheid* legislation. As it was, its failure to stand up to the Nationalist Government encouraged some on the liberal wing to break away. Firstly, the multiracial Liberal Party, founded in 1953, increasingly began to appreciate the need to resist *apartheid* by more than engaging with the white electorate and advocating merely a qualified franchise for non-whites. As it was, its electoral appeal among white voters was limited at best, with the "Liberals pretty well wiped out" in the 1959 provincial elections.[51] As the party became radicalised, non-racial in its aims and began to work with non-white organisations, so its members were arrested, harassed and imprisoned. The Progressive Party proved to have rather greater impact, both internationally and in white politics. Even so, for many years (between 1961 and 1974) Helen Suzman was the party's sole MP and a lone voice: As Colin Eglin said after her death:

> When civil liberties and the rule of law were under assault from the *apartheid* government and the official opposition was either compromising or capitulating, Helen single-handedly stood up against detention without trial, spoke out against racial discrimination and fought for civil liberties and the rule of law.[52]

Outside the white parliament there were other liberal voices – in business, in the judiciary and in the English-speaking press which managed to be "both conformist and critical."[53]

It was the ANC and the South African Communist Party (SACP) which provided the main resistance to the elaboration of the *apartheid* state, alongside Indian and Coloured organisations. The ANC was originally founded, in 1912, as the South African Native National Congress (SANNC), to campaign against injustice and for the rights of Black Africans. In 1923, SANNC became the ANC, but it was not until the 1940s that the organisation became a mass movement. As the *apartheid* screw tightened, so the ANC stiffened its reaction, following the Youth League in a Programme of Action that included boycotts, strikes, protest demonstrations and passive resistance. As Mandela put it: "We in the Youth League had seen the failure of legal and constitutional means to strike at racial oppression; now the entire organisation was set to enter a more activist phase."[54] In December 1951, with Mandela now President of the Youth League, Walter Sisulu the ANC Secretary-General and Oliver Tambo on the National Executive, the Annual Conference in Bloemfontein launched the Defiance Campaign against unjust laws. Despite the misgivings of some (such as Mandela), the campaign united Africans, Coloured and Indians. In a statement the conference declared:

> All people . . . who have made South Africa their home are entitled to live a full and free life. Full democratic rights with a direct say in the affairs of the government are the inalienable right of every South African.[55]

In support of these principles, mass demonstrations were organised for 6 April 1952 to coincide with the 300th anniversary of white Dutch settlement on the Cape. Of the 10,000 taking part in the protest, over 8,000 were arrested, including Nelson Mandela. On 26 June 1955, at Kliptown, the Congress of the People, attended by 3,000 people, officially adopted the Freedom Charter. Its opening demand was "The people shall govern!," and the document set out the belief in non-racial democracy for all South Africans and articulated the other core principles of the South African Congress Alliance.[56] Pointing to the involvement of white members of the banned SACP in the Alliance, the government responded by claiming that the Freedom Charter was a communist-inspired document. In December 1956, in a dawn raid by the police, 140 people, of all races, were arrested and taken to Johannesburg. As a month passed, others were added to the charge sheet with, at its peak, 158 accused of treason under the Suppression of Communism Act. The prosecution attempted to base its case on evidence gathered at the Congress of the People at Kliptown and on the text of the Freedom Charter. The Treason Trial was to drag on until March 1961 when it ended with the acquittal of the remaining twenty-eight defendants.

Early opposition also came from prominent priests such as Michael Scott, Trevor Huddleston and Ambrose Reeves. Huddleston, a member of the Community of the Resurrection based at Mirfield, West Yorkshire, had been sent out to Sophiatown in South Africa in 1943. As he set about his ministry, in what was then

*Figure 3.2* Protestors gather outside the Johannesburg Drill Hall as the Treason Trial begins, 1956. Commonwealth Secretariat.

a multiracial community outside Johannesburg, he increasingly found himself at odds with the government, as *apartheid* law began to bear down. In February 1955 he was among those who helped lead the opposition to the forced removal of 65,000 African, Coloured, Indian and Chinese residents of Sophiatown to Meadowlands in the satellite township of Soweto and to other locations. Under the Group Areas Act, Sophiatown was designated a white residential area named Triomf ('triumph'). A community established in 1904 was therefore destroyed (except for Huddleston's church of Christ the King in Ray Street). Also expunged were the rights of those who owned freehold property in the town (a right which Black people had enjoyed prior to 1913). Most cruel of all, the government's racial classifications (linked to separation into designated group areas) meant that families, as well as neighbours, were split up and forced to live in different locations.

Huddleston was unwavering in his opposition to the government and *apartheid*, declaring: "Any doctrine based on racial or colour prejudice and enforced by the state is therefore an affront to human dignity and 'ipso facto' an insult to God himself."[57] It was a theological perspective shared by Ambrose Reeves, the Bishop of Johannesburg: "It is not merely that *apartheid* is erroneous; it is a heresy, doing violence to the Christian faith in God and in the nature and destiny of man." He continued: "God has some better thing in store for all the peoples of this country than the way of *apartheid*, which has shown all too clearly that it is the way of death and not of life."[58] Debates about Queen, Commonwealth and a South African republic had little relevance. "There is no purpose in a loyalty to Queen or Commonwealth if neither meets your life at any point," explained Huddleston. "Commonwealth citizenship means nothing . . . except to accentuate the ugly fact that . . . his sovereign must condone the state of servitude in which he lives."[59] Huddleston was to be recalled to the UK in 1955 from the Sophiatown he loved, and Ambrose Reeves was deported by the South African authorities in 1961. But it was a Christian message about *apartheid* later proclaimed no less fervently by Beyers Naude, Allan Boesak, Frank Chikane and Desmond Tutu, among many others.

## 6 Britain, South Africa and a Changing Commonwealth

What of Britain and South Africa? Hyam expresses the dilemma facing Britain as being between "the demands of national interest and the necessities of international reputation."[60] Indeed, the relationship was a conflicted one in many ways. True, there were long-standing ties of kinship with the white English community and a shared history in the development of the Union. South Africa was one of the British Commonwealth's 'central' Dominions. It had been a powerful, if slightly unpredictable, military ally in two world wars and an important force not only in the Commonwealth but in the League of Nations and, certainly at the outset, the United Nations also. With the onset of the Cold War, the closure of the Suez canal and growing Soviet naval power, South African surveillance and support facilities (particularly at Simonstown) on the Cape route were seen as particularly important in meeting a "Soviet resolve (that) could become the gravest threat since Hitler to a free world order."[61] This was also true of air communications and overflying rights. Then there were extensive – and growing – economic and commercial interests. South Africa was a significant market for British goods and fertile ground for inward British investment. South African gold was largely traded through London, and its supply offered the international financial system an important source of liquidity.

Set against that were uncertainties. A 'white' Dominion it may have been, but South Africa's leadership was now predominantly Boer rather than English. "The fact that the Boers were not British," commented Mazrui, "often made Britain more flexible in her relations with them and more wary of offending their sensibilities."[62] After all, there was a degree of unfinished business arising out of the Act of Union of 1910. Britain had acquiesced in the suppression of the aspirations for a non-white franchise across the Union and witnessed increasing racial discrimination and measures of segregation against the non-white majority populations well before the advent of *apartheid*. Even then, such developments did not match the British commitment, to its colonies, for measured steps towards self-government within the Commonwealth. For Benson, Britain's role in South Africa was nothing less than "a prolonged and profitable betrayal."[63] However, in 1910, the British had at least resisted the Union's attempts to incorporate the three High Commission territories into the Union precisely because it felt a responsibility to the Black population in those areas and an obligation to secure their eventual political emancipation. Equally, South Africa's envious gaze never left these tasty morsels on its doorstep.

Like the 'mandated' territory of South-West Africa, incorporation, legally or illegally, was a constant threat.

The UK also feared South African pressure further north. In 1951, the Secretary of State for the Colonies, Jim Griffiths, and the Secretary of State for Commonwealth Relations, Patrick Gordon Walker, together urged the Cabinet to counter South African pressure. "The danger is real and urgent," the Ministers argued, and they set out some startling figures. "Afrikaner infiltration into both Southern and Northern Rhodesia is proceeding apace – at present the flow of immigration from the Union is almost double that from the United Kingdom."[64] Unless Britain takes steps to create a powerful central African federation (at that stage dubbed 'British Central Africa'), the consequences would be serious.

> If we do nothing, and so prevent the Southern Rhodesians from linking with their northern neighbours, they will inevitably tend more and more to look southwards. The absorption of Southern Rhodesia into the Union would then probably be only a matter of time.[65]

If that happened, both Northern Rhodesia and Nyasaland would be vulnerable to 'encroachment by the Union'. This would be disastrous for African interests, the Ministers believed.

It was also becoming increasingly obvious that the evolution of the Commonwealth as a multiracial association would bring it into direct conflict with South Africa. "So far as South Africa is concerned," Lord Swinton, the Secretary of State for Commonwealth Relations, told the Cabinet in 1953,

> it is clear that the admission of territories governed by Africans would be unacceptable to the present (South African) government . . . this would probably apply equally in the case of any territory where the population has considerable admixture of African blood e.g. the West Indies.[66]

Britain's relationship with the Union of South Africa had been deeply ambivalent, treating it as "half-ally and half untouchable at the same time, (walking) the tightrope between provocation and conciliation."[67] But the moment of truth was coming closer when a choice would have to be made. This was articulated as early as 1954 by a British spokesman:

> If at any time Britain was compelled to choose between the white settlers, practising racial discrimination in Africa, and "Gold Coast democracy", she would be bound in her own self-interest and in the interests of Commonwealth unity to come down on the African side.[68]

## 7 Conclusion

At the beginning of 1960, Harold Macmillan spent a month visiting a number of African countries and colonies. On 3 February, having arrived in South Africa, the British Prime Minister addressed members of both Houses of Parliament in Cape

Town. His message to his silent and largely disapproving audience was an uncomfortable one. "The wind of change is blowing through this continent. Whether we like it or not, this growth in national consciousness is a political fact." His speech signalled that South Africa could no longer expect unquestioning British support at the United Nations, saying:

> As a fellow member of the Commonwealth, we have always tried to give South Africa our support and encouragement, but I hope you will not mind my saying frankly that there are some aspects of your policies which make it impossible for us to do this without being false to our own deep convictions about the political destinies of free men to which, in our territories, we are trying to give effect.[69]

South Africa's premier, Dr Verwoerd, had not seen an advance copy of Macmillan's speech and was visibly shocked. But he responded:

> There must not only be justice to the black man in Africa, but also to the white man. We see ourselves as part of the Western world – a true white state in Southern Africa, with a possibility of granting a full future to the black man in our midst.[70]

While some argue that "the direction of the 'wind of change' was already set by the time the Conservative Party came into power in 1951," the speech drew as strong a disapproving reaction from the Conservative Right as it gathered plaudits from Liberals and the Left.[71]

A few months later, events at Sharpeville, close to Vereeniging in the Transvaal, would confirm that the moment of truth had indeed arrived with the UK and the Commonwealth set to grapple with the consequences for its emerging multiracial organisation.

## Notes

1. Commonwealth Secretariat, *The Commonwealth at the Summit (Vol.1)*, 14.
2. "South Africa: The Political Scene," *The Round Table: A Quarterly Review of the Politics of the British Commonwealth* 35:140 (1945), 376.
3. "Partnership and policy," *The Round Table*, 3.
4. Alan Paton, *Hofmeyr* (Cape Town, London, NY, Toronto: OUP, 1971), 338.
5. "South Africa and the United Nations," *The Round Table: A Quarterly Review of the Politics of the British Commonwealth* 37:146 (1947): 133.
6. Resolution A/RES/65(1): "Future status of South West Africa," UN General Assembly, 14 December 1946, Accessed 12 May 2018, www.undocs.org/en/A/RES/65(1).
7. India was one of the founding members of the United Nations, joining in October 1945 under the British Raj, two years before independence.
8. "Colour policy in South Africa," *The Round Table* 37:145 (1946): 32.
9. Vineet Thakur, "Jan Smuts, Jawaharlal Nehru and the legacies of liberalism," 18 May 2016, *E-International Relations*, Accessed 11 May 2020, www.e-ir.info/2018/05/18/jam-smuts-jawaharlal-nehru-and-the-legacies-of-liberalism/,1.
10. *The Hindustan Times*, 5 December 1946.
11. Jonathan Hyslop, "'Segregation has fallen on evil days': Smuts' South Africa, global war, and transnational politics, 1939–46," *Journal of Global History* 7 (2012):458.

12 Resolutions of the United Nations General Assembly (1946–1960), Accessed 18 October 2018, www.un.org/en/sections/documents/general-assembly-resolutions/index.html.
13 Saul Dubow, "Smuts, the United Nations and the rhetoric of race and rights," *Journal of Contemporary History*, 43(1) (2008): 46.
14 Commonwealth Secretariat, *The Commonwealth at the Summit (Vol.1)*, 55.
15 Mole, "Mandela and the Commonwealth," 612.
16 Hilary Sapire, "African loyalism and its discontents: The royal tour of South Africa, 1947," *The Historical Journal* 54:1 (2011): 222.
17 Statement, Secretary of State for Dominion Affairs (Viscount Addison), 28 January 1947, House of Lords, Hansard Vol.145 cols 165, Accessed 16 May 2017, www.hansard.parliament.uk/Lords/1947-01-28/debates/7aadaOle-4e55-454a-a795-cc28eOb6c223/TheRoyalVisitToSouthAfrica. The first visit was to Canada, in 1939.
18 Princess Elizabeth, "Broadcast to the Commonwealth," 21 April 1947, Cape Town, *BBC archives*, Accessed 5 May 2020, www.bbc.co.uk/archive/the-21st-birthday-of-princess-elizabeth/zmq68xs.
19 Sapire, "African loyalism and its discontents," 226.
20 "The Crown itinerant," *The Round Table: A Quarterly Review of the Politics of the British Commonwealth* 37:147 (1947): 211.
21 Sapire, "African loyalism and its discontents," 239.
22 Ibid.
23 Paton, *Hofmeyr*, 350.
24 "The Crown itinerant," 207.
25 "Divided Dominion: South Africa and the British Empire," *The Economist*, 10 May 1947, Economist Historical Archive, Accessed 6 June 2020, www.economist.com/unknown/2013/12/05/divided-dominion.
26 "South Africa: The general election," *The Round Table: A Quarterly Review of the politics of the British Commonwealth* 151 (1948): 722.
27 Other slogans used included '*Rooi Gevaar*' (Red Peril), '*Die kaffir op sy plek*' (The kaffir in his place) and '*Die koelies uit die land*' (The coolies, or Indians, out of the country).
28 Nelson Mandela, *Long Walk to Freedom* (London: Abacus, 1994), 127.
29 Shula Marks, "White masculinity: Jan Smuts, race and the South African war," Raleigh Lecture, 2 November 2000, *Proceedings of the British Academy* 87 (2001): 205.
30 Kruger, *The Making of a Nation*, 236.
31 Mandela, *Long Walk to Freedom*, 128.
32 Allister Sparks, *The Mind of South Africa: The Story of the Rise and Fall of Apartheid* (London: William Heinemann Ltd, 1990), 183–4.
33 Paton, *Hofmeyr*, 14.
34 Marks, "White masculinity," 202.
35 Ibid., 202, 213.
36 Ibid., 202.
37 Saul Dubow, "How British was the British world? The case of South Africa," *Journal of Imperial and Commonwealth History* 37:1 (2009): 15.
38 Correspondence from Alfred Milner to Herbert Asquith, 18 November 1897, quoted in Janet Robertson, *Liberalism in South Africa 1948–1963* (Oxford: Clarendon Press, 1971), Introduction.
39 Marks, "White masculinity," 203.
40 Speech by Jan Smuts, South African Institute of Race Relations, 1942, in Jonathan Hyslop, "'Segregation has fallen on evil days," 439.
41 Willem Gravett, "Jan Christian Smuts (1870–1950) in context: An answer to Mazower and Morefield," *The Round Table: The Commonwealth Journal of International Affairs* 106:3 (2017): 272.
42 The official title of the body was *The Native Laws Commission*.
43 Hyslop, "'Segregation has fallen on evil days," 452.
44 Ibid., 452; see also Gravett, "Jan Christian Smuts," 272.

45 Nicolaas Diederichs referenced in "The doctrine of *apartheid*," *The Round Table: The Quarterly Review of British Commonwealth Affairs* 39:153 (1948): 33.
46 Marks, "White masculinity," 206.
47 Paton, *Hofmeyr*, 329.
48 Gravett, "Jan Christian Smuts," 271.
49 Saul Dubow and Alan Jeeves (ed.) *South Africa's 1940s: Worlds of Possibilities* (Cape Town, Juta, 2005), 2.
50 Yvonne Muthien, *State and Resistance in South Africa, 1939–1965* (Aldershot: Avebury, 1994), 3.
51 Margaret Ballinger, *Diaries*, 28 October 1959, UCT archives, Margaret Ballinger Collections, BC 345.
52 Colin Eglin, "Helen Suzman: An appreciation," *The Journal of Liberal History* 66 (2010): 35.
53 Saul Dubow, *Apartheid 1948–1994* (Oxford and New York: OUP, 2014), 128.
54 Mandela, *Long Walk to Freedom*, 130.
55 Resolution of the ANC Annual Conference, 8 November, Bloemfontein, Accessed 28 May 2020, www.sahistory.org.za/archive/report-joint-planning-council-anc-and-south-african-indian-congress-november-8–1951.
56 Apart from the ANC, the other members of the alliance were the South African Indian Congress, the South African Congress of Democrats, and the Coloured People's Congress.
57 Trevor Huddleston, *Naught for Your Comfort* (Glasgow: William Collins & Son Ltd, 1956), 16.
58 Ambrose Reeves, *Shooting at Sharpeville: The Agony of South Africa* (London: Victor Gollancz, 1960), 103.
59 Huddleston, *Naught for Your Comfort*, 116.
60 Ronald Hyam and William Louis, *The Conservative Government and the End of Empire (1957–1964)* (London: TS0, 2000), 436.
61 Lionel Gelber, "Britain, Soviet sea-power and Commonwealth connections," In *Commonwealth Policy in a Global Context*, ed. Paul Street and Hugh Corbet (London: Frank Cass & Co., Ltd, 1971), 43.
62 Mazrui, *The Anglo-African Commonwealth*, 30.
63 Mary Benson, *The Struggle for a Birthright* (Harmondsworth, UK: Penguin Books, 1966), 10.
64 Memorandum by the Secretary of State for the Colonies and the Secretary of State for Commonwealth Relations, "Closer Association in Central Africa," 3 May 1951, TNA, CAB/129/45, 3.
65 Ibid., 2.
66 Memorandum by the Secretary of State for Commonwealth Relations, "The Colonial territories and Commonwealth relations," 8 April 1953, TNA, CAB/129/60.
67 Hyam and Louis, *The Conservative Government and the End of Empire*, 469.
68 Mansergh, *The Commonwealth Experience*, 183.
69 Harold Macmillan, "Wind of change" speech report, *The Guardian*, Thursday, 4 February 1960, Accessed 28 May 2020, www. theguardian.com/theguardian/1960/Fb/04/great.speeches.
70 Ibid.
71 Horne, *Macmillan* (1), 313.

## References

Alan Paton, *Hofmeyr* (Cape Town, London, Toronto: OUP, 1971).
Alistair Horne, *Macmillan: The Official Biography* 2008

Allister Sparks, *The Mind of South Africa: The Story of the Rise and Fall of Apartheid* (London: William Heinemann Ltd, 1990).
Ambrose Reeves, *Shooting at Sharpeville: The Agony of South Africa* (London: Victor Gollancz, 1960).
Commonwealth Secretariat, *The Commonwealth at the Summit (Vol.1)*, Op.Cit
Janet Robertson, *Liberalism in South Africa 1948–1963* (Oxford: Clarendon Press, 1971).
Kruger, *The Making of a Nation*, Op.Cit.
Lionel Gelber, "Britain, Soviet Sea-Power and Commonwealth Connections," In *Commonwealth Policy in a Global Context* (ed.), Paul Street and Hugh Corbet (London: Frank Cass & Co., Ltd, 1971), 43.
Mansergh, *The Commonwealth Experience*, Op.Cit.
Mary Benson, *The Struggle for a Birthright* (Harmondsworth, UK: Penguin Books, 1966).
Mazrui, *The Anglo-African Commonwealth* (Oxford: Pergamon Press, 1967), 30.
Nelson Mandela, *Long Walk to Freedom* (London: Abacus, 1994).
Ronald Hyam and William Louis, *The Conservative Government and the End of Empire (1957–1964)* (London: TS0, 2000).
Saul Dubow and Alan Jeeves (ed.), *South Africa's 1940s: Worlds of Possibilities* (Cape Town, Juta, 2005).
Saul Dubow, *Apartheid 1948–1994* (Oxford, New York: OUP, 2014).
Trevor Huddleston, *Naught for Your Comfort* (Glasgow: William Collins & Son Ltd, 1956).
Yvonne Muthien, *State and Resistance in South Africa, 1939–1965* (Aldershot: Avebury, 1994).

# 4 Sharpeville and South Africa's Commonwealth Exit

## 1 Introduction

South Africa's acrimonious exit from the Commonwealth is often explained in simple terms: that it represented a clash between deeply entrenched institutional racism and an increasingly multiracial organisation embracing values that were sharply at variance with those of the South African state. It is also characterised being the first time an international organisation had challenged Article 2(7) of the UN Charter and the principle that sovereign states would be shielded from wider interference in their internal affairs. This development heralded a change of tone and purpose at the United Nations, a more engaged Commonwealth, and South Africa's increasing pariah status. Reference is sometimes made to the unexpectedly warm reception that Verwoerd received on his return from London to South Africa and to the consolidation of Afrikaner power thereafter once its ultimate objective had been rather unexpectedly achieved. While none of this is invalid, the reality is more complex and nuanced than is generally portrayed.

As a case in point, the Commonwealth is keen to record South Africa's departure from the association as a signal triumph over racism. Its own version of events states:

> At the 1961 summit . . . Commonwealth leaders confronted South Africa, bringing to a head many years of criticism and attempts to persuade it to reform its racial policies. . . . The rest of the Commonwealth wanted nothing less than a willingness by South Africa to end *apartheid*.

It concludes: "South Africa was, in effect, expelled, the first of many expulsions from international councils."[1] This is undoubtedly the prevailing Commonwealth narrative, now enshrined in its mythology. Yet whatever the differing motivation of Commonwealth member countries, until 1961 their combined efforts did not suggest a concerted and determined assault on the growing *apartheid* state, as suggested earlier. Nor would it be accurate to characterise South Africa as being 'expelled' from the organisation, although Verwoerd gloried in "the triumph of Commonwealth expulsion" which had created "a happy day for South Africa."[2]

There is little evidence of collective Commonwealth action over *apartheid* before that date, although pre-independence India had, in December 1946, at one of the earliest sessions of the new United Nations, vigorously opposed racial discrimination in South Africa even before the formal advent of *apartheid* in 1948. Even so, despite the growing opposition of India, Pakistan and Ceylon to *apartheid*, Commonwealth leaders saw the United Nations, rather than the Commonwealth, as the appropriate forum for contesting the issue. It was only in 1960, after Sharpeville, that South Africa's racial policies were first discussed in the Commonwealth itself, and only a year later, in 1961, that Commonwealth leaders pushed their criticisms of *apartheid* to a decisive conclusion.[3]

A further reason to focus on South Africa's departure from the Commonwealth is to explore more deeply the perspective of other parties to these events. The Nationalists had long argued for an independent white South Africa, as an Afrikaner Republic outside the Commonwealth, as the ultimate ideal. One of the party's foremost ideologues was Hendrik Verwoerd, and, on assuming the office of Prime Minister in 1958, he lost little time in setting out his ambition for a republic.[4] Even if there were more immediate objectives, "he had planted a seed and could afford to bide his time."[5] Why was he therefore prepared to offer South Africa's white electorate a republic within the Commonwealth, and how genuine was his commitment to South Africa's continuing Commonwealth membership? The isolation of South Africa after 1961, as it was steadily ostracised internationally, is frequently presented as a key factor in hastening *apartheid's* demise. At the same time, there are those who argue that it had the opposite effect; that, in common with other totalitarian regimes of the century, external condemnation and the cutting of international linkages, merely served to bolster the regime and increase its psychological grip over its population. Indeed, a focus on this seemingly favourable outcome for Afrikaner nationalism appears to support this narrative. Vatcher argues: "The establishment of the Republic and the departure of South Africa from the Commonwealth climaxed the development of Afrikaner nationalism as an organised political force."[6]

While in the 1960 referendum campaign Verwoerd had been prepared to offer white English-speaking voters a continuing presence in the Commonwealth as the price for their support for a republic, there were aspects of membership which jarred. Apart from the pressure to recognise Black diplomats from Africa's newly emergent nations, the connection to the British monarchy (with the Queen as Head of the Commonwealth) remained awkward. As some Afrikaners saw it: "For England, the Queen is a symbol of unity; for South Africa, disunity."[7]

Verwoerd's triumph in the referendum and the break with the Commonwealth, argues Hepple, wrote "his name indelibly in South Africa's history."[8] Some suggest that these events therefore encouraged the development of a South African patriotism, despite the uncompromising racial context in which they were set. Today, in contemporary South Africa, there is evidence that the republic and the exit from the Commonwealth are widely characterised as the final break with British colonialism and imperialism. Van Vuuren's recent reference to "independence from the British Commonwealth in 1961" is a case in point.[9] Given this shared context, reference to these events in the literature of African liberation is often absent or presented in dismissive terms. However, while African leaders held no particular brief for the Commonwealth or the British monarchy, their involvement in the campaign against South Africa marked an important moment.

Undoubtedly, Verwoerd had hoped to enter the referendum campaign having resolved the technicality of lapsing Commonwealth membership. To this end, at the 1960 Commonwealth summit Verwoerd's Foreign Minister, Eric Louw, had tried to extract from Commonwealth leaders' confirmation of South Africa's membership in the event of a change in its constitutional status. Leaders dashed these hopes (faced with what they considered a hypothetical question), and it was clear that a protracted two-stage decision-making process would be necessary. Firstly, the Commonwealth, in or out, would become a bitterly contested issue in the referendum itself. Secondly, only once a decision in favour of the republic had been reached could the procedures requiring reaffirmation of Commonwealth membership be triggered. A five-month period therefore opened up after the referendum result before matters could be concluded. This was to mean that Verwoerd's sincerity in fulfilling his promise on South Africa's continuing Commonwealth membership would be tested in discussion with other Commonwealth leaders.

It also presented the non-white majority – Black African, Indian and Coloured South Africans, who had been excluded from the referendum – with a real opportunity to use the intervening months to extend their campaign. At home, they could seek to use the change to a republic to raise far more fundamental issues, about the rights and status of all South Africa's citizens. Abroad, the impending decision by the Commonwealth in London would provide the chance to work with newly independent African and Asian Commonwealth countries, and with the emerging global AAM, to bring external pressure to bear.[10]

In widening the scope of the inquiry to include the part the Commonwealth, as an issue, played in the Republic referendum campaign, and the implications of the two-stage decision-making process on South Africa's membership as it impacted on the eventual outcome, there are neglected aspects of the matter which require attention. These include looking at the campaigning role of the African liberation groups (and the leadership of Nelson Mandela) and their links with emerging independent African nations in membership of the Commonwealth. There are also the links with the embryonic global AAM and its role in the campaign, including the testimony of some of those involved. Further, the chapter takes a much more critical view of the 1961 Commonwealth Prime Ministers' Meeting itself. Far from being a carefully prepared application of agreed principle, the Commonwealth's collective actions were disorganised, unpredictable and could so easily have turned out otherwise (with what would have been catastrophic consequences for the 'new' Commonwealth). In that sense, the 1961 outcome was not a product of the 'new' Commonwealth but rather the messy and dying convulsions of the old 'imperial' Commonwealth. Even so, it provided a pointer to the unique diplomatic method which the Commonwealth was to claim in the decades that followed.

Finally, the chapter seeks to analyse the impact of the outcome on South Africa's internal politics: principally, the triumph of Afrikaner ideals and the strengthening of the *apartheid* state which had unwittingly resulted. I also explore the disintegration of the English-Speaking white opposition and the consolidation of most white voters behind the Nationalists; the polarisation of internal conflict; and the disappearance of largely outdated concepts of the Commonwealth, held by many, which were now steadily discarded. Externally, South Africa had taken a step into the isolation which in the end it would find suffocating – even as British ambivalence over its relationship with white South Africa, and covert military, diplomatic and intelligence linkages, continued.

## 2 Sharpeville, the Referendum and the Republic

Barely a month after Harold Macmillan's 'Wind of Change' speech in Cape Town came the Sharpeville massacre, with the killing of sixty-seven unarmed Africans and the wounding of 186. Of the fatalities, 70% had been shot in the back. At the subsequent Commission of Inquiry into the shootings, Colonel Pienaar, the police commander, was questioned about his conduct. At the conclusion of his cross-examination, he was asked if he had learnt any useful lesson from the evidence of Sharpeville. "Well, " he replied, "we may get better equipment."[11] The shots at Sharpeville sounded across a horrified world. In vain did the government's defenders argue that the police were still infuriated by the killing of nine young policemen in January 1960 at Cato Manor, near Durban, while searching for illegal beer brewing, or alleging that the crowd gathered at Sharpeville was in fact a "threatening mob... unruly... armed with... some firearms."[12] An unrepentant South African Government responded by declaring a State of Emergency and issuing emergency regulations. These allowed for the banning of processions and gatherings and permitted indefinite detention without charge. Around 1,900 people of all races were immediately arrested, and the ANC and the Pan-African Congress (which had organised the Sharpeville protest) were banned. As South Africa slipped further into darkness, the first international organisation to force South Africa from its membership had begun the necessary processes. A year later, South Africa would no longer be a member of the Commonwealth of Nations.

If many white political leaders had seen 'fusion' of the English-speaking and Afrikaner white communities as a key component in nation-building (under white leadership), other, more ideological Afrikaner *Broeders*, took the opposite view. After what they saw as 'a century of wrong' and the absorption of the two Afrikaner republics into a British-devised Union in 1910, a young Hofmeyr thought "one did not have to kiss the enemy's hand because he took his foot off your neck."[13] Afrikaners agreed that the unity of the white races would undoubtedly be essential in sustaining white supremacy. But they were convinced that this needed to be achieved on Afrikaner terms once the key elements of the Afrikaner republic had been realised. The Afrikaner people, in their eyes, not only had suffered deep injury, injustice and humiliation but also had to endure inequalities (within the white system) which they believed left them the minor white partner across many facets of life, including business, language and culture. In reaction to the merger of Smuts's South African Party and Hertzog's Nationalist Party in 1934, a desire for a 'purified' Afrikaner identity not only had its political expression but also led to much greater attention to constructing a vision of the ultimate Afrikaner state: the republic. Verwoerd was "one of the small group of *Broederbond* intellectuals who applied themselves . . . to working out their master plan which was to achieve Akrikaner unity and Afrikaner domination of South Africa."[14] The onset of the Second World War threw these alternate visions of the future into sharp relief to be recast in the changed circumstances of the war's aftermath.

However, even in the highly racially charged atmosphere of the white election of 1948, Malan chose not to highlight the republic issue. It remained an aspirational rather than a practical political aim. That was also the approach of Strijdom, his successor, despite his earlier fierce advocacy of the issue. It was the party ideologue, Hendrik Verwoerd, who decided to press ahead with the republic, following his succession to the premiership in 1958.[15] In January 1960, Verwoerd declared that a vote on the republic would be held in October of that year. This announcement came only weeks before the visit to South Africa of the British Prime Minister, Harold Macmillan. While Verwoerd did not know of the content of Macmillan's 'wind of change' speech, he was almost certainly aware that the British Government was contemplating a shift in its hitherto uncritical support for South Africa at the United Nations.[16] If, as some argue, Verwoerd's intent in the timing of his announcement on the referendum was to create distance between the South African and British Governments, then it is likely to have hardened British resolve over Macmillan's speech. For Verwoerd, it may have been a means of demonstrating the South Africans Government's independence, emphasising its attachment to the principle of 'non-interference' and reducing the possibility of pressure from the British and other international forces. For the UK, it was a further indication that change was needed, as continuing decolonisation accentuated growing tension between independent Black Africa and the *apartheid* state.

As Macmillan explained:

> The dilemma is easy to state, but difficult to escape. If we rest too much upon the legal and constitutional position, we shall certainly please the old Commonwealth countries like Australia and of course South Africa itself, but we risk gravely offending the Asian and African members.[17]

He continued: "The rigidity, and even fanaticism, with which the Nationalist Government in South Africa have pursued the *apartheid* policy have brought about . . . a dangerous . . . situation in that country. How it will end, I cannot tell." He concluded: "I fear . . . I see a very difficult period facing the Commonwealth."[18]

What also changed after Sharpeville was the Commonwealth's previous reluctance to debate *apartheid* at its periodic summit meetings, preferring instead that critics like India and Ghana should take their criticisms to the United Nations. Malan, representing South Africa's new nationalist government, had welcomed the 1949 London Declaration and the changes it had introduced because it seemed to offer a route to the Afrikaner republic. With the benefit of hindsight, the principal consequence of the agreement in London was a rapid growth in membership, particularly from Africa and Asia, and later from the Caribbean, the Pacific and the Mediterranean. This was to transform the Commonwealth and its attitude to international issues, not least to *apartheid*. It was also to bring the South African regime face to face with the external inconsistences of *apartheid's* relationship with its Black neighbours in Africa. If the logic of *apartheid* was to lead the government to reject non-white visiting athletes and women, so too would it mean not accepting non-white diplomats and High Commissioners. As an academic commentator remarked of the Minister for External Affairs, "[s]o Mr Louw will not exchange diplomatic representatives with the Black States of Africa. . . . South Africa cannot ignore the march of African nationalism, nor resist it."[19]

The equivocal approach of the British Government did little to encourage a more accommodating attitude by the *apartheid* regime towards its neighbours, despite the UK's changed stance at the United Nations. In January 1961 – ten months after Sharpeville – the goodwill visit to South Africa of the Royal Navy aircraft carrier, *HMS Illustrious*, revealed a long-standing 'whites only' practice for British naval crews visiting the country. Before reaching its destination, *Illustrious* had called at Gibraltar and off-loaded its six non-white crew members, having earlier left three Black ratings in Plymouth. "It has been the practice for some years not to send coloured personnel in Her Majesty's ships visiting South Africa, except in special circumstances," Ian Orr-Ewing, the Civil Lord of the Admiralty, told parliament.[20] This was to protect crew from racial discrimination ashore, he explained. This drew a barrage of criticism from Labour and Liberal MPs, prompting Reg Paget MP to protest that "the world should at least realise that the 'wind of change' had blown through the British Admiralty."[21] Further controversy dogged *Illustrious* when the ship's Marine Band the next month gave a public performance in Cape Town from which non-whites were excluded (despite purchasing tickets). Under renewed pressure from MPs, Orr-Ewing, intentionally or otherwise, volunteered the government's primary motivation: "I cannot get away from the fact that this is an extremely important strategic route for the British Commonwealth. It is that which dictates our visit to the Cape, not *apartheid*."[22]

More than a decade before, such attitudes were commonplace. The British Government's banishment of Seretse Khama from Bechuanaland and as Kgosi of the Bamangwato people, after his interracial marriage to Ruth Williams, revealed "deeply felt racism" among British Ministers and officials.[23] It also showed a readiness by the UK government to pander to South African pressure and the views of white settler regimes further north. South Africa still expected to secure formal control over the mandated territory of South-West Africa and continued to cast a covetous eye over the High Commission territories and Southern Rhodesia where substantial post-war emigration from South Africa was having an effect.[24] There were also important defence and economic links with South Africa which weakened the UK's tenuous grasp on the principle of racial equality. In any case, the British Government, in administering the Commonwealth, had not decided its approach to a 'post-Dominion' model of membership. A 'two-tier' ranking of countries was seriously considered, and at this point the British Government favoured granting independence only to much larger federated units, such as the Central African Federation (CAF), rather than to the much smaller nations that eventually emerged.[25] This obstacle would have made decolonisation seem a distant prospect.

White South Africa was further buttressed by the reassuring presence of Portuguese colonial possessions further north, where talk of freedom was firmly rebuffed. Hyslop points out that "too often South Africa is seen as exceptional within the empire," but this was certainly not evident in the early days of *apartheid*.[26] Dubow suggests that the Commonwealth was "a relatively protected space" for South Africa to be involved in international affairs.[27] The reality at this time was that the Commonwealth was "a congenial place for South Africa."[28]

In this context, it is scarcely surprising that the South African Government should have seen the London Declaration not as a dangerous first step to a multiracial Commonwealth but instead as an open door leading to the Afrikaner Republic. Of course, the Afrikaner leadership had repeatedly made it clear that the ultimate goal was a republic outside the Commonwealth: "Afrikaner hegemony in a white supremacist, *apartheid*, republic state."[29] This was an article of faith, though not necessarily practical nationalist politics at this stage. Whatever the optical importance of the severance of any formal link with the UK and its former imperial possessions, there were pressing reasons why the matter needed to be treated carefully. The foremost of these was that the white referendum needed to be won and, even with the addition of white voters from South-West Africa, the abolition of the Coloured roll and the lowering of the voting age to 18, this was by no means certain. Nor was it just a matter of winning the vote: it was also a case of winning English-speaking hearts and minds, if 'Afrikaner' fusion could be achieved. The decade since the Nationalists' assumption of power had seen a further chiselling away of the British connection, such as the removal of the Queen's head from stamps and coins, and of the appeal to the Privy Council, the Union flag, and 'God Save the Queen'.[30] But residual loyalty to Crown and Commonwealth remained strong, especially in Natal, and not just among whites, as the Royal Tour of 1947 had demonstrated.[31]

Earlier in the decade, Patrick Duncan (the son of the former Governor-General and later a determined anti-*apartheid* activist and Pan-Africanist Congress of Azania ambassador) had lamented that English South Africans, since 1948, had to "reconcile themselves to being a subordinate and ruled minority in their own land," conceding that in all the previous regimes of the Union "the English South African continued to run South Africa in fact, if not in appearance."[32] Once the decision to seek a republic had been taken, Verwoerd wanted to establish that there would be no difficulty in South Africa remaining in the Commonwealth. Speaking in the white parliament, days before Sharpeville, he said: "Now I ask honourable members: Do they really think that if we want to be a member there will be anybody who would want to kick us out?"[33] While this was assumed by South Africa to be a formality, it could only be determined by Commonwealth Prime Ministers according to established procedures.

A few months later, at the beginning of May 1960, Commonwealth Prime Ministers met in London. The Federation of Malaya, led by the father of its independence, Tunku Abdul Rahman, was the newest Commonwealth member. South Africa was represented by its External Affairs Minister, Eric Louw, following the assassination attempt on the Prime Minister in April. Louw duly gave notice that

*Figure 4.1* Harold Macmillan welcomes Archbishop Makarios of Cyprus to the Commonwealth, 1960. Commonwealth Secretariat.

South Africa would shortly be holding a referendum on the question of republican status. He was reminded that, if South Africa voted to become a republic and wished to remain in the Commonwealth, it would have to follow the usual procedure and reapply for membership. The Commonwealth could not offer any kind of guarantee based on a hypothetical question: it had to deal with the realities of changed circumstances.[34]

The discussion thus far was constrained. But it was evident that Sharpeville had precipitated a sea change in attitudes. It was not long before anger over *apartheid* bubbled over, with Nkrumah, Diefenbaker and Nehru among South Africa's fiercest critics. The communiqué recorded:

While reaffirming the traditional practice that Commonwealth conferences do not discuss the internal affairs of member countries, Ministers availed themselves of Mr Louw's presence in London to have informal discussions with him about the racial situation in South Africa. . . . Mr Louw gave information and answered questions . . . and the other Ministers conveyed to him their views on the South African problem.

The statement concluded: "The Ministers emphasised that the Commonwealth itself is a multiracial association and expressed the need to ensure good relations between all member states and peoples of the Commonwealth."[35]

With the date of the referendum later set for 5 October 1960 and the next Commonwealth summit not due until March 1961, the decision on republic and Commonwealth was bound to be a two-stage process and a rather protracted one at that. On the face of it, this had advantages to the republican campaign, enabling it to argue that the changes were practical and procedural, an essential step in modernising the constitution but without disturbing the structure of South Africa's external relations. There would be no departure from the Commonwealth, and nor would it open any rift in principle with the British. It would allow the retention of the diplomatic, military and economic alliances the Union enjoyed with the UK and with other former 'dominion' governments. It was, perhaps, inconvenient that the post-1949 Commonwealth involved recognition of King George VI, and later Queen Elizabeth II, as the Head of the organisation. But this was a voluntary external agreement and did not impact on South Africa's constitution or its sovereignty. At the same time, it offered some reassurance to the Union's English-speaking whites (as well as others) that the link to the crown would not be broken. Arguably, it also meant that there would be time for any passions aroused by the referendum to subside and wounds to heal.

But Verwoerd's decision to retain Commonwealth membership was not unconditional. South Africa would remain a member 'for now'. However, this was only so long as there was no interference in its domestic policies and no other threat from the newly multiracial association. He had made little secret of the fact that, ultimately, the destiny of the South African republic would be outside, rather than within, the British-inspired Commonwealth of Nations. If the two-stage process facilitated the triumph of the Nationalists in the referendum, pushing the question of Commonwealth membership to a future date, it also gave the excluded opposition, namely Black, Indian and Coloured South Africans, the chance to campaign against the regime at a moment when it faced international exposure. As Black opposition to the new *apartheid* state intensified, so contacts with neighbouring African countries increased. African nationalists saw the freedom of the oppressed in South Africa bound up with the liberation of Africans elsewhere in the continent. The 1955 Bandung Conference, in drawing delegates from Africa, Asia, and the Middle East, pointed to a global anti-colonial movement and the desire to break free of the geopolitical straitjacket of the Cold War. In 1957, Ghana (previously the Gold Coast) became the first Black African member of the Commonwealth. A year later, it saw legal opportunities to bring pressure on South Africa for flouting its UN mandate over South-West Africa. This was a prelude to the case filed by Ethiopia and Liberia two years later in the International Court of Justice challenging South Africa's mandate. While this ultimately unsuccessful legal challenge did not directly involve the Commonwealth, it helped focus attention, after the Sharpeville massacre of March 1960, on calls for South Africa's expulsion from the Commonwealth.

The year 1960 was proclaimed 'Africa Year' and the Second All-African Peoples' Conference (AAPC) met in Tunis on 25–30 January in a mood of optimism as a succession of African nations achieved independence. The ANC had noted Harold Macmillan's 'wind of change' speech and the promise of British decolonisation for seventeen African countries, but there was scepticism about whether the UK's support for South Africa at the United Nations would change.[36] The 'outburst of horror' at Sharpeville and Langa increased internal unrest, accelerated white emigration, and hit business confidence and foreign investment.[37] It also drew intensified repression from the *apartheid* regime. But it electrified the Black opposition, already buoyed by the steady disintegration of the Treason Trial. In the view of Lodge: "All of these developments encouraged African and left-wing leaders in South Africa to perceive the authorities as vulnerable." Their ability to mobilise a mass following and generate large-scale protest led them to believe that "there was a substantial constituency ready for revolt."[38]

At the same time, the departure of some 'Africanists' from the ANC in November 1958, over disagreements with the Freedom Charter and in protest at collaboration with 'non-African' organisations, led to a fissure in the liberation movement. The Pan-Africanist Congress, formed in April 1959 and led by Robert Sobukwe, stole a march over the ANC by organising the protests at Sharpeville and Langa. Not only did the PAC's reputation in the townships rise substantially but the ANC leadership, including Mandela, were to find that weaning newly independent Black African states from supporting the PAC was a challenging task. That said, both the ANC and the PAC expressed confidence that *apartheid* would be overthrown in a few short years or even months.

Mandela, and London-based allies such as Dr Yusuf Dadoo, saw the political opportunity arising out of Verwoerd's determination to hold a referendum among South Africa's white electorate on the issue of republican status. They held no brief for the monarchy or for the 'imperial' Commonwealth for that matter. For the non-white citizens of South Africa, this was a vote about a 'white Boer republic'. It was an issue about which they had not been consulted and a decision from which they were excluded. For the ANC and others, they could not be passive bystanders: their rights and their future as South Africans were at stake. They would therefore campaign for an alternative constitutional settlement.

In its enabling legislation for the referendum, the Nationalist government had aimed for clarity and a minimum of state disruption. The vote itself, while aggregated according to provinces, would be counted as a whole, requiring a simple majority to effect change. The resulting constitutional amendments would also be kept to a minimum. The Queen would simply be replaced as Head of State by a ceremonial State President. In advocating a 'Yes' vote, the Nationalists argued that the republic was the only way to unite and entrench white hegemony. Verwoerd himself made a personal appeal to individual white voters in what appeared to be a hand-written, four-page letter from the Prime Minister's official residence, Libertas.[39] In it, Verwoerd invited voters to decide the future of the country and its people. "By answering 'Yes' through your cross on the voting paper, you become one of the founders of our Republic of South Africa . . . a democratic republic within the Commonwealth." The alternative, he warned, would be dire: "If you do not take this step . . . we (and our children certainly) will experience the sufferings of the whites who have been attacked in, and driven out of, one African territory after another."[40]

In particular, he cited the recent eruption of violence in the Congo. He continued: "Should South Africa remain a monarchy, it will suffer time and again, from instigated racial clashes and economic setbacks, since these are the weapons used to prevent the coming of the Republic." The leader of the opposition UP, Sir De Villiers Graaff, in advocating a 'No' vote, also cited stability and security. In his view, the 'British' Commonwealth offered economic protection, as well as a political defence against Communism and 'hot-eyed African nationalism'.

Nationalist campaigners argued that South Africa was merely seeking to continue its membership, not make a reapplication, and that assent need not be unanimous.[41] Verwoerd pronounced that he was reassured by what he had heard from other Commonwealth Prime Ministers, particularly the British. "The most heartening feature," declared Coetzee, "is the clear desire to keep the Commonwealth together and the obvious belief of many members that nothing will be solved by merely ejecting us, which from the nature of things can be a 'gesture' only."[42] Zach de Beer of the small Progressive Party riposted:

> What constitutes the threat to our membership is our identification with racialism which sets us apart from all other Commonwealth states and from the western world. Until we are prepared to abandon . . . race discrimination we cannot become a republic and be confident of staying in the Commonwealth.[43]

Others used more colourful imagery. Clough warned that a vote for a republic would be to take "a dark, unknown and uncertain road."[44] Nolteno warned that it would be a "step on the road to serfdom."[45]

When the results emerged, it transpired that despite these dire warnings a narrow majority had voted for the republic, with 850,458 votes (52%) in favour against 775,878 (48%) voting against. Of the four provinces of the Union, only Natal stood against the tide, mustering big majorities against the republic on an exceptionally high turnout. Douglas Mitchell, the inflammatory and 'crude white supremacist' leader of the UP in Natal, continued to stoke the secessionist fires for some months after the result.[46] He caused "a major sensation" in the parliamentary debate on the Republic Bill, declaring: "We live under a hostile Government and this is tyranny and rule by force," warning "the day of reckoning is coming."[47] Privately, he even explored the possibilities of Natal detaching itself from the Union either to join with the Federation of Rhodesia and Nyasaland to the north or reverting to British protection under the Crown.⁴⁸ Mitchell's ardour was effectively punctured by the British High Commissioner, Sir John Maud, who pointed out that any constitutional arrangement involving Britain would have to be on the basis of one man, one vote. Since Mitchell's approach to racial issues was indistinguishable from those of the National Party (NP) (despite his vociferous opposition to Verwoerd on the monarchy and the Commonwealth), the idea of a Zulu majority in Natal had little appeal.⁴⁹ By the end of the year, lingering resistance to the republic in Natal effectively fizzled out.

It was also clear that De Villiers Graaff would not challenge the legitimacy of the vote or the enabling legislation for the establishment of the republic. In a lengthy press statement, he began by saying that "by no stretch of the imagination can that slender majority be described as representing the broad will of the people," but he conceded that nonetheless the government had a mandate for change but that it would be "a sectional Republic and not a South African Republic."⁵⁰ The British High Commission was sceptical, reporting to London that the "[w]hite electorate has given the Nationalists about the only genuine popular majority they have ever enjoyed," not to rewrite the constitution but on the "indisputable fact that more South Africans want a President than a Governor-General."⁵¹ Nevertheless, in declaring the UP "a Commonwealth Party," Graaff argued that no steps should be taken to introduce legislation implementing the republican constitution "before we have the certain knowledge that we shall remain in the Commonwealth."⁵² To that end, Graaff offered his services in securing the necessary Commonwealth support.

If Verwoerd felt disinclined to take up Graaff's offer, there were others, most particularly, those excluded from the process of white consultation and decision-making, who again saw the potential for arraigning the *apartheid* regime in the court of world opinion. In May 1960, the Commonwealth Prime Ministers' Conference had taken place barely a month after the massacre at Sharpeville. Nevertheless, newly independent African and other Commonwealth governments, backed by protests outside the London conference, forced a fractious debate on *apartheid* with South Africa's Foreign Minister, Eric Louw. Now a new opportunity beckoned with, exceptionally, another Commonwealth Prime Ministers' Meeting a year after the last. The anti-*apartheid* coalition was also given precious months between the referendum result (in October 1960) and the summit itself (March 1961) to lobby governments and to organise protests. Indeed, in June of that year, the second Conference of Independent African States, meeting in Addis Ababa, adopted a resolution on South West Africa and on South Africa that, inter alia, invited "independent African states which are members of the (British) Commonwealth to take all possible steps to secure the exclusion of the Union of South Africa from the (British) Commonwealth."⁵³ The conference had also called for economic sanctions against South Africa.⁵⁴

Verwoerd was aware of growing African hostility, but he was optimistic that there would be no difficulty in South Africa retaining its Commonwealth membership now that it was transitioning to a republic. He would have been encouraged in this view both by media comment and by the public statements of Commonwealth leaders as they gathered for the 1961 Commonwealth Prime Ministers' Conference.

Verwoerd duly informed his colleagues of the results of the referendum. He then told the meeting that it was South Africa's desire to remain within the Commonwealth as a republic.

Macmillan, in the chair, sought to delink the formal approval of South Africa's continuing membership from any debate on *apartheid*. One should follow the other. This device was resisted by leaders and undermined by Verwoerd himself, who readily agreed that the two matters be debated together.[55] Even so, by the second day of the conference it seemed as though leaders would content themselves with a strong statement condemning *apartheid*. *The Times* headline declared: "S. Africa's Place Safe in Commonwealth," commenting that "it seems fair to say now that the issue is already decided."[56] A leaked draft communique seemed to confirm that view.[57] However, as the conference entered the new week, criticism of South Africa's *apartheid* policy intensified. This time, the principal critics were joined by Sir Abubakar Tafawa Balewa, the Prime Minister of newly independent Nigeria, as well as Archbishop Makarios, President of Cyprus. In vain did the British Prime Minister and Robert Menzies of Australia attempt to stem the tide. South Africa's position had become untenable, and a bruised and angry Verwoerd withdrew his country's application for membership. He declared that he was "amazed at, and shocked by, the spirit of hostility and even vindictiveness" shown towards South Africa. It marked, he believed, "the beginning of the disintegration of the Commonwealth."[58] Two days later, he told the South African Club in London that "for South Africa and the United Kingdom and the other old friends this decision means new opportunity. We must seek to develop in other ways, untrammelled by the former problems."[59]

Macmillan had hoped for a compromise solution that would have kept South Africa within the Commonwealth but also recorded the detestation by all the other Prime Ministers of South Africa's racial policies. But he conceded that this might fatally undermine Balewa and would not hold off an eventual motion to expel South Africa. Later that day, Lord Home wrote to Harold Macmillan, praising him for the "gallant way you have tried to save the day." It was, said Lord Home, a very sad day, but he conceded that "the only alternative was the break-away of all the Asian and African members," adding: "That could not be faced."[60]

## 3   South Africa's Commonwealth Exit: The Aftermath

Verwoerd returned to South Africa to a warm welcome. Margaret Ballinger recorded: "The press now reports that the Nats are closing their ranks and Verwoerd is to be given a great reception."[61] As Kruger put it:

> Afrikaner nationalists were not unduly perturbed about the exclusion of South Africa from the Commonwealth which they had always regarded as a disguised Empire. They saw no benefit from any further association with a Commonwealth which had utterly changed its character and with which South Africa had far less in common than with many other States outside.[62]

Observing the outcome, the British Ambassador Sir John Maud reported that Verwoerd had returned to a 'hero's welcome', adding: "In his heart, I think, he really was delighted: the Commonwealth was no club for Verwoerd."[63] Gillian Slovo, the daughter of Jo Slovo and Ruth First, both prominent SACP activists, had a similar view: "While most white people applauded this declaration by the *apartheid* state that it no longer cared what the world thought, my parents organised the General Strike which was the ANC's response."[64]

For the ANC and the burgeoning AAM in London the outcome was a triumph. A vigorous campaign had enlisted the support of some of the newer Commonwealth Prime Ministers, and there was a wide degree of political, public and media support in the UK. The campaign had its roots in the All-African Peoples Conference and the formation, in 1959, of the Boycott Movement, led by Tennyson Makiwane of the ANC and Patrick van Rensburg of South Africa's small Liberal Party. Support in the UK for the Boycott Movement spread to the Labour and Liberal parties and to the trade unions. The young Labour MP, Barbara Castle, who had come to national attention with a passionate denunciation of colonial atrocities in the Hola camp in Kenya, was among the most prominent. Unusually among British politicians, she had met Nelson Mandela as early as 1956, in South Africa, impressed by his quiet authority which masked what she felt was 'a man of steel'.[65] It was Castle who, with Yusuf Dadoo, Vella Pillay and Abdul Minty, conceived the idea of a seventy-two-hour continuous vigil outside Lancaster House, the venue of the 1961 Commonwealth Conference. "That was our first major campaign and we succeeded," recalled Abdul Minty: "Nobody thought we would . . . but Barbara Castle was tireless."[66] Minty's organisational skills and Castle's tenacity helped recruit a large band of prominent clergy, writers, actors and parliamentarians, each willing to take a two-hour slot on the picket line on the approaches to Lancaster House, standing in complete silence. The press suspected a hoax and visited the demonstration in the early hours but, as Castle said of the protestors: "We were there!"[67] There was also a march through central London led by Oliver Tambo, Dadoo, Fenner Brockway and other African leaders.[68]

There was no doubting the international impact of the news. The ANC's message from London (drafted by Dadoo) was that South Africa's enforced withdrawal was "a resounding victory for our people, and marks an historic step forward in our struggle against *apartheid*."[69] In May, Mandela wrote to Sir de Villiers Graaff urging action to stop the inauguration of the republic, telling him: "We have been excluded from the Commonwealth and condemned 95 to 1 at the United Nations."[70] Later, Mandela spoke of the successful campaign to oust South Africa from the Commonwealth and praised the role played by Ghana, Nigeria, and Tanganyika.[71] It was the first successful campaign by what had become the AAM and the first in which its partnership with a coalition of Commonwealth countries was to prove such a potent force. Many years later, Castle mused that "the people of this country were ashamed of the fact that at the heart of what was a multiracial Commonwealth, of which we were proud, we had the absolute centre of *apartheid*. And people began to think that this was wrong."[72] However, if this was a defeat for Verwoerd, it was not one which he and his supporters recognised. Contrary to Mandela's hopes,

South Africa's increasing isolation and international ostracism made no observable impact on Verwoerd, the great architect of *apartheid*, who now set about destroying all opposition and consolidating the regime.

Margaret Ballinger, officially the Natives' representative in the South African Parliament, was on board ship, on route to Cape Town, when she heard the news. "It was like a physical blow – or a declaration of war which in effect it is . . . but no one had really foreseen what did happen."[73] She later wrote that the decision had "profoundly shocked overseas opinion everywhere – and now again White South Africans have become, in effect, one group in the eyes of the outside world . . . today, we are friendless indeed in a hostile world."[74] Quentin Whyte, the one-time director of the South African Institute of Race Relations, uttered a great cry of despair which reflected his loss of identity and his fear of growing isolation:

> I feel cut adrift and there is no sub-conscious Commonwealth, British backing for my confidence. . . . I must identify myself ever more completely with my country and must look inwards not outwards. I am deprived of the family and kinship of Commonwealth and cannot now derive from them the expansive, expanding outlook and creativity which could be harnessed for the greater good of my country for I am no longer acceptable; I am an outcast.

*Figure 4.2* Nelson Mandela on a visit to London, 1962. Commonwealth Secretariat.

I am a foreigner, a South African, identified only with South Africa and its presently deplorable policies.[75]

This was the reality of a second-class white citizenship where, as Keppel-Jones has observed, one portion has nationality, the other only language.[76]

What was the future for English-speaking whites? Ballinger, later removed from power by the abolition of the Native Representative Council and their white representatives in Parliament, became active in the small, multiracial Liberal Party. A section of the discredited and disintegrating UP broke away to form the Progressive Party, but in the 1961 elections only one of their number, Helen Suzman, representing the Johannesburg constituency of Houghton, retained her seat. Although the new party polled well in some areas, Suzman was to be the sole liberal voice in parliament for the next thirteen years. Others, such as those in the Liberal Party, clung to pacifism and constitutionalism but were increasingly harassed by the state. In 1965, seven Cape Liberals were banned from political activity, prompting leading members of the party to protest: "You can ban us, gaol us and have your political police snoop on us, but you will never prevent us from continuing to hold our beliefs."[77] Yet it was those liberal beliefs which, in the eyes of Afrikaner nationalists, were "evidence of disloyalty to the state."[78] In 1968, legislation banning multiracial parties finally forced the party's voluntary dissolution. The party declared that the new laws "make it impossible for the Liberal Party to continue without prostituting itself."[79] The liberal *Cape Times*, writing on the twentieth anniversary of the accession to power by the Nationalists, commented: "The Liberal Party is committing hari kiri as the most honourable way to react to the Bill forbidding 'political interference' across the colour line. One side of the political spectrum thrives; the other dies."[80]

In the face of increasing government repression after Sharpeville, including bannings, harassment and detention without trial, some white members of the Liberal Party and others contemplated violence against state infrastructure and services (while, initially, eschewing violence against people). Like the decision of the ANC to establish MK and to resist the state by violence, the National Committee of Liberation (later, the African Resistance Movement) began small-scale acts of sabotage of powerlines, bridges and railways. Even as the security police were breaking up and arresting the group, in July 1964, one of their number, John Harris, placed a time bomb in Park Station in Johannesburg during the evening rush hour. A warning was telephoned to the authorities, but the device exploded, killing an elderly woman and seriously injuring twenty-three others. John Harris was later hanged, the only white South African to be executed for a political crime. The *Cape Times* condemned those who thought they could "solve human problems with dynamite," declaring it "a silly, disastrous episode."[81]

By 1965, many anti-*apartheid* activists had fled South Africa with a considerable number of exiles settling in London. Those liberals that remained had little enthusiasm for the new Commonwealth and did not rejoice at the decision which precipitated their increased isolation. Whyte commented:

The major and salient fact is that our racial policies are quite unacceptable to the Commonwealth and the world. Externally, we face the probability of strong U.N. and other international pressures and actions. Internally, we must be prepared for greater friction, and we must expect more control of aspects of our common life.[82]

And the majority? After the proclamation of the republic, Ballinger had written:

Dr Verwoerd has apparently persuaded himself . . . that a change from monarchy to republic can and will effect some mystic change . . . if only the English people can be cut adrift from their old loyalties they will come together to help . . . the survival of the white man in this country.[83]

And yet, mystical or otherwise, that was what happened. Verwoerd's gamble had seemingly achieved the domestic effect he was seeking, at least in the short term. In white elections from 1961 to 1981, the NP consolidated its dominance of white politics. In the eyes of the world, and within South Africa itself, it seemed that *apartheid* reigned supreme. White opposition, apart from the Progressive Federal Party, was equivocal and diminishing.

However, this apparent white fusion in support of *apartheid*, which reached its electoral peak in 1977, was not as complete as it seemed. Afrikanerdom itself was beginning to splinter, with defections on the right, first to the HNP and later to the Conservative Party (CP). The divide between *verkrampte* ('conservative') and *verligte* ('liberal') had always been a facet of Afrikaner culture, but now it was again being expressed in a political context. Equally, the support of many English-speaking white voters for the Nationalists in the high water of *apartheid* masked clear and persistent cultural, political and social differences among the younger generations, including contrasting degrees of identity with the South African state and nation. A study of Afrikaner and English-speaking students concluded: "Afrikaners and English-speaking South Africans may be citizens of the same nation-state, but in a social-psychological sense they inhabit two different worlds as far as national identity is concerned."[84] By the final days of *apartheid*, even these divisions were breaking down as white voters adjusted to the new reality.[85]

Finally, what of South Africa's relationship with Britain? Confronted with the unenviable choice, the UK had chosen the Commonwealth rather than the *apartheid* state. However, it quickly became clear that in many respects it would be business as usual. As regards military cooperation, the Chiefs of Staff contemplated imminent South African withdrawal and concluded that "from a military point of view it is clearly desirable to preserve, as far as possible, the links between the UK and the South African Armed Forces." The status of military missions would have to change but "special arrangements should be made for service liaison," given the UK's "considerable defence interest in South Africa."[86] Even South Africa's attendance at staff colleges should continue "though there were likely to be strong political objections to this, particularly from the new Commonwealth countries."[87] In introducing the UK government's 'standstill' Bill in the House of Lords, the

Duke of Devonshire spoke of South Africa's departure as a "melancholy landmark" in the Commonwealth's evolution but "a milestone and not a gravestone."[88] He confirmed that a country which moves outside the Commonwealth "can no longer expect to benefit from the same privileges as one which remains" but nor would the UK "needlessly destroy such bilateral relations as we might normally expect to enjoy with a friendly foreign power."[89] The AAM later complained that "if the South Africans are able to retain the practical benefits of Commonwealth membership, or if we fail to snatch at this opportunity further to isolate the Nationalists, the victory will prove meaningless."[90] In 1962, the AAM lobbied against the renewal of the South Africa Bill, pointing out that the system of Commonwealth preferences (worth some £51 million annually to South Africa) was unchanged and that "this devalues the worth of Commonwealth membership."[91]

Close diplomatic liaison between South Africa and the UK continued at the highest level, particularly over action at the United Nations. In November 1963, the South African Ambassador in London called on the Foreign Office to say "that the UK had been very helpful at the UN by voting against oil sanctions."[92] A few weeks later, the Ambassador called again to be told by the Permanent Under-Secretary (PUS) that the "position in New York was very difficult, but the alternative was likely to be something worse." Britain's overriding concern was "to avoid economic sanctions."[93] If politically British ambiguity was becoming tortuous, its economic relationship with South Africa flourished, as did continuing British immigration into the republic. Indeed, the five years following South Africa's exit from the Commonwealth "were the most prosperous in South Africa's history," allowing Verwoerd to boast that the exit was "an act of providence."[94]

## 4  Conclusion

It was by no means certain that the Commonwealth was bound to reach the view it did in 1961. Before the Prime Ministers' conference, the position of many of the participants had not crystallised, and Britain worked hard to keep South Africa inside the association. There was no Secretary-General and independent Secretariat to help channel opinions at an early stage, and the individual interventions of certain Commonwealth leaders, particularly Canada, proved crucial in shifting opinion, though so too did Verwoerd's amiable obstinacy.

What would have been the consequences had the decision gone the other way? Sir John Maud is in no doubt: "Had the Republic been a member of the Commonwealth through the 'sixties and 'seventies, the prospects of peace in Southern Africa would now, I think, be worse than they are."[95] It would certainly have changed the character of the Commonwealth and had profound repercussions. Rhodesian Unilateral Declaration of Independence (UDI), only a few years later, roused great passions and almost split the Commonwealth apart. How much deeper would those divisions have been had the British Government been flanked by an assertive *apartheid* regime, supporting white supremacy in Rhodesia, and without the restraining hand of a Commonwealth Secretary-General? This in turn would have encouraged a more equivocal British stance on Rhodesia and might have arrested the UK's decision to cease its steady support for South Africa at the United Nations. All this would have been more than enough for some of the newer members to walk out and for a future generation of members not to join in the first place. The rupture with South Africa might have come later, in 1965, or in 1971, but it is inconceivable to imagine South Africa retaining membership after 1976 when Soweto's students lit the fires of internal revolt against the *apartheid* state. Whatever the timings, it would have left a much diminished, compromised and fractured Commonwealth.

In 1961, South Africa was not expelled from the Commonwealth, nor consciously excluded. Had the change to South Africa's constitutional status not presented its critics with a procedural opportunity, it is difficult to imagine Commonwealth leaders having the collective will to eject South Africa in 1961 or in the immediate years which followed. Rather, it was the actions of Verwoerd, in resolving that he would take no more criticism, which put the Commonwealth on the right side of history and hastened South Africa's isolation.

South Africa, by virtue of its decision, may have chosen the lonely path of the pariah but, to many whites, it was an act of liberation. After a period when the question of the republic was carefully disentangled and separately debated from the issue of Commonwealth membership, the two were once again conflated. All vestiges of British colonialism, and of monarchy, had now been exuberantly rejected. The proclamation of the Republic on 31 May 1961 became, for the Afrikaner, a decisive moment in nation-building and "the victorious end to the republican struggle."[96] The *apartheid* state stood supreme, its enemies scattered, imprisoned or in exile. The economy was booming and the pattern of relations that South Africa enjoyed with many in the world remained unaffected. The British Government covertly ensured that its security and intelligence links were unaffected, and economic and trading links flourished. The UK's new post-Commonwealth relationship with the *apartheid* state looked much like the old one.

Indeed, paradoxically, the Commonwealth may have unwittingly contributed to what some have described as *apartheid's* 'golden age' – a decade or more of unchallenged supremacy stretching into the 1970s. Certainly, it allowed Verwoerd to confound his white parliamentary opposition. Verwoerd clearly had no real long-term commitment to the Commonwealth but was prepared to offer English-speaking whites continued membership 'for now' as a device for winning the referendum. Once achieved, South Africa's reapplication for membership, determined six months later, was free of any conditionality. In deciding to walk out of the Commonwealth in the face of a chorus of criticism, he turned an apparent defeat into a great Afrikaner victory. Verwoerd, at a stroke, also removed the UP's one claim to be a distinctive opposition as the 'Commonwealth Party'. Now all that was left for Graaff's hapless party was a racial policy which dutifully followed in the Nationalist Party wake. Accused of pandering to his conservative and neo-nationalist wing (most of whom ended up in the NP in any case) and ignoring the remaining liberal elements his party became "stultified and directionless, making its eventual collapse inevitable."[97]

No wonder that the movement of increasing numbers of English-speaking whites into support for the Nationalist Party and *apartheid* accelerated. Cut off from their cultural ties and increasingly ostracised abroad, where their accent and skin colour would be enough to provoke instant negativity among many they might meet, the reassuring embrace of Afrikanerdom provided comfort and security. Whatever their previous attachment to the British Crown and to the 'imperial' Commonwealth, there was no meeting of minds with the new multiracial Commonwealth, and little prospect that there might be so. Even those remaining white liberal forces working fruitlessly for peaceful change felt international abandonment.

The Commonwealth thus became the first international organisation to drive South Africa from membership of a global body. But it was fortunate to be presented with a procedural opportunity to question South Africa's status, and it was only in the latter stages of the 1961 Commonwealth meeting that this chance was finally taken. Had the decision gone the other way, it is doubtful if the Commonwealth would have survived the turmoil which would have undoubtedly followed. As it was, the character and governance of the Commonwealth was to change radically, and the informal and disorganised attempts of the 'new' Commonwealth to work and coalesce around issues of race became more substantial and effective in the years that followed. Gone too was the passive approach to *apartheid*. The Commonwealth, almost by accident, had begun its active contribution to the anti-*apartheid* cause.

South Africa's government was unperturbed. The Afrikaner ideal had been realised, and a substantial proportion of English-speaking whites were forced to abandon an outdated attachment to an 'imperial' Commonwealth and chose to muster behind the Nationalists. In the short term, the *apartheid* state had turned defeat into triumph. South Africa would not return to the Commonwealth fold for another thirty-three years: this time, as a free and democratic nation.

## Notes

1. Commonwealth Secretariat, *Racism in Southern Africa: The Commonwealth Stand* (London: Commonwealth Secretariat, 1987), 6.
2. James Hamill, "South Africa and the Commonwealth," *Contemporary Review* 267:1554 (1995): 16.
3. Commonwealth Secretariat, *The Commonwealth at the Summit (Vol.1)*, 67.
4. Kruger, *The Making of a Nation*, 315.
5. Ibid., 316.
6. Henry Vatcher, *White Laager: The Rise of Afrikaner Nationalism* (London: Pall Mall Press, 1965), 177.
7. Vatcher, *White Laager*, 170.
8. Hepple, *Verwoerd*, 185.
9. Hennie Van Vuuren, *Apartheid, Guns and Money: A Tale of Profit* (London: Hurst & Company, 2017), 6.
10. Stuart Mole, "Mandela and the Commonwealth," *The Round Table: The Commonwealth Journal of International Affairs* 106:6 (2017): 612–3.
11. Reeves, *Shooting at Sharpeville*, 93.
12. Kruger, *The Making of a Nation*, 325.
13. Paton, *Hofmeyr*, 14.
14. Hepple, *Verwoerd*, 86.
15. Ibid., 142.

16 Miller, *Survey of Commonwealth Affairs*, 141.
17 Harold Macmillan, *Pointing the Way (1959–1961)* (Extract) Letter to HM The Queen, 3 April 1960, 486.
18 Ibid.
19 Prof. Du Plessis, "Co-existence in Africa," *The Cape Times*, 7 April 1959, UCT archives, BC 345 E6.36.
20 House of Commons Debate, HMS 'Victorious' (Visit to South Africa), 30 January 1961, *Hansard* Vol.633, cc603, Accessed 5 February 2018, www.api.parliament.uk/historic-hansard/commons/1961/jan/30/hms-victorious-visit-to-south-africa.
21 Ibid., cc608.
22 House of Commons Debate, South Africa (HMS Victorious) 1 March 1961, *Hansard* Vol.635 cc1575–7, Accessed 5 February 2018, https://api.parliament.uk/historic-hansard/commons/1961/mar/02/south-africa-visit-of-hms-victorious.
23 Williams, *Colour Bar*, 74.
24 Cabinet Paper, "The future of Commonwealth membership" by Sir Norman Brook, 21 January 1952.
25 Memorandum by the Secretary of State, "Closer Association in Central Africa," 3.
26 Hyslop, "Segregation has fallen on evil days," 453.
27 Dubow, "The Commonwealth and South Africa," 294–5.
28 Miller, *Survey of Commonwealth Affairs*, 132.
29 Hepple, *Verwoerd*, 167.
30 Miller, *Survey of Commonwealth Affairs*, 128.
31 Sapire, African loyalism and its discontents, 215–240.
32 Patrick Duncan," The English in South Africa – a subordinate minority," June 1953, *The Forum*, UCT archives, BC 668, C1.4, 22.
33 Hendrick Verwoerd, Speech in SA Parliament, Hansard 21 March 1960, Col.3779, quoted in a Progressive Party Briefing Paper: "South Africa and Commonwealth membership," UCT archives, BC 668, C1.4.4.
34 Miller, *Survey of Commonwealth Affairs*, 157.
35 Commonwealth Secretariat, *The Commonwealth at the Summit* (Vol.1), 63.
36 Benson, *The Struggle for a Birthright*, 220.
37 Ibid.
38 Lodge, *Mandela*, 89.
39 *Libertas*, in the suburb of Bryntirion in Pretoria, is now the official residence of the President of South Africa and has been renamed *Mahlamba Ndlopfu* (*New Dawn* in the Tsonga language).
40 Hendrik Verwoerd, "Letter to voters," 21 September 1960, UCT archives, BC 347 B3V.1.5.
41 G.A. Coetzee, *The Republic: A Reasoned View* (Johannesburg-Cape Town: Afrikaanse Pers-Bockhandel (EDMS) BPK, 1960), UCT archives, BAP 320.968.
42 Coetzee, *The Republic: A Reasoned View*, 53.
43 Zach de Beer, Statement by the Chairman of the National Executive of the Progressive Party, 6 September 1960, UCT archives, C1.4.4.
44 Owen Clough, *Republicanism in South Africa: A Statement of Case* (1956), UCT archives, BAP 320.968, 31.
45 D. Molteno, *A Republic of Serfs – Unless We Get Guarantees* UCT archives, BAP 320.968.31.
46 Alex Mouton, "No Prime Minister could want a better leader of the opposition," *African Historical Review*, 46(1), 48–69.
47 Correspondence from BHC Cape Town to Commonwealth Relations Office, *London*, 3 February 1961, TNA, SA 43/3 (DO 180/4), 13.
48 William Stewart, "Natal and the 1960 Republican Referendum," MA thesis (University of Natal, 1990), 163.

49 Ibid., 182.
50 De Villiers Graaff, Press Statement on behalf of the United Party, 8 October 1960, Johannesburg, reproduced in Stewart, "Natal and the 1960 Republican Referendum," 189.
51 Correspondence from Peter Foster, BHC Cape Town to R.G. Britten, Commonwealth Relations Office, London, 4 February 1961, TNA, SA 43/3 (DO 180/4), 3.
52 Stewart, "Natal and the 1960 Republican referendum," 190.
53 Peter Calvocoressi, *South Africa and World Opinion* (London: Oxford University Press, 1961), 61.
54 Ibid.
55 Miller, *Survey of Commonwealth Affairs*, 155.
56 J.D.B. Miller, "South Africa's departure," *Journal of Commonwealth Political Studies* ed. Kenneth Robinson and J.D.B. Miller, Vol.1, (1961): 61.
57 Ibid., 65–66.
58 Nicholas Mansergh, "The Commonwealth: A retrospective survey," In *A Decade of the Commonwealth, 1955–1964*, ed. W.B. Hamilton et al (USA: Duke University Press, 1966), 15.
59 Hendrik Verwoerd, Speech to the South African Club, 17 March 1961, London, Accessed 9 November 2018, https://www.hedrikverwoerd.blogspot.co.uk/2010/12/march-17-1961-prime-minister-verwoerd.html.
60 Lord Home in conversation with Ayub Khan, quoted in Hyam and Louis, *The Conservative Government and the End of Empire*, 323.
61 Margaret Ballinger, *Diaries*, UCT archives, BC 345, B3.5.1.
62 Kruger, *The Making of the Nation*, 335.
63 Maud, *Memoirs of an Optimist*, 91.
64 Gillian Slovo, *Every Secret Thing: My Family, My Country* (Boston: Little, Brown and Company, 1997), 77.
65 Clarity Films, "Have you heard from Johannesburg?" documentary series, 10 December 2013, Accessed 21 March 2018, www.youtube.com/watch?v=xgB7nHj6NyO.
66 Abdul Minty, interviewed by Sue Onslow, *Commonwealth Oral History Project*, 12 February 2013, Geneva, Switzerland, Accessed 5 July 2019, www.commonwealthoralhistories.org, http//sas_space.sas.ac.uk/6531/1/abdul_minty_transcript, 2.
67 "Barbara Castle talks about leading an anti-*apartheid* demonstration at Commonwealth Summit," *Beastrabban\'s Weblog*, 12 May 2016, Accessed 26 May 2020, beastrabban.wordpress.com/2016/05/12/barbara-castle-talks-about-leading-an-anti-*apartheid*-demonstration-during-commonwealth-summit.
68 Picture, Commonwealth Conference March 1961, Accessed 25 May 2020, htpps://www.aamarchives.org/archive/history/1960/Pic6103-commonwealth-conference-march-1961.html.
69 Message to the South African people, "Forced withdrawal of South Africa from the Commonwealth," March 1961, Padraig O'Malley archives, Accessed 3 February 2020, www.omalley.nelsonmandela.org/omalley/index.php/site1q/031v01538/041v01600/051v01617/061v01620.htm.
70 Correspondence from Nelson Mandela to de Villers Graaff, 23 May 1961, Padraig O'Malley archives, Accessed 3 February 2020, htpps://www.omalley.nelsonmandela.org/omalley/index.php/site1q/031v01538/041v01600/051v01617061v01622.htm.
71 Mandela, *Long Walk to Freedom*, 351.
72 BBC News, Interview with Barbara Castle, 27 April 1994, London, Accessed 14 July 2018, BBC Motion Gallery, www.gettyimages.co.uk/videos/bbc-interview-barbara-castle-27-april-1994?collection=bba,bbr,bbe&phrase=BBC%20intervoew%20Barbara%20Castle%2027%20April%201994&sort=best#license.
73 Ballinger, *Diaries*, B3.5.1.
74 Margaret Ballinger, *Sunday Express*, 16 April 1961, UCT archives, BC 345, B3.51.

75 Quintin Whyte, "Withdrawal from the Commonwealth," Draft article, not published, University of Witwatersrand archives, Alan Paton Papers, 2A, HPRA, AD 1502, Bb2.59.
76 Quoted in Dubow, "How British was the British world?" 16.
77 "Seven Cape Liberals banned," 13 March 1965, *The Guardian*, UCT archives BC 345, D5.14.
78 Dubow, "How British was the British world?" 16.
79 Editorial, *Transkei Liberal News*, April 1968, UCT archives, BC 345 D5.71.
80 Editorial, "One thrives, the other dies," 26 May 1968, *The Cape Times*, UCT archives, BC 345, D5.99.
81 Ibid.
82 Whyte, "Withdrawal from the Commonwealth," 4.
83 Margaret Ballinger, "The outlook for the South African Republic 1962," *International Affairs* 38:3 (1962), UCT archives, BC 345 E2.23.
84 Stanley Morse, J. Mann and E. Nel, "National identity in a multi-nation state: A comparison of Afrikaners and English-speaking South Africans," *Canadian Review of Studies in Nationalism* 5 (1978): 242.
85 Peter Stewart, *Segregation and Singularity* (Pretoria: UNISA Press, 2004), 173.
86 Chiefs of Staff Committee, "Defence implications of South Africa's decision to leave the Commonwealth," 11 May 1961, TNA, COS (61) 160, 3.
87 Ibid., 5.
88 Duke of Devonshire, Statement by the Joint Parliamentary Under-Secretary of State. Debate on Republic of South Africa (Temporary Provisions) Bill, 11 May 1961, Accessed 25 May 2020, www.api.parliament.uk/historic-hansard/lords/1961/may/11/republic-of-south-africa-temporary.
89 Ibid.
90 AAM pamphlet, "South Africa out of the Commonwealth – what now?" Accessed 25 May 2020, www.aamarchives.org/archive/history/1960s/60s05-south-africa-out-of-the-commonwealth-what-now.html.
91 Memorandum, "The South Africa Bill," 22 February 1962, AAM archive, Bodleian Library, MSS AAM 818.
92 Telegram, Foreign Office to BHC, Pretoria, 19 November 1963, TNA, UN4/31/IA (DO 181/1), 82.
93 Telegram, Foreign Office to BHC, Pretoria, 2 December 1963, TNA, UN4/31/1A, 731.
94 Hepple, *Verwoerd*, 184.
95 Maud, *Memoirs of an Optimist*, 92.
96 Hepple, *Verwoerd*, 165.
97 Book Review, "Div Looks Back – the Memoirs of Sir De Villiers Graaff," *South African Historical Journal* 30:1 (1994): 202.

## References

Alan Paton, *Hofmeyr*, Op Cit.
Alex Hepple, *Verwoerd*, Op. Cit.
Ambrose Reeves, *Shooting at Sharpeville*, Op.Cit.
Commonwealth Secretariat, *Racism in Southern Africa: The Commonwealth stand* (London: Commonwealth Secretariat, 1987).
Commonwealth Secretariat, *The Commonwealth at the Summit (Vol.1)*, Op Cit.
Gillian Slovo, *Every Secret Thing: My Family, My Country* (Boston: Little, Brown and Company, 1997).
Harold Macmillan, *Pointing the Way (1959–1961)*.
Hennie Van Vuuren, *Apartheid, Guns and Money: A Tale of Profit* (London: Hurst, Company, 2017).

Henry Vatcher, *White Laager: The Rise of Afrikaner Nationalism* (London: Pall Mall Press, 1965).
John Maud, *Memoirs of an Optimist*.
Kruger, *The Making of a Nation*, Op Cit.
Mary Benson, *The Struggle for a Birthright*, Op.Cit.
Miller, *Survey of Commonwealth Affairs*.
Nelson Mandela, *Long Walk to Freedom*.
Nicholas Mansergh, "The Commonwealth: A Retrospective Survey," In *A Decade of the Commonwealth, 1955–1964*, ed. W.B. Hamilton et al (Durham: Duke University Press, 1966), 15.
Peter Calvocoressi, *South Africa and World Opinion* (London: Oxford University Press, 1961).
Peter Stewart, *Segregation and Singularity* (Pretoria: UNISA Press, 2004), 173.
Tom Lodge, *Mandela* (New York: OUP, 2007).
Williams, *Colour Bar*, Op.Cit.
William Stewart, "Natal and the 1960 Republican Referendum," MA Thesis (University of Natal, 1990).

# 5 The Rhodesian Rebellion, Arms to South Africa and the 'New' Commonwealth

## 1 Creating a New Commonwealth

Marlborough House, the creation of Sir Christopher Wren and his son in the early years of the eighteenth century, is set back from Pall Mall, behind high walls and large black gates. Built on land leased to the Duke and Duchess of Marlborough by Queen Anne in 1709, the House and its gardens later reverted to the Crown and became a royal residence, most notably the home of the future Edward VII during his long years as Prince of Wales. In 1953, its last royal occupant, Queen Mary, the widow of George V, died, and for some years after the building was largely unoccupied.

Queen Elizabeth's royal warrant of 1959 signalled a new phase in the life of Marlborough House. It was now designated a Commonwealth Centre, and its wings began to show a discreet Commonwealth presence in the shape of several Commonwealth liaison bodies. More publicly, it was the venue for the 1962 Commonwealth Prime Ministers' Meeting, a summit dominated by animated debate over Britain's application to join the European Economic Community (EEC). Having met the year before in Lancaster House, rather than Downing Street, leaders could now enjoy their own conference centre. Of the fifteen countries (and one colony) represented, a clear majority were from the 'new' Commonwealth.[1] Despite the summit's billing as a meeting of Prime Ministers, two of its participating heads of government were executive presidents.[2] The new Prime Ministers of Sierra Leone, Tanganyika, Jamaica and Trinidad & Tobago all took their seats around the conference table, representing an addition to the association's total population of 15 million. With Uganda reaching independence later in the year (adding a further 7 million as Commonwealth citizens), the 'Africa-Asia' takeover of the old 'British' Commonwealth was clearly established, if not yet complete.

The 1961 meeting had culminated in dramatic fashion with the forced withdrawal of South Africa from membership over the policy of *apartheid*. Verwoerd had reapplied for Commonwealth membership in 1960, having just won a referendum of white voters in South Africa approving a republican constitution. While this had long been a goal of fervent Afrikaner nationalists, such as Verwoerd, the South African Prime Minister had assured English voters that he intended no challenge to the country's place within the Commonwealth. Nonetheless, the organisation's

*Figure 5.1* Queen Elizabeth II with Commonwealth leaders, Commonwealth Prime Ministers' Meeting, London 1962. Commonwealth Secretariat.

processes required an application for readmission following a change of constitutional status. Normally considered a formality, this had become much less certain in South Africa's case following the Sharpeville massacre of March 1960. Macmillan, as Chair of the meeting, attempted to steer a middle course between doing nothing about *apartheid*, on the one hand, and provoking South Africa to secession on the other. Achieving this improbable balancing act was not helped, by the uncompromising line being taken by Canada's Prime Minister, John Diefenbaker, thought Macmillan. "If the Whites take an anti-South African line," he confided to his diary: "how can we expect the Browns and the Blacks to be more tolerant?"[3] As it was, it was Verwoerd and not Diefenbaker who tipped the scales against a compromise once he had made clear that South Africa would not receive the diplomatic representatives of newly independent Black African Commonwealth members. Nigel Fisher thought this "the last straw" and "absurd for South Africa to remain in the Commonwealth and for Verwoerd to meet his fellow Prime Ministers at Marlborough House yet decline to grant the usual civilities to their ambassadors in the Union."[4] Faced with a clear majority of members who were determined to link South Africa's continuing membership with critical scrutiny of its policies on race, Verwoerd withdrew South Africa's application and walked out of the meeting.

South Africa's departure from the Commonwealth served to embitter, rather than sooth, internal relations. UK–South Africa bilateral relations seemed to be undisturbed by the latter's new status, and there were well-founded suspicions that the UK had taken covert steps to ensure that crucial areas of cooperation, whether in trade, intelligence or military cooperation, continued much as before. Besides, the *apartheid* regime now seemed to be moving into a new era of dominance, self-confidence and economic self-reliance even if South Africa could no longer count upon the UK to be an uncritical partner of its policies at the United Nations.

Issues of decolonisation and race were also looming ever larger as the CAF began to disintegrate. In 1953, the UK's Conservative government had favoured establishing a federation combining the self-governing colony of Southern Rhodesia with the protectorates of Northern Rhodesia and Nyasaland because it had the makings of a future Commonwealth dominion, standing in the way of further South African expansion from the south. This reflected the then British view of the Commonwealth as being, in the words of David McIntyre, "a small club for big members."[5] Naturally, the proposal also found favour with the white settler population in all three components both for its economic advantages and because it allowed the dominant Southern Rhodesia to control the mineral resources of Northern Rhodesia while also benefitting from plentiful supplies of Black African labour. More to the point, it was a constitutional arrangement that allowed 196,000 whites (less than 3% of CAF's population) to exercise political power over 7 million Black Africans. Unsurprisingly, the Federation was formed without consulting the overwhelming body of its people, and Black nationalist sentiment in all three territories grew steadily. After violence in Nyasaland and an attempt by the colonial administration there to supress African political activity, the Devlin Report condemned the actions of the Nyasaland government as a 'police state', using illegal and repressive methods.[6] It was now obvious that the Federation had no legitimacy in the eyes of the Black majority. With the lessons of Hola and Devlin ringing in British ears, it was clear "that colonial governments must avoid confrontation and enlist the cooperation of African leaders."[7]

Consequently, the Republics of Zambia (formerly, Northern Rhodesia) and of Malawi (formerly, Nyasaland) would soon emerge from the wreckage of the Federation as independent nations, each with African majorities, in full membership of the Commonwealth. Rhodesia (as the Crown colony was more usually known) had enjoyed responsible self-government since the 1920s under a constitution which, while not excluding Black people from the vote, applied property and educational requirements which made any appreciable enfranchisement of the Black African majority a distant and unlikely possibility. Its Prime Ministers had also been invited to attend Commonwealth Prime Ministers' Meetings in the past and believed that the colony's claim to independence was as strong as its neighbours. At the same time, with hostility to *apartheid* mounting, Darwin noted that "British complicity in creating a second independent 'settler regime was almost unthinkable. . . . This was the dilemma that Labour inherited from the Conservative government, which had carefully prevaricated."[8] Rhodesia was therefore left "high and dry" with neither independence nor Commonwealth membership.[9] The agitation among the white population for unilateral action in declaring the colony's independence increased markedly.

## 2 The UK Turns to Europe

However, the 1962 Commonwealth meeting had to address controversies of a different kind. Its 'primary object' was to review progress in Britain's application to join the EEC and, specifically, to consider the likely safeguards which might be offered for protecting Commonwealth trade.[10] While Macmillan gave every impression of sharing in the Conservative Party's sentimental attachment to the Commonwealth – a political party "so long and intimately linked with the ideal of Empire" – he was also a moderniser and a realist.[11] He was increasingly attracted to early attempts at European integration. As a soldier who had fought in the trenches in the First World War, and been repeatedly wounded, the political merits of a united Europe had a deep appeal to Macmillan, quite apart from its economic merits. In any case, public rhetoric apart, the newly emerging Commonwealth, over which the British would have less and less control, was generally a less attractive prospect for the UK.

That much had been apparent at the 1961 Commonwealth Prime Ministers' Meeting in the passionate debates about South Africa and *apartheid*. Although other issues had been discussed as well, such as disarmament, the United Nations and the Congo, Europe had not been mentioned. That changed after the UK's formal application to join the EEC in July 1961. It was soon evident in the UK's consultations with the rest of the Commonwealth that there was widespread alarm and unhappiness about the British application. Alex May has concluded that "only the Malayan government (whose major exports would be unaffected) seemed relatively sanguine."[12] Early in 1962, Diefenbaker sent a message to Macmillan acknowledging the value of briefings Canada had so far received from British officials on the state of negotiations but remarking that "the implications for the Commonwealth of Britain's membership in the EEC are so great that ... a meeting of Commonwealth Prime Ministers should be held before a final decision is reached."[13] A month later, Macmillan responded readily confirming his intention to convene a Prime Ministers' Meeting, proposing 10–19 September and promising "the fullest possible consultation."

In May, a Canadian diplomat in Accra reported that President Nkrumah was "thinking seriously about whether Ghana should stay in the Commonwealth," should the UK definitely join the EEC. This, said the diplomat, was because Nkrumah "has made up his mind that the Common Market is a neo-imperialist conspiracy."[14] He felt the consequences could be disastrous, creating a domino effect and warning that the "loss of its African members would be a grievous blow to the continued existence of the Commonwealth and its utility." In July, Canada's High Commissioner in London, George Drew, lunched with Philip de Zulueta, at that point Macmillan's Private Secretary (PS) for Foreign Affairs. In ranging over the prospects for what both agreed might be a very difficult Commonwealth conference, de Zulueta accepted that some Commonwealth countries, particularly African ones, might withdraw from membership and start "an unravelling process." To the High Commissioner's evident consternation, this prospect didn't appear to trouble de Zulueta in the least, who added that "it might not be a bad idea if some of the new members were to withdraw."[15] While Ottawa was informed that these views were "presumably personal," there are indications that they were not far removed from those of the British Prime Minister. At the beginning of September, as the UK government was making its final preparations for the Commonwealth Conference, Macmillan commented on a secret Cabinet paper assessing progress in the negotiations with the EEC, remarking:

> The new Commonwealth countries are pretty well looked after and can have no economic grievances. . . . Moreover, to be frank, they carry little political weight in this country. Sentiment towards the Commonwealth is really centred upon the old Commonwealth countries, especially Australia and New Zealand.[16]

Macmillan described the opening day of the conference as "a broadside attack on us" though the temperature was lowered for the next three days by the meeting breaking into separate study groups to deal with the special problems of the various regions and the older Commonwealth countries.[17] As the summit ended, Fisher reflected, rather optimistically, that "there was no question of the break-up of the Commonwealth and the most formidable problem in the Common Market negotiations had been overcome." However, even through the restrained language of the meeting's communique, the apprehensions of Commonwealth governments were clear. They expressed "anxieties about the possible effects of Britain's entry" into the EEC and the danger that it might "weaken the cohesion of the Commonwealth or its influence." They explained "the extent to which their interests had not so far been met" in the negotiations and stressed that "only when the full terms were known would it be possible to form a final judgement."[18] However, the outright opposition of the Australian Prime Minister, Robert Menzies, had been deflected at the last moment.

The day after, Macmillan broadcast to the nation, rejecting the notion that the UK faced a choice between the Commonwealth and Europe, insisting that "both are quite different and the membership of one can help membership of the other." In dismissing a 'Commonwealth Common Market' as not a practical proposition, he reiterated his wish "to preserve and strengthen the Commonwealth." But he concluded that many were "impatient of the old disputes, intolerant of the obsolete conceptions; anxious that our country should play its part in all these new and hopeful movements." Given the right terms, entry into Europe was "the right way ahead for us," he concluded.[19]

After a rousing speech to the Conservative Party conference in October, Fisher reported that Macmillan had secured the twin objectives of "pacifying the Commonwealth" and winning support for his European policy in the constituencies.[20] His victory seemed complete. Yet three months later the British application was brusquely vetoed by the French president, De Gaulle, and Macmillan was left in despair.[21]

More broadly, the Commonwealth was not pacified. Even before the developing crisis in Southern Rhodesia brought race back to the Commonwealth agenda, the abortive British application to join the EEC, according to Alex May, "left a legacy of bitterness in some Commonwealth countries, particularly the old Dominions."[22] Many felt there had been a lack of frankness by the British with diminishing confidence in British leadership. It was becoming increasingly evident that the interests of the UK could no longer be viewed as synonymous with those of the Commonwealth as a whole. From temporary alliances (for example, over South Africa's membership), new networks of influence were forming (such as between Canada, India and Ghana). The UK government, with its eyes now set on the distant European prize, was finding the Commonwealth a far less malleable extension of British influence. Some began to wonder aloud if it was worth the effort. As McIntyre put it, "[t]here was a sense of lack of direction, growing cynicism and apathy."[23]

## 3   The Commonwealth Secretariat

The changes to the composition of the Commonwealth and its growth into a multiracial association, coupled with disagreements over race and equality and the direction of the organisation, prompted general soul-searching. This included work by a Planning Unit within the UK's Commonwealth Relations Office which came up with a bundle of practical undertakings, labelled "The Way Ahead," to put before the next Commonwealth Prime Ministers' Conference in 1964. Other governments, organisations and individuals across the Commonwealth also suggested initiatives. Prominent among these was the proposal for an independent Secretariat and staff to provide impartial support to Commonwealth countries and to coordinate the membership's consultations.

The notion of a Commonwealth Secretariat was proposed unexpectedly at the 1964 Commonwealth Prime Ministers' Conference, though the idea was not new and had not been part of "The Way Ahead" proposals circulated on the eve of the conference by the British Government. Nkrumah, attending his fifth Commonwealth summit, argued that it was global inequality, rather than the Cold War, which should be their primary concern. Such matters required a 'central clearing house' serving the membership as a whole. He added that the Commonwealth "was no longer an association of like-minded countries deriving their institutions from Britain: the main bond was respect for each other's independence, and if it was to have any future strength its members needed to accept new obligations."[24] He was supported by others, including Eric Williams of Trinidad & Tobago and Milton Obote of Uganda. The chair of the meeting, Sir Alex Douglas-Home, concluded the discussion by saying that senior officials would consider further the Secretariat and other proposals over the weekend before the conference reconvened on the Monday morning. Privately, British officials were suspicious of the idea of a Secretariat, fearing that it could be used to pressurise the UK government and diminish its control over Commonwealth affairs. Nevertheless, the Cabinet Secretary, Sir Burke Trend, reported that there had been a 'surprising amount of enthusiasm' among Commonwealth officials, and he and his colleagues thought it better to "go along with the proposal rather than stifle it."[25] By the time the meeting ended, two days later, support for the idea had grown and officials were instructed to consider "the best basis for establishing a Commonwealth secretariat," albeit with a limited functional role.[26] This Secretariat would be at the service of all Commonwealth Governments and would be "a visible symbol of the spirit of co-operation which animates the Commonwealth."[27] Despite gathering storm clouds on Southern Rhodesia and a frustrated attempt to commit the Commonwealth to impose economic sanctions on *apartheid* South Africa, there was an air of optimism as government representatives dispersed. Pathe news enthused about "a family of (eighteen) free and equal nations in open discussion."[28] Lord Carrington, speaking for the British Government in the House of Lords, was similarly upbeat, remarking that there had been "a good deal of misapprehension that, with so many problems in the air . . . this meeting would prove to be the breaking point of the new Commonwealth. This has not been so" and adding, "In fact, the reverse has happened."[29]

Barely a year later, Commonwealth Heads of Government, their numbers bolstered by the addition of Malta, Zambia and the Gambia to membership, again met in Marlborough House. Before them were draft agreements prepared by senior officials which were the results of two working party meetings and which reflected the sometimes uneasy balance between those who feared anything more than a highly restricted organisation and those who foresaw a far more expansive role for the new Secretariat. The Agreed Memorandum declared that the Secretariat should not "arrogate to itself executive functions," but a major part of its work should involve facilitating and promoting consultation which is "the life blood of the Commonwealth association."[30] This would involve preparing and circulating papers of common concern and arranging meetings as requested. At the same time, such papers "should not propagate any particular sectional or partisan points of view, contain no policy judgements or recommendations . . . and . . . not touch upon the internal affairs of a member country."[31] At the same time, the Memorandum accepted that while the Secretariat should begin modestly, it should have a constructive role to play and "its staff and functions should be left to expand pragmatically."[32]

If there was caution about a Secretariat, there was even greater trepidation on the part of some at the idea of a Secretary-General. How high-powered a figure should this be? Australia doubted that the appointment should be at the level of a senior High Commissioner or Ambassador, preferring someone 'less distinguished' and more like an officer-in-charge of a common services organisation. British officials were concerned about the selection procedure and suggested "an interim appointment of a retired British colonial governor as acting Secretary-General for one year while further attention was given to procedure."[33] The dilemma was expressed in an editorial in *The Times* of London:

> The main division is between those governments who want a dynamic personality as Secretary-General to get the organisation off to a good start, and those who fear that anyone but the most retiring official might get it off to much too good a start.[34]

*Figure 5.2* Arnold Smith (L.) meeting Commonwealth law officers, Marlborough House, London, 1966. Commonwealth Secretariat.

The new Commonwealth Secretariat came into being on 1 July 1965 with Canada's former Ambassador in Moscow, Arnold Smith, as the first Commonwealth Secretary-General. Whether perceived as a 'dynamic personality' or a 'retiring official', the British Commonwealth Relations Office's informal induction processes seemed to have assumed the latter. Every attempt was made to limit Smith's access to Heads of Government, and British officials even indicated that Harold Wilson, the new British Prime Minister, should issue Smith with a letter of appointment. This Smith quickly rejected, reminding the Commonwealth Relations Office (CRO) that the Agreed Memorandum made clear that his appointment was made by "Commonwealth Heads of Government collectively."[35] His title was a matter of dispute with the British referring to him as 'Secretary-General of the Commonwealth Secretariat', as opposed to Smith's preference: 'Commonwealth Secretary-General'.[36] Wilson himself erroneously confided to his diary that Smith had been appointed "the new and independent full-time Secretary-General *of the Conference*."[37] Confusion about Smith's title in turn led to a dispute about the number plate ('CSG1') on his official car, as well as the location and size of his office. Marlborough House, now regularly used for Commonwealth conferences, was designated as the home of the Secretariat, but the CRO attempted to confine the new SG to the East Wing, by

Sir Christopher Wren's kitchen, rather than making available any of the fine rooms in the central part of the house. In all these matters, Smith eventually prevailed, though these small battles were wearisome and belittling. Finally ensconced in Queen Mary's former bedroom, on the first floor, Smith became convinced that Marlborough House had been bugged and took to walking in the gardens when he wanted to discuss particularly confidential matters.[38]

For many, the establishment of an independent and politically neutral Secretariat and Secretary-General marked the Commonwealth's transition into an association with global reach, possessing all the hallmarks of a recognisable intergovernmental, international organisation. To others, such a notion was ridiculous and a betrayal of its origins. Now confronted with a series of crises, from the Indo-Pakistan war over Kashmir to the Rhodesian regime's Unilateral Declaration of Independence (UDI) in November, few would have given Arnold Smith much chance of building a viable and long-lasting organisation.

## 4   The Rhodesian Rebellion

Concern over the future of Southern Rhodesia had been rising since the dissolution of the CAF in December 1963. With the whiter settler regime threatening to declare independence unilaterally, many feared that the British Government might be tempted to grant independence without convening an Independence Conference and on terms which fell short of majority rule. At the 1964 Commonwealth summit, the British Prime Minister, Sir Alec Douglas-Home, repeated that full sovereignty would be granted to Rhodesia "as soon as her governmental institutions were sufficiently representative." But he was at pains to reiterate what he saw as the proper limits of the Commonwealth's concern. "The Prime Minister of Britain," read the meeting's communique,

> said that he would give careful consideration to all views expressed by other Commonwealth Prime Ministers. At the same time, he emphasised that the Government of Southern Rhodesia was constitutionally responsible for the internal affairs of that territory and that the question of the granting of independence was a matter for decision by the British Parliament.[39]

The debate over Rhodesia was largely even-tempered partly because Douglas-Home "had managed to defuse a potentially explosive problem that could have wrecked the Prime Ministers' Meeting."[40] This was the question of whether Ian Smith, the Rhodesian Prime Minister, should be invited to the summit as Prime Ministers of the CAF had been in the past. Smith claimed he was entitled to attend as of right, whereas Douglas-Home responded that such rights only applied to fully independent member countries. An invitation would therefore require consultation with the rest of the Commonwealth. Unsurprisingly, their approval was not forthcoming. A second development which may have helped the mood of the meeting was the adoption, for the first time, of a statement on race relations which recorded the belief of all Commonwealth governments in building, in each country, a "society which offers equal opportunity and non-discrimination for all its people, irrespective of race, colour or creed."[41]

However, by the time of the 1965 Commonwealth Prime Ministers' Meeting, in mid-June, feelings were running high. In May, Ian Smith had called a general election in the colony, winning an overwhelming majority among white voters and taking all fifty seats reserved for whites. His Rhodesian Front (RF) party did not contest any of the fifteen seats reserved for 11,000 African voters (out of 4 million Black residents) but still gained the two-thirds majority necessary to alter Rhodesia's constitution. As important, the RF's campaign was a thinly disguised referendum on proceeding ahead with independence "with or without Britain's permission."[42]

As the now twenty-one member countries of the Commonwealth gathered, African leaders voiced their alarm, warning the UK that they expected decisive action in resisting Rhodesian independence and protecting the rights of the overwhelming African majority. The British Government was clear about its negotiating position (which later became the 'Five Principles') and in particular the necessity of unimpeded progress towards majority rule. But it was much less clear about how it would give effect to those principles in the face of Rhodesian resistance. Privately, since neither the UK nor the governments of Canada, Australia and New Zealand were prepared to commit to the use of force in the event of open Rhodesian rebellion, there were no other actions, including the threat of economic and other sanctions, likely to deter Rhodesia from UDI.[43] The debate on the communique was fierce and prolonged, but it was nothing compared with the outcry which was shortly to erupt.

News of Rhodesia's UDI, on 11 November 1965, was conveyed to Harold Wilson as he chaired a meeting of the Cabinet and while the meeting considered the latest reports from Salisbury. Wilson had spoken to Smith the previous day, pressing upon him a proposal for a Royal Commission to break the impasse, but Smith had responded that "the positions of the two Governments were irreconcilable."[44] Now that UDI was a reality, it was agreed that the British Government should immediately call for a meeting of the UN Security Council. It was acknowledged that there would be pressure in the United Nations for military action, but this would be ineffective unless a major Power participated (and there was some anxiety that the Soviet Union might offer to intervene). The United Nations should therefore be diverted from military action by "emphasising our conviction that economic measures, if firmly applied, could bring the rebellion to an end." However, the minutes then recorded their admission that "the economic measures we proposed to take might not in themselves be sufficient to achieve this purpose," and a UN oil embargo would be needed.[45] A limited range of sanctions against Rhodesia were introduced immediately and further measures followed on 1 December. A year later, the UN Security Council was to vote for selective mandatory sanctions. This would cover 90% of Rhodesia's exports and would be accompanied by a ban on the sale of oil, arms, motor vehicles or airplanes to the territory.[46]

Nevertheless, the news of Rhodesian UDI and the British Government's failure to respond with military intervention raised a storm of anger and criticism, especially in Africa. Emeka Anyaoku, then working with the Nigerian Mission at the United Nations, recalls a crisis meeting of the Africa Group on Rhodesia. Afterwards, a Senegalese diplomat remarked to him: "Look, racism seems to be an Anglo-Saxon characteristic," contrasting British inaction in dealing with the Rhodesian rebellion with France's willingness to fight one million white settlers in Algeria.[47] Nkrumah was among those urging the OAU to act, declaring that "the Rhodesian situation is a serious and direct threat to the peace of Africa."[48] Accordingly, OAU Ministers resolved that African Commonwealth countries should break diplomatic relations with the UK if it failed to restore legitimate government in Rhodesia by 15 December 1965. This, Anyaoku considered, was "a mistake on the part of the OAU because it was not a realistic position."[49] Nevertheless, two African Commonwealth nations, Tanzania and Ghana, responded to the call and severed relations with the UK, though they remained in the Commonwealth. This modified action at least recognised Arnold Smith's contention that recurrent threats by member governments critical of Britain to leave the Commonwealth were misplaced. The association was no longer the 'British' Commonwealth and no longer a personal Britannic fiefdom. Withdrawing from a body where a majority of its members were non-white developing countries would serve only to undermine one of the few international forums for North-South dialogue.

The depth of anger among new Commonwealth members about the British Government's failure to intervene militarily in the event of UDI (or even to keep open the threat of force) looks all the more understandable more than half a century later. Undoubtedly, there would have been military challenges to such an operation. Only Zambia offered a suitable assembly and launching point for any military action, with *apartheid* South Africa and Portuguese-controlled Mozambique protecting much of Rhodesia's remaining borders. There were concerns about extended lines of communication and supply, the availability and deployment of an invasion force of at least three brigades, and fears that the Rhodesian forces might have resisted strongly (and, in that event, worries about how British troops might have responded). Given the much more hazardous military calculations around the recapture of the Falkland Islands seventeen years later, the approach by the Wilson Government, and the advice of service chiefs, now looks excessively cautious. But other political and economic factors were likely to have weighed at least as heavily with the Labour Government as military ones. Firstly, Labour had inherited an £800 million balance of payment's deficit and were struggling to stave off devaluation of the pound. Despite Wilson's determination for the UK to remain "a world power, and a world influence," the ability of the UK to underpin its foreign and military commitments financially was becoming unstainable. At the time of UDI, the UK was involved in a considerable commitment to Malaysia in the confrontation with Indonesia. Secondly, domestic and political opinion was divided. Wilson's parliamentary majority was fragile, and any kind of rebellion on his backbenches would have forced him to rely on the votes of Liberal MPs. Although there was a vocal pro-Rhodesia lobby in the Conservative Party, Tory MPs were to split in three directions over the imposition of oil sanctions, let alone military action. Opinion polling suggested that public opinion was similarly divided and might have rallied behind the government, given a strong lead. However, the result, in the view of John Darwin, "was a diplomatic fiasco."[50] Worse, from the outset, Wilson (and his Cabinet colleagues) had publicly signalled that the UK would not countenance the use of force. Wilson recorded that "we would not attempt to restore legality by an expeditionary force," and he threatened to block any attempt to enforce mandatory action in the UN Security Council by using the British veto.[51] In the view of Carl Watts, the "failure to implement a successful deterrent was perhaps the most lamentable aspect of the Wilson government's policy on Rhodesia." It was, he considers, "a profound error of judgement . . . with which successive British Governments were burdened unnecessarily for the next fifteen years."[52]

It was therefore no surprise that, barely a month after UDI, the Commonwealth should meet in crisis, at the first of two summit meetings in 1966, each dominated by the Rhodesian issue. The specially convened meeting of Commonwealth Prime Ministers, held in the Federal Palace Hotel in Lagos in January 1966, was the first leaders' conference to be assembled by the new Commonwealth Secretary-General and serviced by the Commonwealth Secretariat. But its location in Nigeria, chaired by the Nigerian Prime Minister, Sir Abubakar Tafawa Balewa (the first time that such a meeting had been held outside the UK), was quite deliberate. While the original intention might have been to break with the tradition of a British host only for one meeting (and for very specific political reasons), the idea of rotating the summit around the Commonwealth quickly took hold. The communique of the meeting declared:

> Observing that this was the first meeting to be held in Africa, they agreed that to assemble from time to time in a different Commonwealth capital would underline the essential character of the Commonwealth as a free association of equal nations, spanning all races and continents.[53]

However, the political divisions among the Commonwealth's membership were deep and acrimonious. Against those countries who advocated the use of force and berated the UK for its failure to act were those (predominantly the old white dominions) who believed that international sanctions would prove effective in quickly toppling the regime. Wilson had gone as far as to state that the cumulative effect of economic and financial sanctions "might well bring the rebellion to an end within a matter of weeks rather than months."[54] This some doubted but, as time slipped away, it became the only option. An additional concern was that in any negotiations with the Rhodesian regime the British Government should not be tempted to grant independence to the colony before majority rule had been established. The UK had caused alarm by a formulation which suggested that a settlement might be reached giving independence before majority rule provided "the people of Rhodesia as a whole are shown to be in favour of it."[55] This in turn prompted speculation about what precisely this 'test of acceptability' might be and the fear that a British sell-out was possible. For much of the Commonwealth, the watchword became NIBMAR (No Independence Before Majority African Rule).

Amyaoku had left the Nigerian Mission in New York and arrived at Marlborough House in April 1966, ready to take up a new post as assistant director of the nascent International Affairs Division. He found that UDI had "engendered a serious crisis for the Commonwealth."[56] Indeed, the prospect of the organisation's collapse was never far away, and Arnold Smith warned the UK government that there was "a crisis of confidence about British intentions" which it needed to address in its handling of the issue.[57] Thereafter, Smith strove to give the Commonwealth purpose and a distinctive role. While there was widespread acknowledgement that the primary responsibility for ending the rebellion lay with the UK, all member countries acknowledged that "the problem was of wider concern to Africa, the Commonwealth and the world."[58] Accordingly, for the first time, two Commonwealth 'standing' committees were established by the Lagos meeting to work with the Secretary-General. The first of these was a Sanctions Committee, which had the task of monitoring the implementation and impact of sanctions on a regular basis, meeting every three weeks or so. There were considerable misgivings about the efficacy of sanctions in achieving the desired results, and the task of the Sanctions Committee was to work with the British Government in increasing the effectiveness of sanctions, with the authority to involve Commonwealth Heads of Government if necessary, or to make recommendations to the UN Security Council. The Committee was also mindful of the difficulties faced by Zambia, as one of Rhodesia's close neighbours, because of the sanctions policy, and a further duty was to help coordinate the flow of aid into Lusaka.[59]

The second Commonwealth body established in Lagos was the Committee on Assistance for Training for Rhodesian Africans. Chaired by the Secretary-General, the aim was to prepare for a future, independent and Black African-majority state (which would in time succeed Rhodesia) by "training Rhodesian Africans to occupy senior positions in their country's administration."[60] Access to Commonwealth scholarships would be made immediately available to those who might qualify, and training courses would also be put in place in various Commonwealth countries with the eventual aim of public administration provision and educational support within Rhodesia itself. This initiative would in time make an important, practical contribution to an independent Zimbabwe and would provide the template for future assistance to those in similar need, whether in Namibia, South Africa or Mozambique.

The September 1966 Commonwealth Prime Ministers' Meeting, back for the moment in its now familiar London location, was as equally a difficult conference as the one in Lagos and, once again, dominated by Rhodesia. Harold Wilson, back in the chair, bitterly remarked during the debate that Britain was being treated 'like a bloody colony' and afterwards judged the meeting "by common consent, the worst ever held up to that time."[61]

Despite Wilson's assurances on the immediate effectiveness of sanctions, it soon became apparent that this was woefully optimistic. Wilson himself ruefully admitted that his 'weeks not months' prediction "appeared at the time to be a safe prophecy."[62] While the newly established Sanctions Committee presented Commonwealth leaders with evidence that sanctions had undoubtedly "depressed the

Rhodesian economy," it was clear that much stronger action would be needed if the UK's political objectives were to be achieved.[63]

As a result, on the initiative of the UK, in December of that year the UN Security Council adopted mandatory economic sanctions in Rhodesia, by eleven votes to nil, with four abstentions. While the scale of the boycott was superficially impressive, it lacked enforcement mechanisms for penalising countries which flouted the UN embargo. In particular, South Africa, supplying Rhodesia with oil and much of its trade, declared that "it had no intention of obeying the resolution." Without severing this vital artery "sanctions seemed doom to fail."[64]

Thereafter, mandatory sanctions were pursued, though to little ultimate effect (with British companies themselves later revealed to be complicit in sanctions-busting, as well as some commercial interests in other Commonwealth countries). Even as Britain enforced a naval blockade of Beira, in Mozambique, to prevent the shipment of oil, plentiful supplies were beginning to flow across the Beit Bridge between South Africa and Rhodesia. Britain made a number of fruitless attempts to reach a negotiated settlement with Smith, while Commonwealth governments sustained the focus on NIBMAR as the vital precondition of any deal. Arnold Smith confided to his memoirs that he and other Commonwealth governments were engaged in a prolonged and unremitting struggle to hold the British Government to the core principles which it had agreed were intrinsic to any settlement of the issue.[65]

Wilson had come to his first premiership in 1964 as 'a Commonwealth man'. Several years of bruising exchanges with newer Commonwealth members, in particular, over race and Rhodesia, caused these views to sour. After the second 1966 Commonwealth Prime Ministers' Meeting, held in London in September, Wilson was in no hurry to host another. He privately remarked that "many of us feared for the future of the Commonwealth and doubted whether it could survive a similar traumatic conference."[66] In any case, the prospect of a second attempt by the UK to join the EEC for some years turned British eyes away from the Commonwealth and towards Europe. However, by 1969, de Gaulle's second veto had shattered any immediate prospects of European integration and Wilson pronounced the 1969 Commonwealth summit "by far the most successful ever held."[67] It was also the largest meeting of Commonwealth Heads of Government ever (as well as the biggest consultative meeting of Heads of Government from all parts of the world since the signing of the UN Charter in 1945).[68]

## 5 Arms to South Africa

However, this new mood of optimism was soon to be deflated by the defeat of Harold Wilson and the Labour Party in the 1970 British general election. This is not to suggest that Commonwealth member countries necessarily had any particular preferences about the colour of the British Government: long experience had encouraged a more sober and pragmatic judgement. President Kaunda's close adviser, Mark Chona, complained that "Labour appeared to have been so good in opposition on a lot of our (colonial) issues, but not in government."[69] Wilson, he judged, was "long on promises but short on action."[70]

However, Arnold Smith soon encountered a marked change of tone coming from Downing Street. Calling on the new British Prime Minister, Ted Health, some months after the election, Smith records that he "found his mood and attitude chilling."[71] While contemplating a new initiative on Rhodesia, Heath seemed to indicate that he would not be bound by previous British Government commitments to the Commonwealth and the United Nations and cast doubt on the need to involve the Commonwealth in the issue. This was in line with a reference to the Commonwealth in the recent Conservative Party election manifesto:

> The independence of each of its members must be respected, and that their internal affairs and individual responsibilities are matters for their individual decision alone, and that jointly they should only consider those matters freely agreed upon as being of common interest.[72]

This warning was accompanied by the more alarming announcement by the Foreign Secretary, Sir Alec Douglas-Home, that the British Government would be resuming arms sales to South Africa. The Commonwealth and Smith would clearly have their hands full in trying to prevent the British Government from reversing its previous stance on South Africa and Rhodesia, with potentially disastrous consequences, increasingly, Rhodesia and South Africa were seen as the two sides of a white supremacist coin.

In August 1963, the UN Security Council had agreed a voluntary arms embargo on South Africa, calling upon all states "to cease forthwith the sale and shipment of arms, ammunition of all types and military vehicles to South Africa."[73] While the UK and France had abstained on the resolution (otherwise passed unanimously), the incoming 1964 Labour Government was elected on a firm commitment "to end the supply of arms to South Africa."[74] Even so, the Wilson administration equivocated on the question of honouring existing contracts with South Africa on the replacement of Westland WASP helicopters. Initially, it had on three occasions confirmed that it would do so. But in December 1967, it told the South African Government that the sale of WASPS would not be permitted.[75]

The newly elected Conservative Government, however, decided that Britain would be resuming arm sales to South Africa. It maintained that its commitments under the 1955 Simon's Town Agreement and its 'vital defence interests' in countering any threats by the Soviet Union to the sea route around the Cape required continuing arms sales to South Africa, albeit on a limited basis. The South African Government hoped that this new policy would include an order for up to six British-built frigates, but it soon became apparent that the British Government's focus would be on what it considered to be a legal obligation to supply additional WASP helicopters and other naval equipment under existing contracts. It did nevertheless leave open the possibility of future orders "provided that the arms supplied would not be used for any other purpose than the defence of the sea routes."[76]

Heath was keenly aware that this change in UK policy would be likely to have an 'explosive' effect on the 1971 Singapore Commonwealth Heads of Government meeting, and he went to great lengths to persuade the Queen not to attend, advice she only accepted with great reluctance. In so doing, she emphasised that normally it was not only desirable but it was her duty to be present at CHOGM in her role as Head of the Commonwealth.[77] Subsequent attempts to dissuade her from being present at Commonwealth CHOGMs, in Ottawa in 1973, in Lusaka in 1979 and in Harare in 1991 were successfully resisted. As it is, her presence in the wings of the Singapore meeting – or more accurately, on board HMY "Britannia" – and her careful cultivation of Commonwealth leaders through both social events and programmed audiences might have soothed tempers and eased the business of the conference. With Nyerere threatening to withdraw Tanzania from the Commonwealth and feelings running high, the controversy over arm sales to South Africa was bound to dominate the headlines. Derek Ingram commented: "Mr Heath did not enjoy Singapore and there is no reason why he should since he had chosen the previous July to insert into the conference a thoroughly divisive issue."[78] Ironically, the protracted debate on UK arms sales to South Africa (held in closed session and running through most of the night) served to squeeze out much debate on what many considered to be Heath's true passion: a further attempt to obtain membership of the EEC.

While other Commonwealth Heads of Government made little progress in dissuading Heath from his intended path, they did all agree to address one of the key issues at the heart of the argument over arm sales. This was on the question of the security of maritime trade routes in the South Atlantic and Indian Oceans – and different perceptions of the threat posed by the Soviet Union, whether at sea or on the continent of Africa, in its support for independence movements and African nationalism.

*Figure 5.3* Lee Kuan Yew, Prime Minister of Singapore, in discussion with the British Prime Minister, Ted Heath, Singapore, 1971. Commonwealth Secretariat.

More significantly, the meeting also took the opportunity to explore their shared values and issue a declaration that would make clear their abhorrence of racism. The result, which was unanimously adopted, was the landmark Singapore Declaration of Commonwealth Principles.[79] This took the Commonwealth a step closer to adopting a formal code of ethics and committed members to improving human rights and seeking racial and economic justice. Abdul Minty, in Singapore to lobby Commonwealth leaders against arms to *apartheid*, described the Declaration as "an eloquent expression of commitment to act against racism and in favour of human dignity and democracy."[80] Kaunda had brought the first draft of the declaration to the summit with the more immediate aim of locking up Heath in "the prison of principles," as Mark Chona put it.[81] However, the British delegation was careful to insert a phrase into the text which made clear that the manner of implementation of the agreement would be for each member country, "in its own judgement."[82]

Nevertheless, the declaration remained an important addition to the Commonwealth's core values. It would be augmented in future by further elaborations of the Commonwealth's fundamental principles, as the association grew. In so doing, as perceived through the Stultz/Donnelly framework referred to earlier, the Commonwealth would be building its 'human rights regime' through what Chan describes as its "dynamic constitutional structure."[83]

Heath left Singapore even less enamoured of the Commonwealth than he had been at the start, considering it an 'old-fashioned jamboree' which needed to be drastically shortened if he were to attend again. The next CHOGM, he thought, should be in 1975 'at the earliest'.[84] He later explained to the British parliament that "much of the old intimacy of discussion" had disappeared and that there was a danger of it developing into "a mini-United Nations," having lost the capacity for "free and frank discussion."[85] Others agreed with at least some of Heath's points, and there was a widespread determination to make the next meeting far more productive and cordial than Singapore had been.

The first issue was the timing of the next meeting. Hitherto, and despite the appointment of a Secretary-General and an independent Secretariat in 1965, the British Government had exercised considerable influence over where and when the Commonwealth should meet, in part because of the pressure the British Prime Minister could exert on the Queen and her availability. However, the 1971 Singapore meeting is often regarded as the first CHOGM, establishing the practice of continuous rotation around the Commonwealth and meeting every two years. This reflected the growing reality of a Commonwealth with 'no centre and no periphery'.[86] Despite Heath's disinclination to meet in 1973, Arnold Smith suggested to his compatriot, Pierre Trudeau, that Canada should host the next meeting in Ottawa and should invite the Queen direct, rather than through the British Government. The Queen accepted Trudeau's invitation, and a perplexed Foreign Office was told that this approach had been made to her in her role as "[t]he Queen of Canada."[87] Thereafter, the biennial cycle of CHOGMs, hosted across the Commonwealth, has only rarely been disrupted.[88]

Secondly, the 'UN-nery' prominent in Singapore – the reading out of pre-prepared texts and speeches and the making of regular public statements outside the meeting – was to be replaced by the convention that leaders should discuss issues informally, without prepared texts, on first name terms and with spontaneous interventions encouraged as part of the process of lively dialogue. This approach was in keeping with the innovation introduced by Trudeau at the 1973 Ottawa meeting, namely, the leaders' only retreat, a closed session without officials present designed to address the most intractable problems before the summit in as open, frank and flexible a way as possible.

On his return to London, the British Prime Minister made a statement to the House of Commons on the Singapore CHOGM. Heath admitted that "[t]he problems of Southern Africa overshadowed the Conference and dominated the discussion," although there were many other questions "to which we could usefully and constructively have given more time."[89] Yet, in countering "growing Soviet naval power in the Indian Ocean," retaining the Simon's Town base and meeting the obligations under the Simon's Town Agreement were necessary. The question of *apartheid*, which his government condemned, was a separate question, Heath argued. Wilson, now Leader of the Opposition, riposted that "his doctrinaire insistence on arms to South Africa . . . is detrimental to British interests . . . and only in the interests of further Soviet and Chinese penetration of the African continent."[90] Denis Healey, Labour's former Defence Minister, described Heath as being regarded in Commonwealth circles "as a one-man walking disaster area."[91] A week later, Heath was again defending the government's stance at Singapore to the House of Commons and received support from the right-winger Duncan Sandys who assured Heath "that his insistence on Britain's right to pursue its own policies and his refusal to be pushed around has given wide satisfaction in this country."[92]

Later that month, based on advice provided by his legal officers on the obligations arising from the Simon's Town Agreement, Heath approved the sale of seven WASP helicopters and various items of naval equipment to the South African Government but pulled back from the supply of further frigates. The Commonwealth Study Group had therefore made little headway before being overtaken by events. In February 1974, with the defeat of Heath's administration, the arms sales policy was reversed by the incoming Labour administration, headed by Harold Wilson, and the last part of the WASPS order cancelled. The Simon's Town Agreement was terminated at the request of the British Government on 16 June 1975.[93]

In November 1977, the UN Security Council agreed Resolution 418, imposing a mandatory arms embargo on South Africa. All fifteen members of the Security Council voted for the resolution, including the UK. By that point, the Rhodesian regime was increasingly beleaguered; and the campaign against *apartheid* was turning to a new weapon in achieving South Africa's total isolation – an embargo on sporting contact with the pariah state.

## Notes

1 McIntyre, *Guide to the Contemporary Commonwealth*, 130.
2 These were President Ayub Khan of Pakistan and Archbishop Makarios, the President of newly independent Cyprus.

3  Diary entry 16 November 1960, *Pointing the Way*, 293.
4  Nigel Fisher, *Harold Macmillan* (London: Weidenfeld and Nicolson, 1982), 240.
5  W. David McIntyre *A Guide to the Contemporary Commonwealth* (Basingstoke and New York: Palgrave, 2001), 32.
6  John Darwin *The Empire Project* (Cambridge and New York: CUP, 2009), 620.
7  Ibid., 621.
8  Ibid., 645.
9  McIntyre, *Contemporary Commonwealth*, 33.
10  Commonwealth Secretariat, *The Commonwealth at the Summit*, 75.
11  Fisher, *Macmillan*, 312.
12  Alex May, "The Commonwealth and Britain's turn to Europe, 1945–73," *The Round Table*, 102:1, 33.
13  Telegram from the Secretary of State for External Affairs, Canada, to Canada's High Commissioner in London, conveying the text of a message from Prime Minister Diefenbaker to Prime Minister Macmillan, 20 February 1962, 311.DEA/50085-K-40.
14  Telegram from Canada's High Commissioner in Ghana to Secretary of State External Affairs, Canada, 2 May 1962, 313.DEA/12304-B-40.
15  DEA/50085-K-40 Telegram 2408, Government of Canada. High Commissioner in UK to Secretary of State for External Affairs, www.international.gc.ca/history-histoire/dcer-drrec/volumes/29/chap_4_commonwealth
16  Harold Macmillan, Memorandum on "The Commonwealth and the common market" (draft), 4 September 1962, TNA CAB 133/262.
17  Fisher, *Macmillan*, 318.
18  Commonwealth Secretariat, *The Commonwealth at the Summit*, 75–79.
19  Harold Macmillan, *Address to the Nation*, 20 September 1962, London, International Institute of Social History, Amsterdam, www.cvce.eu/obj/address_given_by_harold_macmillan_london_20_september-1962-en-22549d81-8281-4ab8-ao70-289c424f2f79.html
20  Fisher, *Macmillan*, 320.
21  Ibid.
22  May, "Britain's turn to Europe," 37.
23  W. David McIntyre, "Britain and the creation of the Commonwealth Secretariat," *The Journal of Imperial and Commonwealth History*, 28:1 (2000), 135.
24  Smith, *Stitches in Time*, 4.
25  McIntyre, "The creation of the Commonwealth Secretariat," 146.
26  Commonwealth Secretariat, *The Commonwealth at the Summit*, 90.
27  Ibid, 90.
28  British Pathe, Report of Commonwealth Conference, London 13 July 1964, www.britishpathe.com/video/commonwealth-conference-1, Accessed 21 January 2022.
29  Lord Carrington, The Commonwealth Prime Ministers' Meeting. HL Debate 29 July 1964, vol 260 cc1100–20, https://api.parliament.uk/historic-hansard/lords/1964/jul/29/the-commonwealth-prime-ministers-meeting, Accessed 22 January 2022.
30  Commonwealth Secretariat, *The Commonwealth at the Summit*, 106.
31  Ibid, 107.
32  Ibid, 106.
33  Smith, *Stitches in Time*, 17.
34  Editorial, *The Times*, Tuesday, 15 June 1965, 13. The Times Digital Archive, link.gale.com/apps/doc/CS17000655/TTDA?u=Exeter&sid=bookmark.TTDA&xid=9c6c3427, Accessed 24 January 2022.
35  Commonwealth Secretariat, *The Commonwealth at the Summit*, 110.
36  TNA, FCO 68/471.
37  Harold Wilson, *The Labour Government 1964–1970: A Personal Record* (London: Weidenfeld and Nicholson and Michael Joseph, 1971), 116–117.
38  Stuart Mole, "From Smith to Sharma: The role of the Commonwealth Secretary-General," in *The Contemporary Commonwealth: An Assessment 1965–2009*, ed. James Mayall (London and New York: Routledge, 2010), 47.

39 Commonwealth Secretariat, *The Commonwealth at the Summit*, 86.
40 Carl Watts, "Moments of tension and drama: The Rhodesian problem at the Commonwealth Prime Ministers' Meetings, 1964–65," *The Journal of Colonisation and Colonial History*, 8:1, (2007), 5.
41 Commonwealth Secretariat, *The Commonwealth at the Summit*, 83.
42 News Report, "Huge Rhodesia election win for Smith," *BBC on This Day*, 7 May 1965, news.bbc.co.uk/onthisday/hi/dates/stories/may/7/newsid_2880000/2880795.stm, Accessed 26 January 2022.
43 Carl Watts, "Britain, the Old Commonwealth and the problem of Rhodesian independence, 1964–65," *Journal of Imperial & Commonwealth History*, 36:1 (2008), 81–85.
44 Minutes of a meeting of the Cabinet, 11 November 1965, TNA CAB/128/39, 3.
45 Ibid, 5.
46 Article, "United Nations: Sanctions against Rhodesia," *TIME*, 23 December 1966, http://content.time.com/time/magazine/article/0,971,840760,00.html, Accessed 31 January 2022.
47 Anyaoku, *The Inside Story*, 66.
48 Shingirai Mutonho, "Nkrumah's views about colonial Rhodesia," *THE PATRIOT*, 12 February 2015, www.thepatriot.co.zw/old_posts/nkrumahs-views-about-colonial-rhodesia/, Accessed 31 January 2022.
49 Anyaoku, *The Inside Story*, 66.
50 Darwin, *The Empire Project*, 646.
51 Wilson, *The Labour Government 1964–70*, 180, 189.
52 Carl Watts, "Killing kith and kin: The viability of British Military Intervention in Rhodesia, 1964–5," in *Twentieth Century British History*, Vol 16. No. 2 (Oxford: OUP. 2005), 415.
53 Commonwealth Secretariat, The Commonwealth at the Summit, 117.
54 Ibid., 119.
55 Ibid., 125.
56 Anyaoku, *The Inside Story*, 68.
57 Carl Watts, "The Commonwealth and Rhodesia, 1965–1980," *The Round Table: The Commonwealth Journal of International Affairs*, 110:6 (2021), 676.
58 Commonwealth Secretariat, *The Commonwealth at the Summit*, 124.
59 Arnold Smith, *Annual Report of the Commonwealth Secretary-General 1966* (London: Commonwealth Secretariat, 1966), 7.
60 Ibid., 8.
61 Wilson, *The Labour Government, 1964–70*, 277.
62 Ibid., 196.
63 Commonwealth Secretariat, *The Commonwealth at the Summit*, 126.
64 *TIME*, "UN sanctions against Rhodesia," 1.
65 Smith, *Stitches in Time*, xx.
66 Wilson, *The Labour Government 1964–70*, 287.
67 Ibid., 592.
68 Commonwealth Secretariat, *The Commonwealth at the Summit* (*No. I*), 137.
69 Interview with Mark Chona, Commonwealth Oral History Project, Institute of Commonwealth Studies, London. 22 March 2016, 4. Https://www.commonwealthoralhistories.org/2016/interview-with-mark-chona/, Accessed 15 February 2017.
70 Ibid., 5.
71 Smith, *Stitches in Time*, 72.
72 Conservative Party General Election Manifesto 1970, A Better Tomorrow, Accessed 19 April 2020, www.conservativemanifesto.com/1970/1970-conservative-manifesto.shtml.
73 UN Security Council, "Non-mandatory UN arms embargo on South Africa," UNSC 181 (1963), 7 August 1963 Sipri.org/sites/default/files/2016–03/181, Accessed 28 March 2022.
74 Labour Party, "The New Britain," 1964 Labour Party Manifesto (B. New Prospects for Peace), www.labour-party.org.ik/manifestos/1964/1964-labour-manifesto.shtml, Accessed 28 March 2022.
75 Thula Simpson, "The Commonwealth and *apartheid*," in Saul Dubow and Richard Drayton (eds) *Commonwealth History in the Twenty-First Century* (Cambridge: CUP, 2020), 211.

76. Allan Du Toit, "The Anglo-South African Simon's Town Agreement," 2009 King-Hall Naval History Conference: "Commonwealth Navies – 100 years of cooperation," Canberra, July 2009. www.navy.gov.au/2009-king-hall-naval-history-conference-proceedings, Accessed 28 March 2022.
77. Philip Murphy, *Monarchy and the End of Empire: The House of Windsor, the British Government and the Postwar Commonwealth* (Oxford: OUP, 2013), 129–131.
78. Derek Ingram, "Report from Singapore: What not to do in future," *The Round Table: The Commonwealth Journal of International Affairs*, 61: 242 (1971), 212.
79. Commonwealth Secretariat, *The Commonwealth at the Summit* (Vol.1), 156–7.
80. Abdul Minty, "South Africa and the Commonwealth" in *The Commonwealth in the 21st Century*, ed. Greg Mills and John Stremlau (Johannesburg: South African Institute of International Affairs, 1999), 56.
81. Interview with Mark Chona, Commonwealth Oral History Project, 15.
82. Commonwealth Secretariat, *The Commonwealth at the Summit*, 156.
83. Chan, *The Commonwealth in World Politics*, 48–50.
84. Murphy, *Monarchy and the End of Empire*, 131.
85. The Prime Minister, "Conference of Commonwealth Heads of Government," Statement and questions, 26 January 1971, HC Deb vol 810 cc321–40, https://api.parliament.uk/historic-hansard/commons/1971/jan/26/conference-if-commonwealth-heads-of-government, Accessed 22 March 2022.
86. Emeka Anyaoku, in conversation with the author, 8 December 1988, London.
87. Murphy, *Monarchy and the End of Empire*, 131.
88. The Brisbane CHOGM, due to be held at the beginning of October 2001, was postponed because of the 9/11 terror attacks on New York, and the 2020 Kigali CHOGM has been postponed twice because of the Covid-19 global pandemic.
89. Prime Minister, HC Deb 26 January 1971, 1.
90. Ibid., 3.
91. Ibid., 7.
92. Prime Minister, "Commonwealth heads of government meeting," HC Deb 2 Feb 1971, vol 810 cc1453–6.
93. Du Toit, "The Anglo-South African Simon's Town Agreement," 14.

## References

Arnold Smith, *Annual Report of the Commonwealth Secretary-General 1966* (London: Commonwealth Secretariat, 1966).
Arnold Smith, *Stitches in Time*, Op.Cit.
Commonwealth Secretariat, *The Commonwealth at the Summit,* Op.Cit.
Emeka Anyaoku, *The Inside Story of the Modern Commonwealth*, Op.Cit.
Greg Mills and John Stremlau (eds.), *The Commonwealth in the 21st Century* (Johannesburg: South African Institute of International Affairs, 1999).
Harold Wilson, *The Labour Government 1964–1970: A Personal Record* (London: Weidenfeld, Nicholson, Michael Joseph, 1971).
James Mayall (ed.), *The Contemporary Commonwealth: An Assessment 1965–2009* (London, New York: Routledge, 2010).
John Darwin, *The Empire Project* (Cambridge, New York: CUP, 2009).
Nigel Fisher, *Harold Macmillan* (London: Weidenfeld, Nicolson, 1982).

Philip Murphy, *Monarchy and the End of Empire: The House of Windsor, the British Government and the Postwar Commonwealth* (Oxford: OUP, 2013).

Saul Dubow and Richard Drayton (eds), *Commonwealth History in the Twenty-First Century* (Cambridge: CUP, 2020).

Stephen Chan, *The Commonwealth in World Politics* (London: Lester Crook, 1988).

W. David McIntyre, *A Guide to the Contemporary Commonwealth* (Basingstoke, New York: Palgrave, 2001).

# 6 Boycotting *Apartheid* in Sport

## 1 Introduction

After initiatives to stop arm sales to South Africa, campaigners now turned to international action against *apartheid* sport. Sport has long been important to all South Africans, despite the common assertion of the *apartheid* regime that participation in sport was only of interest to the white population. On the contrary, South Africa was arguably a key influence in globalising sport from the end of the nineteenth century, and issues of race were never absent from its sport, at home and abroad.[1] Sport was also an important part of South Africa's membership of the Commonwealth, though the country's segregationist racial policies began to intrude internationally, even before the advent of *apartheid*. Notwithstanding initial gains in the first decade of *apartheid* by opponents of segregated sport, international pressure against *apartheid* South Africa in international sporting events was to grow rapidly. In particular, the Commonwealth, with its long-standing sporting linkages, was able to help achieve South Africa's near total sporting isolation. It is also surprising that this form of boycott should have proved such a potent weapon against *apartheid* at a time, at least initially, when internal opposition to the regime had been all but destroyed, in the "nadir of the South African liberation struggle."[2] By contrast, *apartheid* seemed to be enjoying a 'golden' era of dominance and prosperity.[3] White sport in South Africa had long been conceived as a symbol of racial superiority and white hegemony, and opposition to *apartheid* sport exposed a vulnerability in the regime and created a previously unanticipated theatre of opposition and resistance. In turn, this led the *apartheid* state to use increasingly elaborate and ingenious countermeasures. Despite continuing repression within South Africa, the regime's growing international isolation, across all sports, not only was a result of diplomatic pressure but also involved mass public protest, including direct action to disrupt and harass South African teams touring internationally. This in itself involved tensions between the recently formed AAM, favouring conventional street demonstrations, and those who later advocated direct action, including physical disruption to matches, harassment of visiting teams and even damage to property, as espoused by the Stop the Seventy Tour (STST) in the UK.[4]

For the Commonwealth, its role in opposing *apartheid* in sport made a significant contribution to the international campaign to end *apartheid*. At the heart of that work was the Commonwealth's adoption of the 1977 Gleneagles Agreement on *apartheid* in sport.⁵ This had the effect of both discouraging contact with segregated South African teams and also promoting wider international action. In the latter respect, this led Shridath Ramphal to assert that the Agreement "pioneered world action against *apartheid* in sport."⁶

However, it was popular protest against *apartheid* in sport, as well as threats to the viability of the four-yearly Commonwealth Games, which spurred Commonwealth governments to eventually conclude an international agreement on the issue. A combination of mass protest and more targeted direct action began in the UK, Australia and New Zealand in the late 1960s and early 1970s and took other, more localised, forms in other parts of the Commonwealth in later years. The awareness that this created, and the divisions and passions that were aroused, undoubtedly helped move Commonwealth governments to act. A primary motivation for member governments, however, was the dawning realization that, unless governments pressed forward together rather than relying on national responses alone, the Commonwealth Games, described as "the Commonwealth's most popular event," would be repeatedly and fatally undermined by boycott.⁷ This reflected the growing willingness of African countries (many of them Commonwealth members) to use the boycott weapon with the Commonwealth Games a more tempting and vulnerable target than the Olympics. In that respect, the Commonwealth could be said to be motivated as much by collective self-interest as by a principled response to *apartheid*.

## 2   South Africa, Sport and Race

Although the British had introduced cricket in the Cape Colony after its repossession from the Dutch in 1806, it was the impact of the Second Boer War which, ironically, helped to cultivate an interest in the game among Afrikaners. At the Siege of Mafeking, the Boer commander, General J.P. Snyman, wishing to defend the sanctity of the Sabbath, threatened to shell the defenders as they played cricket on Sunday. Later, a fellow commander, Sarel Eloff, proposed to Colonel Baden-Powell, in charge of the British defences, that his Boer soldiers should join Imperial troops on the cricket field. 'B.P.', using a cricketing metaphor, courteously declined "until the match in which we are presently engaged is over." He told Eloff that his team had "so far scored 200 days not out against the bowling of Cronje, Snyman, Botha and Eloff, and we are having a very enjoyable game."⁸ This bears out Allen's assertion that "as sport was training for war, war would be the ultimate form of sport."⁹

Undoubtedly, the introduction of British Victorian sports, particularly rugby union and cricket (and to a lesser extent association football), was part of the imperial project. In often hostile settings, sports grounds marked out a physical space that was quintessentially 'English', as well as demonstrating the social distance between coloniser and subjects (just as social distinction has permeated these sports throughout much of the UK's recent history). Vidacs has argued that sports were introduced "with the purpose of satisfying colonial ideas of, and needs for, order and discipline among the dominated populations."[10] Sport was also seen as an exemplar of British values and part of its national consciousness.[11] As a result of this development, modern sport in South Africa was to be riven by paradox and myth. Firstly, while a significant section of the white population remained unreconciled to the British imperial state politically, sport was a different matter. As a result, South Africa played a prominent part in globalising the three sports of rugby, cricket and football, largely through imperial and British Commonwealth mechanisms. Thus, the Imperial Cricket Conference (ICC) was formed in 1909, largely on the initiative of South Africa.[12] The first international rugby team to tour South Africa was from the UK in 1891.[13] In 1926, the South African Football Association, reaffiliated to the English FA, proposed the formation of a British Commonwealth Association to arrange Overseas and Dominion tours on a uniform basis.[14]

Secondly, despite protestations that non-whites had no interest or aptitude for sports, the popularisation of cricket, rugby and football among all races in South Africa spread rapidly in the latter part of the nineteenth century. In 1899, a Black football side, sponsored by the Orange Free State, toured the UK and France, the first South African team of any racial composition to play internationally.[15] There was considerable enthusiasm for cricket among Black communities, as well as white, and in the 1880s cricket pitches and clubs proliferated. Interracial matches were common with Black teams regularly beating white.[16] Matters came to a head when the outstanding 'Coloured' fast bowler, 'Krom' Hendricks, was recommended for inclusion in the South African national team due to tour England in 1894. He was passed over, supposedly at the insistence of Cecil Rhodes, but not before he had agreed to the humiliating condition that he could only join the team if he was taken as a baggage man and servant.[17] Another outstanding mixed-race player, Charles Llewellyn, was later treated in a similar fashion. The barriers of racial segregation and prejudice were thus steadily put in place. Years later, under *apartheid*, government ministers would protest that there were no laws which actually prohibited interracial sport, while making clear that it was for the separate population groups to "control, arrange and manage their own sport matters."[18]

In the process, the values applied to sport which once underpinned an empire became a more explicit mutation of the doctrine of white racial supremacy. In the short term, it was obvious that excluding talented players like Hendricks and Llewellyn because of their colour made the chances of a South African national team winning against international competition much less likely. But, came the response, South Africa should abjure the 'victory at any cost' attitude and "learn to take a licking like white men."[19] In the longer term, as non-white players were excluded from competing with white teams (or with teams across different racial groups) and were denied facilities to train and play, the question of lost talent was no longer visible and therefore faded from white consciousness. By the 1920s, most of Black cricket was "deliberately written out of South African sports history."[20] The same was true of other sports. Even as late as the 1950s, all-white South African football teams were competing abroad, though sometimes against mixed Black and white sides. This, says Bolsmann, revealed the contradiction that "all-white South African club, provincial and national sides competed against racially mixed sides in front of mixed crowds abroad, but refused to do so at home."[21]

At the same time, the incongruity of international sporting contact with a regime whose odious racial policies were increasingly apparent troubled many. For some, however, the impact of South Africa's racial policies on sport was already well appreciated. As early as 1956, the International Table Tennis Federation (ITTF) expelled the white South African body because of racial discrimination and recognised instead the South African Table Tennis Board which, while representing Black South Africans, was nonetheless pledged to non-racialism. The South African regime responded to these early developments by hardening its approach and by making absolutely clear that its racial policies extended to the heart of sport. The Interior Minister, Dr T.E. Donges, spelt out the key elements, which included:

- Whites and non-whites should organise their sport separately;
- No mixed sport would be allowed within South Africa;
- International teams coming to South Africa to play against white South African teams should be all-white 'according to local custom';
- Passports would be refused for 'subversive' Black sportsmen seeking international recognition.[22]

The philosophy behind this approach was made clear a few years later by the Afrikaner nationalist newspaper, *Die Transvaler*:

> Social mixing leads inevitably to miscegenation. . . . If they mix first on the sports fields, then the road to other forms of social mixing is wide open. With an eye to upholding the white race and its civilisation, not one single compromise can be entered – not even when it comes to a visiting rugby team.[23]

In the face of such intransigence, attempts at a gradualist approach to non-racial sport by the recently established coordinating body for Black sports organisations, the South African Sports Association (SASA), were repeatedly frustrated. This stiffened the resolve of the leaders of non-racial sport to campaign for the total abolition of racism in sport and to seek international recognition for their campaign. In 1962, the South African Non-Racial Olympic Committee (SAN-ROC) was formed with the aim of supplanting the more limited objectives of SASA. Instead of acceptance or compromise, "peaceful resistance" was the goal.[24] The driving force was Sam Ramsammy who was "a powerful agent in the evolution of global sports protest against South Africa" until victory was finally won.[25] A breakthrough was achieved in 1963 with the suspension of South Africa from the Olympic Movement and, the next year, its removal from the 1964 Tokyo Olympics. It would ultimately be expelled from the Olympic movement in 1970. These developments galvanised international pressure in sports such as football, fencing, tennis and boxing. SAN-ROC, with most of its members in exile, in prison or otherwise restricted, decided to leave South Africa and base its operations in London. It also reorganised to concentrate on non-Olympic sports and "refocus the strategies of SAN-ROC upon the Commonwealth and the United Nations."[26]

Why should sport have been so important to the promoters of *apartheid* – and why did it prove such a powerful weapon in the anti-*apartheid* struggle? Peter Hain, who grew up in South Africa, explained: "I understood the white South African psyche: they were sports mad, Afrikaners especially fanatical about rugby."[27] It is an irony that while the quest of Smuts and others for white 'fusion' largely remained a chimera politically, the white population rallied as one to the cause of Springbok rugby and cricket and to sport in general. Nixon sees it as "a crucial arena of white self-esteem" and contends that their obsession with the sports boycott was "rooted in an ethnic nationalist exasperation at being denied just such opportunities to compensate for the smallness of their population, their geographic marginality and their political ostracism."[28] Segregated sports grounds were not enough, especially in international matches where Black spectators invariably cheered for the visitors, in the hope of seeing the all-white Springboks being beaten. In 1955, fear of this behaviour caused Bloemfontein City Council to ban non-white spectators from watching the British Isles play South Africa at rugby on the grounds that it would 'cause friction'.[29]

If Trevor Huddleston had seen the value of boycotting *apartheid* sport, fellow anti-*apartheid* activists dismissed such a campaign as being concerned with 'petty *apartheid*' and of only marginal significance.[30] Yet as the sporting boycott developed a high profile in the late 1960s, it exposed the tenets of *apartheid* to rigorous scrutiny in an arena where concepts like fair play, teamwork and respect were all important. Just such an illustration of the absurdities and injustices of *apartheid* as applied to sport was provided by the D'Oliviera affair. Basil D'Oliviera was a talented all-round South African cricketer who excelled with bat and ball. Born in Cape Town, to 'Cape Coloured' parentage, D'Oliveira went on to captain South Africa's non-white national side, though excluded from 'white' cricket. With the help of the BBC cricket commentator John Arlott, D'Oliveria left South Africa in 1960, came to the UK and became a regular member of the Worcestershire County team. Before long, he was selected for the England side and was playing Test cricket. When the MCC announced that a cricket team would be touring South Africa in 1968, the South African Minister of the Interior stated that if D'Oliveira was selected, the team would be refused entry. When the team was announced, D'Oliveira was omitted, prompting many to believe that the England selectors were pandering to South Africa's racial policies as they had in the past.[31] Amidst a furore, another player, Tom Cartwright, withdrew as a result of injury and D'Oliveira's inclusion became inevitable. With the MCC finally selecting D'Oliviera, it was now the turn of South Africa's Prime Minister, John Vorster, to rage: "For a government to submit so easily and so willingly to open blackmail is to me unbelievable."[32] The MCC cancelled the tour but left open the possibility of future tours.

Outrage at the D'Oliveira affair had a powerful effect on British public opinion and helped generate a broad-based opposition to *apartheid* sport, involving the churches, trade unions, civic and community groups, students and politicians. John Arlott had visited an African township during England's tour of South Africa in 1948–1949 and was appalled by the desolate living conditions he witnessed. He now saw how the injustices of *apartheid* could be meted out to his sporting protégé. Despite his misgivings about sport as an arena for political action and his admiration for Springbok cricketers like Graeme Pollock, he told the BBC that he could not cover the impending South African tour of England in 1970. He explained: "A successful tour would offer comfort and confirmation to a completely evil regime."[33]

Those campaigning against the 1970 cricket tour now had several opportunities, across several sports, to protest against racially selected South African teams. If the D'Oliveira affair excited public opinion, there was also a fresh tactic, namely non-violent direct action, and new and energetic leadership in the form of Peter Hain and the STST Campaign. Hain, then a Young Liberal, and his fellow activists had first honed their tactics in the summer of 1969 at a Great Britain–South Africa Davis Cup match in Bristol. There were also protests against a touring South African cricket team, the Wilf Isaacs XI. Later in the year there were major protests and disruption of the Springboks rugby tour of the British Isles, including sit-ins, pitch invasions and even the short-lived kidnap of several South African players.

What had changed? Undoubtedly, the issue of *apartheid* in sport had touched a public nerve and the AAM estimates that some 50,000 were involved in protests of one sort or another.[34] For many, this took the form of conventional protests outside playing arenas. However, some turned to direct action within them. Such tactics continuously and effectively disrupted the sporting spectacle, diminished the enjoyment of spectators and undermined the performance of the players. It also markedly escalated the security costs and measures that needed to be put in place as a result. STST had managed to sustain their campaign across all twenty-six rugby fixtures over a period of three months. It was a high-risk strategy and, as Gurney admits, "there were tensions between AAM and STST."[35] Some in the AAM feared that direct action would be counterproductive. No doubt in some cases, this was so. But, in addition to generating much greater publicity and comment (not all of it positive), it raised the question of whether a cricket tour could be protected and at what cost.

## 3   The Commonwealth, *Apartheid* Sport and the Gleneagles Agreement

There was early evidence that a barometer of Commonwealth opinion, and later a powerful means of influence, was the prospect of participation in the Commonwealth Games. In 1934, the second British Empire Games, due to be hosted by Johannesburg, was moved to London, principally because of concerns about the impact of South Africa's colour bar on visiting athletes.[36] Exceptionally, the 1958 British Commonwealth Games in Cardiff attracted protests from South Wales miners and others against the inclusion of an all-white South African team.[37] By 1962 and the time of the next British Commonwealth Games in Australia, South Africa was out of the Commonwealth and therefore excluded from the Games. At the same time, traditional Commonwealth sports, particularly cricket and rugby union, were dominated by the old imperial arrangements for their administration. This served as an insulation from external political pressure. It also encouraged the various internal administrative bodies to skirt round the issue of *apartheid* sport, rather than confronting it directly. Matches between white South African and non-white Commonwealth teams were largely avoided, or alternatively there was an unspoken willingness to pander to the racial conditions clearly specified by the *apartheid* regime. Sport was not the only area where there were discreet steps taken in planning visits to South Africa to exclude any non-white participants and to 'respect the local culture'. This was also true of military exchanges and goodwill visits.

Trevor Huddleston, in saying his farewells to South Africa in 1956 after twelve years as a priest in Sophiatown, was one of the first to raise the spectre of a sporting boycott to bring South Africa to its senses. "Just because the Union is so good at sport, such isolation would shake its self-assurance very severely . . . it might be an extraordinarily effective blow to the racialism which has brought it into being."[38] Two years later, in 1958, Huddleston, Fenner Brockway and others formed the Campaign Against Race Discrimination in Sport with the South African team at the Cardiff Games an immediate target.[39] However, prior to the Sharpeville massacre in 1960, the newly formed Boycott Movement (later to become the AAM) called for the shunning of South African produce, like fruits, cigarettes and alcohol, rather than action against *apartheid* in sport. It was only after the fierce repression that followed Sharpeville, including the crushing of internal dissent and a decision by the ANC and PAC to turn to armed struggle, that the notion of a sporting boycott began to gather support. In 1965, the South African cricket tour of Britain attracted protests, and neither the Queen nor the Prime Minister made their customary visits to the opening day's play at Lords.[40] The AAM, in encouraging a boycott of the tour, declared: "*apartheid* permeates every aspect of sporting life."[41] But it was only after the D'Oliveira affair in 1968; the barring of US tennis star, Arthur Ashe; and, up until 1970, South Africa's continued rejection of Maori players as part of New Zealand's visiting All Blacks' teams, that attitudes markedly changed.[42]

This is one of the contextual reasons why the Commonwealth collectively was slow to act on *apartheid* sport. Despite the widespread international publicity given to protests against the 1969 Springboks rugby tour to England, and the subsequent cancellation of the 1970 cricket tour, there is not a single reference to *apartheid* and sport in any of the Commonwealth's official summit communiques between 1966 and 1975.[43] Nor does the issue appear in any of the Secretary-General's biennial reports to Commonwealth leaders.[44] The only reference in Arnold Smith's memoirs is to the Gleneagles Agreement, which was concluded two years after he had demitted office.[45] Apart from some press cuttings, compiled for monitoring purposes, Commonwealth's archives have no other material on *apartheid* sport prior to 1975.[46]

Some might argue that since South Africa was no longer a member of the Commonwealth, *apartheid* was less of a concern. This was not the case. Not only was Rhodesia a constant and major preoccupation, but Southern Africa more generally (including *apartheid* in South Africa and Namibia) was a regular feature of official Commonwealth pronouncements between 1966 and 1975. As Sonny Ramphal said of the period: "Over those years, the Rhodesia problem has come to be seen more clearly as the issue of liberation in southern Africa."[47] This was also the approach of the AAM which lobbied the 1969 Commonwealth summit in opposition to Wilson's "Fearless" proposals for a settlement in Rhodesia, arguing that "four million Africans are being abandoned to *apartheid*."[48]

It was also the case that international sporting boycotts, though not unknown, were not particularly effective prior to the Montreal Olympics in 1976.[49] In the 1970s, the Caribbean was conflicted by the actions of prominent cricketers playing and coaching in South Africa, leaving governments divided and lacking clear leadership.[50] Boycott as a weapon only became widespread after the call by the UNGA, following the 1977 Gleneagles Agreement, for a shunning of *apartheid* South Africa by all sports bodies.[51] The other difficulty for those who wished to see more effective international action was that in many countries (particularly in the Commonwealth) sporting administration was decentralised and largely autonomous. It was not only the International Olympic Committee, the International Rugby Football Board or the International Cricket Council with some say over the conduct of their respective sports through international competition but the national administrators of the various games also had considerable influence and were not noted for their willingness to listen to politicians or to entertain radical ideas.

Harold Wilson's Labour Government was keen to demonstrate its anti-*apartheid* credentials over the D'Oliveira affair. However, direct action and mass protest against the 1969 Springboks rugby tour, coupled with the threat of

*Figure 6.1* UK Prime Minister Harold Wilson and Mrs Mary Wilson welcome India's Minister for External Affairs, Sardar Swaran Singh, Commonwealth Prime Ministers' Conference 1966. Commonwealth Secretariat.

a credible African and Asian boycott of a 'UK' Commonwealth Games (in Edinburgh), spurred the British Government to act by bringing maximum pressure on the Cricket Council to cancel the 1970 South African cricket tour. Wilson was acutely aware that his best opportunity to seek re-election before his five-year term expired was in the summer of 1970. The last thing he wanted were scenes of prolonged public disorder along with escalating policing costs, which would be a gift to the opposition Conservative Party. Further, nationalism was awakening in Scotland (after the election of Winnie Ewing in the 1967 Hamilton by-election). Damage to Scotland's first Commonwealth Games as host would do Labour's electoral prospects north of the border no good at all. While the Cabinet had secretly discussed prosecuting Hain (a future Labour Cabinet Minister) for conspiracy, the government decided to bring full pressure to bear to stop the tour. Within days of the first Test match at Trent Bridge, Nottingham, the Cricket Council bowed to a formal request from the Home Secretary, Jim Callaghan, to withdraw the invitation to the South Africans. On 22 May, a statement calling off the tour declared: "[W]ith deep regret the Council were of the opinion that they had no alternative but to accede to this request."[52] In the view of Peter Hain, who inspired the anti-*apartheid* campaign in the UK from 1969, "it was African Commonwealth pressure linked to the campaign in Britain that was crucial to the stopping of the Seventy Tour."[53] There were also pressing electoral reasons why Wilson wanted controversy over cricket to end. With a general election underway a week later, Wilson might have hoped that the England's men's football team, winners of the 1966 World Cup, would help carry him to victory. Instead, Wilson went down to an unexpected general election defeat, four days after England's male footballers had succumbed to West Germany in the quarter finals.

Commonwealth African members were thus involved in the successful campaign to 'stop the '70 tour'. But there would have been little scope, and scant support from Commonwealth members generally, for Smith and his new Secretariat to seek a role in the events of 1969–1970. The Secretariat's staff numbers and its budgets were at that stage modest. In 1968–1969, its total budget was £557,805, and there were 176 staff.[54] It was in any case almost overwhelmed by a host of challenging international issues, from Rhodesia and Kashmir to Biafra and the birth of Bangladesh, out of a bloody civil war. A Canadian commentator described Smith as "living in the eye of the hurricane."[55]

There were also some official voices (predominately in the 'old' Commonwealth) who were suspicious of anything other than a strict and narrow interpretation of the 1965 Agreed Memorandum on the Commonwealth Secretariat.[56] Smith and his nascent Secretariat were often in conflict with the former imperial power. "The Secretariat was immediately cordially disliked by Whitehall," comments Verrier, "and every effort was made not merely to limit its effectiveness but to interfere with its tasks."[57] Smith singled out the CRO as the arm of British Government which felt most threatened by him and his team, adding: "the larger and more active the Secretariat, the greater the perceived threat."[58] The British response was to limit Smith's status and influence.[59]

In any case, with the cancellation also of the South African cricket tour to Australia in 1971, again after the intervention of the national government, Smith had every reason to believe that member countries individually would take care of sport and that the Commonwealth's primary contribution to the anti-*apartheid* cause would be to assist an acceptable solution in Rhodesia.

The election of Shridath Ramphal as the Commonwealth's second Commonwealth Secretary-General, in 1975, provided new leadership and fresh impetus to the anti-*apartheid* cause. It also came at a time of far-reaching change. True, the Rhodesian issue seemed no nearer peaceful resolution, though an intensifying and increasingly bloody guerrilla war pointed to the gloomy conclusion that the Black majority would only assert their democratic and human rights through violent struggle. Elsewhere in Southern Africa, the geopolitics of the region had altered dramatically. From a position of apparently unchanging South African dominance, the outer bastions of the citadel were crumbling. The Commonwealth itself now had a 'third world' champion as its chief officer, backed by an established Secretariat, with expanding programmes and growing confidence.

The Commonwealth's membership had also changed beyond recognition. A majority had come to independence only in the post-war period, many recently. Their leaders were the heroes of an emerging new world: Kwame Nkrumah, Jomo Kenyatta, Jawaharlal Nehru, Indira Gandhi, Julius Nyerere, Kenneth Kaunda, Lee Kuan Yew, Michael Manley, Seretse Khama and others to come. Even the old 'white' Dominions were undergoing change with the radical Gough Whitlam in Australia battling a conservative, Malcolm Fraser, whose own foreign policy approaches were distinctly liberal. 'Trudeau-mania' in Canada had left its mark on the Commonwealth in a variety of ways with Canada stepping out of its imperial past and into its chosen destiny as a 'middle power' at the service of global order and justice. Even Harold Wilson and the Labour Party had survived the 'swinging sixties' and were now back in Downing Street.

Ramphal was in temperament and outlook a man for such times. Coming from an Indo-Caribbean background in Guyana, he was keenly aware of the path his family had trod through the pillared institutions of slavery in the West Indies. His Indian great-grandmother had travelled across the oceans and into bondage as an indentured labourer on the sugar plantations of Demerara. Ramphal saw *apartheid* as slavery's modern-day equivalent. In the inhumanity and brutality of systemised 'otherness', and in the voices of those who were *apartheid's* apologists, he heard the echoes of an earlier crime against humanity.[60] Its destruction became a driving passion from his earliest days as Foreign Minister of Guyana. Unless the new, multiracial Commonwealth could confront and vanquish this gross distortion of difference, it would be exposed as an organisation without meaning or substance.

As planning began for the celebrations of the Queen's Silver Jubilee in 1977, it was Queen Elizabeth herself, as Head of the Commonwealth, who encouraged Wilson to propose that the UK should be the venue for the 1977 CHOGM. The summit had outgrown Marlborough House (used for earlier summit meetings), and Lancaster House, close by, was chosen as the venue for the five-day gathering. Another significant change was the innovation of a Heads-Only Retreat, with the Gleneagles

Hotel, set in Perthshire's Ochill hills, as the 1977 venue. In the eyes of many contemporary commentators, the CHOGM did not seem particularly noteworthy. Peter Lyon remarked: "For all its festive setting, and the problem of Amin's Uganda, this meeting was a sober, low-key affair."[61] The noted Commonwealth journalist, Derek Ingram, felt it had been "a rather quiet Heads of Government gathering."[62] Interviewing Ramphal, he commented: "Seen in retrospect, it is difficult to pick out what were its highlights and achievements." Ramphal replied: "On the whole, I would rather Commonwealth Heads of Government Conferences be less headline catching and more practically orientated and substantive in achievement and I am glad that the London meeting qualified on that account."[63] And yet it was the Gleneagles Retreat which would be the setting for a landmark Commonwealth agreement on *apartheid* in sport with far-reaching political implications.

By this point, the campaign for non-racial sport had seen South Africa challenged in virtually every international sporting arena. In 1970, in addition to South Africa's expulsion from the Olympic movement, thirteen of the country's white sporting organisations had been either suspended or expelled from international sport. A year later, South Africa had been virtually excluded from all international cricket. Even so, rugby, so beloved by white South Africans, proved more resistant to change. Following the significant protests in the UK during the 1969 Springboks tour, the South African rugby team met a similar storm in Australia in 1971. Within a year, and the election of a new Australian government, an official policy of opposing *apartheid* sport was adopted. Despite periodic challenges, not least from individual sporting figures, the policy was sustained thereafter.

As a keen sporting nation, New Zealand had come face to face with some of these challenges. In particular, opposition had been growing to the proposed rugby tour of South Africa in 1970. This was aggravated by reports from within South Africa that Maori members of the All-Blacks might not be welcome. Dr Albert Hertzog, a right-wing Cabinet Minister, led the opposition, complaining that the Maoris would 'sit at the table with our young men and girls, and dance with our girls'. At the same time, the New Zealand Athletics Union withdrew an invitation to its white South African counterpart to tour the country in 1970, fearful that such an invitation might scupper New Zealand's participation in the 1970 Commonwealth Games. In the event, the All Blacks tour went ahead after South Africa agreed to accept a mixed-race team. Chris Laidlaw, a talented half-back in that team (and later New Zealand's first resident High Commissioner in Zimbabwe), remarked:

> I had resolved personally to go on the tour if New Zealand was able to take non-white players on the grounds that this was a step forward. . . . Immediately after the tour I was pessimistic about the prospects of further reform and began to believe I had done the wrong thing. A decade later I realised that this tour had helped crystallise the whole issue.[64]

With a Springboks tour due in March 1973, the Commonwealth Games was again used as a lever of influence. India, and several Commonwealth African countries, announced they would boycott the 1974 Games, due to be held in Christchurch,

South Island. The newly elected Labour Prime Minister, Norman Kirk, notwithstanding an election pledge to the contrary, persuaded the NZ Rugby Union that the tour had to be abandoned, infuriating the rugby fraternity. The Christchurch Games were saved and, in an outpouring of emotion and camaraderie, earned the four-yearly sporting event the enduring soubriquet of the 'Friendly Games'.

That mood was to be swiftly punctured by the election, in 1975, of the National Party Leader, Robert Muldoon. The pugnacious Muldoon had made the question of racist tours, politics and sport an election issue, arguing that "sportsmen should be free to play with whomsoever they wished."[65] Emerging victorious, he promised the reinstatement of sports exchanges with South Africa. While Muldoon saw the issue as a domestic one, playing well to sections of New Zealand's electorate, its international implications were alarming. Despite a visit to New Zealand in May 1976 by Sonny Ramphal to head off the "total articulation" of New Zealand policy, a month later the National Government bade official farewell to the All Blacks team as they embarked on their tour of South Africa. The timing could not have been worse. The Soweto uprising by Black school students had just begun and already nearly two hundred had been killed and many more injured. Against such a dreadful backdrop, twenty-eight African nations (eleven from Commonwealth Africa), along with Guyana and Iraq, announced that they would be boycotting the 1976 Olympic Games in Montreal, beginning in July. Quite apart from New Zealand's plummeting international reputation, it was increasingly evident to other Commonwealth member governments, and to the Commonwealth Secretariat, that unless something was done, the impact on the 1977 Commonwealth summit, the Queen's Silver Jubilee celebrations and the 1978 Commonwealth Games in Edmonton would be disastrous.

This was the prelude to the Gleneagles Agreement. As the London CHOGM approached, Ramphal had frankly laid out two particularly pressing issues for the meeting. Writing in his biennial report to Heads, he pointed to General Idi Amin and the problem of human rights in Uganda and also to Prime Minister Muldoon and New Zealand's policy on sporting contacts with South Africa.

The juxtaposition of these two issues, wrote Anthony Payne,

> was highly embarrassing to New Zealand and served to underline the seriousness with which Ramphal intended to force the Commonwealth to find a practical way of translating its rhetorical opposition to *apartheid* into a common policy on the matter of sporting contact with South Africa.[66]

Initially, any excitement at the opening of the CHOGM was consumed by the Ugandan issue with rumours rife that Idi Amin would make a surprise appearance. Otherwise, five days of formal Executive Sessions proceeded at a pedestrian pace with no mention of *apartheid* and sport. Ramphal had his eye on the Retreat for what he subsequently described as "my first excursion into quiet diplomacy."[67]

When Heads eventually decamped to the Gleneagles Hotel, Ramphal followed a pattern that he was to use at subsequent CHOGM retreats to great effect. Most Commonwealth leaders were encouraged on to the golf course or to relax in some other way. At the same time, Ramphal assembled a small group of Commonwealth Heads under the leadership of Michael Manley to try and find a way forward. Apart from Manley and Muldoon himself, there was Lee Kuan Yew, Pierre Trudeau, Shehu Musa Yar 'Adua of Nigeria; and Aboud Jumbe, the Vice-President of Tanzania. Although Muldoon was on his own, the tone of the discussion was about finding a solution rather than indulging in recrimination, working on a draft prepared by the Secretariat. In the end, it was left to Manley to close the deal, in a one-to-one meeting with Muldoon. The New Zealand Prime Minister later claimed that he and Manley had knocked up the agreement in a bar at Gleneagles.[68]

Two final concessions had to be made. One was that they should draw "a curtain across the past" and the other was to blame past misunderstandings and difficulties in part on "inadequate inter-governmental consultations."[69] Nevertheless, Ramphal felt this was a price worth paying. Beginning with the Singapore Declaration of Commonwealth Principles of 1971, the Agreement reaffirmed the Commonwealth's fundamental opposition to racism and to *apartheid* in sport. Secondly, it dealt decisively with the issue of sporting contact with *apartheid* South Africa, stating that such contacts "encourage the belief (however unwarranted) that they are prepared to condone this abhorrent policy or are less than totally committed to the principles in their Singapore Declaration."[70] Thirdly, notwithstanding the past, it committed each and every one of its leaders to the "urgent duty" to combat *apartheid* "by withholding any form of support for, and by taking every practical step to discourage contact or competition by their nationals" with those who practise *apartheid*. Fourthly, while acknowledging that it was for each government to determine implementation of the agreement "in accord with its law," they warned that the "effective fulfilment of their commitment" was essential to the future harmony of Commonwealth sport. In that respect, they added that they did not expect to see in future any sporting contact "of any significance" with *apartheid* South Africa.[71]

By the evening, the draft had been circulated to all the other Heads, none of whom dissented from it. The next day, in London, the Agreement was swiftly adopted by consensus in formal session. The host of the summit, Jim Callaghan, commented: "This agreement was a victory for all Commonwealth countries since they had all agreed to use their best efforts . . . to break down the system of *apartheid* in sports," adding that each country would work to "sustain and strengthen" the consensus brokered at the summit.[72] Sam Ramsammy, for SAN-ROC, remarked: "The Gleneagles Agreement is a huge achievement for us. For the first time an international governmental organisation has signed up to our cause."[73] The 1978 Edmonton Games seemed secure. For Ramphal, the Gleneagles Agreement was one of "substantial achievement."[74] He added: "I believe it has a good chance of sticking."

## 4 Conclusion

In the immediate aftermath, this certainly seemed to be the case. In the eyes of the Commonwealth Secretariat, it had "an immediate and significant effect in diminishing sporting contact with South Africa."[75] On 14 December that year, the UNGA,

*Figure 6.2* Commonwealth leaders, hosted by UK Prime Minister Jim Callaghan, at their Gleneagles Retreat, 1977. Commonwealth Secretariat.

which had called for a sporting boycott of South Africa as early as 1968, adopted the International Declaration against *Apartheid* in Sport.[76] It was then adopted – or at least imitated – by the OAU, and also the Council of Europe, in 1978; by Nordic countries in 1979; and by many other individual countries thereafter. As Anthony Low put it: "The Commonwealth's Gleneagles Declaration of 1977 against sporting links with South Africa managed over the years to grow some remarkably strong teeth."[77] It was, thought Peter Hain, "a major advance."[78]

However, there were to be fierce disputes over the implementation of Gleneagles with various Commonwealth countries, most notably New Zealand and the UK. Both were later accused of contravening Gleneagles, and both protested that they had sought "the effective fulfilment" of their commitment to halt racist tours in the absence of legal powers to prohibit sporting exchanges by their independent games' organisations.[79]

Given his previous record on sporting exchanges with South Africa and his initial scepticism about Commonwealth collective action, New Zealand's premier might have been among those baulking at the full implementation of the Gleneagles Agreement. However, in February 1979, with several New Zealand rugby players invited to tour South Africa with a multinational team, Muldoon wrote to Ramphal reassuring him that "the responsibilities the Gleneagles Agreement places on governments to give a lead are clear. We have observed them meticulously and we will continue to do so." He added a caveat:

## 108  *Boycotting* Apartheid *in Sport*

It would, however, be wrong in principle and contrary not only to Gleneagles but also to everything the Commonwealth stands for to allow a sporting tour undertaken by a few individuals against their Government's counsel to embitter the relations between states and peoples.[80]

Within a few months, a change of government in the UK would have a dramatic impact on the Commonwealth agenda and the intertwining of the Rhodesian crisis, and its resolution, with the implementation of Gleneagles and the campaign against *apartheid* in sport. The election of Margaret Thatcher, with her provenance in right-wing politics, promised a markedly different approach to both issues.

### Notes

1. Chris Bolsmann, "White football in South Africa: Empire, *apartheid* and change 1892–1977," *Soccer and Society* 11:1–2 (2010): 31.
2. Christabel Gurney, "In the heart of the beast: The British Anti-*Apartheid* Movement 1959–1994," In *The Road to Democracy in South Africa*, 287.
3. Thula Simpson, "Rethinking '*Apartheid's* Golden Age': South Africa, c1966–1979," *South African Historical Journal* 69:2 (2017): 151–2.
4. Hain, *Don't Play with Apartheid*, 166, 196.
5. Commonwealth Secretariat, *The Commonwealth at the Summit (Vol.1)*, 198.
6. Ramphal, *Glimpses of a Global Life*, 426.
7. McIntyre, *The Significance of the Commonwealth*, 236; Jamaica, Trinidad & Tobago, Guyana and Barbados were among those Commonwealth countries threatening to boycott the 1970 Commonwealth Games over the planned South African cricket tour to England that year.
8. Quoted by Dean Allen, "Bats and bayonets: Cricket and the Anglo-Boer War, 1899–1902," *Sport in History* 25:1 (2005): 28.
9. Allen, "Bats and bayonets," 32.
10. Ibid., 334.
11. Bruce Murray and Christopher Merrett, *Caught Behind: Race and Politics in Springbok Cricket* (Johannesburg: Wits University Press, 2004), 13.
12. Ibid., 9.
13. Tony Collins, "The Oval World – Rugby and 'globalisation' in the nineteenth century," 24 January 2016, *The Oval World*, Accessed 14 September 2019, www.tony-collins.org/rugbyreloaded/2016/1/24/the-oval-world-thoughts-on-the-global-oval.
14. Bolsmann, "'White football in South Africa," 33.
15. Ibid., 31.
16. Murray and Merrett, *Caught Behind*, 10.
17. Ibid., 15.
18. Cable from Cape Town to FCO, relaying the transcript of a message by Piet Koornhof MP, Minister of National Education, Sport and Recreation, 31 December 1978. TNA, FCO13/88/76–78.
19. Murray and Merrett, *Caught Behind*, 14.
20. Ibid., 35.
21. Bolsmann, "White football in South Africa," 37.
22. Commonwealth Secretariat, *Apartheid and South African Sport* (London: Commonwealth Secretariat, 1976), 2–3.
23. Paul Martin, quoting *Die Transvaler*, 7 September 1965, in "South African sport: *Apartheid's* Achilles heel?" *The World Today* June (1984): 236.
24. Richard Lapchick, "South Africa: Sport and *apartheid* politics," *The Annals of the American Academy of Political and Social Science* 445 (1979): 162.

25 Marc Keech, "At the centre of the web: The role of Sam Ramsammy in South Africa's admission to international sport," *Culture, Sport Society* 3:3 (2000): 43.
26 Ibid., 45.
27 Peter Hain, *Inside Out* (London: Biteback Publishing Ltd, 2012), 48.
28 Rob Nixon, "*Apartheid* on the run: The South African sports boycott," *Transition* 58 (1992): 72–3.
29 Martin, "South African sport," 235.
30 Marc Keech & Barrie Houlihan, "Sport and the end of *apartheid*," *The Round Table: The Commonwealth Journal of International Affairs* 88:349 (1999): 118.
31 Guy Fraser-Sampson, *Cricket at the Crossroads: Class, Colour and Controversy from 1967 to 1977* (London: Elliott & Thompson Ltd, 2011), 86–96.
32 Martin Williamson, "When politics killed a tour," *ESPN Sports Media*, 14 July 2012, Accessed 17 September 2019, www.espncricinfo.com/magazine/content/story/571799.html.
33 John Arlott, 'Why I'm off the air," *The Guardian* 17 April 1970, The Guardian archive, Accessed 19 April 2020, www.theguardian.com/news/1970/apr/17/leadersandreply.mainsection.
34 "The Anti-*Apartheid* Movement in the 1960s," Accessed 19 April 2020, www.aamarchives.org/history/1960s/79-history/124-the-anti-aparttheid-movement-in-the-1960s.html, 6.
35 Gurney, "In the heart of the beast," 289.
36 Philip Barker, "When South Africa gave up the 1934 Empire Games," *BizNews*, 11 March 2017, Accessed 9 September 2019, www.insidethegames.biz/writers/24090)/philip-barker.
37 Christabel Gurney, "A great cause: The origins of the Anti-*Apartheid* Movement, June 1959–March 1960," *Journal of South African Studies* 26:1 (2000): 129.
38 Huddleston, *Naught for Your Comfort*, 150.
39 Hakan Thorn, *Anti-Apartheid and the Emergence of a Global Civil Society* (Oxford: Springer, 2006), 62.
40 AAM explanatory text for "It's not cricket" (1965), "The Anti-*Apartheid* Movement in the 1960s," Accessed 20 April 2020, www.aamarchives.org/history/1960s/po193-it's-not-cricket-1965.html.
41 AAM Leaflet, "*Apartheid* isn't cricket," AAM archives, Bodleian Library, Oxford, L. Commonwealth 1960–85, MSS AAM 2227, 145.
42 Lapchick, "South Africa: Sport and *apartheid* politics," 162.
43 Commonwealth Secretariat, *The Commonwealth at the Summit* (Vol.1), 115–182.
44 Biennial Reports of the Commonwealth Secretary-General 1969–1975, Commonwealth Secretariat archives, COMSEC/CPAD/RSG, 1969–75.
45 Smith, *Stitches in Time*, 235.
46 Country monitoring began in 1973: "*Apartheid* in sport" (6 February 1973–1 April 1977), Commonwealth archives 140/73/02.
47 Shridath Ramphal, *Report of the Commonwealth Secretary-General 1977* (London: Commonwealth Secretariat, 1977), 4–5.
48 AAM Leaflet, "No Munich in Rhodesia, no sell-out to Smith," AAM archives, Bodleian MSS AAM 1231.
49 At the 1956 Olympics, Egypt, Iraq and the Lebanon withdrew, citing the Anglo-French attack on the Suez Canal; Spain, Switzerland and the Netherlands boycotted the Games because of the Soviet invasion of Hungary; and China declined to take part in protest at the International Olympic Committee's continuing recognition of Taiwan.
50 Aviston Downes, "Sport and international diplomacy: The case of the Commonwealth Caribbean and the anti-*apartheid* campaign, 1959–1992," *Sports Historian* 22:2 (2002): 27–28.
51 UN General Assembly, *International Declaration Against Apartheid in Sports*, 14 December 1977, Accessed 19 September 2019, www.digital library.un.org/record 624279/A_RES_32_105M_EN pdf.

52 BBC News, "1970: South Africa cricket tour called off," *On This Day*, 22 May 1970, Accessed 14 June 2018, htpps://www.news.bbc.co.uk/onthisday/hi/stories/may22/newssid_2504000/2504573.stm.
53 Hain, *Don't Play with Apartheid*, 226.
54 Arnold Smith, *Third Report of the Commonwealth Secretary-General (November 1968–November 1970)* (London: Commonwealth Secretariat, 1971), 51.
55 Blair Fraser, quoted in Smith, *Stitches in Time*, 20.
56 Commonwealth Secretariat, *The Commonwealth at the Summit* (Vol.1), 105–111.
57 Anthony Verrier, *The Road to Zimbabwe 1890–1980* (London: Jonathan Cape, 1986), 145.
58 Smith, *Stitches in Time*, 41.
59 Exchanges between L.E.T. Storar and A.L. Mayall (Protocol), 1972, TNA, FCO 68/471.
60 Ramphal, "Glimpses of a global life," 395–406.
61 Peter Lyon, "The Commonwealth's jubilee summit," *The World Today* 33:7 (1977): 250.
62 Derek Ingram, "A quiet conference," *The Round Table: The Commonwealth Journal of International Affairs* 268 (1977): 314.
63 Ibid., 314.
64 Chris Laidlaw (former All Black and diplomat), telephone interview from NZ with the author, 14 June 2012.
65 Nigel Roberts, "The New Zealand General Election of 1975," *The Australian Quarterly* 48:1 (1976): 108.
66 Anthony Payne, "The international politics of the Gleneagles Agreement," *The Round Table: The Commonwealth Journal of International Affairs* 80:320 (1991): 420.
67 Shridath Ramphal (former Secretary-General), in conversation with the author, 31 May 2012, London.
68 Jeremy Pope, email to the author, 3 June 2012, personal copy.
69 Commonwealth Secretariat, *The Gleneagles Agreement on Sporting Contacts with South Africa*, 15 June 1977, Accessed 19 September 2019, www.thecommonwealth.org/sites/default/files/inline/Gleneagles-Agreement.pdf,1.
70 Ibid.
71 Ibid., 2.
72 Commonwealth Secretariat, "From the archives: The Gleneagles Agreement on sport," 9 November 2016, Accessed 19 April 2020, www.thecommonwealth.org/media/news/archive-gleneagles-agreement-sport, 2.
73 Sam Ramsammy and Edward Griffiths, *Reflections on a Life in Sport* (Cape Town: Greenhouse, 2004), 75.
74 Ingram, "A quiet conference," 321.
75 Commonwealth Secretariat, *Racism in Southern Africa*, 16.
76 United Nations General Assembly Resolution 32/105M 14 December 1977, Accessed 12 February 2020, www.research.un.org/en/docs/ga/quick/regular/32.
77 Anthony Low, *Eclipse of Empire* (Cambridge: CUP, 1991), 334.
78 Peter Hain, *Inside Out*, 76.
79 Commonwealth Secretariat, *The Commonwealth at the Summit* (Vol.1), 199.
80 Correspondence from Robert Muldoon to Shridath Ramphal, 13 February 1979, Commonwealth Secretariat archives, 2010/055,1.

## References

Anthony Low, *Eclipse of Empire* (Cambridge: CUP, 1991).
Anthony Verrier, *The Road to Zimbabwe 1890–1980* (London: Jonathan Cape, 1986).
Arnold Smith, *Stitches in Time*, Op.Cit.
Arnold Smith, *Third Report of the Commonwealth Secretary-General* (November 1968–November 1970) (London: Commonwealth Secretariat, 1971).

Bruce Murray and Christopher Merrett, *Caught Behind: Race and Politics in Springbok Cricket* (Johannesburg: Wits University Press, 2004).
Commonwealth Secretariat, *Apartheid and South African Sport* (London: Commonwealth Secretariat, 1976).
Commonwealth Secretariat, *Racism in Southern Africa*, Op.Cit.
Commonwealth Secretariat, *The Commonwealth at the Summit (Vol.1)*, Op.Cit.
Guy Fraser-Sampson, *Cricket at the Crossroads: Class, Colour and Controversy from 1967 to 1977* (London: Elliott, Thompson Ltd, 2011).
Hakan Thorn, *Anti-Apartheid and the Emergence of a Global Civil Society* (Oxford: Springer, 2006).
Huddleston, *Naught for Your Comfort*, Op.Cit.
Peter Hain, *Don't Play with Apartheid* (London: Allen & Unwin Ltd, 1971).
Peter Hain, *Inside Out* (London: Biteback Publishing Ltd, 2012).
Sam Ramsammy and Edward Griffiths, *Reflections on a Life in Sport* (Cape Town: Greenhouse, 2004).
Shridath Ramphal, *Glimpses of a Global Life*, Op.Cit.
Shridath Ramphal, *Report of the Commonwealth Secretary-General 1977* (London: Commonwealth Secretariat, 1977).
Sifiso Ndlovu (ed.), *The Road to Democracy in South Africa: International Solidarity (Vol.3)*, Op.Cit.
W. David McIntyre, *The Significance of the Commonwealth*, Op.Cit.

# 7 Implementing Gleneagles and Problems of Implementation

From New Zealand to Moscow

## 1 Introduction

Many applauded the adoption of the 1977 Gleneagles Agreement in helping achieve South Africa's wider international isolation in sport. Indeed, the sporting boycott played an important part in a pattern of escalation that led, a decade later, to widespread economic and financial sanctions against the *apartheid* regime, including by the Commonwealth.

However, the devil now lay in the far from watertight detail. Much of the Commonwealth may have shared popular sports, but the relationships between individual governments and their national sporting bodies was very different, even where the sincerity of the government concerned to live up to its Commonwealth commitments was not in dispute. As it was, the conjunction of the Zimbabwe settlement in 1979–1980 and the Western boycott of the Moscow Olympics (following the Soviet invasion of Afghanistan in December 1979) provided the UK with 'cover' which otherwise might have encouraged greater boycott pressures on the 1982 Brisbane Games with the UK as the principal focus of discontent.[1]

In examining the difficulties the Commonwealth faced in the implementation of the Gleneagles Agreement, it is worth recalling that it was the Commonwealth's sporting traditions, not least in rugby, cricket and field sports, which in a South African context proved to be so susceptible to boycott and isolation and which were so keenly felt by the South African white population. It also achieved a huge resonance among those outside the privileged white population. As Peter Hain put it, "[t]o non-white South Africans, alone, isolated and forgotten, stripped of all their rights, the campaign was a clarion call in the wilderness – a flash of light into the darkness."[2] This news did more than raise morale. In local South African communities, the rising clamour for non-racial sport presented a powerful counterpoint to the international sporting boycott, breaking down the *apartheid* structures by creating new practical realities.[3]

## 2 Challenges to Gleneagles

The British General Election, of 3 May 1979, has widely been described as a 'political watershed'. Not only did it result in the appointment of the UK's first female Prime Minister, but it also marked a distinct break from the consensual politics of the post-war era. This style of politics ended when the minority Labour government of Jim Callaghan lost a parliamentary 'no confidence' motion and was forced to go to the country. Margaret Thatcher's Conservative government emerged triumphant, recording a 5.2% swing to the party, the largest since 1945.[4] With a healthy parliamentary majority, Thatcher's right-wing radicalism was set to challenge many of the UK's prevailing policy and institutional assumptions, particularly on the economy, employment and the trade unions.

Change was also expected in the UK's foreign relations. On Southern Africa, while Thatcher's initial instinct was to recognise Rhodesia's 'internal settlement' and the government of Bishop Abel Muzorewa, there were also signs of fresh attempts to 'normalise' South Africa's sporting links with the UK in a direct challenge to the Gleneagles Agreement. Encouraged by a rugby tour of South Africa in May–June by six British rugby clubs, the four Home Rugby Unions issued an invitation to a South African Barbarians team to undertake a countrywide UK tour in October 1979. Danie Craven was among those who created an overseas touring squad which, for the first time in South Africa's rugby history, was notionally multiracial, containing eight white, eight Coloured and eight Black players. Despite this, Stop All Racist Tours and the AAM condemned this as a "stooge tour," declaring: "White South Africa is trying to hoodwink us into believing that the tour is multiracial. It is not."[5] However, despite pitch invasions and protests at the various tour venues, the numbers demonstrating against the tour were relatively modest. At the final match, at Newport, over 500 marched through the town and nine were arrested.[6] Ivey has argued that the tour "sparked an international crisis."[7] If so, it was a crisis of modest proportions. True, letters of protest were received, including from some Commonwealth governments. There were threats of retaliation, including a possible boycott of the UK's participation in the 1980 Olympic Games. Hector Munro, the UK Sports' Minister, insisted that the government had condemned the tour and had done all in its power to press for its cancellation. Ivey speculates that the tour threatened not only British international sporting contacts but also the UK's foreign policy aims in Southern Africa, specifically the prospects for a settlement in Rhodesia.[8] In reality, controversy about the tour left the negotiations at Lancaster House untroubled. As the conference inched to a successful conclusion at the beginning of December, Ramphal met Thatcher and Carrington to discuss outstanding issues, but the subject of *apartheid* sport was not raised.[9] The Lancaster House Agreement was finally signed on 21 December.[10]

Four days earlier, the Supreme Council for Sport in Africa, meeting in Yaoundé, Cameroon, had passed a resolution which threatened to "break off all bilateral sporting relations with Great Britain," along with other measures until the UK adhered fully to the Gleneagles Agreement.[11] While deciding against an African boycott of the Moscow Olympics if Great Britain attended, the SCSA warned that this position would change if the proposed Lions tour of South Africa went ahead.

Despite these ominous developments, Thatcher and Carrington, visiting New York and Washington, basked in international adulation. On 18 December, Ambassador Salim Salim, President of the UNGA, offered his "profound congratulations" on the successful conclusion of the conference. He told the British Prime Minister that when the initialling of the ceasefire was announced the previous day, UNGA broke into "spontaneous applause," adding that this was "a rare accolade."[12] Later in the day, the British pair met the UN Secretary-General, Kurt Waldheim, who was fulsome in his praise.[13] On their return to the UK, Thatcher told the Cabinet that they had been "most warmly received during their recent visit."[14] Waiting for the Prime Minister was a letter of congratulations from Ramphal expressing his "deep sense of gratification."[15]

Looming difficulties over the Gleneagles Agreement, with a renewed challenge from British and Irish rugby beginning to gather pace, had been smothered by the good news from Lancaster House. At last it seemed that the long-running Rhodesian rebellion would be ended with the birth of a new African nation: Zimbabwe. Both the UK government and the Commonwealth had been absorbed by the all-party negotiations – neither had paid too much attention to the South African Barbarian's tour which, in any case, had aroused only modest public interest. However, by the end of 1979, it was becoming clear that the Barbarians tour had been only a prelude to a far more ambitious undertaking: an imminent British Lions rugby tour of South Africa and, potentially, a resumption of full sporting links with the *apartheid* state.

Some have speculated that a Conservative Government under Margaret Thatcher would never have assented to the Gleneagles Agreement.[16] At the same time, while she never disavowed the agreement in office, her approach was often lukewarm at best. Later in her premiership, she was asked to approve a draft letter, to be signed by her, to Raman Subba Row, the Chairman of the Test and County Cricket Board (TCCB), about a 'rebel' cricket tour to South Africa. The draft set out the full commitment of the British Government to the Gleneagles Agreement, stated that its policy was to discourage sporting contact by both teams and individuals with South Africa and concluded: "I must make our position clear on this matter which could go far wider than the immediate issue."[17] This was presented to her by her PS, Charles Powell, under a handwritten note which read: "Prime Minister – I think this is probably right. We write stating the Government's position but not trying to exercise any pressure. Agree?"[18]

Her first challenge on Gleneagles was the 1980 British Lions Tour to South Africa. In November 1979, the Four Home Unions committee organising the tour decided to go ahead as planned, and the individual rugby unions of England, Ireland, Scotland and Wales all subsequently gave their assent. Thatcher's decision to act in conformity with the Gleneagles Agreement and 'discourage' the Lions tour came towards the end of 1979. While the Lancaster House conference had not yet reached its conclusion, sporting contact with South Africa was also a matter of considerable concern to Commonwealth countries, particularly in Africa. The UK would need to be seen to be upholding the organisation's opposition to *apartheid* in sport. However, the context dramatically changed at the end of December 1979 as Soviet forces intervened in Afghanistan, displacing and executing the country's President, Hafizullah Amin, replacing him with their own nominee, and taking control of the country with a 100,000-strong army of occupation.

The apparent difficulties facing the UK over sporting contact with South Africa were transformed. In the middle of December, the SCSA had threatened Britain's involvement in the 1980 Moscow Olympics, invoking the spectre of an African-led boycott. By the end of the month, the UK was among those Western countries which quickly supported the US-led boycott of the 1980 Moscow Olympics. The timing of the Lions tour and the Summer Olympics, if not overlapping, were in close sequence. Inevitably, in two instances of 'politics intruding into sport', the British Government had to be seen to be acting consistently and, in that respect, Gleneagles could be viewed as providing the government with additional 'cover' in its approach to the Soviet boycott. This standpoint was captured in a letter from the Prime Minister to Mrs Glen Haig of the Amateur Fencing Association, in May 1980, assuring her that sport should operate in the UK with the minimum amount of interference. Thatcher continued: "Very occasionally – particularly in international affairs – sport and politics come together, and decisions have to be made for political reasons. The Summer Olympics and the Gleneagles Agreement are two such cases."[19]

This was the public case for equivalence between the two issues. But what was the reality in the application of the government's policies? Government records reveal a marked difference in approach. In the case of the British Lions Tour, Thatcher allowed her Minister for Sport, Hector Munro, to undertake the task of persuasion with the Rugby Football Union (RFU). After lobbying from several African Heads of State, Thatcher responded to Abraham Ordia, President of the Supreme Council for Sport in Africa, assuring him that the British Government was against *apartheid* and fully accepted the Gleneagles Agreement. She told Ordia that Munro had both spoken and written to the chairman of the organising committee "asking that the invitation to the British Lions should not be accepted." She added: "I have made clear in Parliament that Mr Munro was acting for the Government as a whole and with my personal support." After this lukewarm call to action she explained that passports could not be withdrawn from players and that therefore "there is nothing more that I, or the government, can do to prevent the tour."[20]

This detached approach was in marked contrast with the pressure the British Government brought to bear on potential British participants in the Moscow Olympics. In an article prepared for the *Daily Express*, shortly before the opening of the summer games, Douglas Hurd wrote: "In the past six months the Government has had a long argument with sporting organisations in Britain," adding that "those who think that sport has nothing to do with politics don't know anything about the Soviet Union." He also revealed that the government had used trade pressure as well, remarking "There are firms and workers in Britain today who are worse off because of what has been done."[21] In a direct appeal to sporting organisations, the Prime Minister used strong language, saying: "I have advised British sportsmen and women and their sporting federations that it would be against British interests and wrong for them to compete in Moscow." They were being asked, she said, "to do something difficult for their country and for the peace of the world."[22] While some organisations had withdrawn from participation, those that still intended to go to Moscow (including the British Olympic Association and its Chairman, Sir

Denis Follows) were subject to relentless pressure, including repeated meetings with Lord Carrington, the Foreign Secretary, and other Ministers.[23] In a letter to Malcolm Fraser, the Australian Prime Minister Thatcher revealed something of her own involvement in the boycott campaign: "We too remain firmly in favour of a boycott," she told him, adding that:

> I and my Ministers have been urging sportsmen and women, though meetings, letter and broadcasts, not to go to Moscow. The House of Commons has supported the boycott by a large majority. I myself have now written four letters to the Chairman of the BOA on this subject.

Their unwillingness to bow to pressure, she said, "frustrate[d] the interests of Britain."[24] At the same time, officials in Downing Street and the Foreign and Commonwealth Office (FCO) kept the Prime Minister informed of a steady stream of anti-Soviet material which was being "fed to the press," both in the UK and overseas.[25]

Thatcher received enthusiastic support for the Moscow boycott from Robert Muldoon of New Zealand. In May 1980, Muldoon met Thatcher in London and reported that "New Zealand sports bodies were pulling out of the Olympic Games one by one." He added: "Although the New Zealand Olympic Committee had refused to bow to pressure from his government, public opinion was now substantially against participation in the Games."[26] On 6 June, the New Zealand Government informed their British counterparts of further withdrawals of athletes from New Zealand's Olympic team and the decision of the Olympic Committee not to use government or private donations to send athletes to Moscow. "Sports associations will now have to find NZ $1,200 per head," declared the cable.[27] However, despite intense political pressure, both New Zealand and the UK sent much depleted teams to Moscow where they competed under the Olympic flag in protest at Soviet action. Sixty-six countries joined the boycott. Only eighty countries took part in the Olympics (some under the Olympic flag), the smallest attendance since 1956. While many African countries travelled to Moscow, "Fifteen sub-Saharan African countries stayed home," records Ivey, including Ghana and Kenya.[28] But this did not "abate their frustrations over the absence of decisive action against South Africa."[29]

Both sporting events went ahead. On the Olympics, Thatcher had brought all her legendary passion and energy to bear: on the British Lions tour there had been lip service only. This was all too evident to Abraham Ordia, Secretary-General of the Nigerian Olympic Committee, who wrote to the Commonwealth Games Federation (CGF) complaining: "If the British Government had spent one tenth of the time it spent persuading the British Olympic Association to boycott the Moscow Olympic Games with the British Rugby Union, the Union's decision might have been different."[30] Downes adds: "Such hypocrisy incensed the African and Caribbean representatives."[31] Indeed, as regards the Commonwealth, Mrs Thatcher's instincts in the summer of 1980 were to respond to those on the right wing of the Conservative Party lobbying for a relaxation of the Gleneagles Agreement boycott (on the dubious grounds that South African sport was appreciably changing).[32] Criticism of the UK's handling of the Lions tour not only had been masked by the boycott of the Moscow Olympics but had also been lost amidst the final days of Rhodesia and, in the first three months of 1980, the gripping denouement of Zimbabwe's birth.

In September 1980, the developing threat to the Gleneagles Agreement intensified when the New Zealand Rugby Union (NZRU), against the advice of the New Zealand Government, invited the Springboks to tour the following year. The Deputy Prime Minister, Brian Talboys, made strong representations to the NZRU urging cancellation, arguing that such contact would be seen as condoning *apartheid* and would affect "how New Zealand is judged in the international arena."[33] Muldoon reasoned that once he had asked the NZRU to cancel the tour, his responsibilities under the Gleneagles Agreement were fulfilled and "any further measures on his part would interfere with the Rugby Union's right to invite whoever it wished."[34]

Once again, the forthcoming Commonwealth Games, this time taking place in Brisbane in 1982, became the target. "Twelve months out from the Games, a boycott was being rumoured by African, Caribbean and Asian countries," recalled the Games' organisers, "the threat for Brisbane was real."[35] Recently released Australian cabinet papers reveal that the option of banning New Zealand from the Games was seriously considered.[36] The diplomatic exchanges between Ramphal and Muldoon became increasingly heated, especially after the Secretary-General began consulting member governments on a proposal from Nigeria that the 1981 Commonwealth Finance Ministers' Meeting (FMM), due to be held in September in Auckland, be shifted to an alternative venue. This, insisted Ramphal, was because "Commonwealth Governments felt that their own stand against *apartheid* would be compromised were they to do otherwise."[37] In response, Muldoon declared that such a decision would be "an insult to New Zealand: a country which has a better record in human rights than any other member of the Commonwealth."[38] If that happened, warned Muldoon, "I shall recommend to my Government and my Government Party in Parliament that we regard the Gleneagles Agreement as being at an end as far as New Zealand is concerned."[39] The Commonwealth did not waver in the face of this threat, and the Commonwealth Committee on Southern Africa issued a further statement which "records its extreme regret that the proposed Springbok tour has not been cancelled . . . [and it] . . . would amount to a devastating setback to Commonwealth and wider efforts against sporting contacts with South Africa."[40] The decision to consider switching venues for the FMM remained in the event of the tour proceeding.

Later in July, the tour began, and the Springboks were met by a wave of protests, involving marches, pitch invasions and acts of civil disobedience. Two of the matches were called off for security reasons. Around 2,000 people were arrested during the eight weeks of the tour, but the protests had a global impact. Ramphal remarked: "The people of New Zealand indeed provided one of the most massive demonstrations ever given in any part of the world in support of the international campaign against *apartheid*."[41] Even so, it left families, and New Zealand itself, bitterly divided.[42] Muldoon protested that the Gleneagles Agreement "had fallen on evil times." He accused Secretary-General Ramphal of encouraging an interpretation of Gleneagles "which is not in accordance with either its letter or the spirit and understanding in which it is drafted."[43] Ramphal, in a robust reply, made clear that it was Muldoon who had let the side down by failing to stand up for the Commonwealth's highest principles. There was nothing wrong with Gleneagles, he argued, "its language is not ambiguous, nor is its intent; it does not imply weasel words designed to mean all things to all leaders. It is a clear statement of political commitment deeply rooted in principle."[44]

Many expected an escalation of the row at the next CHOGM in Melbourne. Curiously, this did not happen, even though the dust from the disastrous Springbok tour had scarcely settled and the FMM had indeed been relocated to the Bahamas. While Muldoon arrived for the Australian summit in a typically combative mood, his speech to the CHOGM was well crafted and well received. Colin Legum thought it 'a remarkable performance', which won praise from no less an adversary than Nyerere, the Chairman of the African frontline states. Legum remarked: "Although Muldoon defended his stand in refusing to ban the tour after his government had declared itself against it, he then went on to make a profound attack on South Africa and its *apartheid* system."[45] Significantly, he signalled that if sanctions were imposed on South Africa, New Zealand would support the decision. In so doing, he joined Australia and Canada in developing a differentiated position on *apartheid* from the UK. Many considered that "the withdrawal of the Finance Ministers' Meeting was a sufficient statement of protest."[46] On *apartheid* and sport, Commonwealth leaders made only a glancing reference, reaffirming their commitment to Gleneagles and to fulfilling their obligations under it. But, noting development at the United Nations on widening measures to prevent sporting contact with South Africa, Heads agreed to "redouble their own efforts."[47]

This deceptive tranquillity masked continuing anxiety about a possible boycott of the Brisbane Games. Muldoon, who had left the summit early, before the conclusion of the final communique, had quickly regained his customary irascibility. Complaining to Fraser, the summit host, that several key statements of his had been left out of the communique, he remarked: "I am afraid that I have been too long in politics to be impressed by the tactics used by the Secretary-General." He continued:

> Both at Lusaka and in Melbourne, there has been an intrusion of the methods which some of our Commonwealth colleagues use in their own countries, but which are entirely alien to countries such as Australia and New Zealand. These things can only damage the Commonwealth in the long term and I believe that it is the countries of the old Commonwealth who must resist such methods and gradually educate our newer colleagues in the ways of democracy and the rule of law.[48]

Little over a month later, Muldoon won re-election in New Zealand's general election, though with a reduced majority.

For a variety of reasons, including tumultuous events in Rhodesia/Zimbabwe, the start of the Soviet-Afghan war and the Moscow Olympic boycott, the UK government's lukewarm implementation of Gleneagles and the British Lions tour of South Africa were shielded from more damaging retribution. At the height of the 1981 controversy, Muldoon protested that

> the British Government places exactly the same interpretation as I do on the Gleneagles Agreement, namely, that governments have undertaken to try and persuade sporting bodies not to have contact with South African teams but that the final decision will be left to the sportsmen and the sporting bodies.[49]

This was fair comment and it begs the question: why was New Zealand criticised so heavily for its stance on the Gleneagles Agreement in relation to the 1981 Springboks tour while the UK received far less attention and opprobrium for its approach to the Lions tour of South Africa a year earlier? Partly the answer lay in the fortunes of timing and the confluence of circumstance as events unfolded in Lusaka, Lancaster House and Kabul. But it was also true that Muldoon had adopted a far more pugnacious approach to boycotts and sporting relations (Moscow excepting) which, until 1981 in any case, served as a dog-whistle issue for his electoral base. The visibility of the two sporting events was also markedly different. The injury-hit Lions tour was relatively low key outside South Africa and was soon eclipsed by the Summer Olympics. The Springboks tour the following year became a protracted global event. In Hamilton protestors chanted "the whole world is watching" and Mandela later revealed that when he heard, in prison, that the Hamilton match had been cancelled it was as "if the sun had come out."[50] John Minto, Halt All Racial Tours' (HART's) National Organiser, said afterwards that the protests against the tour "didn't stop it. But the cost has been so high that it should ensure that this is the last tour by a racist South African team."[51]

Members of the UK's Conservative Government (conscious that Scotland would host the 1986 Commonwealth Games in Edinburgh) realised that it would be folly to push for a relaxation of Gleneagles. As Hector Munro, in his last days as Minister of Sport, explained to Carrington:

> While many of our supporters in the House and in the country would like to see some relaxation of Gleneagles, in practical terms this seems likely to be very difficult. Events over the last month in New Zealand add to that conclusion.[52]

There had also been consternation among the British delegation at the Melbourne CHOGM at news reports that a South African provincial rugby team was about to tour the UK. The Cabinet Secretary, Sir Robert Armstrong, accompanying Thatcher, fired off an immediate cable to the Home Secretary, Leon Brittan (then acting Prime Minister), urging action: "Very important that HMG should be seen to take every possible step open to it to discourage the sport authorities concerned from proceeding." He added: "Much of the criticism of Muldoon, both in NZ and outside, is that he did not himself try hard enough to prevent the Springbok tour of NZ."[53] This inevitably begged the question of Thatcher's own leadership on the issue if the UK was to avoid what Carrington warned was "the growing risk of Britain's isolation in sport."[54]

If this was the view of the Foreign and Commonwealth Office, quite different guidance was coming from Downing Street. The new Minister of Sport, Neil McFarlane, had spoken to Ian Gow MP, Thatcher's Parliamentary PS (and her close confidant) who was also with the Prime Minister in Melbourne. Macfarlane's PS wrote to his counterpart in No. 10 with an account of the conversation. His Minister and Gow had agreed that the right amount and type of publicity had now been achieved, he recounted, and to do more might "create hostility amongst the rugby world and indeed the Government's own supporters. The Government had broken a precedent in its implementation of the Gleneagles Agreement by dealing directly with clubs and it was now best to sit pat."[55]

Ramphal had taken a bold step in encouraging Commonwealth governments to strip New Zealand of the hosting of the 1981 FMM. This was as much about preventing significant collateral damage to Commonwealth intergovernmental relations as it was inflicting a sanction on New Zealand even if Muldoon viewed it as the latter. The FMM, an annual meeting, was the most important of the Commonwealth's ministerial meetings, chiming with the annual meetings of the World Bank and the IMF, and at that time carrying forward several important Commonwealth initiatives. A meeting derailed by boycott and acrimony would do these other significant causes no good at all. By the same token, whatever his private sympathies for those tempted to boycott the Commonwealth Games over *apartheid*, the Games were a major Commonwealth institution and its greatest source of public exposure. As the Commonwealth's principal servant, he was duty-bound to do all he could to protect the Games.

While Ramphal told Macfarlane that shifting the FMM had 'saved the Brisbane Games' he realised that more needed to be done.[56] Ramphal had a considerable ability for spotting and recruiting rising talent across the Commonwealth to work in the Secretariat, sometimes at salaries well below the jobs they had left. Among these were two New Zealanders deeply immersed in sport who would prove to be invaluable to the cause. One was Chris Laidlaw (a former All Black rugby player) who became his Special Assistant and the other was Jeremy Pope (a lawyer who had left New Zealand in 1976 after incurring the displeasure of Muldoon) who became Ramphal's principal Legal Adviser.[57] Pope in particular was responsible for liaison with Sam Ramsammy of SAN-ROC and bodies like HART in New Zealand, as well as the AAM generally. Ramphal was aware of the shortcomings of the Gleneagles Agreement. At the time, Ramsammy conceded: "There is no doubt that we would have preferred a firm commitment to stop all sporting contact with South Africa."[58] Trevor Richards of HART, who was frequently in touch with Ramphal's Private Office, described Gleneagles as "a barely adequate compromise document drawn up to settle an urgent dispute. Like many such documents, it is open to a wide range of interpretations. Much of the document is vague and non-specific."[59] Nonetheless, Richards had used the Commonwealth agreement to advise the United Nations on its own International Declaration Against *Apartheid* in Sport, adopted by the General Assembly in December 1977. The OAU Council of Ministers had also adopted its own declaration in July 1977, and the Commonwealth presence in both the leadership and the membership of the OAU was always strong. This meant that African Commonwealth members would naturally work through the OAU, and its successor body, in the anti-*apartheid* campaign. In sport, however, its primary weapon was in promoting the boycott of events, such as the Olympic or Commonwealth Games, as a way of bringing pressure to bear on those perceived as bringing comfort to Pretoria.

Compared with Gleneagles, the UN Declaration was undoubtedly a stronger document but, as Canada (one of the promoters of the draft) conceded, individual countries differed widely in their approach to sport and its organisation, as well as to tourism, visas and the free movement of their citizens. The Canadian representative argued that the declaration should be regarded as 'a framework' and hoped that member states would not decline to support the UN resolution "as a result of a narrow or too exclusively legalistic interpretation."[60] Nevertheless, the UK, New Zealand (and Ireland) were unconvinced and among the fourteen abstentions when it came to the vote.[61]

It therefore seemed to Ramphal and his advisers that it was only by getting into the heart of Commonwealth cooperation in sport, and in particular the organisation and regulation of the Commonwealth Games, that further pressure could be brought to bear and the Games themselves protected from the blunt instrument of repeated boycott. However, Ramphal was aware that he could not rely on the CGF alone to be the vehicle for change. It was, at that stage, a rather old-fashioned organisation with antiquated procedures. Some of its members exhibited racist attitudes, such as Arthur Tunstall, the Australian sports administrator, who advocated a one-metre springboard diving event for 'Black folks'.[62] Generally, it was not an organisation equipped to deal with the high-pressure politics of *apartheid* and the sporting boycott, despite the best efforts of its benign Chairman, Sir Alexander Ross.[63]

In encouraging the CGF to adopt a Code of Conduct tightening up Gleneagles, Ramphal went to extraordinary lengths to make sure that the necessary changes were adopted. A Special Meeting of the CGF was needed to propose changes which could be adopted by the CGF General Assembly (to be held in the wings of the 1982 Brisbane Games). Ramphal offered Marlborough House (the site of the Secretariat's offices) as the venue and wrote to all Heads of Government, ensuring that attendance would be high and that participants would be in no doubt about the political significance of the event or the proposed changes.[64] He inserted his own staff, including Jeremy Pope, to deal with legal and drafting issues. It led the British Government to comment: "Mr Ramphal and his staff effectively ran the Special Assembly."[65] In so doing, the meeting delivered a recommended Code of Conduct which would allow the CGF to police the agreement (rather than member governments) and deal with any national member association, if necessary, by suspension, which stood accused of 'gross non-fulfilment'. Despite continuing reservations by the British and New Zealand governments, the constitutional changes were approved at the CGF General Assembly in Brisbane in the expectation that the Commonwealth Games would be protected from boycott.

It was not to last. If Ramphal thought that the Code of Conduct would be sufficient to insulate the Games from boycott in future, he was being unduly optimistic. Earlier in 1982, a further challenge to Gleneagles had emerged in the shape of a tour of South Africa by a 'rebel' English cricket team, led by Mike Gatting. The English Test and County Cricket Board took swift and firm action, banning the players concerned from Test match selection for three years. However, Thatcher once again appeared equivocal, being accused of being 'mealy mouthed' and prompting the resignation of the Black campaigner Paul Stephenson from the Sports Council because of her reluctance to personally condemn the tour.[66] This Thatcher denied, though she annotated Ramphal's letter to her with the comment: "The fact is that our capacity to *stop* people going to South Africa is *very small indeed*" (her emphasis).[67]

Two years later, a wholly different challenge emerged in the shape of a 17-year-old white South African athlete, Zola Budd. Budd had shown world-class promise as a long-distance runner but failed to get international recognition because of the sporting boycott of South Africa. In a grotesque parody of the D'Oliveira affair, David English, the editor of the *Daily Mail*, brought Budd to the UK and pressed the British Government to grant her immediate UK citizenship so that she could compete in the British team in the 1984 Los Angeles Olympics. While Budd had grounds to claim British citizenship through her British grandfather, her sincerity in embracing her new mother country was unconvincing and the speed with which she was granted citizenship was quite exceptional. Consideration of her case also coincided with the decision of the RFU to send an international side to South Africa. In vain did the Foreign Secretary, Sir Geoffrey Howe, urge the Home Secretary, Leon Brittan, to delay his approval and consider the wider implications: "I think we need to be careful to avoid giving the appearance of an unseemly rush. . . . The whole question of sport and South Africa is, as you know, a political minefield," and he warned that there might be "serious practical implications for the 1986 Edinburgh Commonwealth Games."[68]

The AAM condemned Budd's "passport of convenience" and protests, and disruption dogged her attempts to train and compete in the UK.[69] Ramsammy declared: "Our opposition to Budd lies in the fact that, by steadfastly refusing to denounce *apartheid*, she has allowed herself to become generally portrayed as a symbol of the system."[70] Although she took part in the 1984 Olympics in the 3,000 metres, she collided with her US rival, Mary Decker, earning the hostility of the crowd and finishing seventh in the race. Later, she and Annette Cowley (a South African swimmer who had also acquired British citizenship) were banned from the 1986 Commonwealth Games in Edinburgh in a vain attempt to stave off a major boycott. Budd later returned to South Africa and competed in the 1992 Olympics as part of the South African team. Llewellyn and Rider (2018) argue that Thatcher's stance on the Budd affair should be seen as part of her developing policy of 'constructive engagement' with South Africa in partnership with Ronald Reagan.[71]

In June 1984 Thatcher controversially received the South African State President, P.W. Botha, though the content of the meeting was later revealed as less supportive of South Africa than her critics alleged.[72] This followed the England Rugby

*Figure 7.1* Children protesting in defiance of the security forces. Commonwealth Secretariat.

tour of South Africa, by an inexperienced team, in May–June. Once again fallout from the English tour seem to have been diminished by a retaliatory socialist nations' boycott of the 1984 summer Olympics in Los Angeles. However, Thatcher's barely concealed disdain for Gleneagles had not gone unnoticed and the rift with the Commonwealth steadily widened, particularly after the 1985 Nassau CHOGM and the disagreement over sanctions. As it was, retribution was comprehensively visited on the 1986 Edinburgh Games, though by then Thatcher's implacable opposition to sanctions on South Africa also drove the boycott.

The actions of both Muldoon and Thatcher illustrate the strengths, and the weaknesses, of a Commonwealth approach that relies on achieving consensus on key issues, rather than by making international policy through majoritarian voting systems, such as in the UNGA. Bourne points out that "if consensus-building is difficult, it is also essential especially in a fractious and heterogeneous family like the Commonwealth."[73] Consensus requires all to be drawn into a commitment to a specific course of action with the expectation that this will be wholly honoured by the group. It can therefore be superior to a majoritarian voting system where the minority simply refuse to abide by the outcome and where deadlock and inaction are the results. The weakness of a consensual approach lies in the power given to the most reluctant participant in effect to reduce action to "the lowest common denominator."[74] Furthermore, on the most contentious issues, that minimal benchmark will almost certainly be achieved only by masking difference with the language of ambiguity and nuance, rather than by any legalistic clarity. In the case of Gleneagles, this vulnerability allowed Muldoon and Thatcher to protest that they remained faithful to upholding the agreement.

New Zealand could, with some justification, complain that Ramphal was less than even-handed in relation to those countries that violated the spirit of Gleneagles. Although he differed with Thatcher on many issues, Ramphal knew that he needed to work with her wherever he could, not only bound by duty to a prominent Head of Government but drawn by the necessities of realpolitik. He saw this as a Manichean struggle to engage her formidable intellect, which could be helpful to the outcome, and to supress her natural instincts, which would invariably complicate matters. He was also aware that confrontation with Thatcher, and her isolation, though sometimes necessary, was not the best ways of winning her round. In Lusaka and at Lancaster House, as in the early days of the sporting boycott, Ramphal had found this approach had worked well. However, after Zimbabwe's independence and as the Commonwealth's campaign against *apartheid* gathered strength, the relationship became much more strained.

As disputes over the sporting boycott turned to disagreements over economic and financial sanctions, Ramphal saw that holding to consensus in all circumstances might not only seriously weaken the Commonwealth's ability to act but also profoundly damage its credibility. The question, asked Ramphal, was whether the Commonwealth would be served by settling for "the lowest common factor of agreement when that means inviting everyone else to acquiesce in what they see as the misguided and, in some respects, contradictory position of a single member."[75] When the single dissenting member is also the one with the most political and economic leverage, the dilemma becomes acute.

The other area of growth after Gleneagles was in 'third party' boycotts. This involved shunning exchanges with not merely South Africa but also those teams and individuals who collaborated with *apartheid* sport. A principal initiator of such actions was the Jamaican Prime Minister, Michael Manley. Shortly after hosting the 1975 CHOGM meeting, he argued that the United Nations should adopt an international convention against *apartheid* in sport, though it was not until 1985 that such a convention was finally agreed and adopted.[76] By then, a Register of Sports Contacts with South Africa had been introduced and proved to be a potent device for influencing sporting figures, administrators and promoters. By the mid-1980s, the inclusion of blacklisted players in touring cricket teams was enough to threaten third-country boycotts, making the prospect of a Black–white split in international cricket much more likely.[77]

Naturally, the *apartheid* regime did all it could to counter the sporting boycott. Pretoria's propaganda offensive included a range of financial and other inducements offered to those who might be encouraged to break the boycott.[78] Sporting contact continued at individual level and, in a new tactic, with the growth of lucrative 'rebel' tours. In 1985, 2,807 sports competitors and coaches visited South Africa, with 1,691 South Africans competing abroad. As late as 1990, Mike Gatting was leading the "rebel" England cricket team to South Africa even as *apartheid* had finally begun to disintegrate. The South African Government also sought to exploit known differences between foreign governments and thereby weaken the resolve and unity of the international forces ranged against the *apartheid* state. For example, in 1983 the Ambassador of South Africa in London conveyed an invitation from Dr Viljoen, South Africa's Sports Minister, to Neil Macfarlane, his British counterpart, to visit the Republic and "acquaint yourself with the latest developments in sport in South Africa." This invitation, the ambassador assured the Minister, was given "in the spirit of constructive dialogue and . . . ensuring objectivity," while adding, disingenuously, that "sport is autonomous in South Africa."[79] In 1982, the Tonga High Commission reported the covert recruitment of three Tongan nationals for an unofficial rugby tour of South Africa, sponsored by a Hong Kong insurance company.[80] Caribbean cricket was also a natural target for South Africa with a 'rebel' West Indies tour arranged in 1983. This, contends Downes, was "more than an expensive buy-out from sporting isolation . . . it represented a serious destabilising insurgency."[81] It would therefore be wrong to conclude that challenges to the boycott were solely in the 'old' Commonwealth, though, individually and collectively, UK sports players were by far the most numerous of those transgressing the boycott.

At the same time, in some sports, such as cricket, there were open attempts in South Africa, both official and unofficial, to remove *apartheid* structures and promote multiracial teams in the quest for international acceptability.[82] This in turn drew the response that there could be no normal sport in an abnormal society.[83] Some developments in non-racial sport were closely aligned with the popular resistance to *apartheid* under the slogan: "One struggle for one democratic nation."[84] In some areas, Sport Action Committees were formed to demand the right to play non-racial sport.[85] Even so, in *apartheid's* final years a clear ambiguity became apparent. The United Nations sought to strengthen the boycott and in 1988 established a UN Commission against *Apartheid* in Sports six months after the International Convention against *Apartheid* in Sport had been ratified.[86] In October of the same year, a secret meeting took place in Harare between Danie Craven and others from South African rugby and a top ANC team, led by Thabo Mbeki. After two days of talks, it was agreed that the ANC would press for the ban on the Springboks to be lifted if South African rugby were reorganised on a non-racial basis. "From now onward," remarked Peter Hain,

> sport – instead of being an important means of confronting whites with the realisation that they had no alternative but to change – became a means of offering them a glimpse of a new post-*apartheid* South Africa in which their beloved sports tours could resume.[87]

Some Commonwealth countries and civil society organisations continued to resist, but the British Ambassador in South Africa assured London: "If we keep up the pressure, the boycott will crumble."[88] In September 1991, at a time when the ANC continued to oppose any lifting of international sanctions against South Africa, its

President, Nelson Mandela, wrote to the International Cricket Council supporting the application of the United Cricket Board of South Africa to be allowed to participate in the 1992 Cricket World Cup.[89] South Africa thus returned to international cricket and to other sports thereafter. In 1987, South Africa had suffered the humiliation of being excluded from the first Rugby World Cup. Less than ten years later, after Mandela's election as President of a non-racial and democratic 'rainbow' nation, the Springboks success at winning the 1995 World Cup became a source of unity for the reborn nation.

## 3   Conclusion

The chapter's primary focus has been on the Commonwealth's role in the sporting boycott of *apartheid*. But its actions also became intertwined with other dimensions of racism in Southern Africa, including the end of the Rhodesian rebellion and the eventual emergence of an independent Zimbabwe. The Commonwealth was also affected by non-Commonwealth issues, such as the Soviet-Afghan war and the boycott of the 1980 Moscow Olympics. Nevertheless, support for the sporting boycott had grown after the visiting All Blacks attempted to complete their 1976 South African tour against the backdrop of widespread township violence, including the killings of school students.[90] The Gleneagles Agreement followed, and the Commonwealth's diplomatic methods, and its capacity for influence, steadily expanded during the period.[91]

Keech and Houlihan have argued that the impact of Gleneagles was modest and that the Agreement "represented the limit of its capacity rather than a first step on a rising scale of sanctions."[92] McIntyre considers that Gleneagles "became the yardstick for governing sporting contacts," though the elaboration provided by a Code of Conduct became necessary.[93] This shifted responsibility for policing sporting contact with South Africa from governments to sports bodies themselves. Overall, the sporting boycott was part of a pattern of escalation which intensified into widespread economic sanctions after the Commonwealth's EPG mission to South Africa and the publication of its influential report in 1986. Excluding South Africans from international sport was not in itself what brought down *apartheid*, but it did contribute to the general isolation of South Africans from international contact of any kind. Gleneagles also helped settle the argument that 'sport should be kept out of politics'. In the case of *apartheid*, the system of 'separate development' had been deliberately entrenched in South African sport from 1956 onwards. This had made the injustice and inhumanity of the system all the more visible, particularly internationally. In the view of Ramphal, to talk of not bringing politics into sport at that point, when sport was already politicised, was "an alibi for perversity."[94] Conversely, as popular internal resistance increased after 1976, the non-white majority took heart from the humbling of Afrikanerdom on the sporting field.

Clearly, the actions taken by the Commonwealth were part of an international response, most notably expressed through the United Nations. While the UN

Special Committee Against *Apartheid* played a pivotal role across a range of organisations in encouraging action, much attention was focused on specific South African rugby and cricket tours between 1969 and 1985. The battleground was not only Britain, Australia and New Zealand but also the Caribbean, Ireland, France and the United States.

In all these conflicts, sympathetic governments maintained close contact with the AAM. After 1977, the Commonwealth Secretary-General and the Secretariat were frequently contacted by anti-*apartheid* groups around the Commonwealth concerned about breaches of the agreement. At first, no formal powers existed to police the agreement, but the perennial threat to disrupt the Commonwealth Games and other international sporting events proved to be a powerful weapon. The British AAM, two years after the adoption of the agreement, said: "The Gleneagles Agreement ... (has been) ... welcomed by all opponents of *apartheid* as a positive contribution to the international campaign against *apartheid*." But it urged: "More determined and vigorous action by the British Government and any other governments which have failed to secure the effective implementation of the Agreement."[95] This mounting criticism eventually contributed to a large-scale boycott of the 1986 Commonwealth Games.

As 'official' exchanges across the major sports dried up, the emphasis for anti-*apartheid* campaigners turned to 'third party' boycotts. This meant condemning official sporting exchanges with not merely South Africa but also those unofficial teams and individuals who collaborated with *apartheid* sport. While the prime initiator of this action was Michael Manley, the Caribbean itself was sometimes conflicted both in regard to government policy and in the attitudes to erring, sometimes high-profile, sporting figures. As Aviston Downes concludes: "West Indians and their governments were often divided and confused in their responses to the anti-*apartheid* campaign."[96] Nevertheless, the contribution of the Caribbean as a whole to the international anti-*apartheid* sport campaign was significant, argues Downes.

As the former colonial power, Britain had special connections to South Africa, both historic and contemporary, which provided opportunities for influence over the *apartheid* regime. This included cultural links with the English-speaking white population (which continued to expand in the post-war years with continuing emigration from the British Isles). These cultural ties were also true of India and South Africa's Indian population, though India's relationship with South Africa was much more detached and confrontational after 1945. In the same way, the geographic proximity of neighbouring African Commonwealth countries gave rise to similar linkages, particularly through migrant labour. But it was the Commonwealth's sporting traditions which opened the way to boycott and international isolation and which had such an effect on the South African white population. Unsurprisingly, it was the 'old' Commonwealth members of Australia, New Zealand and the UK (though not so much Canada with its rather different sports) which were in the firing line of the sporting boycott. It was the Commonwealth Games which repeatedly offered ideal leverage in upholding Gleneagles.[97]

## Notes

1. James Ivey, "Double standards: South Africa, British Rugby, and the Moscow Olympics," *The International Journal of the History of Sport* 36:1 (2019): 115.
2. Hain, *Don't Play with Apartheid*, 211.
3. Leaflets of the Western Province Council of Sport, UCT archives, Cape Town, Sport and *Apartheid* BAP 796.0968 SPOR.
4. BBC report, "3 May 1979," *BBC Politics 97*. www.bbc.co.uk/news/special/politics97/background/pastelec/ge79.shtml, Accessed 6 April 2022.
5. Leaflet, Stop All Racist Tours (SART), MSS AAM 1438, Accessed 2 June 2020, www.aamarchives.org/archive/campaigns/sport/spo09-stop-the-barbarians.html.
6. BBC News, "Anti-racists tackle South African rugby tourists," 3 October 1979, *BBC on This Day*, Accessed 2 June 2020, www.news.bbc.co.uk/onthisday/hi/dates/stories/October/3/newsid_2486000/2486623.stm.
7. Ivey, "Double standards: South Africa, British Rugby, and the Moscow Olympics," 107.
8. Ibid., 109.
9. Record, Ramphal and Thatcher, TNA, PREM 19/116.
10. Report, *Southern Rhodesia Constitutional Conference*, Lancaster House, September–December 1979, Accessed 2 June 2020, www.sas-space.sas.ac.uk/5847/5/1979_Lancaster_House_Agreement.
11. Ivey, "Double standards: South Africa, British Rugby and the Moscow Olympics," 109.
12. Record of a meeting between Margaret Thatcher and Salim Salim, 18 December 1979, New York, TNA, PREM 19/116.
13. Record of a meeting between Margaret Thatcher and Kurt Waldheim, 18 December 1979, New York, TNA, PREM 19/116
14. Conclusions of Cabinet, 20 December 1979, TNA, 128/66.
15. Correspondence from Shridath Ramphal to Margaret Thatcher, 19 December 1979, TNA, 19/116.
16. Matthew P. Llewellyn and Toby C. Rider, "Sport, Thatcher and *apartheid* politics: The Zola Budd affair," *Journal of Southern African Studies* 44:4 (2014): 578.
17. Draft correspondence from Margaret Thatcher to Raman Subba Row, 1 August 1989, TNA, PREM 19/3568/125.
18. Ibid., 126.
19. Correspondence from Margaret Thatcher to Mary Glen Haig, 27 May 1980, TNA, PREM 19/376, 3/98.
20. Correspondence from Margaret Thatcher to Abraham Ordia, 12 May 1980, TNA, PREM 19/3568/243.
21. Douglas Hurd, Text of article for the *Daily Express*, Friday, 27 June 1980, TNA, PREM 19/376.
22. Correspondence from Margaret Thatcher to sporting organisations, 16 June 1980, TNA, PREM 19/376/32.
23. Correspondence from P. Lever (PS to Lord Carrington) to M. Alexander (Prime Ministers' Office), 10 June 1980, TNA, PREM19/376/46.
24. Correspondence from Margaret Thatcher to Malcolm Fraser, 4 June 1980, TNA, PREM/376/76, 77.
25. Correspondence from Lever to Alexander, 9 June 1980, TNA, PREM19/376/69.
26. Record of a meeting between Margaret Thatcher and Robert Muldoon, 31 May 1980, TNA, PREM 19/376.
27. Cable from Smedley, FM Wellington, to FCO, 6 June 1980, TNA, PREM 19/376.
28. Ivey, "Double standards: South Africa, British Rugby, and the Moscow Olympics," 115.
29. Ibid., 114.
30. Correspondence from Abraham Ordia to K.S. Duncan, 20 November 1980, Commonwealth Secretariat archives, London, 2011/118/1, 86.
31. Downes, "Sport and international diplomacy," 32.

32 John Carlisle, "How the West has been fooled in South Africa," *The Guardian*, 9 June 1980, Commonwealth Secretariat archives, 2012/074/1, 46.
33 "From Montreal to Gleneagles," *NZ History*, Accessed 5 June 2020, www.nzhistory.govt.nz/culture/1981-springbok-tour-battle-lines-are-drawn.
34 Donald Macintosh and Michael Hawes, *Sport and Canadian Diplomacy* (Montreal & Kingston: McGill-Queen's University Press, 1994), 111.
35 AUS Commonwealth Games website, "Brisbane 1982: Patriotism, Moments and Matilda," Accessed 19 April 2020, www.commonwealthgames-com-au/Brisbane-1982-patriotism-moments-and-matilda/.
36 Radio New Zealand, "Australia considered option of NZ Games ban," 13 June 2012, Accessed 19 April 2020, www.radionz.co.nz/news/national/108121/australia-considered-option-of-nz-games-ban.
37 Circular letter from Shridath Ramphal to Commonwealth governments, "Venue of Commonwealth Finance Ministers' Meeting 1981," 20 June 1981, Commonwealth Secretariat archives c/on I 40/73/2.
38 Correspondence from Robert Muldoon to Shridath Ramphal, 21 June 1981, Commonwealth Secretariat archives, c/on I 40/73/2 32b.
39 Ibid., 1.
40 News Release by the Commonwealth Secretariat, "Springbok tour of New Zealand," 13 July 1981, Commonwealth Secretariat archive APP/81/11.
41 Shridath Ramphal, "A time to be forward looking," Opening remarks, Special Meeting of the Commonwealth Games Federation, Marlborough House, London, 5 May 1982, Commonwealth Secretariat archives, 2014/093, 2/2, 4.4.
42 Donald McKinnon, "Mandela and the Commonwealth: Identifying and upholding Commonwealth values," *The Round Table: The Commonwealth Journal of International Affairs* 106:6 (2017): 648.
43 Robert Muldoon, "Why my small country is now being rent asunder," *The Times*, 28 July 1981, London.
44 Shridath Ramphal, "How Muldoon let the side down," *The Times*, 5 August 1981, London.
45 Colin Legum, "Muldoon silences African critics," *The Observer Syndication Service*, 2 October 1981, Melbourne, UCT archives, Colin Legum Papers, BC 1329 06.1.7.
46 Macintosh and Hawes, *Sport and Canadian Diplomacy*, 111.
47 Commonwealth Secretariat, *The Commonwealth at the Summit* (Vol.1), 225.
48 Correspondence from Robert Muldoon to Malcolm Fraser, 27 October 1981, Commonwealth Secretariat archives, 2012/074/1, 102.
49 Text of Robert Muldoon's television address, 6 July 1981, Commonwealth Secretariat archives, APP/81/11.
50 "1981 Springbok tour: Impact," *NZ History*, Accessed 5 June 2020, www.nzhistory.govt.nz/culture/1981-springbok-tour/ompac-if-the-tour, 8.
51 Alastair Carthew, "New Zealand-South Africa rugby: No-win situation for both countries," 14 September 1981, *The Christian Science Monitor*, Accessed 2 June 2020, www.csmonitor.com/layout/1981/0914/091433.html.
52 Correspondence from Hector Munro to Lord Carrington, 8 September 1981, and attached Memorandum: Sport in South Africa: Towards non-racialism, TNA, PREM 19/3568/224.
53 Cable from Robert Armstrong to Leon Brittan, 1 October 1981, TNA, PREM 19/3568/216.
54 Telegram from Lord Carrington to Margaret Thatcher, TNA, PREM 19/3568/212–214.
55 Correspondence from W.L. Smith, PS to Minister of Sport, to Willie Rickett, PS No.10, 2 October 1981, TNA, PREM 19/3568/206.
56 Minutes of a meeting between Neil Macfarlane and Shridath Ramphal, 20 September 1982, TNA, PREM19/3568/171.
57 When Ramphal next met Muldoon, following Pope's recruitment, he informed the New Zealand premier of the appointment in line with the usual Commonwealth protocol.

"You can keep him!" was Muldoon's reported response (email, Max Gaylard to the author, 23 June 2020).
58 Ramsammy and Griffiths, *Reflections*, 74.
59 Report by Trevor Richards, "The international campaign against *apartheid* in sport: Policy and organisational requirements," January 1979, Commonwealth Secretariat archives, 2010/055/1, 8.
60 Official Records of the UN General Assembly, Thirty-Second Session, Wednesday, 14 December 1977, Accessed 7 September 2019, www.research.un.org/A_32_PV.102-EN (1).
61 Ibid., Resolution 32/105M/212.
62 Correspondence from Ordia to Duncan, 2.
63 Sir Alexander Ross was Chairman of the CGF 1968–82. A New Zealand-born banker and rower, he had won a bronze medal in New Zealand's Coxless Fours at the British Empire Games in 1930.
64 Circular letter from Shridath Ramphal to Commonwealth Heads of Government, 22 April 1982, TNA, PREM19/3568/179,180.
65 Correspondence from W.L. Smith to M.A. Arthur, 23 September 1982, TNA, PREM 19/3568/169.
66 Correspondence from Paul Stephenson to Neil McFarlane, 8 March 1982, TNA, PREM19/3568/199.
67 Correspondence from Shridath Ramphal to Margaret Thatcher, 11 March 1982, TNA, PREM19/3568/188.
68 Memorandum from Geoffrey Howe to Leon Brittan, 23 March 1984, TNA, PREM 19/3568/157.
69 Annual Report of the Anti-*Apartheid* Movement, September 1984, Accessed 3 June 2018, Aluka Digital Library www.aluka.org/action/showMetadata?doi=10.5555/AL.SFF.DOCUMENT.aam00062.
70 Ramsammy and Griffiths, *Reflections*, 95.
71 Llewellyn and Rider, "Sport, Thatcher and *apartheid* politics," 576.
72 Martin Plaut, "What really happened when Margaret Thatcher met South Africa's P.W. Botha," *New Statesman*, 3 January 2014, Accessed 19 April 2020, www.newstatesman.com/world-affairs/2014/01/'what-really-happened-when-margaret-thatcher-met-south-africas-p-w-botha.
73 Richard Bourne, "Forging Commonwealth consensus: The buck stops with the Secretary-General," *Opinions*, Commonwealth Advisory Bureau, Institute of Commonwealth Studies (London: CAB, 2012), 4.
74 Ibid., 6.
75 Shridath Ramphal, "Preserving the Commonwealth heritage," Address to the Diplomatic and Commonwealth Writers Association, 15 July 1986, London, Commonwealth Secretariat archives, C.152–40/3/2 HGM (1986) COMGEP, 2.
76 Resolution 40/64G of the United Nations General Assembly, 10 December 1985, Accessed 12 February 2020, www.research.un.org/en/docs/ga/quick/regular/40.
77 Murray and Merrett, *Caught Behind*, 209.
78 Conference paper from the African National Congress (ANC), "*Apartheid* propaganda offensive," Commonwealth media workshop on countering *apartheid* propaganda, 20–22 May 1985, Marlborough House, London, 10–21.
79 Correspondence from Marais Steyn, Ambassador for South Africa, to Neil McFarlane, 30 August 1983, TNA, PREM 19/3658, 168.
80 Correspondence from Inoke Faletau, High Commissioner for Tonga, to Shridath Ramphal, 9 August 1982, Commonwealth Secretariat archives, 2014/093, 66.
81 Downes, "Sport and international diplomacy," 35.
82 Martin, "South African sport: *Apartheid's* Achilles heel?" 242–3.
83 Douglas Booth, "Hitting *apartheid* for six? The politics of the South African sports boycott," *Journal of Contemporary History* 38:3 (2003): 492.

84  Leaflet by Western Province Council of Sport (supporting SACOS), UCT archives, BAP968/19a.
85  Leaflet by SACOS, "Sports action committees: Why they are necessary," UCT archives, BAP968.
86  By 1990, fifteen Commonwealth countries were among the sixty states ratifying the Convention, Accessed 19 April 2020, www.whatconvention.org/en/ratifications/303.
87  Hain, *Inside Out*, 77.
88  Cable from Robin Renwick to FCO (Commonwealth posts), February 1991, TNA, PREM19/3568, 120.
89  Correspondence from Nelson Mandela, President ANC, to Colin Cowdrey, Chairman ICC, 25 September 1991, TNA, PREM 19/3568, 016.
90  McIntyre, *The Significance of the Commonwealth*, 102–3.
91  Chan, *The Commonwealth in World Politics*, 41.
92  Keech and Houlihan, "Sport and the end of *apartheid*," 119.
93  McIntyre, *The Significance of the Commonwealth*, 103.
94  Ingram, "A quiet conference," 322.
95  Report by the Anti-*Apartheid* Movement, "Britain and *apartheid* sport," to the 1979 CHOGM, Zambia, Anti-*Apartheid* Movement archives, Bodleian Library, Oxford, MSS AAM 1297.
96  Downes, "Sport and international diplomacy," 40.
97  Donald Macintosh, Donna Greenhorn and David Black, "Canadian diplomacy and the 1978 Edmonton Commonwealth Games," *Journal of Sport History* 19:1 (1992): 51.

## References

Commonwealth Secretariat, *The Commonwealth at the Summit (Vol.1)*, Op.Cit.
Murray and Merrett, *Caught Behind*, Op.Cit.
Peter Hain, *Don't Play with Apartheid*, Op.Cit.
Peter Hain, *Inside Out*, Op.Cit.
Ramsammy and Griffiths, *Reflections, Op.Cit.*
Stephen Chan, *The Commonwealth in World Politics*, Op.Cit.
W. David McIntyre, *The Significance of the Commonwealth*, Op.Cit.

# 8 Zimbabwe's Birth – Thatcher's Triumph?

## 1 Introduction

While profound disagreements over the British Government's handling of UDI in 1965 aroused deep passions and brought the Commonwealth close to collapse, it encouraged the new organisation, and particularly the Secretary-General, to create collective and autonomous mechanisms and policies which were key to the association's development. At the heart of this growth over the next fifteen years was the Commonwealth's claim to be developing a distinctive and effective diplomatic method. This in turn raised the broader issue of whether the effectiveness of the Commonwealth's operating processes was uniquely bound up with the leadership skills and other attributes of individual Secretaries-General or whether the involvement of the office, as an initiating and coordinating mechanism, was sufficient in itself. This was the question posed by Chan in contemplating Ramphal's retirement at the end of his fifteen years' tenure: "Can the Secretariat sustain itself as an international actor if . . . the Secretary-Generalship devolves upon a person of less capacious gifts?"[1]

Arnold Smith had proved himself the right person to be entrusted with the difficult task of establishing the Commonwealth Secretariat and carving out a distinctive and substantive role both for the organisation and for the high office he filled. In 1975, with Smith's health faltering, Shridath Ramphal, the young and dynamic Minister of Foreign Affairs from Guyana, was elected by Heads of Government to succeed Smith at the Kingston CHOGM, chaired by the Jamaican Prime Minister, Michael Manley. It was to be some months before Ramphal would take up office, but, once again, Southern Africa took up much of the summit's agenda. In a novel development, Bishop Abel Muzorewa, the President of the African National Council, led a united delegation of nationalists, including the Zimbabwe African National Union (ZANU) and the Zimbabwe African People's Union (ZAPU) to meet with Commonwealth leaders. After some discussion about the sanctity of a Heads-Only summit, the leaders decided that they should meet the delegation in 'informal session', a point reinforced by the Canadian Prime Minister, Pierre Trudeau, who left his official seat for more casual seating near the nationalist group.[2]

Commonwealth governments recognised that new realities were taking hold in the region. International sanctions were clearly proving ineffective, and Heads "took note" of the determination of African freedom fighters to achieve independence on the basis of majority rule, an objective which had their total support, to be achieved peacefully if at all possible. However, they recognised the "inevitability of intensified armed struggle" should peaceful avenues be blocked by the regime.[3] That certainly now seemed the most likely course. Within Rhodesia, low-level guerrilla activity had been overtaken by a much more intensive liberation war, the 'Second Chimurenga'. In turn, the Rhodesian Army was responding with a more aggressive approach, including extensive mining operations, 'hot pursuit' beyond its borders, including attacks on guerrilla bases in neighbouring countries and the deployment of chemical and biological weapons. Externally, a military coup d'état in Portugal in 1974, against the *Estado Novo* of Marcelo Caetano, had ushered in the 'Carnation Revolution' and opened the way to democracy. It had also led to the collapse of Portugal's African empire. After Portugal's hasty withdrawal from Mozambique, Rhodesia was now surrounded on three sides by hostile neighbours. At the same time, South African military and financial support began to waver, as the *apartheid* government came to appreciate the impossibility of propping up the beleaguered Rhodesian regime over the long term. Some kind of negotiated settlement to the conflict now became inescapable.

The eventual agreement which began to take form in Lusaka in August 1979 and finally solidified into a deliverable outcome at Lancaster House, in December 1979, is sometime presented as Mrs Thatcher's greatest foreign policy triumph. However, the influence of the Commonwealth in shaping the outline of the settlement and supporting the inclusion of the Patriotic Front of Zimbabwe (PF) in any agreement was critical in enabling the birth of the new nation through Zimbabwe's national elections in March 1980. The Commonwealth presence at the British-administered polls was substantial, both through the deployment of a Commonwealth Observer Group (COG), led by Ambassador Rajeshwar Dayal, of India, and through a Commonwealth Monitoring Force (CMF) charged with supervising the ceasefire and facilitating a peaceful transition of power. Judged on the results, the overwhelming victory of Robert Mugabe and his ZANU-PF party came as a considerable shock to the British Government and suggested a profound policy miscalculation which did not produce the consequences that the British Government's actions had intended. Arguably, this was to colour Thatcher's dealings with the Commonwealth thereafter.

## 2 The Lusaka CHOGM 1979

Thatcher's electoral triumph in May 1979 presented the Commonwealth with an immediate challenge on Rhodesia. In line with the Conservative's manifesto commitment, she wished to move to early recognition of Bishop Muzorewa's government of 'Rhodesia/Zimbabwe', after an internal settlement and elections which many internationally considered to be 'flawed'. In the eyes of the United Nations, it was an agreement which was "illegal and unacceptable."[4] At the same time, it had become abundantly clear that a prolonged and bruising guerrilla war and Rhodesia's virtual encirclement rendered military resistance ultimately futile. A decisive factor was South Africa's unwillingness to commit to all-out conflict on Rhodesia's behalf.[5] All this had helped move the Smith regime towards a negotiated outcome, though not necessarily one based on the principles which British, Commonwealth and international opinion had deemed essential. The question was, would Thatcher's commitment to the 'internal settlement' prevail, or would a more inclusive, and internationally acceptable, agreement be possible?

There is a body of literature which argues that a constitutional settlement was achieved through three factors. Firstly, that there was a significant change of mindset within the British Foreign Office which in turn changed the thinking of the new Foreign Secretary, Lord Carrington. This was based on the argument that the UK alone needed to take the lead in delivering a solution in negotiation with the principal parties, rather than through a multilateral framework. Secondly, that securing Commonwealth support for this approach was successfully achieved by Thatcher in charming Commonwealth leaders at the Lusaka 1979 summit. Thirdly, that it was the skill and persistence of Lord Carrington alone which secured a constitutional settlement at Lancaster House and that it was the diplomacy and leadership of Lord Soames, as the temporary Governor of 'Southern Rhodesia', that managed to keep together all the parties through the process of demilitarisation and largely peaceful elections to achieve the ultimate goal of independence and an end to colonial rule.[6] It is thus frequently presented as a British triumph and, more personally, as evidence supporting the view that "Thatcher qualifies as an international statesman of the first rank."[7]

There are several reasons to challenge this prevailing Anglocentric discourse and to give far greater weight to the role of the Commonwealth in these events. The Commonwealth's first formidable task was to dissuade the newly elected Conservative Government from implementing its manifesto commitment to recognise the Smith-Muzorewa government and the 'internal settlement'.[8] From May 1979 until the opening of the Commonwealth summit in August, all Commonwealth effort was thrown into this immediate task. Initially, Carrington seemed at one with his Prime Minister in wanting to recognise Muzorewa's mandate, stating that "it would be morally wrong to brush aside an election in which 64% of the people cast their vote."[9] He was therefore minded to accept the judgement of his political colleague, Viscount Boyd of Merton, that the elections were free and fair. By contrast, the Liberal Peer, Lord Chitnis, who had also been present in a separate observer group, declared the elections "fraudulent."[10] Thatcher herself was convinced that "the UK no longer had any basis for maintaining the illegality of Rhodesia's situation."[11] Indeed, on a visit to Australia in June she came close to public recognition of the interim government.[12]

However, Carrington's early enthusiasm began to subside. He told the Cabinet that moving too quickly could have "adverse consequences for our international interests." While the Prime Minister accepted this approach, she added: "We should not assume that we had much time before we would need to reach and announce a firm decision on recognition."[13] Nonetheless, Carrington argued that it was the British Government's duty "to achieve a return to legality in conditions of the widest possible international recognition." He added: "I attach special importance to the closest possible consultations with our partners in the Commonwealth."[14] In turn, Ramphal was quick to point out to Carrington the shortcomings of the internal settlement constitution, arguing that "at best, the Constitution is a 'transitional' document, but no end to the transitional period is assured or predictable."[15] It therefore became increasingly unlikely that Carrington would be able to secure the widespread recognition for Muzorewa he had sought. Much more resistant to persuasion was the Prime Minister herself, but she was at least encouraged to take no precipitous action, such as recognition or promising to lift sanctions, that might have caused difficulties at the impending Commonwealth summit.[16] The other aspect of preventing recognition of a flawed 'internal settlement' lay in seeking to neutralise the lobbying of Bishop Muzorewa. Despite this, on 15 July, Muzorewa confided that he thought his government was "close to recognition."[17] By then, the Lusaka CHOGM was a mere two weeks away, and any statement of recognition by the British Government would have been highly provocative.

There was also the question of what role, if any, the Lusaka summit might play in shaping British policy. A succession of British Prime Ministers since Harold Wilson had discovered the uncomfortable realities of the modern Commonwealth. Many had seen the CHOGM as an occasion to be endured. Accordingly, Carrington warned Thatcher that Lusaka would be "a damage-limitation exercise."[18] Thatcher feared for her personal safety and was also concerned about "provocative action" by Soviet agents believed to be in the Zambian capital.[19] Ramphal helped allay these concerns, and he helped negotiate a ceasefire by the Zimbabwe People's Revolutionary Army (ZIPRA), based in Zambia, which might have threatened air traffic. In particular, he urged Commonwealth leaders to surprise Mrs Thatcher with their 'calm reason'. In turn, he assured the British Prime Minister that there would be no 'ganging up' by other Heads, and he advised her to send them a 'positive signal'. With the FCO team (particularly Anthony Duff and Robin Renwick) urging an approach that would see responsibility for agreement returning to Britain and being accompanied by negotiations on a new constitution in line with other independence settlements, some sort of all-party constitutional conference became increasingly likely.

In the event, that appeal to positivity triumphed with a mood of conciliation and a desire to find a workable solution apparent at the conference's opening session at Mulungushi Hall. Thatcher assured her colleagues that her government was "wholly committed to genuine black majority rule in Rhodesia," adding: "The aim is to bring Rhodesia to legal independence on a basis which the Commonwealth and the international community as a whole will find acceptable; and which offers the prospect of peace for the people of Rhodesia and its neighbours."[20] Malcolm Fraser declared: "As formidable as the differences on some issues are . . . they are differences about means and timing, not about ends. We must not allow means to dominate ends."[21] Members of the accompanying British press corps were struck by the British Prime Minister's moderate tone, following as it did the absence of the expected recognition of Bishop Muzorewa. *The Observer* ascribed this shift to the influence of Lord Carrington, saying: "The voice was Mrs Thatcher but the guiding hand was unmistakably that of Lord Carrington."[22]

*Figure 8.1* President Kenneth Kaunda, Ziaur Rahman, President of Bangladesh, and Mrs Margaret Thatcher (with Lord Carrington) at the opening session of the 1979 Lusaka CHOGM. Commonwealth Secretariat.

After a productive debate, Ramphal drew on the discussion to identify areas of agreement and give shape to a draft 'Heads of Accord'. He then convened a small and carefully balanced group of key Heads – Kaunda, the Zambian host (along with his key adviser, Mark Chona); Nyerere of Tanzania; Fraser of Australia; Manley of Jamaica; Adefope, representing Nigeria; and Thatcher and Carrington. After intensive work, what was to become the Lusaka Accord was born. It was, judged Ramphal, "a monumental achievement for the Commonwealth," adding: "The Commonwealth accomplished more in three hours than in nearly twenty years of often bitter argument."[23] Despite a flurry of final difficulties, the draft Accord was approved by Heads of Government as a whole before being released to the waiting media. "When the crunch came to save the Lusaka Accord," declared Ramphal, "it was Mrs Thatcher's nerve that held."[24] Indisputably, the Zambian summit was a personal triumph for Thatcher. "We knew what we wanted and we got it," recorded Carrington.[25] Thatcher was no less definitive: "Many had believed that we could not come out of Lusaka with an agreement on the lines we wanted. We had proved them wrong."[26]

But the Lusaka Accord was also a Commonwealth triumph. While it was clear that it was the constitutional responsibility of the British Government to give legal independence on the basis of genuine Black majority rule, the imprint of the

Commonwealth in framing the context of that task was unmistakable. The internal settlement constitution was dismissed as "defective in certain important respects."[27] It was recognised that "the search for a lasting settlement must involve all parties to the conflict," including the liberation forces of the PF, despite Thatcher's earlier description of them as "terrorists" with whom she would not do business.[28] The independent government that emerged would need to be chosen by free and fair elections "properly supervised under British Government authority, and with Commonwealth observers."[29] A cessation of hostilities and an end to sanctions would be linked to the implementation of a lasting settlement. Such a settlement would come, urged Commonwealth leaders, from the British Government calling a constitutional conference involving all the parties, and this the British Government now intended to do. The Lusaka CHOGM therefore extracted a range of concessions from the British Government. But in return it provided the international legitimacy for the process which Carrington sought. On 9 August, fresh from Lusaka, he wrote:

> I believe that we must now move quickly to take advantage of the agreement reached at Lusaka. We have been in close touch with Bishop Muzorewa throughout and he already knows, from his talks with the Prime Minister in London, what we have in mind.[30]

The next day, Carrington told the Cabinet:

> The Bishop would be expected to attend the conference and the Patriotic Front would probably do so, under pressure from the Front-Line Presidents. At the conference, agreement with the Patriotic Front might well not be reached, but if so they would appear in a bad light and we could hope to carry moderate international opinion with us over independence arrangements we would then reach with Bishop Muzorewa.

Carrington went on to acknowledge that if agreement was reached with all the parties

> there would be even greater difficulties to be overcome as regards the transitional arrangements, including the elections to which it has been necessary to agree in the Lusaka document as the natural corollary of the new constitution, but these would be under British supervision and would be a price worth paying in order to end the war.[31]

At the end of August, Mrs Thatcher reinforced this dual approach:

> The Prime Minister, summing up a short discussion, said that while the chances of reaching agreement all round at the Constitutional Conference were not good, we should be well placed to convince moderate international opinion that any breakdown was the fault of our opponents.[32]

138  *Zimbabwe's Birth – Thatcher's Triumph?*

The first four months of Thatcher's premiership had passed, and the dominant issue had been Rhodesia and the looming Commonwealth summit in Lusaka. By contrast, the UK government's approach to the Gleneagles Agreement on sporting links with South Africa had not registered in Commonwealth circles as a matter of immediate concern. It had not been flagged by Ramphal as an item for debate at the Lusaka CHOGM in his annotated agenda letter to all Heads of Government in June.[33] To the surprise of the British Government, the implementation of the Gleneagles Agreement did not even arise in August during the Lusaka discussions, though British officials recognised the issue as "very much a matter of Commonwealth concern."[34] Clearly, Commonwealth leaders had more immediate pressures on their minds.

## 3  The Lancaster House Agreement

In September 1979, at the opening of the Lancaster House conference in London, Carrington gave generous recognition to the Commonwealth's contribution. "The agreement reached at Lusaka," he said, "has made it possible for the British Government to convene this Conference with the very real hope that it will lead to an internationally acceptable settlement." He continued: "I would like to pay tribute to the Commonwealth Heads of Government and the Commonwealth Secretary-General, all of whom worked so hard at Lusaka to establish an agreed position."[35] But he also made it clear that this was not a Commonwealth initiative. No Commonwealth delegation was invited to attend, and, in the eyes of the UK government, the Commonwealth's work was now done. In any case, as Carrington privately confided, given the Commonwealth's robust support for the Patriotic Front, Ramphal had "no credibility as an impartial observer."[36] How therefore could the Commonwealth hope to contribute to the successful conclusion of the Lancaster House talks?

If the Commonwealth was not permitted to be in Lancaster House, its presence in proximity to the conference, based at Marlborough House, was constant, vocal and visible. Ramphal saw the association as collectively responsible for the proper implementation of the Lusaka Accord, and he used all the means at his disposal to give substance to the viewpoint of the Commonwealth and the active pressure it could therefore bring to bear. He arranged for a senior FCO official to brief Commonwealth High Commissioners daily, if necessary, on progress in the conference. By the time the negotiations had been concluded, around thirty such meetings had been held. They served as an immediate channel of intelligence from the London diplomatic representatives of Commonwealth member countries to their capitals and governments. Ramphal also convened regular meetings of the recently established Commonwealth Committee on Southern Africa. This body, which had replaced the Commonwealth Sanctions Committee and was similar in composition to the High Commissioners' briefings, provided a forum for developing Commonwealth policy and exerting suitable pressure as the conference progressed.

The other crucial channel of communication between Ramphal and the Commonwealth was with Heads of Government themselves – in particular, African

*Figure 8.2* Simon Muzenda, Robert Mugabe and Joshua Nkomo of the Patriotic Front at the Lancaster House Constitutional talks, London, 1979. Commonwealth Secretariat.

leaders such as Kaunda, Nyerere and Olusegun Obasanjo (of Nigeria), as well as Manley and Fraser. Ramphal was constantly on the telephone to leaders who in turn instructed their representatives on what should be said in London; to which the Secretary-General could then respond. Ramphal's mandate as the Commonwealth's public servant was thus the product of a living, vibrant and symbiotic relationship. Chan, who witnessed these events at first hand, remarked: "Ramphal's role, both at the Lusaka summit and throughout the Lancaster House talks, significantly extended the role of the Commonwealth Secretary-General. His was an activist role, played from the position of a responsive servant of the Commonwealth."[37] Like at the Retreat in Gleneagles in 1977, Ramphal proved adept at overcoming obstacles and moving forward by marshalling multiple points of diplomatic pressure.

There were three key issues on which Commonwealth intervention proved to be decisive. Firstly, the Commonwealth had taken upon itself the role of being the principal supporter and resource of the PF parties, and it insisted that the PF could not be excluded from any viable solution. This was in opposition to Lord Carrington's approach of 'divide and rule'. In a time-honoured imperial tactic, Carrington would play off one party against the other, reaching agreement with one, only for this 'solution' to be presented to the other, with a deadline for its acceptance. At times,

Carrington seemed quite prepared to accept the second-best option of an agreement concluded by only some of the parties. Driven by his bottom line of ABM (Anyone But Mugabe), Carrington was suspected of manoeuvring to secure for Bishop Abel Muzorewa (or perhaps a Muzorewa/Nkomo coalition) that outcome which the late 'internal settlement' could not.[38] Whether in dialogue with the British Government or, sometimes, with the PF, the Commonwealth insisted that the Conference hold on to the Lusaka principle of 'inclusivity': that, in the words of the Lusaka Accord, "the search for a lasting settlement must involve all parties to the conflict."[39] In the end, that view prevailed.

Secondly, the Commonwealth argued forcefully for a solution to the land issue, which the liberation forces and many others in Africa saw as central to any lasting solution. In the opening speeches at the start of the Lancaster House conference, Joshua Nkomo asked rhetorically: "What will be the future of the people's land?"[40] It was clear that the British Government had no answer to that question or plans to address the land issue, other than to enshrine property rights in the Independence Constitution, which would be protected from amendment during the ten-year transitional period. It took the intervention of Ramphal with the US government to help establish a fund for land redistribution under the Constitution. Once the British Government had been encouraged to participate in this multinational donor fund, the way was clear to keep the Patriotic Front on board. In Ramphal's view it "saved the conference."[41]

Thirdly, the Commonwealth resisted attempts to dilute any role the organisation might have in the observation of the elections and the monitoring of the transition. The Lusaka Accord had spoken of the new Zimbabwean government being chosen "through free and fair elections properly supervised under British Government authority, and with Commonwealth observers."[42] The presence of Commonwealth observers had only been accepted by the UK with some reluctance, the British Government preferring a reference to 'international observers'. At Lancaster House a row now broke out about the interpretation of this commitment. Did it mean, as the British maintained, that observers would be invited from individual Commonwealth countries to be embedded into the arrangements organised by the Governor, Lord Soames, the sole authority in the transition period? Or was it to be a collective Commonwealth presence, aiming to operate independently, with its own advisers and support staff, and seeking to deliver a unified Commonwealth view on the validity of the elections (rather than having its voice fragmented, uncoordinated and diminished in possibly contradictory national viewpoints). In the end, and marshalling all the Commonwealth strength he could muster, Ramphal's interpretation of the Accord prevailed. "The Commonwealth Observer role which assisted in confirming the validity of those elections would be a seal of assurance of great importance to Zimbabwe's future," he declared.[43] By 3 December, Nkomo confided that he was 'on the bus' and a more reluctant Mugabe was expected to follow.[44] The British Government's tenacity and patience had been rewarded and a historic settlement achieved. But it was an agreement made possible by the Commonwealth's active, if off-stage, involvement.

## 4 Zimbabwe's Birth

Lancaster House had delivered an inclusive constitutional settlement, but the final outcome would be determined by elections overseen by a British governor and by the temporary reversion of 'Southern Rhodesia' to the status of a crown colony. The elections would be monitored by a Commonwealth Observer Group, and a Commonwealth military force, with personnel drawn from the UK, Australia, Fiji, Kenya and New Zealand, would make up the CMF. This would help uphold the ceasefire and then facilitate the peaceful mustering of former combatants at designated assembly points.

During the Lancaster House talks the suspicion had arisen that the Commonwealth's strenuous attempts to prevent the PF leaving the conference were actually frustrating a covert aim of British policy. Declassified papers later revealed that on 1 November, Carrington told the Cabinet: "If the PF withdrew, we would carry out our transitional plan in agreement with Bishop Muzorewa. We could not then expect much general international support . . . independence would be conferred at the end of the transitional period."[45] Lord Luce, then a junior Foreign Office Minister, recounts that Duff and Renwick "contributed to the influence on Carrington at a certain

*Figure 8.3* Commonwealth election observers meet a white voter, Rhodesia/Zimbabwe, 1980. Commonwealth Secretariat.

stage that we should do a deal just with Joshua Nkomo and exclude Mugabe."[46] When Luce and his ministerial colleague, Ian Gilmour, got wind that this was Carrington's intention they both threatened resignation, and the matter was dropped.[47]

Even so, the British Government seemed to have a fall-back position. Carrington had conceded that Muzorewa should step down from office to contest the elections, to the Bishop's evident dismay. The British Foreign Secretary had also eventually accepted proposals for a collective and independent Commonwealth monitoring presence at the elections (making the electoral disqualification of Mugabe and ZANU-PF far less likely). But, despite this, there was a universal British view, also supported by Rhodesian and South African intelligence forces, that even if Muzorewa and Sithole were not able to win outright, the most likely result would be one resulting in a Muzorewa/Nkomo coalition.[48] In vain did Commonwealth opinion attempt to persuade the British Government otherwise. Indeed, so strong was the British view, it probably served to neutralise any pre-emptive military action by General Peter Walls, who seemed convinced that Thatcher could be trusted to frustrate a Mugabe victory.[49] Once the election result was known, it was far too late to mount a successful coup, though there is evidence that contingency plans had been put in place but never activated.

The triumph of Mugabe and ZANU-PF, winning 63% of the popular vote, while no surprise to the Commonwealth, came as a devastating blow to Thatcher and Carrington. As Hugo Young put it, "Robert Mugabe . . . was not meant to win the election." He continued: "The British expectation, and certainly hope, was for a more malleable independent government, formed by an alliance between Joshua Nkomo and Bishop Muzorewa."[50] Former Conservative Minister, Mark Robinson, remarked: "It was a gigantic miscalculation."[51] Lord Carrington confided to his diaries this masterly understatement: "I cannot say that the Election's results . . . were exactly what we had anticipated or that they gave to the British Government undiluted pleasure." He later spelt out the domestic hazards the British Government faced: "Politically, we stood to suffer a lot of criticism – a misconceived settlement, an inappropriate election, a corrupt result, a betrayed kith and kin. I was unrepentant at our efforts but I can't pretend I was happy."[52] His intentions had thus been the complete opposite of those sometimes ascribed to him.[53] As for the Prime Minister, far from being her greatest foreign policy triumph, Thatcher had reason to rue the smooth blandishments she received from the Foreign Office and privately regretted that "we have given it to the Communist."[54]

Zimbabwe's joyous independence celebrations took place on 18 April, presided over by the Prince of Wales and in the presence of many international leaders who had helped the new country's birth. The initial mood of reconciliation, particularly with Zimbabwe's whites, extended to sport. The new nation had no difficulty in sending a partially integrated national rugby team to tour the UK, while simultaneously being involved in a regional boycott of the Lions rugby tour to South Africa.[55] It did not join the boycott of the Moscow Olympics, and its (all-white) women's field hockey team caused a major upset by winning the gold medal, Zimbabwe's first in any category. It seemed that the UK had been fortunate not to attract greater criticism of the Lions' South African tour. A report to Carrington after the visit had ended mused: "Superficially at least, the 1980 Lions' tour did the morale of white South Africans no end of good." The official concluded his report by stating that although the government had opposed the tour, it had gone ahead and "in the context of South Africa today I believe both decisions were right."[56] If that assessment captured the dominant political mood, it was certainly not the approach of the FCO generally.

## 5 The Fifth Brigade, Matabeleland and the *Gukurahundi*

If the UK's relations with South Africa during the *apartheid* era were riven by ambiguity, this ambivalence was also true of the British relationship with Commonwealth Africa. Mugabe's decisive victory in Zimbabwe's independence elections, in March 1980, had come as a complete shock to Thatcher and to her government, though not to the Commonwealth Monitoring Group supervising the ceasefire on the ground.[57] Prior to independence, and during the Lancaster House talks, it has become evident that Thatcher and Carrington were complicit in encouraging a covert South African military presence in Rhodesia/Zimbabwe. Even so, Carrington emphasised that South African soldiers "must be dressed in Rhodesian uniforms, and not come to notice in formations."[58] Similarly, General Peter Walls, the commander of the Rhodesian forces, believed that he had a private understanding with the British Prime Minister and her Foreign Secretary, that any political settlement in the new state would exclude Mugabe.[59] However, if Thatcher had misgivings about handing over the British colony of Southern Rhodesia, "to a professed Marxist," these feelings were soon suppressed by regional realpolitik.[60]

Despite much talk of reconciliation and the return of many whites who had fled the country before independence, evidence of a much deeper malaise surfaced early in 1983 with reports of massacres in Matabeleland. This was the coming of the *Gukurahundi*.[61] The rivalry of Zimbabwe's two nationalist forces – Mugabe's ZANU and Nkomo's ZAPU – was long-standing and mirrored historic divisions between the majority Shona people and the minority Ndebele. While Nkomo had supported Zimbabwe's first government (and expected high office in it), there had been sporadic evidence of dissident activity in Matabeleland and parts of the Midlands from independence, some of it apparently financed and armed by South Africa. This deepened Mugabe's suspicions of Nkomo. By the beginning of 1983, it quickly became apparent that the 'Gukurahundi' Fifth Brigade, standing outside the Zimbabwe Army's normal command structures and trained by the North Koreans, was engaged in indiscriminate killings, mass rape, burnings and terror, encompassing the local population as a whole rather than targeting dissidents. Over a nine-month period, it is estimated that the Fifth Brigade killed between 10,000 and 20,000 with "many more suffering severe physical or psychological harm" from persistent beatings or from being made to witness extreme cruelty, often to their own family members.[62]

Was this not confirmation of Thatcher's worst fears, marking a souring of British diplomatic relations with the new state? Hazel Cameron's research suggests otherwise.[63] The massacres were soon within the public domain, both within Zimbabwe and internationally. The UK government was aware of graphic coverage by British journalists like Donald Trelford and Jeremy Paxman.[64] Deep concerns were also being raised by Garfield Todd, then a Senator.[65] Despite the weight of evidence of atrocities, including from the Zimbabwe Catholic Bishops' conference citing "incontrovertible evidence," the muted reports out of the British High Commission in Harare gave credence to Cameron's accusation of "wilful blindness" on the part of the UK government.[66]

Dumiso Dabengwa, the ZIPRA commander jailed after independence, has accused Thatcher and the British of being behind the massacres, though without substantiating his claim.[67] A more telling accusation has come from Nokhuthula Moyo who in 2007 spoke of the growth of ZANU government's culture of impunity and its widespread use of violence. "There are varying degrees of violence," he remarked: "and Gukurahundi was the university where these degrees were obtained."[68]

The British High Commissioner in Harare at that time was Robin Byatt. He later reflected that the Zimbabwe government's actions in Matabeleland were a "disastrous mistake" which divided the country terribly and left behind deep-rooted resentment.[69] His wife, Jilly, defended her husband for failing to intervene with Mugabe: "It was very important to keep good relations. . . . Aggressive criticism would have got us nowhere. It would just not have worked."[70]

There is little evidence of any collective action by the Commonwealth where some would have regarded the issue as an internal matter, a rekindling of known animosities between Nkomo and Mugabe. "There was no official Commonwealth view, as far as I knew," commented Moses Anafu, a political officer specialising in Africa, concluding rhetorically: "What do you think the Secretariat could have done?"[71] Pressed by Sue Onslow, Ramphal was asked if the Commonwealth had taken a stand. "You know, we didn't, because we were becoming caught up in South Africa."[72] The Commonwealth had claimed with some justification that it had played an important part in creating the success story which was the new state of Zimbabwe. The end of the bush war, all-party negotiations and a democratic transition seemed to have been attained peaceably, largely without bloodshed and with every indication of a reconciliation between Black and white. There were few who had any appetite for disrupting that positive narrative so early in the life of the new nation.

As far as the British were concerned, former Deputy Prime Minister, Michael Heseltine, has been among those who has drawn a distinction between Thatcher's visceral passions and her undoubted intellect. He has spoken of "the thinking Margaret, not the gut Margaret."[73] Her instincts led her to protest against initialling the successfully concluded Lancaster House Agreement, declaiming: "I am not going to shake the hands of terrorists."[74] While there was no ideological reconciliation, her intellect led her to take a more pragmatic view. "Much to the amazement of officials at the Prime Minister's Downing Street office, Mugabe would drop in for informal chats with Mrs Thatcher during private visits to London."[75] As late as 1988, this close relationship led to the UK intervening with "prophylactic action" to forestall a raid "by British nationals and mercenaries" to free South African agents being held in Chikurubi prison (after a bloody cross-border raid on an ANC house in Bulawayo).[76] Mugabe always spoke approvingly of his ability to work with Thatcher. "You could trust her," he judged.[77]

## 6  Conclusion

The techniques, structures and diplomatic methodology which first began to emerge in the 1960s over the Rhodesia crisis and at the 1971 Singapore CHOGM over arms sales to South Africa came to be refined and extended at Gleneagles in 1977 and at Lusaka and Lancaster House in 1979. The Sanctions Committee (and the programme of support for Zimbabwean exiles) was institutional recognition of a distinctive Commonwealth interest. It was to become the Commonwealth Committee on Southern Africa, which was to have a particularly important role in coordinating the input of Commonwealth governments alongside the Lancaster House negotiations. The Secretary-General, and his senior Secretariat team, engaged with Heads of Government at the highest level, beyond what might have been envisaged in 1965.[78] But Ramphal, rather as Arnold Smith had done before him, always presented publicly as the servant of member governments, responsive to their wishes and impartially guarding the association's core values and established conventions. The biennial CHOGM experimented with an 'in camera' session in 1971, and Trudeau developed this into a full-blown 'retreat' at the Ottawa CHOGM in 1973.[79] The Retreat would become the space where Ramphal's inner and outer circles of conciliation and consensus-creation could operate unhindered by civil servants and advisers. Commonwealth policy-making was also accompanied by agreed declarations or statements expressing the values and principles on which all were approaching the issue in question. In an organisation of such difference, these were the essential building blocks of its unity and mission (to be codified in a Charter only in 2012).

In all this, the Secretary-General might need to face down the national aspirations of individual governments in the interests of the association as a whole. This occasionally led some Heads and Ministers to object to the Secretary-General's 'interference'. Ramphal later reflected:

> "Interfering" is the epitaph most Secretaries-General (not only of the Commonwealth) must endure for being dutiful to the higher values of their organisations, when national policy threatens them. To that extent, rejection is an occupational hazard and "interfering" a badge of honour.[80]

If the Secretary-General's relationship with Heads (directly, as and when needed) and with Commonwealth High Commissioners in London (on a day-to-day basis) was a crucial element in the organisation's methodology, so too was the connection to the global AAM. Roger Fieldhouse, an AAM activist, concludes: "For a quarter of a century, between 1964 and 1990, AAM lobbied and pressurised the Commonwealth Secretariat and conferences and its various sub-groups and committees in an effort to strengthen its actions against *apartheid*."[81] Gurney argues that the resolution of conflict in Rhodesia and the experience of the sporting and other boycotts enabled the AAM to respond to the new conditions of the 1980s. As a result, it was able to "create a coalition of anti-*apartheid* forces and reach out to people who had never been involved in a formal political organisation, but who wanted to express their instinctive feeling that *apartheid* was wrong."[82]

Were these various ingredients uniquely given form, energy and direction by the alchemy of 'Sonny' Ramphal? While Ramphal's 'capacious gifts' were difficult to match, his lieutenant, Emeka Anyaoku, was to become Secretary-General in 1990 and to use these same methods and techniques in the final stages of *apartheid's* demise. This will be further elaborated in the chapters which follow.

**Notes**

1 Chan, *The Commonwealth in World Politics*, 55.
2 Anyaoku, *Inside the Modern Commonwealth*, 250.
3 Commonwealth Secretariat, *The Commonwealth at the Summit*, 174.
4 UNSC Resolution 423, 14 March 1978, Accessed 2 June 2020, htpps://www.undocs.org/S/RES/423/1978.
5 Chris Saunders, "The Cold War in southern Africa 1976–1990," In *The Cambridge History of the Cold War*, ed. Melvyn Leffler and Odd Arne Westad, Vol.III (Cambridge: CUP, 2010), 222–243.
6 Farley, *Southern Africa in transition*, 448.
7 Paul Sharp, *Thatcher's Diplomacy: The Revival of British Foreign Policy* (London, Macmillan Press Ltd, 1997), 35, 41.
8 The Conservative Party, 1979 General Election Manifesto, 11 April 1979, Margaret Thatcher Foundation archive, Accessed 19 April 2020, www.margaretatcher.org/document/110858.
9 Peter Carrington, *Debate on the Address*, House of Lords, 22 May 1979, HL Deb 22.5.79 Vol.400 cc 241, Accessed 19 April 2020, www.api.parliament.uk/historic.hansard/sittings/1979/may/22.
10 Pratap Chitnis, *Debate on the Address*, cc 294.
11 Minute of the Prime Minister's meeting with Roy Jenkins, 21 May 1979, TNA, CAB/128/66.
12 Stephen Chan, *Southern Africa: Old Treacheries and New Deceits* (New Haven and London: Yale University Press, 2011), 15.
13 Ibid., 2.
14 Carrington, *Debate on the Address*, cc 249.
15 Memorandum from Jeremy Pope to the Secretary-General, 22 May 1979, Commonwealth Secretariat archives, 2011/120 (Rhodesia).
16 Philip Murphy, *Monarchy and the End of Empire: The House of Windsor, the British Government and the Post-War Commonwealth* (Oxford: OUP, 2013), 139.
17 Ramphal, *Glimpses of a Global Life*, 340.
18 Robin Renwick, *A Journey with Margaret Thatcher: Foreign Policy Under the Iron Lady* (London: Biteback Publishing, 2013), 33.
19 Correspondence from Bryan Cartledge to John Hunt, Cabinet Secretary, "Briefs for PM for Lusaka CHOGM," 31 May 1979, TNA, PREM 19/9.
20 Margaret Thatcher, Speech, Lusaka CHOGM: 5th Session, 3 August 1979, Margaret Thatcher Foundation and TNA, HGM (979), 91.
21 Ramphal, *Glimpses of a Global Life*, 353.
22 Colin Legum, "The gentling of Mrs Thatcher," *The Observer*, 5 August 1979, UCT archives, Colin Legum Papers, BC 1329 06.1.7.
23 Ramphal, *Glimpses of a Global Life*, 362,359.
24 Ibid., 364.
25 Carrington, *Reflecting on Things Past*, 300.

26 Margaret Thatcher, *The Downing Street Years* (London: Harper Collins, 1993), 76.
27 Commonwealth Secretariat, *The Commonwealth at the Summit* (Vol.1), 205.
28 Annotations by Prime Minister on correspondence from J.S. Wall, FCO, to B.G. Cartledge, No.10, 29 May 1979, TNA, PREM 19/106.
29 Commonwealth Secretariat, *The Commonwealth at the Summit* (Vol.1), 205.
30 Memorandum on Rhodesia from the Foreign Secretary to the UK Cabinet, 9 August 1979, TNA, CAB/129/207/3 – C (79)33.
31 Conclusions of Cabinet, 10 August 1979, TNA, CAB/128/66/13 – CC (79)13.
32 Conclusions of Cabinet, 30 August 1979, TNA, CAB/128/66/11.
33 Correspondence from Shridath Ramphal to all Commonwealth Heads of Government, 13 June 1979, TNA, PREM 19/9.
34 Departmental Memorandum by Roger Barltrop, Commonwealth Coordination Department, on the Lusaka CHOGM, TNA, HCM 021/38, DS(L)1388, 8.
35 HMSO, Report of the Constitutional Conference on Southern Rhodesia, Lancaster House, London, September–December 1979, Cmnd 7802, 3.
36 Carrington, *Reflecting on Things Past*, 300.
37 Stephen Chan, *The Commonwealth Observer Group in Zimbabwe: A Personal Memoir* (Gweru: Mambo Press, 1985), 12.
38 Matthew Neuhaus, "The Commonwealth in contemporary crises: Britain and the Commonwealth with special reference to Rhodesia" (MPhil Dissertation, University of Cambridge, 1986), 46.
39 Commonwealth Secretariat, *The Commonwealth at the Summit* (Vol.1), 205.
40 HMSO, Report of the Constitutional Conference on Southern Rhodesia, 9–12.
41 Martin Plaut, "U.S. backed Zimbabwe Land Reform," *BBC News*, 22 August 2007, Accessed 19 April 2020, www.news.bbc.co.uk/go/pr/fr/-/1/hi/world/africa/6958418.stm.
42 Commonwealth Secretariat, *The Commonwealth at the Summit* (Vol.1), 205.
43 Minutes of the Commonwealth Committee on Southern Africa, 23 November 1979, Commonwealth Secretariat archives, 2011/120, 6.
44 Record of a meeting between Shridath Ramphal and Margaret Thatcher, 3 December 1979, London, TNA, PREM 19/116.
45 Minutes of Cabinet, Thursday, 1 November 1979, TNA, CAB/128/66/19.
46 Richard Luce, (former UK Minister), interviewed by Sue Onslow, for "The road to settlement in Rhodesia," 25 January 2006, CCBH Oral History Programme, 16.
47 Richard Luce, interviewed by the author, 14 March 2017, which corroborates Onslow's interview on the same point; Richard Luce, *Ringing the Changes: A Memoir* (Norwich: Michael Russell Publishing, 2007), 89.
48 Luce, Onslow CCBH interview, 27.
49 Record of a meeting between Margaret Thatcher and Peter Walls, 6 December 1979, TNA, CAB/128/66.
50 Hugo Young, *One of Us* (London: Macmillan, 1989), 182.
51 Mark Robinson (former MP and Minister), in conversation with the author, 31 January 2017, Bristol.
52 Carrington, *Reflecting on Things Past*, 303.
53 Julia Langdon, "Lord Carrington's Obituary," 10 July 2018, *The Guardian*, Accessed 9 June 2020, https://www.theguardian.com/politics/2018/july/10/peter-carrington-lord-carrington-obituary.
54 Ramphal, *Glimpses of a Global Life*, 362.
55 James Ivey, "Double standards: South Africa, British Rugby, and the Moscow Olympics," 116.
56 Ibid., 115.
57 Miles Tendi, "Four decades of underestimating Mugabe: How the British never expected he would win Zimbabwe's 1980 election," 22 December 2015, *The Conversation*, https://theconversation.com.four-decades-of-undersetimating-mugabe-how-the-british-never-expected-he-would-win-zimbabwes-1980-election-50276.

58 Record of a meeting between Lord Carrington and Pik Botha, 28 November 1979, TNA, PREM 19/115 f60, 4
59 Record of a meeting between Lord Carrington and General Peter Walls, 6 December 1979, TNA, PREM 19/116 p2.f.162, 5
60 Xan Smiley, "Zimbabwe, Southern Africa and the rise of Robert Mugabe," *Foreign Affairs* (1980), 58 (5), 1060
61 Gukurahundi is chiShona for "the early rain which washes away the chaff before the spring rains."
62 Jason Burke, "UK downplayed killings in Zimbabwe to guard its interests, study claims," *The Guardian*, 16 May 2017, www.theguardian.com/world/2017/may/16/uk-downplayed-killings-zimbabwe-mugabe-guard-interests-study-claims
63 Hazel Cameron, "The Matabeleland massacres: Britain's wilful blindness," *The International History Review* (2018), Vol 4, 1, 1–19
64 Ibid, 14
65 Judith Todd, *Through the Darkness: A Life in Zimbabwe* (Cape Town: Zebra Press, 2007), 49
66 Cameron, Matabeleland Massacres, 14, 15
67 Staff reporter, "Margaret Thatcher was behind the Gukurahundi massacres, claims Dabengwa," *Bulawayo 24 News*, 9 April, 2013, https://bulawayo24.com/index-if-news-sc-regional-byo-28690-article-Margaret+Thatcher+was+behind+the+Gukurahundi+massacres+claims+Dabengwa
68 Meeting summary, "Zimbabwe's Gukurahundi: Lessons from the 1980–1988 disturbances in Matabeleland and the Midlands," 4 September 2007, *Chatham House*, Speech by Nokhuthula Moyo, Legal Resource Foundation, 5
69 Robin Byatt, interviewed by Alasdair MacDermott, 24 February 2016, British Diplomatic Oral History Programme, Churchill College Cambridge, DOHP 148, 17
70 Jason Burke, "UK downplayed killings in Zimbabwe to guard its interests, study claims," 16 May 2017, *The Guardian* www.theguardian.com/world/2017/may/16/uk-downplayed-killings-zimbabwe-mugabe-guard-interests-stidy-claims
71 Mose Anafu, interviewed by Sue Onslow, 6 May 2015, Commonwealth Oral History Project, Institute of Commonwealth Studies London, https://commonwealthoralhistories.org/2015/interview-with-moses-anafu/pt.1, 6
72 Shridath Ramphal, Interviewed by Sue Onslow, 17 April 2015, Commonwealth Oral History Project, Institute of Commonwealth Studies, London, https//: commonwealthoralhistories.org/2015/interview-with-sir-shridath-ramphal/pt.2, 19
73 Michael Heseltine, 26 May 2019, "Sunday," *BBC Radio 4*.
74 Moore, *Margaret Thatcher* (Vol.1), 503
75 Richard Dowden, "British policies have not helped Zimbabwe – yet," in *The Day After Mugabe: Prospects for Change in Zimbabwe*, eds. Gugulethu Moyo and Mark Ashurst (London: Africa Research Institute, 2007), 140
76 Martin Plaut and Sue Onslow, "When Margaret Thatcher rode to Robert Mugabe's rescue," 23 July 2018, *New Statesman America* www.newstatesman.com/world/Africa/2018/07/when-margaret-thatcher-rode-robert-mugabe-s-rescue/
77 Peta Thornycroft, "Robert Mugabe claims he could trust Margaret Thatcher," 25 May 2013, *The Telegraph*, https://www.telegraph.co.uk/news/worldnews/africaandindianocean/Zimbabwe/10080131/Robert-Mugabe-claims-he-could-trust-Margaret-Thatcher-but-Tony-Blair-was-dishonest-in-new-documentary/
78 Commonwealth Secretariat, *The Commonwealth at the Summit* (Vol.1), 105–111.
79 Minutes of a meeting with Edward Heath, 19 January 1971, Singapore, TNA, PREM 15/277.
80 Ramphal, *Glimpses of a Global Life*, 368.
81 Roger Fieldhouse, *Anti-Apartheid: A History of the Movement in Britain* (London: Merlin Press, 2005), 242.
82 Gurney, "The 1970s: The anti-*apartheid* movement's difficult decade," 487.

## References

Charles Moore, *Margaret Thatcher (Vol.1)*.
Commonwealth Secretariat, *The Commonwealth at the Summit*, Op.Cit.
Emeka Anyaoku, *Inside the Modern Commonwealth*, Op.Cit.
Gugulethu Moyo and Mark Ashurst (eds), *The Day After Mugabe: Prospects for Change in Zimbabwe* (London: Africa Research Institute, 2007).
HMSO, *Report of the Constitutional Conference on Southern Rhodesia* (London: Lancaster House, 1979), Cmnd 7802.
Hugo Young, *One of Us* (London: Macmillan, 1989).
Jonathan Farley, *Southern Africa in Transition*, 448.
Judith Todd, *Through the Darkness: A Life in Zimbabwe* (Cape Town: Zebra Press, 2007).
Margaret Thatcher, *The Downing Street Years* (London: Harper Collins, 1993).
Matthew Neuhaus, "The Commonwealth in Contemporary Crises: Britain and the Commonwealth with Special Reference to Rhodesia," MPhil Dissertation (University of Cambridge, 1986).
Melvyn Leffler and Odd Arne Westad (eds.), *The Cambridge History of the Cold War (Vol.3)*, (Cambridge: CUP, 2010).
Paul Sharp, *Thatcher's Diplomacy: The Revival of British Foreign Policy* (London, Macmillan Press Ltd, 1997).
Peter Carrington, *Reflecting on Things Past* (London: Harper Collins, 1998).
Philip Murphy, *Monarchy and the end of Empire: The House of Windsor, the British Government and the Postwar Commonwealth* (Oxford: OUP, 2013).
Richard Luce, *Ringing the Changes: A Memoir* (Norwich: Michael Russell Publishing, 2007).
Robin Renwick, *A Journey with Margaret Thatcher: Foreign Policy under the Iron Lady* (London: Biteback Publishing, 2013).
Roger Fieldhouse, *Anti-Apartheid: A History of the Movement in Britain* (London: Merlin Press, 2005).
Shridath Ramphal, *Glimpses of a Global Life*, Op.Cit.
Stephen Chan, *Southern Africa: Old Treacheries and New Deceits* (New Haven, London: Yale University Press, 2011).
Stephen Chan, *The Commonwealth in World Politics*, Op.Cit.
Stephen Chan, *The Commonwealth Observer Group in Zimbabwe: A personal memoir* (Gweru: Mambo Press, 1985).

# 9 Mission to South Africa – Negotiating with *Apartheid*

## 1 Introduction

The 1986 mission to South Africa of the Commonwealth Eminent Persons Group involved the Commonwealth in a sustained diplomatic attempt to encourage a negotiated end to *apartheid*. The EPG initiative resulted from an intensification of the Commonwealth's campaign against *apartheid* and the adoption of the 1985 Nassau Accord on Southern Africa.[1] This agreement, made the same year at the Commonwealth summit in the Bahamas, is often seen as a compromise between the many Commonwealth voices calling for economic and other sanctions against South Africa and the firm opposition to sanctions articulated by the UK government led by Margaret Thatcher. While all Commonwealth governments agreed at Nassau to a modest set of sanctions (or 'signals', as Thatcher preferred to call them), this was accompanied by approval for a diplomatic mission to South Africa. The latter was given the daunting task of negotiating an end to *apartheid* or at least facilitating the conditions which might allow all-inclusive negotiations to begin. Differing perceptions of the mission threatened the viability of the initiative from the outset. Was it, as Bob Hawke intended it to be, a genuinely 'dual' approach – an offer to facilitate an internal process of authentic negotiations as an alternative to the progressive tightening of the sanctions ratchet?[2] Or was it, as Huddleston feared, a ruse cooked up by the British Government to stave off Commonwealth and international sanctions and which might become a near-permanent delaying mechanism, rather as the Contact Group of Western nations on Namibia had been widely viewed?[3] Once permitted entry to South Africa and neighbouring states and provided with extraordinary access to all shades of opinion, what progress did the Commonwealth make in its stated aim of achieving a negotiated end to *apartheid*? And once the diplomatic mission had ostensibly failed, what effect did the speedy publication and promotion of the EPG's report have on Commonwealth governments and on the international campaign for economic and financial sanctions against South Africa? Inevitably, the breakdown of the mission and the conclusions of the report were to trigger marked disagreements with the UK government which were to plague the Commonwealth for the next four years.

Some specialist Commonwealth writers have touched upon the EPG initiative in detail. David McIntyre provides one of the fuller accounts.[4] Major Commonwealth figures like Emeka Anyaoku and Shridath Ramphal, who were deeply involved in the process, provide valuable insights.[5] For Ramphal, it was "the most ambitious and delicate undertaking the Commonwealth had ever managed."[6] He did not join the EPG in the field, remaining mostly in London so that he could play a wider role as needed. He continued to be deeply sceptical about the good faith of the *apartheid* regime, and some FCO sources privately, if unjustly, suspected him of wanting the mission to fail.[7] Anyaoku successfully insisted to Ramphal that he should head the EPG's support team, provided by the Secretariat, rather than Moni Malhoutra, and Anyaoku was therefore closely involved in the negotiations.[8] As an African, his feelings about *apartheid* were profound, but his diplomatic style was less flamboyant than Ramphal's. An important perspective has also been provided by Hugh Craft, a key member of the EPG support team, who gives prominence to the mission in his doctoral thesis.[9] Craft places his critique of the EPG within the thematic context of conflict resolution. For Craft, the EPG "acted as a circuit-breaker in the process of achieving a lasting settlement."[10] He quotes the South African activist, Mkhuseli 'Khusta' Jack, who told him that "the Commonwealth gave us the language of negotiation."[11] Although Craft draws on his extensive interviews rather than primary archival sources, he provides a thorough assessment of the context for negotiations and the particular aspects of the Commonwealth's diplomatic method. This was centred around the EPG's mandate and purpose, its operational principles, its specific time frame, its confidence-building procedures and its legitimacy as a mediator. In this respect, Craft carries forward earlier work by C.R. Mitchell.[12]

A number of *apartheid* scholars, such as Saul Dubow, also cover the mission. Dubow judges it "a long-term success" because it gave impetus to a "Possible Negotiating Concept" for direct negotiations between the principal parties, including Mandela.[13] Alistair Sparks judged it "the most remarkable attempt at foreign mediation in the South African conflict so far undertaken."[14] Some analysed the initiative at the time, including a confidential study prepared by various South African and foreign academics for the South African Institute of International Affairs.[15] Adrian Guelke uses Deon Geldenhuys's framework for assessing the different methods by which the international community sought to influence the South African Government.[16] Of Geldenhuys's four categories of external action, Guelke argues that mediation only arose towards the end of the *apartheid* era but nonetheless "had a profound impact" on South Africa's transition.[17] In this he accords early prominence to the EPG, within a mediation process which culminated in 1994. Generally, however, the EPG intervention is either misrepresented, fragmented or largely ignored by the literature with suggestions that its impact has been exaggerated.[18]

Surprisingly, South Africa's own official history of the struggle, commissioned by President Mbeki, and in particular the volume dealing with international solidarity, makes no mention of the EPG mission in its brief summary of Commonwealth activities against *apartheid*.[19] Abdul Minty, a veteran anti-*apartheid* campaigner and, after 1994, senior South African diplomat, has written a tribute to the Commonwealth's 'major role' and its 'remarkable achievement' in the struggle against *apartheid* but does not refer to the mission of the EPG.[20] Christabel Gurney, the AAM activist and historian, mentions the EPG but emphasises the AAM's conviction that 'there was no prospect of any meaningful dialogue' and that the 'visit' would merely give credibility to the Botha government's controversial reforms.[21] Worden records that "[i]n May 1986, a high-ranking Commonwealth delegation (a concession granted to Thatcher by Commonwealth leaders) arrived in South Africa to investigate the situation and talk to the government."[22] Tim Shaw, a former Director of the Institute of Commonwealth Studies in London, refers only to the 'innovative' EPG and its task "to visit and report in the late 1980s."[23] Even the distinguished Commonwealth analyst and academic, Stephen Chan, undervalued the work of the EPG by saying that the group "reported on a sensitive and specific issue of international relations," adding his view that this was 'one step up' from a consultative group and 'a few steps up' from an expert group.[24]

Where does the truth lie? Beyond the prevailing discourse a more significant and complex interpretation is evident. This is discernible by drawing extensively from a range of occasionally contrasting primary archival sources, rather than relying on sometimes flawed secondary sources alone. Archival evidence is also useful in challenging, confirming or prompting oral histories or biographical accounts. The resulting analysis supports a more extensive and multi-layered assessment of the mission. Firstly, it is clear that this was an intensive and multifaceted diplomatic demarche, beyond the scope of any individual government and on a scale unusual for a multilateral, global organisation, outside the United Nations itself. Certainly, in size, cost and difficulty, it was unique in the Commonwealth's experience. No mission of this kind had previously been granted access to South Africa by the *apartheid* regime. Secondly, the chapter points to the hitherto unparalleled access the group obtained to all shades of political opinion, both within South Africa and within the region (including to groups engaged in the armed struggle). This involved unprecedented access to Nelson Mandela in Pollsmoor prison. Thirdly, the "Possible Negotiating Concept" developed by the EPG in the course of its consultations (and later put to the principal parties) provided the basis on which future multi-party negotiations were to begin some four years later, as Pik Botha has confirmed.[25] In that respect, Mandela's involvement in the Commonwealth initiative ought to be seen as the start of a sustained period of covert negotiation and confidence-building. New archival evidence directly links Mandela's discussions with the EPG with those who, albeit tentatively, subsequently took forward dialogue with Mandela from the government side. These secret tripartite consultations were to settle into a pattern, involving Mandela from his prison cell, key figures within the South African Government, and (through Mandela) the ANC leadership in exile. There were also other, lower-level, contacts. In this context, it is difficult to characterise the EPG as an isolated, brief and one-off initiative.

Finally, it is argued that despite its failure to achieve its primary objective – namely, a negotiated end to *apartheid* – the report of the mission and the widespread dissemination of its findings nonetheless provided a powerful boost to the international campaign for increased sanctions on South Africa. This served to undermine the position of the British Prime Minister, Margaret Thatcher, and the US President, Ronald Reagan, challenging their joint policy of constructive engagement. All in all, Craft is correct to conclude that the three enduring outcomes of the

EPG initiative were to deepen South Africa's isolation, galvanise the imposition of further sanctions and lay the groundwork for a negotiated solution.[26]

## 2  After Zimbabwe: The Commonwealth, the UK and Southern Africa

The genesis of the EPG was at the Nassau CHOGM, and it arose out of a crescendo of voices demanding sanctions against South Africa, despite the fervent opposition of Thatcher and the British Government. The proposal that a programme of sanctions be linked to a diplomatic mission, probing the prospects for negotiations, was advanced by Australia, rather than Britain, and formed a distinct dual strategy around which the association could unite. Furthermore, deep tensions evident at Nassau, and conflicted approaches to dealing with *apartheid*, paradoxically made the work of the EPG mission possible, providing it with breadth and reach, securing its unparalleled and untrammelled access to all parties, and bringing it close to success. It is therefore important to trace the development of the *apartheid* issue within the Commonwealth in the years after the independence of Zimbabwe in 1980. In particular, how could obvious differences in policy and method become the basis for common endeavour?

The attitude of Thatcher's government towards Zimbabwe, and to its African neighbours, was consistent with her policy of 'constructive engagement' towards *apartheid* South Africa and symptomatic of Thatcher's developing partnership with Reagan after 1980. Seen, inevitably, through the prism of the Cold War, such an approach saw Southern Africa as an important cockpit of conflict, particularly in Namibia and Angola, and in the other border lands of the *apartheid* state. The veteran right-winger Julian Amery was speaking for a vocal section of the Conservative Party in urging the Prime Minister to "halt the tide of Soviet imperialism in Southern Africa."[27] For their part, the newly independent African nations of the region had found common cause against the *apartheid* enemy along a new frontier. They saw *apartheid* as the root cause of violence and instability in the region. Resistance was, in their eyes, a political and moral imperative. However, these frontline states faced an unenviable choice between economic co-option and coercion, or subversion and conflict. These were the twin prongs of South Africa's "Total Strategy": to offer trade and prosperity in the region, though on Pretoria's terms, or to destabilise its neighbours through cross-border attacks, covert action and the use of locally created proxy forces.

The FLS had been formally recognised as a separate entity in 1975, at that stage comprising Botswana, Tanzania and Zambia. By 1980, their ranks had been swollen by the addition of the former Portuguese colonies of Angola and Mozambique, by Malawi, Swaziland and Lesotho, and by newly independent Zimbabwe. In April 1980, their attempts to loosen South Africa's economic grip on the region led to the formation of the Southern African Development Coordination Conference (SADCC), later to become the Southern African Development Community

(SADC) and including post-*apartheid* South Africa. But in 1980, the region was beset by conflict. Many FLS countries provided operational and training bases for the ANC and the PAC, and, while the impact of the liberation forces on South Africa was limited, these were more than matched by SADF cross-border raids. Far more sustained fighting took place in Namibia, Angola and Mozambique.

The FLS had other avenues for exercising their new-found muscle, including the NAM; their parent body, the OAU; and of course the United Nations. While the United Nations provided a constant focus on *apartheid*, particularly through the work of the Special Committee, and was a powerful forum for articulating the policies and norms of the international community, it had its practical limitations. As Reddy has acknowledged, the leaders of the liberation movement did not expect it "to deliver freedom and democracy to South Africa."[28] The role of the international community was in that respect "secondary and supportive."[29] Its capacity to give voice to the totality of world opinion on *apartheid* was no guarantee that its policies could be implemented. For example, in 1985 Malcolm Fraser became chairman of the UN Panel of Eminent Persons on the Role of Transnational Corporations in South Africa, but the panel members were denied access to South Africa, and the panel's New York hearings were largely boycotted by the corporations they were hoping to influence.[30] Similarly, in March 1988, a draft resolution of the UN Security Council seeking selective mandatory sanctions on South Africa was vetoed by the United States and the UK.[31]

While not an alternative to the United Nations, membership of the Commonwealth offered African (and other) countries a particular opportunity to work on what has been coined the "We-They" frontier.[32] The organisation was in any case very different from the 'imperial' Commonwealth of the immediate post-war years, and the leverage that Commonwealth Africa could now bring to bear on the UK and its policies towards *apartheid* made it a tempting prospect.

The UK had long-standing links with white South Africa (including around 800,000 'English' whites with residency rights in the UK), as well as significant economic investments and a substantial trading relationship.[33] Since 1960 and Macmillan's 'wind of change' speech, the UK had publicly parted from South Africa on *apartheid* and ceased to defend the regime's policies at the United Nations. It professed to an approach which avoided violent change and economic disruption, but which also brought about reform of the *apartheid* state and an end to institutionalised racism. Nevertheless, together with the United States, it still saw South Africa as an important strategic ally in the final stages of the Cold War. As international and regional pressure on South Africa intensified after the resolution of the Rhodesian conflict, the UK Cabinet needed to respond to the rising clamour for economic sanctions against the *apartheid* regime. The conclusion of the Foreign Secretary was that in defending its interests the UK should do "all in our power to avoid the choice between applying or vetoing sanctions."[34] It would prove to be an impossible balancing act.

Prior to Thatcher's first CHOGM, Lusaka in 1979, Ramphal as Secretary-General had urged other Heads of Government not to provoke the new British Prime Minister. It proved to be an effective approach. By 1983, however, the relationship between Thatcher and Ramphal was becoming more strained. Ramphal, a Guyanese voice from the 'South', offered a radical and activist leadership which was attracting a new generation of Commonwealth leaders, such as Bob Hawke of Australia, Brian Mulroney of Canada and Rajiv Gandhi of India. As Hawke put it, "We had a very good relationship. I liked him. I thought he was a genuine man."[35] Unsurprisingly, there were some in the British Government who took a different view. Lord Carrington, the former Foreign Secretary, had been so irritated by what he saw as Ramphal's interference in the 1979 Lancaster House negotiations that he later said he would 'swim the Atlantic twice over' to frustrate Ramphal's ambitions to become UN Secretary-General.[36] Douglas Hurd, who served under Carrington and was himself to become Foreign Secretary also, described Ramphal as "a loud mouth. He talked a lot. He blew his own trumpet anywhere he could and, in a way, I think that reduced the total of good that he did."[37] Nevertheless, Ramphal's was a voice the British Government could not ignore. His help was invaluable, for example, on the UK's approach to the Gleneagles Agreement on sport and *apartheid* and in mustering Commonwealth support for the UK in the Falklands War.

However, as the issue of further measures against South Africa, including sanctions, rose to the top of the Commonwealth's agenda, there were signs that Ramphal's patience was wearing thin. As he later reflected, "Mrs Thatcher was much less receptive to the demand for change in South Africa . . . she never seemed to see *apartheid* as the transcendent evil it was."[38] Defenders of Thatcher insist that she repeatedly made clear her opposition to *apartheid*.[39] President Nyerere was among those who accepted the sincerity of her stated position.[40] Her difficulties in likewise persuading all her critics were twofold. Firstly, for every clear statement expressing her personal opposition to *apartheid*, there were other comments which seemed to be lukewarm or equivocal on the issue. This was in marked contrast to her condemnation of Communism and the Soviet Union and was apparent in her differing approaches to the 1980 Moscow Olympics and the British Lions Tour of South Africa the same year.[41] Her legendary passion was much more evident in her robust rejection of economic and financial sanctions, her argument that they would bear disproportionately on the Black majority and her belief that the *apartheid* system was unsustainable economically in the long term. Liberal economies would, in time, change illiberal states, she thought. Even if the South African economy could be described in those terms, the problem, argues Sharp, was that "it depended on seeing the operation of the market economy as the principal engine of social change in South Africa, rather than as the principal beneficiary of racial oppression."[42]

The second argument explaining Thatcher's equivocation on *apartheid* was presented in terms of her vigorous pursuit of 'constructive engagement'. If she resisted public denunciation of *apartheid*, it was so that she could maximise her private leverage with President Botha. In this task she had an ally in President Reagan, with whom she forged a particularly close personal and ideological relationship. This was despite the hiccup to their relationship caused by the 1983 US invasion of Grenada, about which the British Prime Minister was not properly consulted.

She hoped it would be treated as "a difficult but isolated incident, rather than a new departure," and this indeed turned out to be the case.[43]

In 1984, Thatcher created considerable controversy by receiving President P.W. Botha on a state visit to the UK. This was met with condemnation and protest, and Botha saw this as a good opportunity to press his new ally on the presence and activities of South African exiles in London which were a constant source of irritation to the *apartheid* regime. On the contrary, while Thatcher remained implacably opposed to sanctions on South Africa and looked for a working relationship with Botha, in the privacy of her Chequers study she took Botha to task. There was no question of the British Government moving against anti-*apartheid* activists in the UK; South Africa must stop its covert and illegal actions against UK residents; *apartheid* must go; and Nelson Mandela must be released. This powerful message was not apparent or appreciated at the time: Archbishop Huddleston had condemned constructive engagement as "double-talk and hypocrisy."[44] However, by the end of the visit even Huddleston and other campaigners privately realised that on this occasion Thatcher's robust dealings with Botha had been positive.[45]

By 1985, the *apartheid* regime in South Africa was increasingly engulfed in crisis. It faced growing resistance internally, with rent boycotts and uprisings in the townships, and little support for its *apartheid* 'reforms'. In August 1985, President Botha addressed the National Party Congress in Natal. The speech had been widely anticipated and was expected to usher in far-reaching change to the *apartheid* system, perhaps involving the release of Nelson Mandela. Despite being billed as the 'Rubicon' speech, Botha made a partly impromptu and wholly defiant speech, declining to cross the point of no return. He declared: "I am not prepared to lead White South Africans and other minority groups on a road to abdication and suicide. Destroy White South Africa and our influence, and this country, will drift into faction strife, chaos and poverty."[46]

Privately, Thatcher was deeply disappointed by Botha's failure to embrace change, though publicly she argued that the speech indicated a willingness to negotiate an end to *apartheid*.[47] This was not the view of her Commonwealth colleagues. For Ramphal, the campaign against *apartheid* had become a "virtual crusade."[48] In preparation for the 1985 Nassau CHOGM he set out the case for sanctions, arguing: "It is irrefutable that the conjunction of a rising tide of anger within South Africa and a rising demand for economic sanctions is making Pretoria pause." He added the thinly veiled warning that "[i]t is unthinkable that any Commonwealth country should offer comfort to South Africa at this time."[49] Shortly before the summit, Thatcher wrote to Botha. She began by providing evidence of South African collusion with RENAMO in fomenting conflict in Mozambique, in breach of the Nkomati Accord. She continued: "You will appreciate that this episode has been a further embarrassment . . . to those of us in the West who wish to maintain sensible policies towards your country and the region's problems." Turning to the future, she remarked on "the increasing drift towards economic sanctions." While firmly opposed to economic sanctions and trade boycotts, pressures for such measures were bound to increase and she warned Botha that his government "should take no action which would undercut our efforts to resist these pressures."[50]

At the same time, Nyerere was among leaders who privately appealed for her support. Admitting that he knew Thatcher would not agree to full, mandatory economic sanctions, Nyerere instead urged her backing for "a meaningful package of selective sanctions."[51] President Masire of Botswana also wrote from the perspective of one of South Africa's closest neighbours. Agreeing that meaningful dialogue between the South African Government and the authentic representatives of Black organisations should be encouraged, Masire warned that the situation was 'explosive' and that he feared the consequences of inaction. "Botswana is held hostage by South Africa," he explained, adding: "We have been threatened and attacked for no reason. Following such traumatic events, we cannot be expected to defend South Africa's position." At the same time, he appealed to the British to help minimise the adverse effects on Botswana of any Commonwealth measures against South Africa and help it to withstand any punitive measures that the *apartheid* regime might take against its neighbour.[52]

The characterisation of a 'binary Commonwealth' suggests an implacable UK facing the unified opposition of the rest of the Commonwealth. Furthermore, there is more than a hint that the divide was between those countries which saw their nation's interests as paramount and those which were responding to a higher moral purpose, riding above national interest. The truth is less stark. In the case of the rest of the Commonwealth, Austin argues that most were willing to approve a policy of sanctions "since the price demanded was either negligible or even favourable."[53] More specifically, he suggests that these countries divided into four broad categories. Firstly, there were those far removed from South Africa which were "not directly concerned," such as Malta, Cyprus, Singapore and the Pacific Islands. The second category included countries like India and Malaysia, and those in West and East Africa and the Caribbean, which were "very much concerned" but not likely to be affected, since they had already terminated their trade with South Africa. Thirdly, there were some countries, such as the former Dominions (Australia in particular), which might actually benefit from sanctions, given that their economies were competitors of South Africa in mining and agriculture. Finally, there were the frontline states who supported sanctions but feared the consequences and required compensation and protection, Botswana in particular.[54] Such a perspective may be unduly cynical, but it does bear out the far more nuanced nature of the division on sanctions than is sometimes presented.

## 3 The 1985 Nassau Summit: Sanctions and a Divided Commonwealth

The Nassau CHOGM is often described in unduly confrontational terms. Some claim that there was 'deadlock' in the plenary sessions;[55] others that the exchanges were 'acerbic' and outraged.[56] Yet others saw the CHOGM as a 'watershed' and "a historic break in the evolution of the Commonwealth on a matter of global significance."[57] This is to equate the storm raised afterwards in the media with an internal Heads' debate which was largely good natured and positive and which eventually led to an agreed position. The policy positions of most governments were largely well understood beforehand. Australia and Canada were among Commonwealth countries who had already announced economic and other measures against South Africa, mirroring developments in the United States, the EEC and Scandinavia.[58] Thatcher, on the other hand, had been clear that economic sanctions were not the way to promote peaceful change. Indeed, she believed that their imposition would be counterproductive.

The Heads of several African countries had been in private correspondence with Thatcher, urging compromise. During the debate, King Moshoeshoe of beleaguered Lesotho movingly appealed for help for his people, while Malaysia's Mahathir pointedly said that sanctions by small countries were an "exercise in futility" and that to be effective they had to be applied by rich countries which did the most trade and financing with South Africa.[59] Thatcher told her colleagues that "she hated *apartheid*" but set out her opposition to mandatory sanctions and instead argued for negotiations.[60] But the loophole she offered the meeting was her willingness to send Pretoria 'signals', on top of what the UK had already done in banning arms sales, nuclear and defence cooperation, North Sea oil exports, the supply of computer equipment for security use and government loans.[61] David Lange, the New Zealand Prime Minister, seized on this, suggesting that "the precise terminology of the message was irrelevant" because "one man's sanctions were another's signals."[62] Furthermore, while Thatcher spoke in general terms about negotiations, it was Bob Hawke, the Australian premier, who the day before had set out detailed proposals for a Group of Eminent Persons "to initiate and encourage a process of dialogue."[63] Hawke returned to the debate after Thatcher had spoken. While welcoming her remarks, he emphasised that his proposal for a negotiating initiative was not a substitute for addressing the question of "restrictive measures or sanctions or signals, or whatever they might be called."[64]

## 4 The Negotiation Initiative – The Eminent Persons Group Is Born

Ramphal became converted to the idea of the EPG but admitted that "for the Commonwealth generally it involved a major strategic change from a policy of Pretoria's isolation to one of dialogue." Maintaining the pressure of sanctions would be essential. Even so, he knew there would be many, whether in Africa or in the AAM, who would have deep misgivings and would need to be won round. It was therefore at the leaders' retreat at Lyford Cay that a small group of Commonwealth Heads of Government, convened by Ramphal, and including Thatcher, began the search for an agreement. The debate was at times brusque, and Thatcher's Private Secretary was dismissive of the other leaders. Their approach, he reported, was "naïve," their knowledge of South Africa "slim" and their drafting skills "rudimentary," revealing the persistence of the FCO's colonial mindset.[65] Nevertheless, as the Retreat progressed the leaders were able to grind out a consensus which later proved acceptable to all. In return for agreement on dialogue with South Africa, the UK reluctantly signed up to a number of additional 'measures' (the term 'sanctions' was eschewed), and the summit adopted the Commonwealth Accord on Southern Africa. In declaring that *apartheid* must be dismantled immediately, the Accord called on Pretoria to take five key steps "in a genuine manner and as a matter of urgency." These included declaring an end to *apartheid*; releasing Nelson Mandela and other detainees; unbanning the ANC and other political parties and allowing political freedom; terminating the state of emergency and, in the context of a suspension of violence on all sides, beginning a process of dialogue with all parties with a view to establishing a non-racial and representative government.[66] To this end, the Accord also set out its decision: "to establish a small group of eminent persons to encourage through all practicable ways the evolution of that necessary process of political dialogue."[67] The situation would be reviewed after six months and, if adequate progress had not been made by then in meeting the objectives set out in the Accord, the adoption of "further effective measures" would have to be considered.[68]

The aims of the EPG mission were extraordinarily ambitious. So too was the expectation that the South African Government would accept such a mission and allow it free and unaccompanied access to opposition leaders over an extended period, anywhere in the country. Even more unlikely was that an imprisoned Mandela would be visited on three occasions and would thereby be part of a dialogue about South Africa's post-*apartheid* future. How could the Commonwealth's disparate diplomatic coalition hope to achieve such a process, let alone a positive outcome?

For her part, back in London, Thatcher wrote confidentially to Botha, giving an account of the Commonwealth summit. She reported somewhat disingenuously that the debate on South Africa "was a highly unpleasant and bitter one; and there is no doubt that the issue of sanctions will not go away, despite my success in preventing the Commonwealth from adopting them at this meeting." Her other main purpose at the meeting, she said, "was to secure Commonwealth backing for dialogue between the South African Government and representatives of the black community in the context of a suspension of violence by all sides." She added: "I hope you will agree that it is no small achievement to have persuaded the Commonwealth to put its name to a suspension of violence." In urging Botha to receive the EPG and allow it to contact various communities, the Prime Minister added: "I can well imagine that you will find this tiresome to say the least. I am under no illusion that much of what it will say and do will be distasteful to you."[69] But the alternative – of refusing to see the EPG altogether – would be much more damaging, she argued. Botha responded that he was "gratified by the strong, principled stand that you have taken against economic sanctions and also by your refusal to meet with the ANC for so long as that organisation remains committed to violence." He continued: "I must however tell you – informally and confidentially since we have not been officially approached to date – that my government will find it impossible to cooperate with the Commonwealth initiative."[70]

Meanwhile, Ramphal lost no time in constituting the EPG. Thatcher decided that the British nomination ought to be the Foreign Secretary, Sir Geoffrey Howe. "She suggested to him," wrote Powell,

> that the other nominations made it likely that the group would be difficult for the South African Government to accept and do business with. We should

need to be able to exercise a strong influence on it. She thought that the Foreign Secretary himself would be the most effective spokesman and the person best able to keep some control of the Group's activities.[71]

When Howe demurred, pleading he would have insufficient time to undertake the mission alongside his duties as Secretary of State, Thatcher reportedly offered to take over as Foreign Secretary in his absence. This can only have increased his anxieties.

A few days later, the Foreign Secretary submitted a formal memorandum to the British Prime Minister on the Commonwealth's EPG initiative (and his own personal involvement). He began by posing a rhetorical question: should the UK government take the proposal seriously, or instead treat it as a damage-limitation exercise, as part of their opposition to further sanctions on South Africa? Howe's answer was: "I believe we should approach the Group with the intention of trying to make it work."[72] Even so, he foresaw a host of difficulties. Firstly, there was "a high risk that the South African Government would refuse to receive the group at all" and cited the negative reaction of the South African Ambassador in London. Secondly, he felt the group was bound to want to see Mandela, with some reluctant to travel to South Africa otherwise, even though access to him had been refused to the three European Community Foreign Ministers (the EC 'Troika') who had visited South Africa in September 1985. Thirdly, the Commonwealth's commitment to a future South Africa where there would be one person, one vote in a unitary state was "totally unacceptable to the South African Government." Finally, he reflected on his own position. There were "serious disadvantages to my participation," he suggested, both because he could not spare the time and because it was necessary for the UK government to keep some distance from the work of the group and any of its likely recommendations. Instead, he proposed the names of Lord (Anthony) Barber, the former Chancellor of the Exchequer, and the FCO and UN diplomat, Sir Anthony Parsons.[73] Thatcher was having none of it. In a letter the next day, her PS wrote to Len Appleyard at the FCO in robust terms: "She remains convinced that the Foreign Secretary should be our nominee for the group. She believes that otherwise the conclusion will be drawn that we are not trying and that the whole exercise will in consequence fail." He added: "The Prime Minister does not consider that either Lord Barber or Sir Anthony Parsons would be suitable."[74]

By now, Thatcher's attempts to nominate the Foreign Secretary and her ambition that he should also chair the group had become public knowledge, following a front-page article in *The Observer*. The reaction was immediate. Tanzania, Zambia and Nigeria publicly declared their opposition to any such plans and moved to disassociate themselves from the EPG initiative. Ramphal, seeing that matters were at a critical juncture, contacted his Nigerian deputy Secretary-General, Emeka Anyaoku. Anyaoku saw that the British move to appoint Howe could not be "anything other than disastrous."[75] He later wrote: "Ramphal asked me to go to Africa to attempt to salvage the initiative by persuading the three Heads of Government to change their minds."[76] While Anyaoku worked to bring the African Commonwealth back into balance, Ramphal contacted other EPG Heads to clarify the understanding (in the minds of the Secretary-General and others, at any rate) that the EPG members "would carry out this task not as representatives of their governments but on behalf of the entire Commonwealth."[77] The Australian premier, Bob Hawke, also told the UK government that it would be "contrary to the spirit of the discussions in Nassau to appoint someone currently in Government to the committee."[78]

Anyaoku accordingly worked on Nyerere and Kaunda in the expectation that this would open the way for Nigeria to reverse their opposition to the initiative.[79] Ramphal prepared to pre-empt the British and announce that General Olusegun Obasanjo, the former Head of Nigeria's military government between 1976 and 1979, and Malcolm Fraser (the former Prime Minister of Australia) would be co-chairs of the EPG. On 18 November, Akinyemi, the Nigerian Foreign Minister, declared that Nigeria would after all participate in the mission and that Obasanjo was their nominee.[80] The deal on the leadership of the group was quickly done, leaving Ewen Fergusson, the FCO Deputy Under-Secretary of State, observing ruefully that it was clear that Ramphal:

> had cooked up this choice of joint chairmanship in his negotiations over membership of the group as a whole. On balance, I suggest we accept the choice of Obasanjo and Fraser as a fait accompli. We would gain little or nothing by being difficult.[81]

## 5 Deploying Diversity and Securing Access

With the chairmanship settled, the names of the other members were made public. These were Dame Nita Barrow, a leading civil society activist from Barbados; two former Foreign Ministers, John Malecela of Tanzania (who later became its Prime Minister) and India's Swaran Singh; Archbishop Ted Scott, from Canada; and, from Britain, Lord Barber. Denied the opportunity to nominate Howe, Thatcher reconsidered her earlier rejection of Barber. His solid Tory background and wide commercial interests in Africa made him ideally suited to support her policies on South Africa (or so she thought).

However, the diplomatic prospects for the mission continued to hang in the balance. Many in Africa, including the leadership of the ANC, perceived the EPG as a British device to stave off economic sanctions. This was also the initial view of the AAM. The noted anti-*apartheid* campaigner, Dr Allan Boesak, expressed his distrust of the mission: "I've cautioned my people not to rush in and give credibility to the group simply to help South Africa out of a difficult situation."[82] They now felt somewhat reassured by the participation of the frontline states and by the leading role taken by Nigeria. The rest of the Commonwealth approved of the composition of the group, which had been carefully selected to be as broad based and balanced as possible. It encompassed the five regions of the Commonwealth (as usually defined); it blended old and new Commonwealth; it contained the Commonwealth's largest economies, as well as some of the smallest, a matter of relevance to the sanctions debate; and it included a solitary woman.

*Figure 9.1* The Commonwealth Eminent Persons Group with Shridath Ramphal, Marlborough House, 1986. Commonwealth Secretariat.

On the other hand, some of these elements of reassurance for those outside South Africa seemed to be having the opposite effect within it. The British Ambassador in South Africa, Sir Patrick Moberly, sent London a gloomy assessment:

> I have yet to meet anyone in the government or among ordinary South Africans who relishes the prospect of a Commonwealth Eminent Persons Group coming to South Africa. There are widespread reservations about a team of outsiders thinking they can help in a situation of which they have no firsthand experience. Less polite critics describe it as unwarranted interference which is liable to increase the difficulties.[83]

Malcolm Fraser, who had made very public comments on South Africa earlier in the year, attracted much criticism.[84] Sir John Hoskyns reported to the FCO on his meeting with President Botha on 4 November. Botha had described Fraser as "utterly biased," adding that "there was no way the South African Government would accept that Fraser had a useful contribution to make." An exasperated Moberly later cabled the FCO, saying: "Has Ramphal any idea of the fiercely low opinion in which Fraser is held by the great majority of the whites?"[85]

There was little British optimism about the South Africans accepting the EPG mission. President Botha had consistently dismissed the Commonwealth plan as unwarranted and unacceptable interference in South Africa's internal affairs. On 12 November, Botha told Thatcher: "My government will find it impossible to cooperate with the Commonwealth initiative. Were it not for your admirable efforts, I would have no hesitation in rejecting the Nassau initiative outright."[86] On 20 November, Moberly reported that the Foreign Minister, Pik Botha, was "extremely negative."[87] FCO officials considered the initiative was "on a knife edge" and one went as far as to suggest that "there is some circumstantial evidence that Mr Ramphal is playing for a South African rejection."[88]

Thatcher, reputedly with the support of Pik Botha, made a final effort to persuade the State President.[89] In a letter of 17 November, she told him: "I am convinced that it would be infinitely more damaging to South Africa's future interests were you to refuse to have anything to do with the Group." She continued:

> May I ask you to consider for a moment the full implications if your government were to reject co-operation with the Group. Your enemies in the Commonwealth would be delighted. We and others who had hoped for progress through dialogue will be told that we should have known better. The international pressure for sanctions against South Africa will fast gather momentum again. Most of the value of my having held the line in Nassau will be lost. My ability to help preserve the conditions in which an internal dialogue of the sort you are seeking has a chance of success will be critically, perhaps fatally, weakened.

She concluded:

> In short, I can see no need for you to take a decision about cooperation with the Group now, let alone reject it publicly. If you value my continuing help, I urge you most strongly not to do so. I do not think I could be plainer.[90]

Within days, a breakthrough had been achieved with the FCO reporting a surprisingly compliant response from South Africa and observing: "Had it not been for the Prime Minister's intervention with President Botha, the Eminent Persons Group would have been rejected out of hand."[91] A formal statement from the South African Government followed, though its acceptance of the Commonwealth mission was expressed in rather grudging terms. "It is obvious that the great majority of Commonwealth members is ill-informed or not informed at all of the South African Government's reform programme and of the current situation in South Africa," declared the regime. It added:

> [T]he South African Government has nothing to hide. Should the Commonwealth group be genuinely interested in acquainting themselves with the prevailing circumstances in this country, the South African Government is

prepared to consider ways and means of making this possible without conceding the right of intervention in the country's internal affairs.[92]

There were still sensitive issues to be resolved, such as access to Nelson Mandela, but Thatcher responded: "You know how much importance I attach to this initiative and I am therefore much encouraged by the positive tone of your response."[93] The mission was on its way, despite the deep reservations of some in the AAM, including its UK President, Trevor Huddleston. He privately confessed that it was only his high regard for Ramphal that prevented him from denouncing the group.

## 6  Mission to South Africa

The EPG, or COMGEP as it became known in the Secretariat, held its first meeting in Marlborough House, London, on 12–13 December 1985. Its task, set out under the Nassau Accord, was to encourage political dialogue and advance by all practical means the fulfilment of the Accord. Quite how that was to be done was left to the EPG. Establishing the group's credibility and securing acceptance of its mission had required sensitive and sustained diplomacy on all sides, but now its work could begin in earnest. This it did without delay in the full knowledge that the situation would be reviewed after six months with a report by the group to a special review meeting of Heads of Government on the progress made. Within its terms of reference, the group determined that it would work in discreet and non-public ways and would keep all its discussions confidential. It would operate independently of the South African Government, and of foreign diplomatic missions, and travel anywhere and meet whosoever it wished. Several members of the group, including Obasanjo, insisted that a meeting with Mandela was essential.

Why should the Commonwealth have been effective as an interlocutor? As the formation of the group illustrated, selecting its membership proved to be a considerable challenge and was linked to the equally troubling issue of securing access to all shades of opinion. However, the disparate and haphazard distribution of Commonwealth membership, largely resulting from historical chance, fortuitously gave it a stake in virtually every continent and region of the globe. It was therefore able to use its breadth of connection to maintain good relations with contrasting constituencies and work for consensual positions. This was particularly true of African, Asian and Western interests in the case of the EPG. Secondly, the Commonwealth was careful to 'deploy its diversity' within the membership of the EPG. This provided a visual reminder of its commitment to racial equality and demonstrated the relative ease with which people from very different backgrounds could work together. This was important in South Africa where the Commonwealth could mirror the diversity of the country's emerging 'rainbow society'. That said, it was instructive that it was the Nigerian soldier, Olusegun Obasanjo, who seemed to strike the best relationship with his white interlocutors, rather than the lanky Australian, Malcolm Fraser.[94] Thirdly, the close links most Commonwealth countries maintained with the former colonial power placed them in a specially privileged position of intergovernmental influence with the UK (and, through Britain, to the

United States). Fourthly, those same links also provided valuable connections to opposition political leaders in the UK and to the heart of the global AAM (in the UK and Ireland). This enabled many countries to work with civil society, as well as through diplomatic and governmental channels, in pursuing the anti-*apartheid* cause.

After their first meeting, all seven members of the EPG gathered at Downing Street for a discussion with the British Prime Minister. Thatcher's PS recorded that the Prime Minister had spoken of an "historic opportunity," adding that she was "encouraged by her meeting with the Group. She was under no illusion about the difficulty of their task. But they were off to a good start. She would certainly do her best to influence President Botha in a sensible direction."[95] The next day, true to her word, she wrote again to Botha, telling him of "the generally sensible, level-headed and helpful approach of the Group," adding: "I hope you will agree that it is worth an effort to preserve this."[96] At the EPG's second meeting, on 12–13 February 1986, the group finalised arrangements for the visit of three of its number to South Africa the following week. Accordingly, Fraser, Obasanjo and Barrow visited Cape Town, Johannesburg, Durban and Port Elizabeth to prepare for the visit of the full group. Among those they met were five government Ministers, Bishop Tutu, and UDF leader, Dr Allan Boesak. At Port Elizabeth, Fraser and Obasanjo demonstrated that a picture can be worth a thousand words by strolling, hand in hand, on a 'Whites-Only' beach.

Following this preliminary visit, five members of the group (Barber, Malecela, Scott, Barrow and Fraser) visited Botswana, Lesotho and Zimbabwe before proceeding to the Zambian capital, Lusaka. They met President Quett Masire of Botswana, President Robert Mugabe of Zimbabwe and King Moshoeshe II of Lesotho, along with Lesotho's military leader, Major-General Lekhanya. In Zambia, the group met President Kenneth Kaunda and engaged in dialogue with the ANC leadership, headed by Dr Oliver Tambo. They were joined by the two remaining EPG members, Singh and Obasanjo, and by Ramphal, who also visited Zimbabwe. Before returning to South Africa, the EPG flew to Luanda for talks with Angola's President Dos Santos. By this stage, the group had met the leadership of most of the frontline states and of the ANC outside South Africa, as well as with many other key figures within South Africa itself.

## 7 Mandela and Dialogue: The "Possible Negotiating Concept"

The group had determined early in its planning that it should meet Nelson Mandela, if possible. His release, along with other political prisoners, was a key demand set out in the Nassau Accord, and Mandela's towering authority, even after the isolation of many years' imprisonment, would be a key component in any process leading to genuine negotiations between the government and the full spectrum of opposition groups. Besides, the release of Mandela and his colleagues, the unbanning of the ANC, the PAC and other political parties and free political activity would be likely to create a highly volatile situation, and his presence might reassure the government and South Africa's whites that political chaos would not be the result. That was certainly the fear of the South African Government even while it contemplated Mandela's release. In February 1985, P.W. Botha had offered Mandela his freedom but only if he agreed to unconditionally reject violence as a political weapon.[97] Mandela's response was uncompromising, rejecting Botha's offer in a statement read out publicly by his daughter, Zindzi and declaring: "What freedom am I being offered while the organisation of the people remains banned? Only free men can negotiate. A prisoner cannot enter into contracts."[98]

In 1982, Mandela and other senior ANC leaders had been moved from Robben Island to Pollsmoor Prison in Tokai outside Cape Town.[99] This made discreet contact rather easier. Even so, very few international figures had managed to visit Mandela over the years, apart from humanitarian visits from the International Committee of the Red Cross.[100] Some foreign and local journalists had also been given access, largely for propaganda purposes.[101] In the main, applications to visit him were regularly rejected.[102] At first, the EPG's request to meet Mandela, conveyed to the Minister of Justice, Kobie Coetsee, seemed likely to be refused. But there were powerful figures in the government, including the Foreign Minister, Pik Botha, who lobbied the Minister of Justice and, later, the State President, in support of the EPG's request. He explained: "I went to PW. I said to him 'You can forget about any further positive results from the EPG if we don't do this. They are here as a result of Margaret Thatcher's intervention'. I used her name."[103] The visit was approved. Much later, Coetsee was to say that it was part of "the strategy of the government, to get Mandela to meet the EPG on an equal footing."[104]

In all, the EPG, in various guises, met Mandela in Pollsmoor three times. The first of these encounters took place in February 1986 during the EPG's preliminary visit to South Africa. Only Obasanjo saw Mandela at this point, and no official Commonwealth record of his meeting exists though there are newspaper reports.[105] The next meeting, on 12 March, took place with the EPG as a whole during the group's first substantive visit. Again, no Commonwealth record is available, although Mandela provided his own account.[106] For the EPG, Archbishop Scott made notes which he wrote up afterwards. He describes Mandela's "immaculate appearance. . . . He stands over six feet tall, very upright with clear piercing eyes looking in extremely good health." Asked by Obasanjo how he saw himself, Mandela replied: "as a deeply committed South African nationalist," though he added that nationalists came in more than one colour. Asked to comment on the charge that the ANC was Communist controlled, Mandela "affirmed immediately that he was not a Communist and Oliver Tambo and many others were not Communists. There were Communists in the ANC and at one time in the early years of the Congress," he said, adding that "he and Oliver Tambo had led an attempt to expel those who were Communist and this had been defeated by the Executive." He added: "If he had been in prison for 24 years and had not changed his position, he did not think that the Communists would be able to change him if he was allowed out of prison."[107] The meeting ranged over a number of issues, including his possible release from prison. He confirmed that he was not prepared to accept a conditional release nor release on humanitarian grounds. He also indicated that, if a free man and in the leadership of the ANC, he felt he would be able to work with people like Chief

Buthelezi and with the growing group of younger leaders of the United Democratic Front (UDF).

The question of violence was of particular interest to the group. It would be crucial to the viability of the "Negotiating Concept" later developed by the EPG. Mandela began by explaining why the ANC had reluctantly taken up arms against the *apartheid* state. In 1985, he had written to President Botha clarifying his position. A copy of his letter should be held in the President's office, though Mandela had not been permitted to retain a copy. However, he went on to emphasise that "violence was never an ultimate solution and (the) working of human relationships required negotiation."[108] He added that the ANC had always been anxious to negotiate. In practical terms, it would be impossible for the ANC to defeat the South African Government by military force, and violence was only useful if it helped to lead to "a point of negotiation." As the EPG members took their leave, Mandela told Scott that the visit had meant a great deal to him and that he believed that what was happening with the visit of the group to himself, to South Africa and to the frontline states "was perhaps the most important thing that had happened in the history of South Africa for some decades."[109] All this was rather different in tone to the response so far from the ANC leadership in Lusaka and, indeed, from Mandela's own wife, Winnie Mandela.

All the members of the EPG (except for Obasanjo, who arrived later) met with the executive of the ANC in Lusaka on 28 February 1986. Accompanying the EPG on this occasion was Secretary-General Ramphal, who had flown in from London. The ANC delegation was led by Oliver Tambo and included Thomas Nkobi, Mac Maharaj, Joe Nhlanhla, James Stuart, Pallo Jordan and Thabo Mbeki (who was then the ANC's Director of Information). Initially, the ANC struck a sceptical note with Tambo telling the EPG that

> their immediate reaction to the setting up of COMGEP was that this put the Commonwealth on the side of the oppressor as COMGEP could contribute to the relief of the pressure on the South African regime which had been building up at the time of the Nassau Heads of Government meeting.[110]

After a full explanation of the EPG's role by Malcolm Fraser, Tambo spoke in more conciliatory terms. "The Commonwealth," he said,"

> was known to people in South Africa as a body which had consistently taken strong positions on the *apartheid* question and at no time had these attitudes been more strongly expressed than at the Heads of Government Meeting (CHOGM) in The Bahamas. The ANC therefore saw the mission of the Group as being an elaboration of the strong lead given at Nassau.[111]

He accepted that COMGEP "was part of a major international effort to bring an end to *apartheid*"[112]

Nevertheless, Tambo was deeply sceptical about the sincerity of the South African Government and its willingness to negotiate seriously. He was particularly concerned that, if no progress was made, the regime might nonetheless play a delaying game and attempt to string out the process. There should therefore be "no attempt to extend the mandate."[113] Tambo, in setting out the historical background which had led the ANC to take up arms against the *apartheid* state, also made clear the ANC's reluctance to accept any cessation of violence until after serious negotiations had delivered positive outcomes. Pressed by Lord Barber on whether the ANC might temporarily suspend violence if it was clear that meaningful negotiations were possible, Tambo remained reluctant, saying the ANC could not act unilaterally and that there were many examples of negotiations which had occurred without the cessation of violence. The EPG left Lusaka grimly aware that much more work would be needed before the ANC could be brought into a possible agreement.

Winnie Mandela had met the EPG at the time of the preliminary visit and before the group's meeting with the ANC leadership. She had told the three members of the EPG present that the country's crisis was deepening from day to day.[114] The government had lost control: it knew where the solution lay but refused to face facts and kept looking for artificial answers. She felt that the group would not find many doors open. Nothing less than the complete dismantling of *apartheid* would be acceptable. All else would be "a waste of time."[115] Asked about Mandela's release from prison, she said it was inconceivable that he should be released into anything other than a free political atmosphere. But she feared that the government wanted to push him into "a highly volatile political atmosphere and, by so doing,

*Figure 9.2* John Malecela and his EPG colleagues meet Winnie Mandela, 1986. Commonwealth Secretariat.

destroying the myth that they believed had built up around him."[116] Mrs Mandela also argued that the government was attempting to 'Muzorewarise' Chief Buthelezi and project him as a future leader of the country. She warned that if the group contacted "the puppets, it would be difficult to justify in the community. Emotions were now so brittle, and Blacks who had collaborated with the government were now seen as part of the government apparatus itself. Buthelezi fell into this category." If the EPG were to see such people, it would be at great cost to their status and credibility with the Black community, and "it was really not negotiable."[117] Winnie Mandela met the group again on at least one other occasion. But it was an impromptu speech she made in Munsieville, near Krugersdorp, on 13 April 1986, which caused widespread concern. "We have no guns," she told the crowd, "we have only stones, boxes of matches, and petrol. Together, hand in hand, with our boxes of matches and our necklaces we shall liberate this country."[118] A draft letter to Malcolm Fraser cataloguing Mrs Mandela's various reported comments, and the press reaction to them, was drawn up within the Secretariat but was never sent.[119]

The EPG's third meeting with Mandela took place on 16 May. By then, the group's proposals had been crystallised into a short document titled "A Possible Negotiating Concept." This had been debated and refined when the EPG met, for a third time, in Marlborough House on 30 April–1 May. It had then been put to the principal parties. The proposals were designed to provide the basis for the start of negotiations between the South African Government and Black and other opposition leaders. It called on the government to remove troops from the townships; release Nelson Mandela and other political prisoners; unban the ANC, PAC and other political parties; and permit normal political activity. For their part, the ANC and the other parties representing the Black majority would enter negotiations and suspend violence.

Some days before the last meeting with Mandela, Ramphal had sent a secret message to the EPG following a meeting he had had in Kuala Lumpur with Tambo. It read:

A   "The ANC's preference will continue to be for at least initial talks preceding a ceasefire arrangement, but alternative COMGEP concept could have a change [*chance?*] provided, repeat provided, there is range of matters in preamble. Without clear agreement on this from SAG no/no deal is likely.
B   There is uneasiness about lack of communication between Mandela and Tambo etc prior to an agreement for negotiations. COMGEP intermediation will help but may not/not suffice. There will be need for inventiveness on this.
C   There is a basic worry about a double-cross and anxiety lest without sufficient assurances COMGEP puts pressure on ANC to go along with what turns out to be major tactical setback. I have emphasised COMGEPs awareness of all dangers and that it will not/not itself recommend arrangements without being satisfied SAG will deliver."[120]

Clearly, the leadership of the ANC outside South Africa was coming around to accepting COMGEP's formulation of a suspension of violence in return for the South

African Government fulfilling the key steps set out in the negotiating concept. But there was also unease that Mandela might agree something out of step with his colleagues, as well as deep distrust of the South African Government.

It was not yet 9 a.m. on 16 May when Mandela welcomed the EPG to the Guest House within the Pollsmoor prison compound. Greeting Fraser, he asked him to compliment Bob Hawke on the suggestion that the group be constituted. "It was a very good idea," he added.[121] They were joined, on the South African side, by the Minister of Justice, Kobie Coetsee; the Commissioner of Prisons, General Willemse; Brigadier Munroe, the Commandant of Pollsmoor Prison; and Mr J. Heunis, a Legal Adviser to the State President. After about ten minutes of informal discussion over coffee, Coetsee and Willemse withdrew, despite Mandela's protestations that they should stay. He emphasised that he would still have spoken perfectly freely, and the Minister would have had a measure of how he viewed things. He added: "The fact of talking would build mutual confidence . . . and it was this lack of confidence that was leading to a serious wastage of the country's human and other resources." If the Minister wished not to be present, he appreciated the reasons but hoped it would not be the last time that they would see each other.[122] Mandela was under no illusion that his talks with the EPG would be private and fully expected that the government would record all his conversations. It was therefore in the likely knowledge that his audience went far beyond the EPG that Mandela continued:

> [I]t was his deep wish to organise discussions with the government in order to allay their fears and assure them of his cooperation, not just as an individual but as a member of the ANC. His view could carry weight only if expressed as part of the ANC. One of the difficulties in Pollsmoor was that he was not in contact with the ANC, either with fellow members of the party in Pollsmoor and other prisons, or out of jail.[123]

The group then presented Mandela with a copy of the "Possible Negotiating Concept." Mandela read the paper and then returned it to Obasanjo. Pressed for his reaction, Mandela said that he had no problem with the document. Although he had not studied it closely, he was already conversant with its general tenor from some press reports he had seen. "The only problem," he added, "was that the Group was interested in his views not just as an individual but as a member of the organisation to which he belonged." He needed to consult his colleagues, but "he did not think he would have many problems in persuading his colleagues to use the Group's ideas as a starting point."[124] Surprisingly, and contrary to the views of others in the ANC, he counselled the group not to insist on a strict timetable for decisions: the South African Government needed to be given a reasonable chance. He was also asked to comment on the view that Chief Buthelezi should be excluded from any negotiations. Mandela said that "his position was very clear. Buthelezi was a freedom fighter in his own right. Although he differed from the ANC and had said harsh things about it, he was a force who could not be ignored."[125] Obasanjo then asked Heunis, the President's Legal Adviser, if he wished to ask a question. Heunis said that he wanted to clarify Mr Mandela's position on the group's negotiating concept. Was he right in assuming that Mr Mandela regarded it as an acceptable starting point and that if the government accepted it, he would accept it too? Mandela replied that he accepted it whether the South African Government accepted it or not. However, he wanted his views to be those of his movement, not just of an individual.

The EPG's meetings with Mandela revealed several important features. Firstly, for the first time, Mandela had, from his prison cell, opened a dialogue about change in South Africa which involved both the South African Government and a third party (in this case, the Commonwealth). Secondly, he had made clear that his responses were inseparable from those of the ANC leadership outside South Africa and emphasised that no agreement could be reached which did not recognise that reality. Thirdly, that notwithstanding, his personal approach appeared to be one of extraordinary flexibility and openness, including on violence and on the inclusivity of any negotiations.

While Mandela's influence helped move the ANC to accepting the suspension of violence, in the context of the negotiating concept, Mandela also emphasised the importance of synchronising responses from both the government and the ANC. At the same time as the ANC suspended violence, the government should also pull out the army and the police from the townships. It was also clear that, while many in the South African Government had concluded that these actions were necessary, they feared the unknown circumstances of normal political activity, with Mandela and other political leaders out of jail and free to operate politically. Some continued to argue for a cessation, rather than a suspension, of violence. This would be completely unacceptable to the ANC.

As far as Coetsee was concerned, Mandela's message could not have been clearer. While the Minister had operational authority for overseeing Mandela's imprisonment (including requests for visits and changes to the conditions under which his most famous prisoner was being held), he first visited Mandela in hospital in 1985, and the two men seemed to get on well. Now it seemed that a far greater opportunity beckoned. However, the immediate usefulness of the Commonwealth channel was about to be abruptly terminated.

## 8 The Breakdown: The EPG Leaves

The EPG had presented its proposals to the government during its third visit to South Africa. The "Possible Negotiating Concept" was neither accepted nor rejected, and it became clear that the Cabinet was divided on the issue and that a struggle for ascendancy was in process. Early on the morning of 19 May, news reached the EPG in Cape Town that units of the South African Defence Force (SADF) had earlier attacked three neighbouring Commonwealth countries, namely Botswana, Zambia and Zimbabwe.[126] Du Toit commented: "The targets held little military significance but the attack was intended to demonstrate the State's military strength and to symbolise the resolve of the PW Botha government not to be dictated to by outsiders."[127] The hardliners had won, and the group had received its answer in dramatic and brutal terms. Kaunda declared the raids: "a dastardly, cowardly action," and Ramphal branded them "a declaration of war."[128] Nonetheless, the group decided not to withdraw at once but to conclude all its scheduled meetings, including with the Cabinet's Constitutional Committee where a formal response had been expected to the Commonwealth's proposals.

The EPG's eventual failure as an exercise in negotiation and conflict resolution proved to be its greatest political success. Admittedly, there were some who have argued that its work was terminated prematurely. Stremlau, while accepting that the initiative was "a politically influential act," concludes that "the Commonwealth lacked the capacity and resolve to gain quick acceptance of the formula" and thus had to wait until local conditions ripened for its voluntary acceptance four years later.[129] It was clear that the British Government would have wished the EPG to continue its work.[130] More intriguingly, Mandela in his later exchanges with the EPG appeared to be open to the mission continuing, despite setbacks.[131] However, this would not have been either acceptable to key parties, most notably the ANC, or feasible practically. Desmond Tutu, the new Anglican Archbishop of Cape Town, described Pretoria's actions as "a slap in the face" for the EPG. He warned that the group would have "no credibility whatever with blacks if it continues to talk with Pretoria." He added: "Only a robust call from the EPG for economic sanctions against South Africa would justify the Commonwealth's effort and vindicate the trust reposed in it."[132] The South African regime made outward protestations of its wish to keep talking. However, Guelke concludes that Pretoria had decided that "the continuation of the mission was no longer in its interest."[133] In all, there was no prospect that the mission might have been rescued without damaging the Commonwealth's credibility or discrediting the prospects of genuine negotiations. Paradoxically, the rejection of the EPG's proposals convinced many that the last days of the *apartheid* system had now come. In the view of veteran journalist John Battersby, it was "the beginning of the end." At that moment "everything conflicted – sanctions were inevitable, *apartheid* was shown in its full horrors, and there was only one way out now, which was negotiations."[134]

## 9 The EPG and South Africa's Negotiated Solution

As an attempt at negotiations, the initiative clearly failed. However, it not only left an important legacy in terms of the framework of issues involved in the "Possible Negotiating Concept" but also fostered contacts and relationships which were to contribute to a series of other, largely covert, meetings. These included gatherings in Dakar and Senegal, as well as Leverkusen in Germany, facilitated by the Institute for a Democratic Alternative (IDASA), where figures in the ANC met prominent Afrikaners for informal discussions.[135] These were designed to explore common ground and to move the public discourse away from confrontation and division and towards engagement and potential accommodation. The Mells House talks, initiated in late 1987 by senior staff in the mining giant Consolidated Goldfields and partly taking place in a stately home in Somerset, had a similar purpose, though its activities were spread over several years and were more covert.[136] Harvey claims that this "prolonged dialogue," that at times included Thabo Mbeki and Willie de Klerk, the elder brother of the future president, was the beginning which led to "the constitutional agreement between Cyril Ramaphosa and Rolf Meyer in 1993."[137] Others were less sure with Robin Renwick insisting it was "not a negotiation."[138] In all, Niel Barnard, the former Head of the National Intelligence Service (NIS), has estimated that between 1983 and 1990 about 1,200 South Africans met representatives of the ANC in exile in 167 gatherings and meetings.[139] Unsurprisingly, Barnard has a low opinion of "these amateur negotiators . . . these self-appointed mediators."[140] His correspondingly high opinion of his own role seems equally misplaced: "Perhaps it was the deep emotional connection we both had with South Africa that brought home both Mandela's and my realisation that negotiations, like a healthy marriage, had no room for outsiders."[141]

It is certainly the case that Mandela saw the visit of the EPG visit as an opportunity to advance his desire for 'talks about talks'. After the EPG's third call on him in jail, he felt optimistic and believed that "the seeds of negotiations had been sown."[142] That was not to be but instead Mandela was able to utilise his growing relationship with the Justice Minister, Kobie Coetsee. In 1988, this personal contact was superseded by a committee of senior officials, including Niel Barnard.[143] This new arrangement lasted until Mandela's release and involved many meetings, but these were more about building confidence and allaying government concerns, in preparation for a meeting with P.W. Botha and, later, de Klerk, rather than substantive negotiations. At the end of the process, Barnard rather plaintively remarks of Mandela that he did not "hold him to statements he had made during our secret talks . . . nor raise it when he took a different stance from that adopted in discussions."[144] Nevertheless, Coetsee's private papers, now held after his death in the archives of the University of the Free State, reveal a clear and growing governmental connection with Mandela in covert 'talks about talks' which originated with the EPG's visit.[145]

## 10 Conclusion

The point has been made earlier that as a diplomatic initiative the EPG's mission was significant, sustained and far-reaching. It is also apparent that the "Possible Negotiating Concept" provided a substantive contribution to the all-party negotiations that began after 1991, as Pik Botha and others have recognised.[146] The unresolved issue in 1986 was the suspension of violence in the context of the release of Mandela, the unbanning of prohibited parties, and free political activity. The *apartheid* regime needed time and the closing of other options to grasp this nettle, but there were little more any external interlocutors could have done at that stage to facilitate further negotiations. Only today, with the availability of hitherto classified documents, can the EPG mission, and its follow-up, be seen in its full context. In terms of process as well as content, the Commonwealth mission should therefore be viewed as a ground-breaking and important contribution to the process of multi-party negotiations that began in Mandela's prison cell in February 1986. It was only after the collapse of the EPG initiative in May that Mandela, in July of the same year, took the further step of requesting a meeting with P.W. Botha. It was therefore the EPG mission, rather than Mandela's letter to Botha as some suggest, which ought to be considered as initiating the pre-negotiation process. Nevertheless, thereafter Mandela recognised that while Botha would always remain 'a symbol of *apartheid*', he should also be remembered: "for the steps he took to pave the way towards the eventual peacefully negotiated settlement in our country."[147]

**Notes**

1. Commonwealth Secretariat, *The Commonwealth at the Summit* (Vol.1), 267–269.
2. Peter Limb, "The anti-*apartheid* movements in Australia and Aotearoa/New Zealand" in *The Road to Democracy in South Africa*, ed. Sifiso Ndlovu, Vol.3, International Solidarity, Part II, 943; Bob Hawke, *The Hawke Memoirs* (Australia: William Heineman, 1994), 318.
3. Correspondence from Trevor Huddleston to Shridath Ramphal, 9 January 1986, AAM Archives, Bodleian Library, Oxford L: CW 1960–1994, MSS AAM 1301.
4. McIntyre, *The Significance of the Commonwealth*, 117–120. See also W. David McIntyre, *A Guide to the Contemporary Commonwealth* (Basingstoke and New York: Palgrave, 2001), 40–43.
5. Ramphal, *Glimpses of a Global Life*, 431–449.
6. Ibid., 434.
7. For fuller details and reference, see page 17.
8. Anyaoku, *The Inside Story of the Modern Commonwealth*, 92–3.
9. Craft, "Between the idea and the reality," 103–160.
10. Ibid., 104.
11. Ibid. 103.
12. C.R. Mitchell, "Conflict management in the Commonwealth," In *The Commonwealth in the 1980s: Challenges and Opportunities*, ed. A.J.R. Groom and Paul Taylor (London: Macmillan, 1984).
13. Saul Dubow, "The Commonwealth and South Africa: From Smuts to Mandela," *Journal of Imperial and Commonwealth History* 45:2 (2017): 302.
14. Alister Sparks, *The Mind of South Africa: The Story of the Rise and Fall of Apartheid* (UK: Mandarin, 1990), 352.
15. Special report for SAIIA Members, *Implications of the Report of the Commonwealth Eminent Persons' Group: June 1986* (Braamfontein, Johannesburg: Jan Smuts House, 1986).
16. Adrian Guelke, *South Africa in Transition: The Misunderstood Miracle* (London and New York: I.B. Tauris, 1999), 137.
17. Ibid., 143.
18. Dubow, "The Commonwealth and South Africa," 303.
19. Enuga Reddy, "The United Nations and the struggle for liberation in South Africa "in *The Road to Democracy in South Africa*, 111–112.
20. Abdul Minty, "South Africa and the Commonwealth: Assessing the challenges ahead" in *The Commonwealth in the 21st Century*, ed. Greg Mills and John Stremlau (Johannesburg and London: South African Institute of International Affairs, 1999), 57–61.
21. Christabel Gurney, "In the heart of the beast: The British anti-*apartheid* movement, 1959–1994" in *The Road to Democracy*, 330.
22. Nigel Worden, *The Making of Modern South Africa: Conquest, Segregation and Apartheid* (Oxford, UK and Cambridge, Mass., USA: Blackwell Publishers, 1994), 135–136.
23. Timothy Shaw, *Commonwealth: Inter- and Non-state Contributions to Global Governance* (London and New York: Routledge, 2008), 40.

24 Chan, *The Commonwealth in World Politics*, 71.
25 Interview with Pik Botha, 13 December 2012, Pretoria, RSA, Accessed 16 February 2015, Commonwealthoralhistories.org/2015/interview-with-rf-pik-botha.
26 Craft, "Between the idea and the reality," 150–6.
27 Note of a meeting between Margaret Thatcher and Julian Amery, 24 July 1979, TNA, PREM 19/108 f.71.
28 Reddy, "The United Nations and the struggle for liberation," 42.
29 Ibid.
30 UN Chronicle, "End *apartheid* by 1 January 1987, Panel of Eminent Persons asks," Nov/Dec 1985, *Questia*, Accessed 28 April 2020, www.questia.com/read/1G1-4003584/end-*apartheid*-by-1-january-1987-panel-of-eminent.
31 Meeting of the UN Security Council, 8 March 1988 (PV.2797), Dag Hammarskjold Library, Accessed 28 April 2020, www.undocs.org/en/s/PV.2797.
32 Arnold Smith, "The we-they frontier: From international relations to world politics" (37th Montague Burton Lecture, 1 November 1982), University *of Leeds Review* (1983): 87–106.
33 Sharp, *Thatcher's Diplomacy*, 229–230.
34 Ramphal, *Glimpses of a Global Life*, 416.
35 Bob Hawke, interviewed by Sue Onslow, 31 March 2014, *Commonwealth Oral History Project*, London, 31 March 2014, Accessed 5 July 2019, www.commonwealthoralhistories.org, 2015/interview-with-bob-hawke, transcript, 6.
36 Ramphal, *Glimpses of a Global Life*, 386.
37 Lord Hurd, interviewed by Sue Onslow, 26 October 2013, *Commonwealth Oral History Project*, London, 26 October 2013, Accessed 5 July 2019, http://www.commonwealthoralhistories.org.2015/interview-with-douglas-hurd, transcript, 8–9.
38 Ramphal, *Glimpses of a Global Life*, 327.
39 Sharp, *Thatcher's Diplomacy*, 227–228.
40 Correspondence from Julius Nyerere to Margaret Thatcher, July 1986, TNA PREM 19/1644, F169.
41 See 126–158.
42 Sharp, *Thatcher's Diplomacy*, 230.
43 Note by David Barclay to Bernard Ingham, 31 October 1983, recording a telephone conversation between the Prime Minister and Charles Douglas-Home on 29 October 1983, TNA, PREM 19/1983/1049.
44 Fieldhouse, *Anti-Apartheid*, 157.
45 Martin Plaut, "What really happened when Margaret Thatcher met South Africa's PW Botha?" *New Statesman*, 1 January 2014, Accessed 14 September 2019, www.newstatesman.com/world-affairs/2014/01/what-really-happened-when-margaret-thatcher-met-PW-botha-?
46 P.W. Botha, Opening Address, National Party Natal Congress, Durban, 15 August 1985, Padraig O'Malley archives, Nelson Mandela Foundation, Accessed 5 July 2019, htpps://www.omalley.nelsonmandela.org/omalley/index.php/site/q.
47 Anyaoku, *The Inside Story of the Modern Commonwealth*, 89.
48 McIntyre, *Guide to the Contemporary Commonwealth*, 40.
49 Ramphal, *Glimpses of a Global Life*, 426.
50 Correspondence from Margaret Thatcher to P.W. Botha, 4 October 1985, Thatcher Foundation, Accessed 5 July 2019, www.margaretthatcher.org/document/111647.
51 Correspondence from Julius Nyerere to Margaret Thatcher, 7 October 1985, TNA, PREM 19/1644/270.
52 Correspondence from Quett Masire to Margaret Thatcher, 11 October 1985, TNA, PREM 19/1644/175.
53 Dennis Austin, *The Commonwealth and Britain* (London: Routledge & Kegan Paul Ltd, 1988), 39.

54 Ibid., 39–40.
55 Ibid., 39.
56 Sharp, *Thatcher's Diplomacy*, 232.
57 S.K. Rao, "Shridath Ramphal and his struggle for peaceful change in South Africa," In *Shridath Ramphal: The Commonwealth and the World*, ed. Richard Bourne (London: Hansib Publications, 2008), 63.
58 Commonwealth Secretariat, *Report of the Commonwealth Committee on Southern Africa*, October 1983–September 1985, presented to the Nassua CHOGM 1985 as HGM (85)5 and annexed to *Minutes of Sessions and Memoranda*, personal papers, 279–280.
59 Commonwealth Secretariat, *Minutes of Sessions and Memoranda*, Commonwealth Heads of Government Meeting, Nassau, 16–22 October 1985, personal papers, 98,100.
60 Ibid., 104–5.
61 Ibid., 107.
62 Ibid., 117.
63 Ibid., 83.
64 Ibid., 109.
65 Correspondence from Charles Powell to Anthony Acland, 21 October 1985, TNA, PREM 19/1688.
66 Commonwealth Secretariat, *The Commonwealth at the Summit*, 267.
67 Ibid., 268.
68 Ibid., 269.
69 Correspondence from Margaret Thatcher to P.W. Botha, 31 October 1985, TNA, PREM/1644, 26.
70 Correspondence from P.W. Botha to Margaret Thatcher, quoted in Ramphal, *Glimpses of a Global Life*, 433.
71 Correspondence from Charles Powell to Len Appleyard, 22 October 1985, TNA, FCO 105/2034.
72 Correspondence from Geoffrey Howe to Margaret Thatcher, 27 October 1985, TNA, FCO 105/2034.
73 Ibid.
74 Correspondence from Charles Powell to Len Appleyard, 28 October 1985, TNA, FCO 105/2034.
75 Emeka Anyaoku (Commonwealth Secretary-General), in conversation with the author, 5 December 2016, Travellers Club, London.
76 Anyaoku, *The Inside Story of the Modern Commonwealth*, 89.
77 Message from Shridath Ramphal to Margaret Thatcher, conveyed through Sir John Thomson, 28 October 1985, TNA, FCO 105/2034.
78 Cable from FM Canberra (Leahy) to Foreign Secretary, 28 October 1985, TNA, FCO 105/2034.
79 Anyaoku, *The Inside Story of the Modern Commonwealth*, 89–92.
80 Cable from FM Lagos to FCO, 19 November 1985, TNA, FCO 105/2034.
81 Correspondence from Ewen Fergusson to the PM's Private Secretary, 20 November 1985, TNA, FCO 105/2034.
82 Broadcast transcript, Allan Boesak interviewed by Graham Leach, 6 p.m. News Bulletin, *BBC Radio 4*, 4 January 1986, Commonwealth Secretariat archives, COMGEP/40/4/1-B(iii).
83 Cable from Patrick Moberly, FM Pretoria, to FCO, 6 November 1985, TNA, FCO 105/2034.
84 Malcolm Fraser had been chairman of the UN Panel of Eminent Persons on the Role of Transnational Corporations during 1985.
85 Cable from Patrick Moberly, FM Pretoria, to FCO, 23 November 1985, TMA, FCO 105/2034.
86 Correspondence from P.W. Botha to Margaret Thatcher, 12 November 1985, TNA, FCO 105/2034.
87 Cable from Patrick Moberly to FCO, 20 November 1985, TNA, FCO 105/2034.

88 Handwritten annotation by Ewen Fergusson on correspondence from Anthony Reeve to the Private Secretary/Permanent Under-Secretary, 20 November 1985, TNA, FCO 105/2034.
89 Pik Botha, interviewed by Sue Onslow, *Commonwealth Oral History Project*, London, 16 February 2015, Accessed 5 July 2019, www.commonwealthoralhistories.org, 2015/interview-with-rf-pik-botha/11.
90 Correspondence from Margaret Thatcher to P.W. Botha, 17 November 1985, quoted in Ramphal, *Glimpses of a Global Life*, 433.
91 Correspondence from Anthony Reeve to the Private Secretary, 26 November 1985, TNA, FCO 105/2034.
92 Press Release, by the South African Government, 26 November 1985, Pretoria, TNA, FCO 105/2034.
93 Correspondence from Margaret Thatcher to P.W. Botha, 9 December 1985, TNA, FCO 105/2034.
94 Anyaoku, *Inside the Modern Commonwealth*, 94–5.
95 Note by Charles Powell of a Meeting between the Prime Minister and Members of the EPG, Friday, 13 December 1985, TNA, FCO 105/2034.
96 Correspondence from Margaret Thatcher to P.W. Botha, 14 December 1985, TNA, FCO 105/2034.
97 Mandela, *Long Walk to Freedom*, 620–621.
98 Ibid., 623.
99 Also transferred at the same time were Ahmed Kathrada, Raymond Mhlaba, Andrew Mlangeni and Walter Sisulu.
100 Andrew Thomson, " 'Restoring hope where all hope was lost': Nelson Mandela, the ICRC and the protection of political detainees in *apartheid* South Africa," *International Review* 98:903 (2017), 799–829.
101 Martha Evans, "News from Robben Island: Journalists' visits to Nelson Mandela during his imprisonment," *Journal of Southern African Studies* 45:6 (2019): 1116–1129.
102 Pik Botha, interviewed by Sue Onslow, *Commonwealth Oral History Project*, London, 16 February 2015, Accessed 5 July 2019, www.commonwealthoralhistories.org, 2015/interview-with-rf-pik-botha/11.
103 Ibid., 11.
104 John Carlin, Interview with Kobie Coetsee, "The long walk of Nelson Mandela," *FRONTLINE*, 6 December 2013. www.pbs.org/wgbh/pages/frontline/shows/mandela/interviews/coetsee.html, Accessed 10 May 2022.
105 Dimeji Kayode-Adedeji, "My encounters with Mandela – Obasanjo," *Premium Times of Nigeria*, 6 December 2013, Accessed 23 June 2020, www.premiumtimesng.com/news/150982-encounters-mandela-obasanjo.html.
106 Mandela, *Long Walk to Freedom*, 628–630.
107 Ted Scott, "Reflections on the visit of the COMGEP on Nelson Mandela," 12 March 1986, Commonwealth Secretariat archives, 40/4/1–6, 3.
108 Ibid., 2.
109 Ibid., 4.
110 Oliver Tambo, speaking at a meeting between the Executive of the ANC and the Commonwealth Group of Eminent Persons, at the Mulungushi Hall, Lusaka, Friday, 28 February 1986, Commonwealth Secretariat archives, COMGEP (SR) 40, 2.
111 Ibid., 4.
112 Ibid., 5.
113 Ibid., 7.
114 These were Rt. Hon. Malcolm Fraser, General Olusegun Obasanjo and Dame Nita Barrow.
115 Record of a meeting between the Commonwealth Group of Eminent Persons and Winnie Mandela, Wednesday, 19 February 1986, Sandton, Commonwealth Secretariat archives, COMGEP/40/3-B, 2.
116 Ibid., 3.

117 Ibid., 5.
118 Emma Gilbey, *The Lady: The Life and Times of Winnie Mandela* (London: Jonathan Cape, 1993*)*, 145–6.
119 Draft telex to Rt.Hon. Malcolm Fraser, initiated by Dominic Sankey and Hugh Craft, 21 April 1986, Commonwealth Secretariat archives, COMGEP/40/3-B, ANC 6.
120 Message from Sonny Ramphal to COMGEP (via Ambassador Lee) marked SECRET for meeting of 13 May 1986, Commonwealth Secretariat archives, COMGEP 40/4/1-B(i).
121 Record of a meeting between COMGEP and Nelson Mandela, Friday, 16 May 1986, Pollsmoor Prison, Commonwealth Secretariat archives, COMGEP (SR) 122 (ANC) 4/1-B(i), 1.
122 Ibid., 2.
123 Ibid.
124 Ibid., 5.
125 Ibid., 9.
126 The *Apartheid* Museum in Johannesburg records the 19 May attack but provides no context and makes no mention of the Commonwealth's EPG initiative.
127 Pierre du Toit, *South Africa's Brittle Peace: The Problem of Post-Settlement Violence* (Basingstoke, UK and New York: Palgrave Macmillan, 2001), 76.
128 BBC News, "South African raids wreck peace bid," *BBC on This Day*, 19 May 1986, Accessed 4 March 2018, htpp://www.news.bbc.co.uk/onthisday/hi/dates/stories/may/19/newsid_3030000/3030995.stm.
129 John Stremlau, "The Commonwealth contributing to civility on the eve of the citizen century" in *The Commonwealth in the 21st Century*, 65–66.
130 Margaret Thatcher, Prime Minister's Questions, 20 May 1986, *Official Record* (98/174–78), Accessed 12 February 2018, www.api.parliament.uk/historic-hansard/commons/1986/may/20/engagements.
131 Record of a meeting between Nelson Mandela and the Commonwealth Group of Eminent Persons, 16 May 1986, Commonwealth Secretariat archives, COMGEP (SR) 122, 4/1-B(i), 7–8.
132 Notes of a telephone conversation between Desmond Tutu and Shridath Ramphal, 29 May 1986, from Janet Singh to Moni Malhoutra, of the same date, Commonwealth Secretariat archives, COMGEP 40/4/1-E, 1.
133 Guelke, *Rethinking the Rise and Fall of Apartheid*, 202.
134 John Battersby, Remarks to a Witness Seminar on "Negotiating with *apartheid*: The mission to South Africa of the Commonwealth Eminent Persons Group 1986," University of London, 13 June 2011. Unpublished report, personal papers, 43.
135 Patrick Salmon (ed.), *The Unwinding of Apartheid: UK-South African Relations 1986–1990*, Documents on British Policy Overseas, Series III, Vol. XI (London and New York: Routledge, 2019), xii–xiv.
136 Robert Harvey, *The Fall of Apartheid* (Basingstoke & NY: Palgrave Macmillan, 2001).
137 Ibid., xv.
138 Ibid., 178.
139 Niel Barnard, *Secret Revolution: Memoirs of a Spy Boss* (Cape Town: Tafelberg, 2015), 191.
140 Ibid., 192.
141 Ibid., 193.
142 Mandela, *Long Walk to Freedom*, 630.
143 Ibid., 636.
144 Barnard, *Secret Revolution*, 265.
145 Private collection of H.J. (Kobie) Coetsee, PV357, Archive for Contemporary Affairs, University of the Free State, Bloemfontein.
146 Pik Botha, interviewed by Sue Onslow, *Commonwealth Oral History Project*, London, 13 December 2012, Accessed 5 July 2019, www.commonwealthoralhistories.org, http//sas_space.sas.ac.uk/5806/i/Pik Botha transcript, 3.

147 Nelson Mandela, "PW Botha: Reaction in quotes," *BBC NEWS*, 1 November 2006, Accessed 20 October 2021, www.news.bbc.co.uk/1/hi/world/africa/6105178/stm.

## References

Adrian Guelke, *Rethinking the Rise and Fall of Apartheid: South Africa and World Politics* (London: Palgrave, 2004).
Adrian Guelke, *South Africa in Transition: The Misunderstood Miracle* (London, New York: I.B. Tauris, 1999).
A.J.R. Groom and Paul Taylor (eds.), *The Commonwealth in the 1980s: Challenges and Opportunities* (London: Macmillan, 1984).
Alister Sparks, *The Mind of South Africa: The Story of the Rise and Fall of Apartheid* (UK: Mandarin, 1990).
Bob Hawke, *The Hawke Memoirs* (Australia: William Heineman, 1994).
Commonwealth Secretariat, *The Commonwealth at the Summit (Vol.1)* (London: Commonwealth Secretariat, 1987).
Dennis Austin, *The Commonwealth and Britain* (London: Routledge, Kegan Paul Ltd, 1988).
Emeka Anyaoku, *The Inside Story of the Modern Commonwealth*, Op. Cit.
Emma Gilbey, *The Lady: The Life and Times of Winnie Mandela* (London: Jonathan Cape, 1993).
Greg Mills and John Stremlau (eds.), *The Commonwealth in the 21st Century* (Johannesburg, London: South African Institute of International Affairs, 1999).
Hugh Craft, "Between the Idea and the Reality," PhD Thesis (Canberra: Australian National University, 2008).
McIntyre, *The Significance of the Commonwealth*, Op.Cit.
Nelson Mandela, *Long Walk to Freedom*, Op.Cit.
Niel Barnard, *Secret Revolution: Memoirs of a Spy Boss* (Cape Town: Tafelberg, 2015).
Nigel Worden, *The Making of Modern South Africa: Conquest, Segregation and Apartheid* (Oxford, UK, Cambridge, Mass, USA: Blackwell Publishers, 1994).
Patrick Salmon (ed.), *The Unwinding of Apartheid: UK-South African Relations 1986–1990, Documents on British Policy Overseas*, Series III, Vol. XI (London, New York: Routledge, 2019).
Paul Sharp, *Thatcher's Diplomacy*, Op.Cit.
Pierre du Toit, *South Africa's Brittle Peace: The Problem of Post-Settlement Violence* (Basingstoke, UK, New York: Palgrave Macmillan, 2001).
Richard Bourne (ed.) *Shridath Ramphal: The Commonwealth and the World* (London: Hansib Publications, 2008).
Robert Harvey, *The Fall of Apartheid* (Basingstoke, NY: Palgrave Macmillan, 2001).
Roger Fieldhouse, *Anti-Apartheid: A History of the Movement in Britain; A Study in Pressure Group Politics* (London: Merlin Press, 2005).
Shridath Ramphal, *Glimpses of a Global Life*, Op.Cit.
Sifiso Ndlovu (ed.), *The Road to Democracy in South Africa (Vol.3)*, (International Solidarity: Op.Cit.)
Stephen Chan, *The Commonwealth in World Politics*, Op.Cit.
Timothy Shaw, *Commonwealth: Inter- and Non-State Contributions to Global Governance* (London, New York: Routledge, 2008).
W. David McIntyre, *A Guide to the Contemporary Commonwealth* (Basingstoke, New York: Palgrave, 2001).

# 10 The Sanctions Campaign and 'Endgame'

## 1  Introduction

The Commonwealth summit in the Bahamas in October 1985 had seen a clear and sometimes bitter division open up over the issue of economic and financial sanctions against South Africa. What had eventually united Commonwealth leaders was the adoption of the Nassau Accord, an agreement which, in the words of British journalist Nicholas Ashford, was "a carefully balanced package of sanctions, threats and inducements."[1] Its purpose was to encourage the South African Government to begin a dialogue with representative Black leaders on ways of ending *apartheid*. Now that Commonwealth efforts to encourage all-party negotiations lay in ruins, the Accord's undertaking that leaders should therefore take further measures against South Africa, including sanctions, came sharply back into focus. The then Bishop of Johannesburg, Desmond Tutu, was blunt: "we face a catastrophe in this land and only the action of the international community by applying pressure can save us."[2]

Mrs Thatcher considered the collapse of the initiative a 'disaster'. The day after the SADF raid which aborted the Commonwealth's mission, she told the House of Commons:

> I totally and utterly condemn the raid by South Africa into the three countries. The Group has now left South Africa because the members of the group thought that that stage of their proceedings was over. It is just possible that they may continue their work.[3]

Pressed by Neil Kinnock, the Leader of the Labour Opposition, on the adoption of "effective sanctions" against South Africa, she replied: "I do not believe that sanctions and the isolation of South Africa are any more likely to achieve the desired negotiations after the raid than they were before."[4] She added that the UK government was continuing its efforts to secure dialogue and discussion and hoped that the EPG would persist in its work, despite its 'setback'. As the EPG met in Marlborough House on 5 June, to finalise its report, the UK Cabinet was clutching at straws. Sir Geoffrey Howe told his colleagues that the EPG had not yet reached any conclusion:

*Figure 10.1* Archbishop Desmond Tutu. Commonwealth Secretariat.

The British member of the Group, Lord Barber, was working hard to keep the Group in being, so that it could carry forward the attempt to engage South Africa in dialogue. The Australian member of the Group, Mr Malcolm Fraser, was giving some support.[5]

After this over-optimistic gloss, Howe continued in a more realistic vein: "COMGEP might not decide to give up its work immediately, but the prospects for its further efforts were not good."[6]

Thereafter, it was clear that the UK government's approach was twofold: Firstly, to keep in being the notion of dialogue and negotiation, either through the Commonwealth or, increasingly, through some other channel; and, secondly, to resist the calls for economic sanctions on South Africa. In the latter respect, a semantic argument developed over what the EPG had meant by its call for 'further effective measures'. The veteran Labour MP, Peter Shore, had quoted the phrase at Thatcher and remarked: "If that is not equivalent to sanctions, I do not know what is."[7] For her part, Mrs Thatcher responded by quoting the report, in saying: "We are not determining the nature or extent of any measures which might be adopted, or their effectiveness."[8] Mindful that the Commonwealth review meeting (of seven Heads of Government, including the UK) was due to convene at the beginning of August to consider the EPG report and

182  *The Sanctions Campaign and 'Endgame'*

consequential measures, the British then sought to pursue both themes. This involved trying to persuade Western allies not to pursue economic sanctions, as well as investing effort in Sir Geoffrey Howe's ill-timed and humiliating demarche to South Africa on behalf of the European Council of Ministers.

## 2   The EPG's Report – And a Change of Direction

Following the failure of its mission, the EPG's next task was to report its findings to the Commonwealth and to the world. An agreement had already been reached that its report would be published as a Penguin Special. Working through the night under the direction of the Assistant Secretary-General, Moni Malhoutra, a writing team in Marlborough House set about preparing a draft report for the Secretary-General. With his own changes and additions incorporated, Ramphal then presented the draft to the EPG, who finalised the text in a formal session from 4 to 7 June. The finishing touches to the document took place over the following weekend with the typed manuscript arriving with the Penguin editor on the morning of Monday, 9 June. Design, typesetting and proofreading took place at breakneck speed. With the cover and illustrations complete, printing of the book started on Wednesday evening with binding beginning during the night. A Secretariat officer, Clive Jordan, was present throughout to advise where necessary. Finished copies left the printer in Suffolk at 9 a.m. on Thursday, 12 June, arriving at Marlborough House in time for its noon launch. Copies were in bookshops the same day.

*Figure 10.2* The EPG in session. Commonwealth Secretariat.

It was reputably the fastest book ever published, and it quickly became a bestseller, supplanting *The Hunt for Red October* in popularity. Penguin's original 55,000 copies sold out in one week, and another 10,000 were printed, followed by a further 4,000 in mid-July. In all, over 80,000 copies were printed in English, though it was also translated into French, Dutch, Japanese and Greek. John Mortimer described it as 'a miracle of publishing at the moment of truth'. David Astor, the newspaper publisher and editor of *The Observer*, wrote to Ramphal, calling the report "magnificent . . . it is a thrilling document and I am certain that it must help the situation." He congratulated Ramphal "on the initiative that you personally took in promoting this great mission which will certainly find its place in the history books."[9] Anthony Sampson, the writer and biographer of Nelson Mandela, wrote in similarly effusive terms:

> It is a publishing feat. Its publication is a major political event. It is a document that will change history; every country's view of South Africa will be changed by it. The report is enormously readable. Its original fresh style gives it enormous impact.[10]

More significant still was the political impact of the report. Bob Hawke, the Australian Prime Minister, declared:

> The report is a powerful and compelling account of the daily agony brought about by the *apartheid* system in South Africa, of the conscientious and dedicated attempts of the seven members of the group to carry out the Commonwealth's mandate from Nassau, and of the obduracy and intransigence of the South African regime.[11]

James Callaghan, the former Labour Prime Minister, added: "I do not think I have ever seen a more damning document prepared by such a diverse group, all of whom are in agreement."[12] Copies (in French) were rushed to the World Conference on Sanctions against South Africa in Paris on 16 June, where it was presented by Ramphal. The final resolution of the conference, inter alia, noted "with appreciation the efforts of the Commonwealth Group of Eminent Persons to provide a just and peaceful solution to South Africa." A Commonwealth Secretariat officer reported: "There were frequent references to the EPG Report as well as SG's speech . . . there was also great demand for the EPG Report and the available copies had to be carefully rationed!"[13] It was a message carried to all parts of the world and picked up by civil society campaigners and the global AAM. It was particularly influential in the decision of the US Congress to pass sanctions legislation in defiance of President Ronald Reagan's threat of veto.

The report's description of *apartheid* was striking:

> None of us was prepared for the full reality of *apartheid*. As a contrivance of social engineering, it is awesome in its cruelty. It is achieved and sustained only through force, creating human misery and deprivation, and blighting the lives of millions. Black and white live as strangers in the same land.[14]

But it also chronicled the EPG's attempts to pursue political dialogue and achieve a negotiated end to *apartheid*. It concluded that, in rejecting the negotiating concept, the South African Government was not yet genuinely ready to engage in negotiations about the establishment of a non-racial and representative government in South Africa. The group concluded that "it is not sanctions which will destroy the country but the persistence of *apartheid* and the government's failure to engage in fundamental political reform." In recommending further measures against the regime, the group concluded:

> The question in front of Heads of Government is in our view clear. It is not whether such measures will compel change; it is already the case that their absence and Pretoria's belief that they need not be feared, defers change. Such action may offer the last opportunity to avert what could be the worst bloodbath since the Second World War.[15]

All seven members of the EPG signed the report. This included Lord Barber, Thatcher's nominee, who wrestled with duty and conscience and eventually joined the call for further sanctions. Barber, a former UK Chancellor of the Exchequer, had been chosen by Thatcher partly because of his extensive business interests in South Africa. As Chairman of Standard Chartered Bank, he had travelled to South Africa many times. He had begun his involvement with the EPG faithfully pursuing the role given to him by his patron and mentor. But the work of the group exposed him to a side of the country he had not seen before and to people and opinions beyond his previous experience. In the end, and despite the counterclaims in one of his obituaries, he found he could not dissent from his Commonwealth colleagues about the need for further sanctions.[16]

As Thatcher struggled to contain the demands for sanctions, new impetus was given to those advocating a boycott of the 1986 Commonwealth Games in Edinburgh. Warnings of action over the XIIIth Games had been building for some time. At the Nassau CHOGM the previous year, the leader of the Nigerian delegation, Commodore Ukiwe, had put on record that the Games "might be a source of conflict, if all those who had continued to interact with South Africa in sport ignored the call by Heads of Government."[17] The original motivation for such a move, by African and Asian nations in particular, was therefore to protest against the UK's equivocal attitude to the Gleneagles Agreement on *apartheid* in sport. However, it was the sanctions row, rather than *apartheid* in sport, which precipitated the effective collapse of the Games as a multiracial competition. Nigeria and Ghana withdrew at the beginning of July and others quickly followed. By the end of July, only twenty-six nations and territories remained in a distinctly monochrome contest. Worse, the Games were the first to be tasked with finding all their funding from commercial sources (with Thatcher confirming that there would be no financial support from the UK government). With the Games already showing a £4m deficit (on a budget of £14m) the organisers found an unlikely saviour in the considerable shape of Robert Maxwell, the former MP, publisher and newspaper baron. Proclaiming that "there is no shortfall," Maxwell steadily propelled the

Games into insolvency.[18] Ramphal did his best to prevent the boycott, but the tide was too strong. He appealed for Thatcher's help in saving the Games, but she replied: "They're not my Games: they're yours."[19] Bateman and Douglas concluded: "There has never been a Games so battered and bruised by conflict, by accountants and by politicians."[20] It was an inauspicious omen for the impending special Commonwealth summit beginning on 3 August.

## 3 The London Review Meeting

Only days after the disastrous large-scale boycott of the 1986 Edinburgh Commonwealth Games, seven Commonwealth leaders gathered at Marlborough House to consider the report of the EPG and its recommendations. Chaired by the host of the Nassau summit, Lynden Pindling, the other Heads of Government present were Gandhi (India), Hawke (Australia), Kaunda (Zambia), Mugabe (Zimbabwe), Mulroney (Canada) and Thatcher (Britain). They were joined at the table by Ramphal. The night before, all eight had been at Buckingham Palace at a private dinner hosted by the Queen. Ramphal recalls that this was a working dinner, rather than a social occasion, and that the Queen left a clear impression that the summit should find unity and not fail in its task.[21] It was one of several reports that suggested that the Queen, as Head of the Commonwealth, was unhappy with the approach of the British Prime Minister.[22]

Certainly, as they began their work, most leaders were mindful of the overwhelming concern of the Nassau CHOGM that there should be further speedy and effective action against the South African regime if it had failed to make adequate progress in dismantling *apartheid* and finding a negotiated solution. For most, that much seemed beyond doubt.

However, unlike Nassau, the debate was difficult from the outset. Mugabe told Thatcher that he found the British position "a little disappointing, to say the least." He "appealed to Britain to demonstrate its leadership role in the Commonwealth."[23] Thatcher responded by accusing Mugabe of suggesting to the meeting "a proposal to give arms to the ANC." This accusation triggered general protests that Mugabe had not made such a proposition, but the British Prime Minister was in no mood to back down, declaring that "the difference between Mr Mugabe and herself was that she rejected violence whereas he did not."[24]

Listing the assistance the UK had given to Africa and the FLS in particular, she regretted that "Britain rarely received any thanks" and hoped that in future she could attend meetings: "without having to listen to some of the unfounded criticisms she has heard."[25] Pressed on the question of further sanctions, she declared that she saw "no proof to convince her that sanctions would bring about internal change within South Africa and, indeed, everything pointed to the contrary. Sanctions had never brought about a change and never would."[26] When her colleagues suggested a ban on air links and the import of iron ore and coal, as well as agricultural products, she protested: "[I]t would be ridiculous to allow the business to pass to someone else."[27] The morning session ended with an appeal from Mulroney. Confirming that Canada would support whatever measures the meeting

*Figure 10.3* The CHOGM Review meeting, Marlborough House, August 1986. Commonwealth Secretariat.

agreed upon, he said that "he did not want the Commonwealth to look preposterous and ludicrous and be seen to be backing away from the fundamental issue." On the contrary, it was essential that the Commonwealth should do the right thing.[28]

In the afternoon, Geoffrey Howe substituted for his Prime Minister and brought a more emollient approach to the conference table. Nevertheless, the UK's policy approach remained broadly unchanged. At the end of the meeting, six of the leaders agreed on a package of eleven sanctions against the *apartheid* regime. These included those envisaged at the Nassau summit the previous year as well as several additional measures. The UK, the seventh country, stood aside from the agreed sanctions but announced that it would accept and implement any decisions by the EEC to ban the import of coal, iron and steel and gold coins from South Arica. It also agreed a 'voluntary ban' on new investment in South Africa and on the promotion of tourism to it.[29] This then marked the emergence of a 'binary Commonwealth'. All Heads regretted the absence of full agreement but recognised, more in hope than in expectation, that "the potential for united Commonwealth action still exists."[30] The six leaders, excluding Britain, concluded their decisions with an appeal for a concerted programme of international action and announced that they would embark on intensive consultations to that end.[31] But they protested that the aim of sanctions was not punitive, as Thatcher feared. As the Australian Prime Minister Bob Hawke had put it (quoting his Foreign Minister, Bill Hayden): "We want to bring them to their senses, not to their knees."[32]

The ANC and the AAM were relieved that the EPG remained impervious to the blandishments of the *apartheid* state and that its conclusions were clear and boosted the sanctions campaign.[33] In turn, pressure for economic and financial sanctions grew, through a widening network of support, though the campaign failed to move significantly its principal target, the UK government. Archbishop Trevor Huddleston, AAM's President, casting aside his previous scepticism, greeted the report with these words:

> I wholeheartedly welcome the report. The policies of the AAM on which we have campaigned for a quarter of a century have been absolutely vindicated. The report is a devastating condemnation of President Reagan's constructive engagement policy and the Prime Minister's servile acceptance of it.[34]

He later wrote: "The Commonwealth initiative and the report Mission to Africa (sic), of the Eminent Persons Group, was of the utmost importance. Just because the authority of the representatives of the Commonwealth was unquestionable, the strength of their recommendation carries immense weight."[35] But there were more critical voices. Helen Suzman, the veteran anti-*apartheid* campaigner and for many years the sole embodiment of South Africa's liberal conscience, told protestors against her anti-sanctions' stance in New York: "I understand the moral abhorrence and pleasure it gives you when you demonstrate. But I don't see how wrecking the economy of the country will ensure a more stable and just society."[36]

The Commonwealth can justifiably claim that the EPG's report and the fierce disputes about sanctions which followed enlarged the debate and helped encourage the imposition of further international sanctions. The report also painted a vivid picture of a racially oppressive and intransigent regime, continuing to incarcerate the world's most famous political prisoner. The promotion of the EPG report and the measures agreed at the Commonwealth's special summit in London, in August 1986, should therefore be intrinsically linked to the EPG's efforts to seek a negotiated solution and the conclusions the group drew once that initiative had broken down. Together, this had "a catalytic effect," argued Ramphal.[37] However, some do not make this connection, preferring to see the mission in isolation from its report and aftermath.[38]

## 4  Internationalising Sanctions

But what could the Commonwealth hope to achieve in the absence of British support? Ramphal argues that the Commonwealth was successful in setting "the benchmark for international sanctions."[39] Within a few days of the Commonwealth summit, the US Senate voted by a large majority for a package of sanctions, including many of those adopted in London. The imprint of the Commonwealth was clear. After the return of the EPG from South Africa and the launch of its report,

188  *The Sanctions Campaign and 'Endgame'*

Obasanjo, Fraser and Ramphal had embarked on a range of visits to key capitals. At the beginning of June, prior to the release of the EPG report, the co-chairmen had written to Senator Edward Kennedy about his Anti-*Apartheid* Bill, recently introduced into the US Congress. They suggested that they might "comment on the sorts of measures which we believe might be most effective."[40] They concluded that their recommendation "probably represents the minimum programme that would carry real weight with the South African Government." They recognised that some would argue for comprehensive sanctions but warned that it would be "far more difficult to get the international community to accept such an approach."[41]

A month later Obasanjo and Fraser were in Washington and lobbying Congress at a time when Reagan's faltering South Africa policy was causing widespread concern. On 23 July, Senator Edward Kennedy announced that he and Senator Weicker were tabling an anti-*apartheid* amendment to the Debt Ceiling Act. He said: "The amendment we propose contains a series of economic and diplomatic sanctions that we believe have broad support. In essence, they are the proposals endorsed by the Eminent Persons Group of the Commonwealth of Nations."[42] While conceding that these measures fell short of the full divestment and total trade embargo adopted by the House of Representatives, Kennedy urged: "These are still far-reaching and effective sanctions."[43] The amendment was passed by a large majority.

In Europe, there was a similar EPG demarche during June 1986, particularly to Bonn, Paris and the EEC, prior to the European summit in The Hague and the UN Sanctions conference in France. The failure of Howe's mission to Southern Africa in July (in his capacity as President of the Council of Ministers) persuaded the EC to agree on further sanctions (as envisaged in June). The imposition of sanctions by the Nordic countries and by Japan followed, though the response was not only from governments. As Ramphal adds, "[w]ithin a month of the London meeting, 21 American states and 65 American cities had taken disinvestment action, and some US$30 billion of pension fund investments were up for imminent withdrawal."[44] In the UK, there was a surge in local authority action against *apartheid*, including cutting financial links to South Africa or Namibia through divesting contracts or investments. However, this was severely constrained in 1988 by the passing of legislation making it illegal for local councils to boycott South African products or suppliers.[45] Nevertheless, student pressure in boycotting Barclays Bank proved increasingly effective. In 1986, Barclays admitted that they had achieved 'poor results' the previous year, largely as a result of "intensive anti-Barclays activity, accentuated by the extensive media coverage afforded to South Africa."[46]

For the Commonwealth, the question was how, without British support, the organisation could now drive the sanctions agenda forward. The 1987 Vancouver CHOGM saw a deepening rift in the 'binary Commonwealth' and acrimonious exchanges. Both sides had reason to argue that the rift suited them: Thatcher, because she was free of the Commonwealth's shackles and therefore able to articulate the breadth of UK policy more clearly; Ramphal, because the Commonwealth had upheld its credibility and integrity and no longer needed to be constrained by the need to accommodate the British viewpoint. Neither benefited from the division in the longer term. An unfortunate side effect was that British diplomatic staff in the Commonwealth Secretariat were on occasions suspected of divided loyalties with their skills under-utilised as a consequence.[47] The mood of the Vancouver CHOGM worsened when, at a summit press conference, Thatcher declared the ANC a "typical terrorist organisation."[48] This was despite the low-level dialogue her government had been conducting with the movement since 1986.[49] The summit produced the Okanagan Statement and Programme of Action on Southern Africa, albeit punctuated by British dissent.[50] McIntyre described it as "a somewhat vague document, laced with the rhetoric of urgency but much less specific than the Nassau Accord."[51] Unlike the previous year, no new sanctions were agreed. At the same time, under the Okanagan Statement, a Commonwealth Committee of Foreign Ministers on Southern Africa (CFMSA) was established under the chairmanship of Canada. Designed to "sharpen the focus of Commonwealth sanctions and sustaining the political momentum," the CFMSA, Ramphal pronounced, was "a major evolution of Commonwealth practice."[52]

Working with the Secretariat, CFMSA was charged with coordinating the implementation of Commonwealth sanctions and safeguarding their effectiveness. The Commonwealth (the UK excepted) also agreed to evaluate the impact of sanctions on a continuous basis and to explore the possibilities of financial measures. What was remarkable about this work (headed by Dr Joseph Hanlon and an independent Study Group) was that it had not been done before. In 1988, as Hanlon began his task, he discovered that there was no directory of sanctions imposed on South Africa and no detailed trade statistics. Without these, Hanlon wondered how the effectiveness of current sanctions could be assessed or how new forms of pressure could be exerted.[53] Their work, Hanlon argued, also "demonstrated that certain other approaches would be less fruitful."[54] This necessarily selective and targeted approach was to create tension with the ANC whose unchanging mantra was 'comprehensive and mandatory sanctions'.

At the 1989 CHOGM, Hanlon's report enabled Commonwealth leaders (and others beyond the organisation) to look dispassionately at the effect of sanctions imposed on South Africa by its major trading partners. At that point, there were twenty-seven countries with economic, financial and other links with South Africa. The bulk were European, others were Commonwealth countries, and the remainder comprised the United States, Japan, Argentina and Brazil, together with the Nordic countries.[55] Van Vuuren contends that sanctions were widely evaded, not only in the West but "by the liberation movement's traditional allies in the Eastern bloc, including Russia and China."[56] While patterns of implementation therefore varied, it was financial sanctions which offered the most scope for further pressure. That was the message coming from Bob Hawke and the Australian Government. They financed a further independent report by two Australian economists, Keith Ovenden and Tony Cole, on *apartheid* and international finance which recommended further sanctions to widespread approval. All this was too much for Thatcher who publicly repudiated a Commonwealth consensus painstakingly negotiated at the summit by her Foreign Secretary, John Major.

However, by the late 1980s, economic pressure on South Africa was now coming from multiple sources: individual and collective, private and public. "It is the action of both formal and informal sanctions which determine the balance of South Africa's economic equation," declared the AAM.[57] Robin Cohen, among many others, has argued that 1985 proved to be a turning point for South Africa. The precipitous fall in the value of the Rand, capital outflows and the drying up of foreign investment, coupled with persistent internal unrest and the government's imposition of a state of emergency called into question those such as Adam (1971), Gann and Duignan (1983) and Schlemmer (1983) who confidently predicted *apartheid's* survival. On the contrary, "[t]he *apartheid* ship of state has sailed permanently into an angry hurricane of protest," thought Cohen, it had reached "a new state of unstable equilibrium."[58]

In addition to mounting economic pressures, South Africa's once-fabled military reputation had been dealt a severe blow at Cuito Cuanavale in 1988. The costs of policing the townships and fighting beyond South Africa's borders were becoming prohibitive, even as its effectiveness diminished. Circumventing the oil embargo was essential, but it came at a hefty price. In 1986, P.W. Botha put the additional cost of buying oil on the black market at R22 billion (nearly R300 billion at 2017 values) in the ten years since 1975.[59] Most importantly, deprived of foreign investment and long-term credits, South Africa had to finance its expenditure by generating a current account surplus. In 1989, the UK Ambassador to South Africa, Robin Renwick, reported that the new Governor of the Reserve Bank, Chris Stals, was hoping to achieve a current account surplus of R4 billion in 1989, adding: "While South Africa is not yet out of the woods, the net outflow of capital in the third quarter had diminished."[60] Dr Desmond Krogh, a key figure in South Africa's attempts to counter sanctions, told the FCO: "As long as sanctions remained selective, non-standardised and non-mandatory, their effect would be limited." However, financial sanctions were a different matter if it deprived South Africa of long-term credits. "There is no prospect of South Africa handling the urbanisation process, achieving economic development and tackling regional problems without long term external finance," admitted Krogh. He continued: "There would be a sharp recession in the first half of next year: the government was already cutting back sharply on spending plans."[61] Privately, the FCO's economic assessment admitted that the Commonwealth's Ovenden & Cole report "makes the case, which no one seriously disputes, that financial pressures have harmed the South African economy and further financial sanctions could inflict further damage."[62] The key question for the FCO was what the political effect of such sanctions might be and, even as *apartheid* began to crumble, the UK held to the judgement that sanctions had no effect on the political process and might well be counterproductive. In assessing the broad mix of pressures which, after 1985, helped edge the South African regime to negotiation and *apartheid's* disintegration, it is important to apportion some weight to sanctions and especially financial ones. In that respect, Hawke was largely justified in his conviction that "the investment boycott was the dagger which finally immobilised *apartheid*."[63] The EPG initiative therefore contributed both to negotiations and to the sanctions campaign. It also considerably raised the profile and the credibility of the Commonwealth as a modern, international organisation.

## 5 Conclusion

At the conclusion of the EPG's mission, it could show an impressive reach. It had met with the South African Government on twenty-two occasions; visited Mandela on three occasions in Pollsmoor prison; and had held talks with all the main opposition leaders in South Africa, across the spectrum, as well as with prominent academic, religious and community figures. It had also consulted the leaders of the FLS and the leadership of the ANC outside South Africa. It had held many other meetings with governments in Africa, Europe, the United States and elsewhere.[64] In all, the EPG mission lasted from December 1985 until August 1986 and was funded by a special Commonwealth Secretariat budget of £1 million, to which the UK was the largest contributor.[65] The Canadian Government also made a substantial in-kind contribution, providing an executive Challenger jet and crew, through the Royal Canadian Air Force, so that the EPG could conduct its shuttle diplomacy across Southern Africa. It was indisputably a significant and sustained exercise in conflict resolution and the largest single initiative of its kind ever mounted by the Commonwealth. As a comparison, the budget for the Mells House process was between £500,000 and £1 million, described by Harvey as "an astonishing figure."[66]

It was to be nearly four years before a newly released Nelson Mandela, after twenty-seven years' imprisonment, could declare that South Africa's long march to freedom was now irreversible. As negotiations began on South Africa's democratic future, it was clear that much in the EPG's original "Negotiating Concept" remained valid. More to the point, the enforced conclusion of the mission laid bare the true nature of the *apartheid* regime and ensured that the EPG's report would reach a receptive global audience, galvanising calls for full economic and financial sanctions against the South African state.

The failure of the mission, however, did nothing for the Commonwealth's relations with its most influential member, the UK. Over the next three years, the Commonwealth's differences with Thatcher and the British Government seemed to grow wider. That said, without her links to P.W. Botha and her influence, the EPG mission would never have been granted entry to South Africa, or the freedom to travel wherever, and meet whoever, it pleased.[67] She repeatedly called for the end of *apartheid* and for the release of Nelson Mandela. Although she was still Prime Minister in February 1990, when Mandela was finally released after twenty-seven years in prison, her resignation followed some months later.

The 1986 mission of the Commonwealth EPG, its report and the part the Commonwealth subsequently played in the developing international sanctions campaign are not widely recognised. Yet the evidence is clear that the organisation made a distinctive and significant collective contribution to the international campaign against *apartheid* in South Africa in this instance. This was recognised at the time by various international organisations, national governments, and commentators: and the initiative generated legacies which proved useful at a further stage in the international campaign against *apartheid*. It was also a timely reminder of the strengths that the Commonwealth could offer in the service of the world – and in the application of its own distinctive 'healing touch'.

## Notes

1. Nicholas Ashford, "Summit accord on *apartheid* hailed as key step," *The Times*, 21 October 1985, Margaret Thatcher Foundation, www.margaretthatcher.org/document/111652.
2. Desmond Tutu, Press Conference St George's Cathedral, Cape Town, 2 April 1986, reported by David Crary, "Tutu calls for economic sanctions against South Africa," Associated Press, 3 April 1986, Accessed 14 September 2019, www.apnews.com/9657ea631dc8cd6ae090453489e61591.
3. Margaret Thatcher, Prime Minister's Questions, Tuesday, 20 May 1986, *Official Record*, 98/174–178, Accessed 12 February 2018, www.api.parliament.uk/historic-hansard/commons/1986/may/20/engagements.
4. Ibid., 174–178.
5. Minutes of a Meeting of Cabinet, Thursday, 5 June 1986, TNA, CAB 128/83/22, 6.
6. Ibid., 6.
7. Margaret Thatcher, Prime Minister's Questions, Thursday, 12 June 1985, *Official Record* 99/491–496, Accessed 12 February 2018, www.api.parliament.uk/historic-hansard/commons/1986/june/12/engagements.
8. The Commonwealth Eminent Persons Group, *Mission to South Africa: The Commonwealth Report* (Harmondsworth, UK: Penguin books, 1986), 140.
9. Correspondence from David Astor to Shridath Ramphal, 18 June 1986, Commonwealth Secretariat archives, COMGEP/40/6.
10. Correspondence from Anthony Sampson to Geraldine Cooke, 16 June 1986, Commonwealth Secretariat archives, COMGEP/40/6.
11. Bob Hawke, Statement on "Mission to South Africa," 12 June 1986, Commonwealth Secretariat archives, COMGEP/40/6.
12. Correspondence from James Callaghan to Sonny Ramphal, 12 June 1986, Commonwealth Secretariat archives, COMGEP/40/6.
13. Memorandum, "World Conference on Sanctions on South Africa," from S.K. Rao to Shridath Ramphal, 4 July 1986, Commonwealth Secretariat archives, COMGEP, I/40/5/34A, 2–3.
14. The Commonwealth Group of Eminent Persons, *Mission to South Africa*, 23.
15. Ibid., 141.
16. Dennis Kavanagh, "Lord Barber: Reluctant and unhappy chancellor," Obituary in *The Independent*, 19 December 2005, Accessed 5 July 2019, www.independent.co.uk/news/obituaries/lord.barber.520040.html.
17. Commonwealth Secretariat, *Minutes of Sessions and Memoranda*, 96.
18. Derek Bateman and Derek Douglas, *Unfriendly Games: Boycotted and Broke, The Inside Story of the 1986 Commonwealth Games* (London: Mainstream PP Ltd, 1986), 53.
19. Ramphal, *Glimpses of a Global Life*, 449.
20. Bateman and Douglas, *Unfriendly Games*, 124.
21. Ramphal, *Glimpses of a Global Life*, 444; Hardman, *Queen of the World*, 398–9.
22. Jason Beattie, "Queen's fury at Margaret Thatcher for 'damaging the Commonwealth' revealed in declassified documents," *Daily Mirror*, 29 December 2017, Accessed 19 September 2019, www.mirror.co.uk/news/politics/queens-fury-margaret-thatcher-damaging-11765243; Robert Hardman, *Queen of the World* (London: Century, 2018), 390–1.
23. Record of Proceedings, Heads of Government Review Meeting, 3–5 August 1986, Commonwealth Secretariat archives, COMGEP 40/4/1-A, 37.
24. Ibid., 37–38.
25. Ibid., 39.
26. Ibid., 40.
27. Ibid., 42.
28. Ibid., 50.
29. Commonwealth Secretariat, *The Commonwealth at the Summit* (Vol.1), 293.
30. Ibid., 294.

31 Ibid., 293.
32 Bob Hawke, *The Hawke Memoirs* (Australia: William Heineman, 1994), 317.
33 Gurney, "In the heart of the beast," 331.
34 Trevor Huddleston, Statement on the release of the EPG report, 12 June 1986, Commonwealth Secretariat archives, COMGEP/40/06.
35 Trevor Huddleston, "Introduction," *Annual Report of the Anti-Apartheid Movement 1985/6*, October 1986, AAM archive, Bodleian Library, B.1.1., MSS.AAM, 13, 2.
36 John Burns and Alan Cowell, "Helen Suzman, relentless challenger of *apartheid* system, is dead at 91," *The New York Times*, 1 January 2009, 3, Accessed 3 March 2019, www.nytimes.com/2009/01/02/worls/africa/02suzman.html.
37 Shridath Ramphal, *Biennial Report of the Secretary-General 1987* (London: Commonwealth Secretariat, 1987), 6.
38 David Welsh and J.E. Spence, *Ending Apartheid* (Harlow: Longman, 2011), 57.
39 Shridath Ramphal, "Mandela's freedom, the Commonwealth and the *apartheid* axis," *The Round Table: The Commonwealth Journal of International Affairs* 106:6 (2017): 625.
40 Correspondence from Olusegun Obasanjo and Malcolm Fraser to Edward Kennedy, 10 June 1986, Commonwealth Secretariat archives, COMGEP/40/4/2-A, 1.
41 Ibid., 4.
42 Edward Kennedy, Statement on the anti-*apartheid* amendment to the Debt Ceiling Act, 23 July 1986, Commonwealth Secretariat archives, I40/5 Part A.
43 Ibid., 1.
44 Ramphal, "Mandela's freedom," 625.
45 Fieldhouse, *Anti-Apartheid*, 368.
46 Circular letter No.239/86, from S.H. Fortescue, General Manager Barclays Bank plc, to undisclosed recipients, 14 July 1986, personal papers, 1.
47 Interview with former member of Commonwealth Secretariat staff, 14 July 2019.
48 Robin Renwick, "Margaret Thatcher's secret campaign to end *apartheid*," *Daily Telegraph*, 11 February 2015, Accessed 6 August 2020, www.telegraph.co.uk/news/politics/MargaretThatcher/11403728/margaret-thatcher's-secret-campaign-to-end-*apartheid*.html.
49 Andy McSmith, "Margaret Thatcher branded ANC 'terrorist' while urging Nelson Mandela's release," *The Independent*, 9 December 2013, Accessed 12 July 2019, www.independent.co.uk/news/uk/politics/margaret-thatcher-branded-anc-terrorist-while-urging-nelson-mandela-s-release-8994191.html.
50 Commonwealth Secretariat, *The Commonwealth at the Summit, 1987–1995* (Vol.2) (London: Commonwealth Secretariat, 1997), 7–12.
51 McIntyre, *The Significance of the Commonwealth*, 120.
52 Shridath Ramphal, *Biennial Report of the Secretary-General 1989* (London: Commonwealth Secretariat, 1989), 8.
53 Joseph Hanlon (ed.), *South Africa: The Sanctions Report – Documents and Statistics* (London: Commonwealth Secretariat & James Currey, 1990), 1.
54 Ibid., 2.
55 Ibid., 5–8.
56 Van Vuuren, *Apartheid, Guns and Money*, 11.
57 Lynda Loxton, "Paying the price of hanging on to *apartheid*, "*Financial Mail*, TNA, FCO 105/3575.
58 Robin Cohen, *Endgame in South Africa* (Paris & London: UNESCO Press and James Currey Ltd, 1986), 88.
59 Van Vuuren, *Apartheid, Guns and Money*, 103.
60 Cable from Robin Renwick to Priority FCO, October 1989, TNA, FCO 105/3575.
61 Correspondence from R.J. Sawers (British Embassy, Pretoria) to Geoffrey Berg (FCO), quoting Dr Desmond Krogh, 28 July 1989, TNA, FC0 105/3575, 1–2.
62 G. Gantley (Economic advisers) to G. Berg (FCO), Memorandum on "Ovenden & Cole: *Apartheid* and international finance," 7 August 1989, TNA, FCO 105/3575, 78, 2.

63 Georgia Hitch, "Bob Hawke looks back at Australia's involvement in the downfall of *apartheid*," *ABC News*, 27 April 2016, Accessed 14 June 2017, www.abc.net.au/news/2016-04-27/bob-hawke-opens-*apartheid*-exhibition-in-canberra/7364762.
64 Commonwealth Group of Eminent Persons, *Mission to South Africa*, 150–156
65 In terms of 2019 values, this equates to a sum of between £3 and 5 million
66 Harvey, *The Fall of Apartheid*, 20.
67 Anyaoku, *The Inside Story*, 103.

**References**

Bob Hawke, *The Hawke Memoirs* (Australia: William Heineman, 1994).
Commonwealth Secretariat, *The Commonwealth at the Summit (Vol.1)*, Op.Cit.
Commonwealth Secretariat, *The Commonwealth at the Summit, 1987–1995 (Vol.2)*, (London: Commonwealth Secretariat, 1997).
David McIntyre, *The Significance of the Commonwealth*, Op.Cit.
David Welsh and J.E. Spence, *Ending Apartheid* (Harlow: Longman, 2011).
Derek Bateman and Derek Douglas, *Unfriendly Games: Boycotted and Broke, The Inside Story of the 1986 Commonwealth Games* (London: Mainstream PP Ltd, 1986).
Emeka Anyaoku, *The Inside Story of the Modern Commonwealth*, Op.Cit.
Hennie Van Vuuren, *Apartheid, Guns and Money: A Tale of Profit*, Op.Cit.
Joseph Hanlon (ed.), *South Africa: The Sanctions Report – Documents and Statistics* (London: Commonwealth Secretariat, James Currey, 1990).
Robert Hardman, *Queen of the World* (London: Century, 2018).
Robert Harvey, *The Fall of Apartheid*, Op.Cit.
Robin Cohen, *Endgame in South Africa* (Paris, London: UNESCO Press, James Currey Ltd, 1986).
Roger Fieldhouse, *Anti-Apartheid: A History of the Movement in Britain*, Op.Cit.
Shridath Ramphal, *Biennial Report of the Secretary-General 1987* (London: Commonwealth Secretariat, 1987).
Shridath Ramphal, *Biennial Report of the Secretary-General 1989* (London: Commonwealth Secretariat, 1989).
Shridath Ramphal, *Glimpses of a Global Life*, Op.Cit.
The Commonwealth Eminent Persons Group, *Mission to South Africa: The Commonwealth Report* (Harmondsworth, UK: Penguin books, 1986).

# 11 Ending *Apartheid* – A Troubled Transition

## 1 Introduction

The last white parliament of South Africa had heard watershed speeches before. In 1985, P.W. Botha had promised to "cross the Rubicon" but at the last moment had remained rooted defiantly on the opposite bank, obdurate in the face of international opinion. This time, however, Botha's successor struck a different note. There is "a growing realisation by an increasing number of South Africans that only a negotiated understanding among the representative leaders of the entire population is able to ensure lasting peace," he said: "The alternative is growing violence, tension and conflict."[1]

With these words, President de Klerk embarked on a course which, in dramatic circumstances, would eventually lead to *apartheid's* end. It would also see a decisive shift in the Commonwealth's approach, away from confrontation and South Africa's isolation and towards a process of engagement in support of peaceful transition. This followed the steps highlighted in de Klerk's speech: the release of Nelson Mandela, the unbanning of the ANC, PAC and other proscribed parties, and the first steps of what can now be viewed as an irreversible process of change.

These momentous events, which seemed to fulfil the Commonwealth's long-held objectives for ending *apartheid*, meant that the association had to respond to these changed circumstances by fundamentally rethinking its approach. If it was to have a continuing contribution to make, the association now had to seek engagement with all the parties, including the South African Government, and find specific ways in which it could assist transition. This included mediation, peace-making, capacity-building, conflict resolution and other support for the negotiation process. In doing so, the Commonwealth also needed to reinvigorate its relationship with the UK.

Apart from one or two biographies, oral histories and relevant journal articles, this aspect of the Commonwealth's relationship with *apartheid* has been particularly neglected. It is a contribution which, for all its three years in length, merits a single line in Enuga Reddy's summary of Commonwealth programmes in his comprehensive account of the role of the United Nations in the anti-*apartheid* struggle.[2] While Reddy cross-references the Commonwealth to some degree in describing UN programmes and concludes that the United Nations worked collaboratively

10.4324/9781003208617-11

*Figure 11.1* Nelson Mandela and F.W. de Klerk exchange greetings. Commonwealth Secretariat.

with other international organisations in helping end *apartheid*, he is otherwise silent on the substance of the Commonwealth's role. Spence mentions the assistance of "monitors and observers" at the elections but, in listing international groups, omits the Commonwealth.[3]

The relevant Commonwealth' archives, now coming into the public domain, tell a different tale, revealing a sustained period of engagement by the Commonwealth with South Africa during the transition from *apartheid*. This was no less significant than earlier periods of Commonwealth action involving, for example, the sporting boycott, the EPG initiative and the beginnings of the negotiation process, or the sanctions campaign (notwithstanding differences with Britain) and the final days of *apartheid's* resistance.

What therefore were the circumstances which enabled the UK and the rest of the Commonwealth to find common cause at the 1991 Harare CHOGM? It was hardly surprising that the search for a new facilitative and supportive role for the Commonwealth in the transition process was initially greeted by de Klerk and his government with scepticism and some hostility. However, an assessment of the 1991 special mission to South Africa, led by the new Commonwealth Secretary-General, Emeka Anyaoku, supports the Commonwealth's claim that it was instrumental in opening the door to an international dimension in the multi-party talks. The chapter then examines the first of two major in-country deployments that grew out of the Commonwealth's re-engagement and which built upon the idea of an international observer presence. The first deployment had its genesis in the upsurge in violence in 1992 which included the Boipatong massacre of 17 June that year. This precipitated a breakdown in the multi-party talks and the withdrawal of the ANC from negotiations.[4]

Whatever the causes of the violence ripping through the townships of the Vaal and of Natal, its effect was to wreck the chances of multi-party negotiations and threaten peace. Further repression and a return to the status quo on the part of the government, or a mass rising by the ANC and its allies by taking the 'Leipzig Option', were unthinkable even if accidental civil war was not.[5] Anyaoku, in his discussions with the principal protagonists, argued that the Commonwealth and international effort should now be directed at "preventing violence from obliterating the prospects of a peaceful solution."[6] Accordingly, he put forward the idea of international observers who could be deployed to the 'hotspots' to seek to contain the violence. Was this, as Anyaoku claims, the origin of the adoption of UN Security Council resolution 772, on 17 August 1992, with its recognition that violence, if it continued "would seriously jeopardise peace and security in the region" and its authority for the deployment of international observers, including from the Commonwealth?[7] How effective were the four international observers missions which resulted, from the United Nations, the OAU, the EC and the Commonwealth? Was their contribution "rather limited" as Abdul Minty has maintained?[8] Or did the Commonwealth mission (COMSA), in particular, make a contribution through conflict resolution and mediation which was distinctive and significant? In particular, how was it that the international observer presence tasked with addressing transitional violence helped make acceptable a far larger international observer deployment at the greatest moment of change – the 1994 'freedom elections'?

## 2  Overcoming a Divided Commonwealth

The release of Mandela on 11 February 1990 had been followed, twelve days later, by the announcement that the UK was unilaterally lifting a number of voluntary sanctions – the ban on new investment and the ban on the promotion of tourism to South Africa. Despite disquiet in Europe and consternation in the Commonwealth, Thatcher declared:

> As you know, two of our voluntary sanctions have been lifted this morning after we had our consultations with Europe. We differ slightly on sanctions but not in the way in which we praise President de Klerk for his bold initiatives and what he has already done.[9]

Mandela was incensed by Thatcher's actions. In the febrile and uncertain period prior to negotiations, the ANC and the UDF were aghast at any suggestion of rewarding de Klerk at this stage or altering the pressures on the government to come to the negotiating table. Two months later, making his first visit to London since 1962, Mandela declined an invitation to meet the British Prime Minister. Instead, he told a rapturous rock concert at Wembley Stadium: "Do not listen to anyone who say that you must give up the struggle against *apartheid*."[10] When the Commonwealth Committee of Foreign Ministers met in Abuja, in May 1990, his anger had not abated. "We would like to point out that we are, to put it mildly, amazed at the behaviour of certain countries," he told the meeting: "There are no grounds whatsoever for lifting sanctions against the racist regime of South Africa or ending its diplomatic and cultural isolation."[11]

However, Anyaoku appreciated that if the Commonwealth was to find a new international role in hastening *apartheid's* end, it could not cling to its full sanctions policy once the process of irreversible change had begun. To do so would make it much more difficult to present the Commonwealth to the South African Government as a credible and impartial interlocutor. Additionally, despite his initial rhetoric, Mandela recognised the importance of reaching out to the private sector and to the major corporations doing business in South Africa. As Anyaoku put it: "[i]t would be in nobody's interests if a new nation was born on the back of a broken economy."[12]

Anyaoku's opportunity to soften the Commonwealth's policy on sanctions came with a further meeting of Commonwealth Foreign Ministers in February 1991. He proposed that the Commonwealth should adopt the 'programmed management' of sanctions. By this he meant that "sanctions on South Africa should not be lifted in a unilateral and uncontrolled way but that, equally, it would be foolish not to respond to positive change in a collective and measured manner."[13] Despite Anyaoku's African credentials and his well-cultivated diplomatic links in the region, his initiative was resisted by the four African Ministers on the CFMSA, particularly Nathan Shamuyarira of Zimbabwe. It took the threat of a phone call to Thabo Mbeki before Shamuyarira would accept that Anyaoku's approach had ANC support.[14] It was a policy then adopted by Heads at the 1991 Harare summit. Any change to the application of sanctions was to be linked to 'real and practical steps' in the ending of *apartheid*. The United Nations arms embargo, underpinned by various Commonwealth measures, would remain in force until the establishment of a post-*apartheid* government. By contrast, people-to-people sanctions (such as visa restrictions, cultural and other boycotts and bans on travel and tourism) would be lifted immediately in recognition of progress made so far. What was more nuanced was the lifting of financial and economic sanctions. Economic sanctions, including trade and investment measures, would be removed once transitional mechanisms had been agreed, allowing all the parties to participate fully in the negotiating process. But financial sanctions, described by Heads as "the most demonstrably effective of all sanctions" and including lending by the international financial institutions such as the IMF and the World Bank, should only be raised after agreement on a new constitution had been reached.[15] The UK dissented from this view and therefore did not agree with the timescale for the lifting of financial and economic sanctions.[16] That apart, a common approach was concluded on the resumption of sporting links with South Africa and plans laid for the Commonwealth's involvement in the reconstruction of a post-*apartheid* South Africa, particularly as regards human resource development.

In November 1990, Mrs Thatcher unexpectedly lost power, after a challenge from within her party, being replaced by her former Chancellor and Foreign Secretary, John Major. Major knew the Commonwealth well, partly from a youthful career assignment in Nigeria and partly from the innovative work he did with other Commonwealth Finance Ministers on debt relief.[17] Major was also instinctively and publicly anti-racist, a belief that he had made evident in his pre-parliamentary days while on Lambeth Borough Council.[18] In the run up to the 1989 Kuala Lumpur CHOGM, the then Foreign Secretary had declared: "*Apartheid* cannot survive and does not deserve to survive. It is something to oppose constantly and comprehensively."[19] This did not spare him the mauling he received in Kuala Lumpur, but it won him lasting friends.

There had also been a change in the Commonwealth Secretariat. After fifteen years as Commonwealth Secretary-General, Sonny Ramphal came to an end of his tenure and was followed by his former deputy, Emeka Anyaoku. The British joined in the acclaim and the honours heaped on Ramphal's shoulders, but there was no denying the debilitating effects upon the UK-Commonwealth relationship of a very protracted and public dispute with Mrs Thatcher over *apartheid* and South Africa. The divisions and suspicions between the UK and the rest of the Commonwealth even infected staff relations within the Secretariat with the then most senior British national in the organisation suggesting that all his UK colleagues should caucus together to defend their perceived interests. Fortunately, other UK nationals robustly rejected the idea, but there were still fences to mend.[20] Anyaoku was an anglophile who recognised the damage done to UK-Commonwealth relations over many years. Having served in the Commonwealth Secretariat almost from its inception, he had taken to heart the repeated accusations of hypocrisy and double standards thrown at the Commonwealth, particularly by the British media, during the bitter debates over *apartheid*. As Robin Renwick put it, "[m]any of those criticising the South African regime themselves were guilty of anti-democratic practices and the British public knew it."[21] That much Anyaoku conceded, agreeing that "the apologists of *apartheid* and white minority rule in Southern Africa, many of whom were critics of the Commonwealth, had a point."[22] This rather grudging acceptance belied Anyaoku's recognition that the Commonwealth was living with an 'internal contradiction' that "while it had members who were either military regimes or one-party states, it still espoused democracy as one of its key tenets."[23] That contradiction had to be resolved. It was not just South Africa that was changing – the Commonwealth itself had to change and become a more credible interlocutor for democracy and human rights.

This process of transformation within the Commonwealth itself had begun at the 1989 Kuala Lumpur Heads of Government Meeting with the formation of a High-Level Group (HLAG) of Ten Heads of Government. Their task was to report on the role and priorities of the Commonwealth in the 1990s and beyond.[24] Senior officials duly prepared a draft declaration for the coming 1991 Harare CHOGM, at which HLAG was due to report. While the content of the draft was unexceptional, it was over lengthy and written in rather turgid prose.[25] A month before the summit, John Major produced an entirely new draft, largely the work of his Cabinet Secretary, Robert Armstrong. Major told Anyaoku:

> The forthcoming meeting is very important for the future of the Commonwealth, and presents us with a golden opportunity, not to be missed or fluffed, to renew the Commonwealth's sense of purpose and direction, and to refocus its energies and activities.

A stronger declaration, he argued, would help "strengthen our commitment to the Commonwealth's guiding principles and our determination to follow them up in what we do, as well as what we say."[26]

Anyaoku's officials warned him that, according to their soundings, the tabling of a British text "may not be warmly received."[27] Some of the tensions apparent in the drafting process surfaced when the ten HLAG Heads of Government met in formal session, immediately prior to the summit. All were conscious that they were attempting a further codification of the Commonwealth's fundamental values, building on the 1971 Singapore Declaration adopted twenty years before. It was to be, in the words of Anyaoku, their 'mission statement' and "an important milestone in the evolution of the Commonwealth."[28] The statement of core principles would be linked (as Major had urged) to targeted and practical programmes. At the Heads' meeting, Major also linked the adoption of the Declaration to the criteria for accepting future applicants into membership. Up to that point, aspiring members invariably had to demonstrate widespread national support for any application, usually through a parliamentary vote, but they were not required to commit to any foundational principles. That would change, and acceptance of the principles and values set out at Harare would become a key requirement which new members were expected to uphold. What was not made clear was what would happen to any new or existing member who clearly flouted those principles. This was a question addressed four years later, in dramatic circumstances, at the 1995 Auckland CHOGM in New Zealand.

It has been suggested that other Commonwealth leaders were distracted by summit discussions on South Africa and paid no attention to the British draft or its detail.[29] The British version, so it is argued, was therefore adopted with only minor changes. Such a view is not borne out by the evidence. The British draft had in fact been circulated towards the end of September, nearly three weeks before the opening of the CHOGM. Redrafting by officials of the Harare Declaration took place at the CHOGM between 16 and 18 October, and the text was finalised by Heads of Government at their Retreat at Elephant Hills on the morning of 19 October. It was released to the media at a press conference the following day.[30]

While the British desire for a "shorter, sharper and more dramatic" text was accepted, there were nonetheless important differences which needed to be resolved in the negotiating process.[31] A clear and persistent tension lay in attitudes to systems of democracy and whether it had primacy over development or vice versa. Many developing nations disliked the suggestion in the British draft that the European ideal of democracy was pre-eminent: "It has been vividly demonstrated in Europe," read the British draft, "that, no matter how long and hard the fight, democracy and justice are essential to economic progress and the well-being of peoples and will prevail."[32] This also implied, many felt, that the decolonising struggles for national self-determination and liberty had not in fact been about democracy and justice, or about economic progress, a view that they would vigorously rebut. That reference was duly deleted, and, on a proposal from Singapore, a more cautious reference to democracy "according to local circumstances" was inserted. Some feared that this could be the thin end of a very undemocratic wedge. Most, however, saw it as a necessary movement away from the "Westminster model" of democracy automatically bequeathed on independence. Other amendments were made which strengthened the Commonwealth's commitment to poverty alleviation, debt relief and development, and removed any suggestion that democracy, human rights and the rule of law were the Commonwealth's overriding priority. This was a tension which was to recur repeatedly in the years that followed.

Anyaoku considered that the adoption of the Harare Declaration "not only defined the priority areas where the activities, energies and resources of the organisation should be directed. It provided an updated definition of the core principles of the Commonwealth, first enunciated in the Singapore Declaration."[33] For his part, John Major records his presence at Harare as the 'happiest' of any summit or conference he attended as Prime Minister. Mandela's release had encouraged the healing of wounds over South Africa, and the Harare Declaration laid down the standards of good government expected of Commonwealth members. "It was an important step," commented Major, "not least because it answered complaints that the Commonwealth harboured dictators."[34] More than that, he told Huddleston, it "mapped out a positive role for the Commonwealth, particularly on good government and human rights."[35] Both at the Harare summit and subsequently, a number of Commonwealth countries which were previously one-party or military regimes moved to multi-party, democratic systems.[36] This helped a coming together of the UK with its Commonwealth partners, especially on the question of *apartheid*.

### 3  South Africa and the 'New' Commonwealth

Overriding all the leaders' discussions on the dramatic developments underway in South Africa was a palpable desire to find a new and more positive way for the Commonwealth to assist the process of change. Waiting patiently in the wings of the Harare meeting was the symbol of that seismic change, Nelson Mandela. As Anyaoku recalled, "I had become convinced that there was a real chance for negotiations and that the Commonwealth was in a position to assist in that negotiation process."[37]

But what could the Commonwealth expect to do? Its last attempt at mediation had been in 1986 with the mission of the Commonwealth EPG. As an attempt to kick-start meaningful negotiations on the ending of *apartheid*, that mission had ended in failure. But it had produced a "Possible Negotiating Concept" which had set out the steps that both the government and the opposition forces needed to take in creating a climate conducive to negotiations. The core elements of the Concept had now been realised: the removal of the military from the townships and the restoration of political freedoms; the release of Mandela and other political prisoners; and the unbanning of the ANC, PAC and other opposition parties in conditions of normal political activity. These steps also went a considerable way to overcoming the five principal obstacles to negotiations identified by the United Nations.[38] But the final remaining blockage in the path of negotiations, compromising the government's efforts not to deploy the military in the townships and not to declare localised 'unrest areas', was violence.

The issue of violence, and reassurances about how this might be contained in conditions of political freedom, had proved to be the stumbling block for the mission of the EPG. Now the reality of violence and disorder was upon South Africa, and it was not clear how the Commonwealth could help. It was unlikely to have a mediatory role. True, its links with the ANC and with Mandela were as strong as they had ever been. At the same time, Buthelezi had felt increasingly sidelined by the Commonwealth even while some in the West had championed his importance over that of the ANC. Despite Buthelezi's best efforts, he had not been invited to the Harare CHOGM alongside Mandela, and this perceived slight had rankled. Similarly, the EPG's relationship with the government, built up during the mission, had dissolved in acrimony. The SADF's attack on three neighbouring Commonwealth countries, in May 1986, had demolished the Commonwealth's openness to negotiation, and the organisation's subsequent crusade for the imposition of worldwide sanctions on South Africa had scarcely endeared it to the *apartheid* state as a potential interlocutor. What could it hope to offer?

Nonetheless, the soundings that Anyaoku had taken before the Commonwealth summit encouraged him to broach the idea of:

> a Special Mission to South Africa to explore with the principal parties concerned ways in which the Commonwealth could assist [and] render every practicable assistance for the reinvigoration of the faltering process of political dialogue including, in particular, the convening of the proposed Constitutional Conference.[39]

At their Elephant Hills' Retreat, Heads agreed that, despite the adoption of the National Peace Accord (NPA) a month earlier, the escalating violence in South Africa was now so serious that it threatened the whole process of change. Choosing their words carefully, their communique read:

> While the terms of a constitutional settlement were for the people of South Africa themselves to determine, Heads of Government believed that the Commonwealth must remain ready to assist the negotiating process in ways that would be helpful to the parties concerned. They therefore decided to request the Secretary-General to visit South Africa at the earliest opportunity to explore with the principal parties concerned ways in which the Commonwealth could assist in lending momentum to the negotiating process.[40]

Even while Anyaoku assembled his mission, he knew that he would have difficulty overcoming the suspicions and reservations of the South African Government. On 18 October, during the Harare meeting, Anyaoku had had a conversation with South Africa's Trade Representative in Zimbabwe, N.M. Nel. Later that day, Nel passed a confidential response from the South African Government to Anyaoku's proposal. It began: "The Commonwealth can do incalculable harm if it sees itself as a pressure group charged with the task of extracting concessions from the government and generally engaged in prescribing solutions to problems which are the sole concern of South Africans."

On a rather more positive note, it continued:

If, on the other hand the Commonwealth wants to be informed of the situation in South Africa and confines itself to promoting peaceful dialogue and, moreover, it can be seen to be unbiased in this respect, a visit by the Secretary-General could serve a useful purpose.

In reiterating its determination to get the multi-party conference off the ground, the government note concluded: "Against this background the Secretary-General is welcome to visit South Africa and to consult with the Government and representatives of political parties and other leaders."[41]

While this was a green light of sorts, President de Klerk soon made his views known about any mediating or facilitating role by the Commonwealth or other international organisation in the negotiating process. "I am dead against international involvement in the internal affairs of South Africa,"[42] he declared, though he did go on to accept that the international community had a legitimate interest in developments in South Africa. "We welcome fact-finding missions but international monitoring of the negotiating process (or the security forces) in the sense of internationalising an all-party congress – or a multi-party conference – I (am) against that, South Africans must find the solutions amongst themselves."[43]

This scepticism was underlined by confidential and anonymous advice to Anyaoku from South Africa (possibly from the British Ambassador, Sir Anthony Reeve): "There is still strong resistance in Pretoria to any direct form of intervention in the transition." But the note continues: "Having said that, there is clearly a far greater openness to international organisations in general and a willingness . . . to normalise relations with such bodies as the Commonwealth." The writer adds:

Pretoria's perception of the Commonwealth is that it has a long way to go on its own democracy/human rights programme before it would have either the credibility or skill to become involved in the intricacies of the South African situation. But it regards the Secretary-General as a person of considerable influence in relation to the ANC and therefore someone who should be cultivated. This is over and above Pretoria's need to normalise relations with the Commonwealth.

The writer therefore saw "a window of opportunity for the future."[44]

Anyaoku was well aware that he would need all his persuasive powers to overcome the South African Government's hostility. But, apart from establishing sufficient mutual trust for a good working relationship, what could the Commonwealth hope to offer? Some in the Secretariat thought Anyaoku might offer himself as a neutral convenor of the proposed all-party Congress or could establish a high-level facilitative group to monitor the processes of constitutional and electoral development. Expert advice could be offered in these areas, and there could be a focus on post-*apartheid* reconstruction.[45] By the time of Anyaoku's departure for South Africa, accompanied by a small team, there was continuing debate about the specifics of any Commonwealth assistance. But it was agreed that the basis of any Commonwealth involvement should be the twin objectives of (a) encouraging the parties to the negotiating table and (b) helping to end the violence.[46] As Anyaoku put it, "[t]here is a growing concern that recent developments, including continuing violence despite the Peace Accord, could undermine the negotiating process." He emphasised that the constitutional future of South Africa "is for South Africans to determine, but I have been given the task of exploring with the parties concerned ways in which the Commonwealth could be supportive of the process."[47]

Anyaoku and his team flew into South Africa in the early morning of Wednesday, 30 October, for a visit that was to last nine days. His first meeting was with Pik Botha, the Foreign Minister and, five years before, a closet supporter of the Commonwealth's EPG mission. Much had happened since, and he was not disposed to treat the Commonwealth mission with any favour. The next meeting, with de Klerk, was no less awkward. The Commonwealth had been consistently hostile to South Africa, remarked the State President. How could it now be its friend? The Commonwealth's hostility had been to *apartheid*, responded Anyaoku, not to his government which had now declared that *apartheid* would be dismantled. As such, their objectives were the same, and the Commonwealth's ability to bridge difference might be useful to South Africa's many communities. At the conclusion of the meeting, a mollified de Klerk led Anyaoku to a joint press conference in the Union buildings. "We focussed on the positive role that the Commonwealth could play in South Africa," declared de Klerk. Both agreed that the Commonwealth role must not affect the sovereignty of South Africa or interfere with its internal affairs.[48]

Apart from further meetings with the government, including with Dr Gerrit Viljoen, the Minister for Constitutional Development, Anyaoku rekindled his relationship with a spectrum of political leaders. This included Oliver and Adelaide Tambo, Nelson Mandela, Cyril Ramaphosa, Thabo Mbeki, Allan Boesak and Jacob Zuma of the ANC; Dikgang Moseneke and colleagues from the PAC; Andries Treurnicht, the CP leader; and Zak de Beer and others from the Democratic Party (DP). But a particular task involved mending fences with Chief Mangosuthu Buthelezi and the Inkatha Freedom Party (IFP). This necessitated a special visit to the KwaZulu capital of Ulundi. There, in the KwaZulu parliament chamber, Buthelezi and the IFP Central Committee greeted Anyaoku and his delegation with a lengthy, pre-printed speech of welcome, much of it complaining of past disagreements or perceived slights. Buthelezi's conclusion was that perhaps Anyaoku's trip would lead to an appreciation of the complexity of the situation and that there was a need "for some months of ongoing dialogue between the Commonwealth and the South African political parties before any kind of finality is reached about what the Commonwealth should do during the next two crucial years."[49]

While Anyaoku was not disposed to take up the Chief Minister's suggestion of a lengthy open-ended dialogue, he took the opportunity to sketch out some of the ideas for Commonwealth involvement that he was later to put to de Klerk in his final meeting with the State President. Anyaoku was also able to build his personal relationship with Buthelezi, something that would be invaluable in the coming years. Apart from the political parties, Anyaoku met business, church and trade union leaders, as well as prominent academics and journalists. Generally, the various parties rejected the idea of any Commonwealth mediatory role, although the PAC argued that the international community should provide a neutral venue outside South Africa for the all-party negotiations and a convenor (or convenors) of suitable standing for the talks.[50] But there was a feeling that the Commonwealth might help facilitate the negotiations and provide support and expertise.

This generally positive response led Anyaoku to put two specific proposals to de Klerk. Firstly, that a team of five or six distinguished Commonwealth citizens observe the inaugural proceedings of the all-party talks as official guests of the conference. This, Anyaoku considered, "could be particularly helpful as an indication of international support for the process and in promoting mutual trust between the various parties."[51] The second proposal was for Anyaoku himself to be available to observe appropriate stages of the negotiations accompanied by a team of advisers from various disciplines whose expertise might be helpful to the process. Responding, de Klerk made clear that both proposals were matters for the all-party conference to decide, though he made clear that he himself was 'not negative'. A definitive answer would be given following further consultation. In a joint statement issued to the media after the meeting, de Klerk and Anyaoku described their discussions as "constructive and fruitful."[52]

These were modest beginnings, perhaps, but it led Anyaoku to report to Commonwealth leaders that the visit "has created a climate in which new opportunities for Commonwealth help to the people of South Africa may well be possible."[53] Michael Manley, the Jamaican Prime Minister, responded: "Let me ... congratulate you on the progress made during those discussions and the confidence you have established with all the parties for a constructive Commonwealth role."[54] The Malaysian Prime Minister, Dr Mahathir, was rather more downbeat, commenting that he had "no problem in endorsing the two proposals which you have put forward."[55] Nevertheless, the Commonwealth's new strategic direction, in aiding the process of transition, was now in progress.

Anyaoku and his team had scarcely arrived back in London when formal confirmation arrived for the start of all-party talks. These were to open, as the Convention for a Democratic South Africa (CODESA), on 20 December 1991 in the World Trade Centre, north Johannesburg. Without question, the issue of international observers at CODESA's opening plenaries was a minor one alongside the central issue of South Africa's transition to democracy, the constitutional principles upon which this would be based, and the degree to which the negotiations would be inclusive of all the parties. But it was symbolic of the world interest in South Africa's hazardous path out of *apartheid*, a cause which the United Nations and other international organisations (including the Commonwealth) had long held dear. In his opening statement, Mandela spoke of the country's "yearning for democracy and peace," adding: "CODESA represents the historical opportunity to translate that yearning into reality."[56] But he also included a welcome to "the guests from the United Nations organisation; the organisation of African unity; the Commonwealth; the European Economic Community, and the non-aligned movement," adding, "we trust that they will avail to the process now unfolding their wisdom, insights and experience gained in many similar initiatives across the world."[57]

Anyaoku's proposal for an international observer presence at CODESA would of course never have been accepted had it been confined to Commonwealth representation. It therefore had the effect of drawing in other international organisations, principally the UN, and making it more likely that there might be internal acceptance of some kind of international role in the transition process in the future. Indeed, one of CODESA's working groups was given the task of exploring the future contribution that the international community might make to transition. Close engagement with CODESA, and the numerous bilateral meetings that took place with various participants in its wings, would have deepened appreciation of many of the tensions and issues evident. Despite a veneer of warm bipartisanship, de Klerk and Mandela clashed, and the IFP (at that moment within the negotiating process) complained of collusion between the government and the ANC and doubted whether the talks could prove to be effective or genuinely inclusive. Others already outside the negotiations, from the CP to the PAC and Azanian People's Organisation (AZAPO), made similar complaints.

The Commonwealth group of observers saw CODESA 1 as "a milestone in South Africa's political evolution."[58] However, they added that "violence continues to be an intractable problem, fuelling suspicion and mistrust."[59] A joint statement by all the international observers declared: "Our presence at Codesa is a testimony of the

*Figure 11.2* Welcome to CODESA, 1992. Commonwealth Secretariat.

profound commitment by the international community to encourage the emergence of a democratic, non-racial South Africa."⁶⁰ Most of those at the initial talks signed a Declaration of Intent, committing all parties to a united, democratic, non-racial, and non-sexist state. Five Working Groups were established and began discussions, and administrative support for the process was put in place. There was considerable optimism that the next CODESA plenary, in May 1992, would see significant progress.

## 4  Combatting Violence

The Commonwealth can legitimately claim responsibility for proposing the presence of international observers at the opening of multi-party negotiations (CODESA 1) in 1991. However, that presence was largely symbolic, suggesting only an active interest in, and support for, the internal process of negotiation by the international community. Anyaoku's later proposal, that international observers could play a sustained role in combatting the upsurge in violence threatening negotiations, was viewed with greater scepticism. Anyaoku had mooted the idea, including with Mandela, during his attendance at the second negotiating plenary, CODESA II, which opened in May 1992.⁶¹ However, he was not the first to do so. In March of that year a delegation of church leaders, headed by Archbishop Desmond Tutu, put to de Klerk the notion of "an international monitoring mechanism" to address the violence. This proposal drew a sharp response from de Klerk who condemned it as "a gross infringement of South African sovereignty and a grave challenge to the legitimacy of his government."⁶²

*Figure 11.3* ANC march against violence in Natal, Johannesburg, July 1990. Commonwealth Secretariat.

The massacre at Boipatong, following the collapse of CODESA II, changed the climate overnight. Many local people believed that the killings had the unmistakable imprint of the security forces, and Ellis states that there was circumstantial evidence that "it was indeed the work of one or other of the covert units."[63] However, the accusation of state complicity in the violence, through a government-sponsored 'third force', led the Goldstone Commission to set up an independent inquiry, headed by the UK criminologist, Dr Peter Waddington. The Waddington Report later declared that the inquiry had "uncovered no information that suggests any complicity on the part of the SAP (South African Police) in the attack," adding that "omissions arose, not from deliberation, but incompetence."[64]

Nevertheless, Ellis describes the violence of the transitional period as a continuation of "low intensity warfare," perpetrated not only by elements within the government and the NP but also by combatants in the IFP and the ANC, while all parties were ostensibly pursuing negotiations.[65] It became clear that the fierce counter-insurgency strategy of the previous decade, which had spawned a variety of irregular, covert 'third force' units, had left a disturbing legacy.

Anyaoku renewed his efforts, making contact with Mandela and de Klerk, as well as with Major and some of his Ministers. His proposal document declared: "Violence in South Africa now threatens not only the current process of negotiations but the very prospect of a successful transition to the new South Africa."[66] Even so, his initial overtures were rebuffed: "[T]he ANC displayed a marked reluctance to involve the Commonwealth," Anyaoku recorded.[67] Cyril Ramaphosa told Anyaoku that the ANC executive had decided to take the matter to the OAU. Anyaoku ruefully reflected: "I had to go along," though he considered the likelihood of anything coming out of the OAU "quite unlikely."[68] Nevertheless, Anyaoku used the OAU summit to pursue the idea with Mandela, whose position began to soften. Likewise, de Klerk's initial hostility began to abate once Anyaoku convinced him that the international observers "would not interfere in the running of South Africa."[69] Later, de Klerk was to praise Anyaoku for "a very constructive role for which I have the greatest appreciation."[70]

While Anyaoku was slowly making headway with a range of South African leaders, including Chief Buthelezi of the IFP, Clarence Mkwetu of the PAC and Constand Viljoen of the far-right Afrikaner Volksfront (AVF) as well as the ANC and NP, it became clear that the UN Secretary-General, Dr Boutros Boutros-Ghali, also had considerable reservations. However, he assured Anyaoku that, providing the Commonwealth could secure South African agreement, the United Nations would be prepared to support such an initiative.[71] By this time, following a meeting of the UN Security Council, Boutros-Ghali had been authorised to appoint a Special Representative, Cyrus Vance, whom Anyaoku also met. With the prospects of the ANC's rolling mass action planned for 3 August descending into 'uncontrollable violence', the United Nations itself decided to despatch a ten-person observer term to cover the event.[72] The Commonwealth was also invited to send a team but was not able to respond in the time available. Nevertheless, this initiative sealed the acceptability of international observers to monitor the violence.[73] It also cleared the way for the adoption, on 17 August 1992, of UN Security Council resolution 772.

This provided the mandate for each of the four international observer missions. Their role was to "assist the people of South Africa to end violence," and they were to deploy their teams "in co-ordination with the United Nations and the structures set up under the National Peace Accord."[74]

Spurred on by the Bisho massacre in September, where twenty-nine died and over two hundred were injured on the Ciskei border, the various observer missions began to travel to South Africa. A thirteen-strong advance group from the United Nations arrived in Johannesburg in September to establish the UN Observer Mission in South Africa (UNOMSA). The first phase of the Commonwealth's involvement began a month later with the deployment of the eighteen members of the Commonwealth Observer Mission to South Africa (COMSA). At the end of the month the fifteen European observers making up the European Community Observer Mission in South Africa (ECOMSA) arrived, and, in November, they were joined by four observers from the Organisation of Africa Unity, constituting OAUOMSA. At the same time, UNOMSA attained its full complement of fifty observers.[75]

All observer teams shared a common broad mandate, namely, to address the violence and to do so in partnership with the United Nations and within the structures of the NPA. Specific areas of concern were "hostels, dangerous weapons, the role of the security forces and other armed formations, the investigation and prosecution of criminal conduct, mass demonstrations and the conduct of political parties."[76] This helped shape the composition of some of the teams. As far as COMSA was concerned, the mission was headed by Justice Austin Amissah, the former Attorney-General and Justice of Appeal of Ghana. The observers were selected with considerable thought from a variety of relevant fields, including in policing, criminology and law enforcement, law and the judiciary, and politics and community relations.[77] This helped determine where, within its broad mandate, COMSA was to develop its efforts. In later phases, electoral experts would be included in the mission as the elections approached.

The UN Secretary-General reported that the various international observers were coordinating their efforts and had "established close working relationships at the field and headquarters levels."[78] Given the number of observers with a police background in both the UNOMSA and COMSA missions, a joint task force was set up to examine and monitor different aspects of the South African Police. At the same time, there were differences between the various international groupings, not only in reporting and methodology but in what the individual teams perceived as the scope of their authority, their programmes and the priorities they should adopt, and how and to where they should deploy.

The challenge that an upsurge in "extreme and brutal violent conflict" posed, not only to negotiations but to the prospect of peaceful and inclusive elections, was formidable.[79] It is estimated that between 1990 and 1994 some 16,000 people died in violence in South Africa, in particular in KwaZulu Natal and in the townships of the East Rand.[80] "The violence," say Taylor and Shaw, "claimed far more lives than did the fight against *apartheid* itself." It was not only deaths. In reporting a 40% surge in violence in South Africa in 1992, compared with the previous year, the Human Rights Commission (HRC) pointed out that politically motivated violence had also left around 6,000 injured (many maimed or scarred for life) and "tens of thousands displaced and homeless."[81] All told, South Africa's prevailing homicide rate made it "one of the most violent countries in the world."[82] Furthermore, the nature of the violence was far more complex than the 'Black on Black' characterisation often portrayed in the media. Far from offering explanation, the Centre for the Study of Violence and Reconciliation (CSVR) felt that such terms "disguise causation by reinforcing the camouflage of racial stereotypes."[83] CSVR expressed concern about not only the big upswing in the levels of violence but "a qualitative shift in the forms and brutality of the conflict."[84] COMSA was of the view that the causes of violence in South Africa were "complex and multi-faceted" and needed to be viewed in a historical context "including the legacy of the *apartheid* system."[85] The CSVR saw a 'culture of violence' acquiring "a pervasive social acceptability as a legitimate means of attaining change." But the CSVR also emphasises that 1990 saw "a dramatic increase in violence against women, children and the elderly (as well as violent crime more generally)."[86] It has been estimated that as many as 300,000 women in South Africa were being raped each year, and in 1990 the rape of young girls increased by 23%, compared with the previous year.[87] Child and domestic abuse also increased, as did family murders, and there was a marked upswing of violence by white homeowners against their Black domestic workers.

It was often difficult to disentangle political violence from general criminality. This is borne out by a special study of violence in Crossroads, in the Western Cape, undertaken by the HRC during 1993. While some of those involved held political office locally, the origins of the violence seem to have been the disputed development of a parcel of land, as well as ongoing 'taxi wars'. The HRC concluded that different community factions were "equally responsible" for the violence.[88]

Kynoch's study of political violence in the townships of Katlehong and Thokoza presents a complex picture of the transition generating "an unprecedented level of communal conflict" where the ANC and IFP "armed and assisted local militias, and fighters aligned with both sides committed atrocities, often against non-combatants."[89] He sees "political violence as the primary enabling agent for the transition-era violence," with nationalist histories and the dominant account of transition violence providing "sanitised versions of the past."[90] Guelke agrees that "violence was a function of political competition."[91] But he goes further in challenging the dominant narratives of the period by arguing that "violence played a part in the strategy of the very parties that negotiated a constitutional settlement," though he concedes that the NP and the ANC also disagreed fundamentally on the nature of political violence.[92] Spence dismisses ethnicity as the key characteristic of violence between township 'comrades' and hostel-dwellers. He points out that "in Soweto, 40% of the permanent inhabitants are Zulu," adding to evidence that "the more settled a community, the less violence there is between members of different ethnic groups."[93] Conversely, ethnicity becomes more of an issue among the most marginalised, such as between squatters and hostel-dwellers. Like Kane-Berman, Spence accepts the significance of socio-economic factors in violence in addition to political motivations.

What therefore could a relatively small number of around one hundred international observers hope to achieve in the face of such a challenging issue and across such a large and diverse country with its population of around 30 million? Boutros-Ghali was in little doubt of their value, telling the Security Council that "the presence of the observers is viewed as having a salutary effect on the situation." He added that, despite the continuing violence, "there is wide agreement that without the deployment of international observers in the country the level of violence would be higher."[94] This was echoed by COMSA which pointed to a nine-month low in politically related deaths in November 1994, attributed by the HRC in part to the presence of international observers.[95]

However, Abdul Minty was more critical. Drawing upon a fact-finding visit to South Africa in November 1992, he felt that the monitors had made "a rather limited contribution."[96] Leaving aside the obvious retort that international observer activity had scarcely begun by that time, it is instructive to itemise the detailed elements of Minty's critique against the more upbeat assessment of Boutros-Ghali. Firstly, Minty acknowledged that the main value of observers "has been in being present at major rallies, meetings, demonstrations and marches." He added: "[T]hey have also made some impact in resolving local disputes on the spot and acting as a deterrent in preventing violent actions." However, Minty accuses the monitors of being "helpless when it comes to taking any preventative action; and they obviously cannot anticipate the various attacks on the trains and in African townships." He adds: "In any case, they are usually remote from the areas of violence."[97]

As regards the accusation of 'remoteness', there were differences between the various international observer groups. UNOMSA, with the largest number of observers, felt it important to have a national presence across South Africa. Its fifty observers were therefore deployed to all eleven provinces, although the deployment was "weighted towards the Witwatersrand/Vaal and Natal/KwaZulu regions, where 70% of the political violence occurs."[98] COMSA, with its smaller numbers, decided that it should be based exclusively in "the two regions of South Africa worst affected by violence: the Pretoria-Witwatersrand-Vaal (PWV) area and Natal," as well as more distant flashpoints.[99] On the other hand, while ECOMSA placed approximately half its fifteen observers in Johannesburg/PWV, where it also had its headquarters, the rest were quartered in Durban, Cape Town and East London. There was strong pressure in the European mission for rotation of personnel, so that observers stationed in PWV could spend time in a less-stressful environment.[100] ECOMSA reported that their work had become more dangerous because there was an increasing tendency: "for us to be used as marshals, Peace Structure Observers and police officers." Nevertheless, ECOMSA was in no doubt that "the physical presence of Observers at rallies, marches and other tense public gathering has had a positive, calming effect on all participants."[101]

While Minty is therefore correct in saying that some international observers were remote from the violence 'hotspots', this was certainly not the case in general or at all in respect of COMSA. Minty himself appears to concede that the random and apparently motiveless acts of terror on commuter trains could not be anticipated. Nevertheless, COMSA designated train violence as a particular area of inquiry, given that its primary impact was in the PWV area where there were 269 train attacks, 259 deaths and 469 injuries in the first ten months of 1992 alone.[102] Having international observers ride a few trains would have been futile and might have provided false reassurance. Instead, COMSA engaged with the South African Rail Commuter Corporation, the SAP, the Goldstone Commission and others to pursue solutions capable of providing a lasting response, such as recruiting a 4,000-strong train guard unit to provide security on trains, introducing video surveillance systems, and enhancing security at station access points.

In other respects, however, the various international missions did attempt to anticipate potential violence by mobilising all their collective forces to be present at major flashpoints. One such event was on Sharpeville Day, on 21 March 1993, in the large township area covering Vosloorus, Katlehong and Thokoza. Both the ANC and the IFP had announced that they would be holding election rallies simultaneously at venues less than 4 kilometres apart.[103] The IFP rally, addressed by Chief Buthelezi, had drawn extensively from hostels across the Reef. IFP supporters left the rally armed and buoyed up, some intent on marauding through neighbouring ANC areas. This tense stand-off was eventually defused with the assistance of IFP and ANC marshals, peace monitors and international observers.[104]

On a smaller scale, international observers were frequently contacted by Local Dispute Resolution Committees (LDRCs), peace monitors or community groups warning of possible trouble and seeking their help. Anglin comments: "[O]n critical occasions like the Chris Hani and Oliver Tambo funerals, their role was decisive." Moreover, "parties and communities continued to request observer 'protection'," even if, over time, "individuals determined on violence were not deterred."[105] Minty had from the outset acknowledged that international observers had sometimes had a positive impact in resolving local disputes. In the case of COMSA, this deserves a fuller analysis, given the Commonwealth's claim to have a comparative advantage in the field of conflict resolution and mediation. In any event, although the value of mediation was recognised by other observer missions, there was some doubt whether this was an appropriate area of activity. ECOMSA reported that while its observers had often acted as facilitators and mediators and had made proposals for conflict resolution, there was "some doubt in the minds of some ECOMSA team members whether these actions do not in fact exceed their mandatory duties."[106] In seeking clarification from the European presidency and individual governments, ECOMSA observed: "[I]t is important to note that the Commonwealth Observer Mission do not accept the UN guidelines but operate under a wider interpretation of the mandate."[107]

COMSA saw working with, and seeking to improve, the peace structures established under the NPA as being a key element of its mandate. The NPA, adopted by the political parties on 14 September 1991, recognised the untold misery, hardship and disruption caused by political violence and declared that it "now jeopardises the very process of peaceful political transformation and threatens to leave a legacy of insurmountable division and deep bitterness in our country."[108] Under the leadership of John Hall, the National Peace Committee worked hard to hold the various political parties to the undertakings given under the NPA. In that respect, COMSA was supportive of attempts to broker a peace summit between Mandela and Butheleizi.[109] This was also an area where the Commonwealth Secretary-General sought to use his good offices. However, securing peace and an end to political violence was at least as much a local and regional issue as it was a national one. The COMSA team deployed to Natal found that only six of the twenty-six LDRCs envisaged for the province had been established, and only two of these were functioning. They reported the widespread perception that Natal was sliding towards 'all-out civil war'.[110]

The COMSA observers identified a major impediment to establishing local peace structures. While the KwaZulu 'homeland' government and the IFP leadership had signed the Peace Accord, the local *amakhosi* (chiefs) had not been included and were suspicious of actions and structures which might be seen as undermining their authority. COMSA therefore worked with the *amakhosi* to achieve reconciliation, peace and reconstruction, particularly by establishing LDRCs. Their focus, in Natal, was on two areas. The first was Umbumbulu on the upper south coast. This rural district, with a population of around 400,000, had the reputation of being the area worst affected by violence in the whole of South Africa. Shortly after COMSA's arrival, it was declared an unrest area. After significant negotiations, involving the political parties, the *amakhosi*, business, the churches and regional bodies, the launch of a LDRC for Umbumbulu was achieved in December 1992 with agreement on the return of refugees displaced from their homes. This was hailed by the 'New Nation' newspaper as "an unsurpassed feat in the strife-torn Natal Upper South Coast."[111] *City Press* asked: "Was a magic wand waved over this area, healing the wounds of the past?" The answer, the newspaper suggested, was more prosaic: "[I]ndependent peace facilitators from the Commonwealth Observer Group were instrumental in kickstarting the whole process."[112]

The Ensimbini Valley in the Port Shepstone area, on Natal's lower south coast, provided the other major focus for COMSA's activities. Despite the presence of a LDRC in Port Shepstone, the Ensimbini Valley was a battleground between traditional forces, supporting IFP, in conflict with ANC-supporting youth. Local media dubbed the area "a wasteland."[113] Following protracted negotiations, peace agreements were concluded in the KwaNdwalane and KwaMavindla localities, and sealed by a series of peace rallies, involving the former protagonists. At the largest of these, 6,000 people in Murchison were addressed by regional leaders of both the ANC and the IFP, urging peace. Reconciliation and Development Committees were established, and a substantial number of refugees were thereafter able to return to the valley. The 'South Coast Herald' described it as "a major breakthrough" with a dramatic fall in the death rate reported.[114] A major figure in COMSA's mediation operations was Dr Moses Anafu, a Ghanaian and a senior political adviser in the Commonwealth Secretariat.

Despite the early success of conflict resolution in KwaZulu-Natal and its positive impact nationally on ANC-IFP relations, the continuation of the Commonwealth mission in Durban was cast into doubt by a potential restructuring of COMSA in its third phase, beginning in June 1993. In this new phase, there were rumours that the Durban team would be withdrawn with an increasing emphasis on election preparations

214   *Ending* Apartheid – *A Troubled Transition*

*Figure 11.4* Observed by Dr Moses Anafu of COMSA, Inkosi Mhlabunzima Wellington Hlengwa successfully appeals for an end to hostilities and the safe return of ANC refugees, Commonwealth-sponsored community meeting in Umbumbulu, KwaZulu/Natal, 1992. Commonwealth Secretariat.

rather than conflict resolution. This prompted a flurry of letters of protest. On 28 April 1993, Mark Butler, a Human Rights Monitor with the Pietermaritzburg Agency for Christian Social Awareness, wrote to Anyaoku expressing his extreme concern "in the light of the unique and crucial role played by your Mission in the process of building peace in Natal." He continued: "People in Natal do not trust easily, and your mission has been able to build trust in areas where we never thought it possible."[115] The Head of COMSA, the Australian criminologist Professor Duncan Chappell, privately told Commonwealth Secretariat staff that "members of the mission are very unhappy about this and feel it is particularly unfortunate that the Natal office is closing in this way; they feel they have done good work there." He added that the changes being proposed "would not build on the progress the mission has made in the first two phases": it would be "starting again from cold."[116] Two days later the Secretary-General had a letter from Rev. Beyers Naude, the noted anti-*apartheid* campaigner (and chair of the Ecumenical Monitoring Programme in South Africa [EMPSA]), asking for official clarification "as a matter of greatest urgency, especially in the light of the significant contribution that the Commonwealth Observer Group in Natal is making towards the cause of peace."[117]

While Anyaoku's office reassured those lobbying the Secretary-General that there were no plans to terminate the mission, in reality COMSA was facing a funding crisis. As earlier as December 1992, Anyaoku had privately admitted that "regrettably, I do not see how we can find the necessary financial resources for sustaining COMSA beyond 16 January 1993."[118] Only by raiding other budgets while preparing a fresh appeal to governments could the mission continue its operations into the early part of the year.[119] However, by the time of Anyaoku's visit to South Africa at the end of May 1993, the Secretary-General was able to make it clear that COMSA's role in KwaZulu-Natal would continue as the broader Commonwealth mission moved into its third phase.

The political context, however, had changed dramatically in April 1993 with the brutal assassination of Chris Hani, the SACP leader and rising ANC star. The perpetrators – the CP politician, Clive Derby-Lewis, and his accomplice Janusz Walus – had intended "to ignite racial fury and wreck the reconciliation process."[120] Derby-Lewis later told the TRC: "Hani had to be the target . . . we were fighting against communism, and communism is the vehicle of the Antichrist."[121] However, in a pivotal moment and in the face of erupting violence, Mandela broadcast to the nation. "This is a watershed moment for us all," declared the ANC leader;

> [O]ur decisions and our actions will determine whether we use our pain, our grief and our outrage to move forward to what is the only lasting solution for our country – an elected government of the people, by the people and for the people.[122]

Despite the political hazards in taking such a stance, Mandela's decisive appeal had the desired effect. It was, Dubow considered, "an act of consummate statesmanship."[123] Multi-party negotiations resumed on a much more inclusive basis than previously, and, on 1 June, the date of South Africa's first non-racial elections was quickly agreed.

It would be a mistake to regard COMSA as solely focused on the practicalities of mitigating the violence. The team had also been chosen to contain a blend of high-quality skills and experience, particularly in policing, security and the law. An important component of the mission's work was to review the administration of justice, particularly the correctional system. At a press conference in December 1992 COMSA's Chairman, Justice Amissah, presented a report which was critical of South Africa's courts, its prisons and the police. "Until the confidence of the people is secured, the police contribution to the control of violence will be flawed," remarked Amissah.[124] The Department of Justice immediately issued a lengthy rebuttal, branding it "a generalised, ill-informed and superficial evaluation" which would create incorrect perceptions.[125] But, in an editorial under the heading "Upholding the Law," *The Star* said these criticisms were to be expected but "there is much truth in what the Commonwealth Observer Mission to South Africa had to say."[126] There were other occasions when COMSA publicly clashed with the government in recommending changes, though the mission was careful to remain impartial between the various parties. If Minty's accusation about the international observers that "[t]hey do not appear to make any independent assessment of the general situation" had been plausible initially, it certainly carried no weight thereafter.[127] Even among these controversies, Foreign Minister Pik Botha was fulsome in his praise of the Commonwealth team, thanking Anyaoku for the quality of the observers and saying that any initial misgivings by the government had been "completely eliminated."[128]

## 5  The National Peacekeeping Force

The Commonwealth had a less happy experience in its attempts to help train the embryonic National Peacekeeping Force (NPKF). The idea of the force was to overcome criticisms of the SADF and SAP that they were not properly impartial and did not enjoy the confidence of the communities to which they were deployed. Instead, a unified force would be built, drawing equally from all the armed formations in the county, including the homelands and the police. This would be used to provide security up to and during South Africa's first democratic elections in April 1994. Anglin has described the establishment of the NPKF as "an imaginative and constructive, but ultimately disastrous, initiative." Although the Transitional Executive Council (TEC) approved the plan in August 1993, with the enthusiastic backing of the ANC, it was not until November than COMSA was informally approached about Commonwealth assistance. In January, COMSA reported to London that "those involved in setting up the force have now come to the international community at the eleventh hour with a desperate request for assistance."[129] Of the four missions, only the Commonwealth was prepared to help, though the Australian Ambassador warned that the South Africans had left the matter too late and "now wanted the international community to pull the chestnuts out of the fire."[130] The Joint Executive Secretaries of the TEC, Mac Maharaj and Fanie van der Merwe, wrote to Anyaoku on 19 January 1994 formally requesting assistance. They declared that they saw "a crucial role for the international community in monitoring and evaluating the performance of the NPKF once the training is complete." They asked that the Secretary-General consult with member governments with a view to "mobilising their bilateral contributions under a Commonwealth umbrella."[131] Despite the TEC's recognition that this was "very short notice," Anyaoku responded that he was confident, in the light of his consultations, that "Commonwealth governments will be in a position to provide the assistance requested."[132] Nevertheless, the timing was impossibly short. Five days after the TEC's request for assistance, the first NPKF recruits began to arrive for training. It was nine days before the opening of the election campaign and three months before polling day. Anglin commented that all four international observer missions had been sounded out, "but only the Commonwealth was in a position to respond quickly and effectively and was willing to do so considering the obvious high risks of failure."[133]

On 10 February, the Commonwealth announced that a Commonwealth Peacekeeping Assistance Group (CPAG) had been assembled to help in the training of the NPKF.[134] Headed by Colonel Cottam of the British Army and A.K. Gupta of the Indian Police Service, CPAG was to be a combined group of eighteen army officers and eight police officers from seven Commonwealth countries, funded at an estimated cost "in excess of £250,000."[135] Given the time constraints, Anglin considers that assembling such a high-powered team was "a remarkable achievement."[136] However, CPAG joined an initiative already facing mounting problems.

With a second batch of recruits arriving on 19 February, making 3,800 in all, it was clear that no more could be trained by the time of the election and that the goal of a force of 10,000 by then was unachievable. The bulk of recruits came from MK, the SADF and the Transkei Defence Force, but these were raw recruits rather than the elite personnel anticipated, and there was minimal screening to assess their suitability. Conditions at the De Brug camp outside Bloemfontein (shared by the CPAG team) were spartan with inadequate facilities, accommodation in tents and limited food. Teething problems were reported, including strikes, insubordination, mutiny and desertion and several lurid instances of violence and racism between various factions.[137] Apart from basic soldiering skills, CPAG sought to provide training in peacekeeping techniques, especially in an electoral context. This included stressing the importance of community support and public confidence and strict adherence to a Code of Conduct and rules of engagement. At the end of the training period, the evaluation by the multinational team was that the bulk of the Force was "undertrained and not ready for deployment in war-like situations".[138] Added to poor command and control issues, the commanding officer appointed, Brigadier Gabriel Ramushwana, was an open supporter of the ANC (and an election candidate for the party). As the military leader in Venda, his democratic credentials were dubious and his integrity questionable. Nevertheless, the TEC's Sub-Council on Defence pressed ahead with deployment. CPAG, and others, reacted with horror to the first proposal that the NPKF be sent into KwaZulu-Natal. The IFP had boycotted the TEC and therefore supplied no formations for the NPKF. Given its leadership and provenance, the Force would have been viewed as an invading army in Natal, and CPAG argued strongly against the deployment. The Sub-Council's decision to deploy the NPKF to the townships of the East Rand instead, also opposed by CPAG, was deeply problematic, given the history of bloody conflict there between ANC Self-Defence Units (SDUs), IFP hostel-dwelling militants, and, from time to time, other armed groups supporting AZAPO and the PAC.

After a hesitant start and without support from the SADF, the NPKF quickly disintegrated in the face of political resistance and an upsurge in violence. Col. Cottam reported that the first three days "did not go too badly," as the NPKF patrolled Thokosa, Katlehong and Vosloorus townships.[139] However, by the fourth day gun battles had broken out between hostel-dwellers and local SDUs, in which the Force was involved. Kynoch contends that the NPKF was widely perceived as an 'ANC army' and that its soldiers cooperated with ANC SDUs in their assault on the Mshayazafe Hostel on 18–19 April. "The NPKF, although operational for a very short time and only deployed in a limited area, clearly backed the ANC."[140] The NPKF requested help from the SADF, and the Force was withdrawn, confined to barracks until after the elections. Col. Cottam remarked: "The NPKD deployment has not been successful because it lacked the necessary support."[141] Anglin contends that "[t]he real blunder was the decision to deploy the NPKF on the East Rand."[142] The TEC wished to persist with the Force and requested that CPAG remain for a further phase of training. Col. Cottam demurred, remarking: "It would be a pity for CPAG to outstay its welcome."[143] Instead, a CPAG withdrawal, he suggested, "can be achieved gradually and with dignity." Some have sought to defend the NPKF,

218  *Ending Apartheid – A Troubled Transition*

arguing: "Where the soldiers were properly supported, they served well . . . and laid the groundwork for a promising future for South African peacekeeping."[144] A more obvious consequence was a new public confidence in the SADF and the SAP, whose support for the 1994 electoral process, in terms of security and logistical support, was widely praised. Seegers rates their performance over the period of polling as "exemplary."[145] As a result, Anglin sees the ANC, as "compelled to undergo a rapid and radical change in their historically-conditioned distrust of the security forces."[146]

## 6    Conclusion

The chapter began with the extraordinary events that took place in South Africa during February 1990. The far-reaching reforms unveiled by President de Klerk to the white parliament were surpassed only by the release of Mandela, so long the icon of South Africa's long struggle against *apartheid*. Internationally, the end of the cold war may not have been a decisive factor in the demise of *apartheid*, but it did have a powerful contributory effect to peace in the Southern Africa region. Both the United States and former Soviet Union moved from supporting proxy wars and arming conflict into facilitating the resolution of long-running disputes. Thereafter, the Communist bogey ceased to have the resonance it once did in the politics of the region and, internally, in South Africa itself.

The Commonwealth, too, was experiencing change. In November 1990, Thatcher was toppled, and John Major emerged as her successor. Earlier in the year, Anyaoku succeeded Sonny Ramphal as Commonwealth Secretary-General. Facing a radically different environment in South Africa, both men played a crucial role in ending the 'binary Commonwealth' and finding common purpose at the 1991 Harare CHOGM. In that respect, the adoption of the Harare Declaration was of profound importance. In Stultz's terms, the agreement may have been a declaratory act in placing a new emphasis for the association on the post-cold war themes of human rights and democracy. However, it also strengthened and elaborated the Commonwealth's human rights regime in ways which were to have far-reaching consequences internally, for both aspiring and existing member countries.[147] Externally, its public adoption may have eased the passage of Anyaoku's mission to South Africa after the Harare summit. This was to open a new chapter in the story of the Commonwealth's role in the ending of *apartheid*. But, in its metamorphosis from implacable opponent of Pretoria to friend and facilitator, how significant was the Commonwealth's contribution to international assistance for the transition process?

The greatest contribution the Commonwealth was able to make to South Africa's transition was in promoting initiatives which were then 'internationalised', particularly in combatting violence and promoting peaceful negotiations. This was the case in terms of Anyaoku's offer of Commonwealth observers at CODESA and in early 1992 his advocacy of international observers to address the growing violence, which eventuated in United Nations Security Council (UNSC) resolution 772 (92). The four international missions which as a result were deployed to South Africa focused on the immediate challenge of violence. However, they also paved the way for a substantial international observer presence at the 1994 elections, which up until the last moment were also threatened by violence. Coupled with Anyaoku's continuing good office contacts with the principal parties, this helped give the international dimension of South Africa's transition form and substance. Landsberg adds:

> While there was almost unanimity amongst South African political parties that they did not want formal mediation by external parties, there was also tacit agreement that they wanted the foreign community to play a supportive role such as putting pressure on opponents to end violence.[148]

That tacit agreement had not been evident at the outset, and the Commonwealth can claim credit in helping it materialise.

It is also the case that, given the calibre of the Commonwealth observers and the less restrictive operational constraints on their actions, COMSA and the election observer mission (Commonwealth Observer Group to South Africa [COGSA]) were able to be more proactive and interventionist than their counterparts in the United Nations, OAU and EC missions. Generally, the actions of COMSA (and later COGSA) drew praise, and its conflict resolution work in Natal was widely commended. Even so, given the scale of the problems faced, the limited numbers deployed and the relatively short-term nature of their deployment, their impact in any given area must have been limited. That said, whatever the threat of violence, it was very largely confined to highly localised areas of the East Rand and Natal, affecting no more than 10% of South Africa's population. The reach of the international observers prior to the elections, being generally focused on these areas, was therefore greater than it might have appeared.

**Notes**

1 F.W. de Klerk, Speech at the Opening of Parliament, 2 February 1990, *Cape Town*, https://omalley.nelsonmandela.org/omalley/index.php/site/q/03lv02039/04lv02103/05lv02104/06lv02105.
2 Reddy, "The United Nations and the struggle for liberation," *The Road to Democracy*, Vol.3, pt.1, 112.
3 J.E. Spence (ed.), *Change in South Africa* (London: RIIA, Pinter Publishers, 1994), 12.
4 Bill Keller, "Mandela, stunned by massacre, pulls out of talks on Black rule," 24 June 1992, *The New York Times*, Accessed 30 September 2019, www.nytimes.com/1992/06/24/world/mandela-stunned-by-massacre-pulls-out-of-talks-on-black-rule.html.
5 David Welsh and Jack Spence, *Ending Apartheid* (Harlow, England: Longman/Pearson, 2011), 131.
6 Anyaoku, "The Commonwealth, Mandela and the death of *apartheid*," 640.
7 United Nations Security Council, Resolution 772 (1992), 17 August 1992, Accessed 3 July 2017, www. digitallibrary.un.org/record/148221?In=en.
8 Abdul Minty, "South Africa: From *apartheid* to democracy," *Security Dialogue* 24:1 (1993): 80.
9 Transcript of a Joint Press Conference, Margaret Thatcher with Guilio Andreotti, 23 February 1990, London, Margaret Thatcher Foundation, COI document 108020.

220  *Ending Apartheid – A Troubled Transition*

10 Steven Prokesch, "Mandela urges support for sanctions," 17 April 1990, *New York Times*, Accessed 3 July 2018, www.nytimes.com/1990/04/17/world/mandela-urges-support-for-sanctions.html
11 Statement by Nelson Mandela, ANC, to CFMSA, May 1990, quoted in Ramphal, *Glimpses of a Global Life*, 470.
12 Anyaoku, "The Commonwealth, Mandela and the death of *apartheid*," 638.
13 Ibid., 639.
14 Anyaoku, *The Inside Story of the Modern Commonwealth*, 105.
15 Commonwealth Secretariat, *The Commonwealth at the Summit* (Vol.2), 90.
16 Ibid., 90.
17 This led to the adoption by Commonwealth Finance Ministers of the Trinidad & Tobago terms, and this package of debt relief was subsequently welcome by the UN and endorsed by the World Bank.
18 John Major, *John Major: The Autobiography* (London: HarperCollins Publishers, 1999), 46–47.
19 Major, *John Major: The Autobiography*, 123.
20 Stuart Mole, interviewed by Sue Onslow, *Commonwealth Oral History Project*, 1 February 2013, Accessed 7 March 2019, www.sas-space.sas.ac.uk/4910/10/stuart-mole-transcropt%201.11.
21 Robin Renwick, *Unconventional Diplomacy in Southern Africa*, 111.
22 Anyaoku, *The Inside Story of the Modern Commonwealth*, 129.
23 Ibid., 128.
24 McIntyre, *A Guide to the Contemporary Commonwealth*, 87–90.
25 HLAG Working Group of Senior Officials, "Draft Harare Commonwealth Declaration," Kuala Lumpur, December 1990, Commonwealth Secretariat archives, Marlborough House SGAN/03/011.
26 Correspondence from John Major to Emeka Anyaoku 26 September 1991, Commonwealth Secretariat archives, SGAN/03/011.
27 Brief for the Secretary-General's meeting with Prime Minister Mahathir, Kuala Lumpur, 8 October 1991, Commonwealth Secretariat archives, SGAN/13/001.
28 Anyaoku, *The Inside Story of the Modern Commonwealth*, 130.
29 McIntyre, *A Guide to the Contemporary Commonwealth*, 89.
30 Confidential note to Heads of Delegation from Emeka Anyaoku, "Harare Commonwealth Declaration," 19 October, Commonwealth Secretariat archives, SGAN/03/011.
31 Correspondence from Major to Anyaoku, 26 September 1991, 1.
32 Submission by the British Government, "Draft Harare Commonwealth Declaration," 18 September 1991, Commonwealth Secretariat archives, SGAN/03/011, 2.
33 Anyaoku, *The Inside Story of the Modern Commonwealth*, 130.
34 Major, *John Major: The Autobiography*, 517.
35 Correspondence from John Major to Trevor Huddleston, 12 November 1991, AAM archives, Bodleian, MSS AAM 1300.
36 Srinivasan, "Principles and practice," in *The Contemporary Commonwealth*, 70–71.
37 Anyaoku, *The Inside Story of the Modern Commonwealth*, 106.
38 UNGA Resolution, "Declaration on *apartheid* and its destructive consequences in Southern Africa," 14 December 1989, Accessed 5 March 2019, www.research.un.org/en/docs/ga/quick/regular/44.
39 Confidential memorandum and draft terms of reference by Emeka Amyaoku, "Special Commonwealth Mission to South Africa," 16 October 1991, Commonwealth Secretariat archives, SGAN/09/025.
40 Commonwealth Secretariat, *The Commonwealth at the Summit* (Vol.2), 89.
41 Correspondence from N.M. Nel to Emeka Anyaoku, 18 October 1991, Commonwealth Secretariat archives, SGAN/09/025.
42 Interview transcript, F.W. de Klerk in conversation with CSM South Africa, 28 October 1991, Commonwealth Secretariat archives SGAN/09/025.
43 Ibid.

44 Memorandum (unidentified author), "Notes on possibilities for international role in the transition to democratic government in South Africa," Commonwealth Secretariat archives, SGAN/09/025.
45 Memorandum from Max Gaylard to Emeka Anyaoku, "Secretary-General's mission to South Africa," 29 October 1991, Commonwealth Secretariat archives, SGAN/09/025.
46 Political Brief, "Secretary-General's mission to South Africa," Commonwealth Secretariat archives, SGAN/09/033.
47 Commonwealth News Release (91/39), "Commonwealth Secretary-General in special mission to South Africa," 29 October 1991, Commonwealth Secretariat archives, SGAN/09/025.
48 R. Dunn, "De Klerk in talks over violence," 1 November 1991, *Daily Telegraph*, Commonwealth Secretariat archives, SGAN/09/025.
49 Memorandum by Chief Buthelezi presented to Chief Emeka Anyaoku, 3 November 1991, Ulundi, KwaZulu-Natal, Commonwealth Secretariat archives, SGAN/09/025, 8.
50 Correspondence from Emeka Anyaoku to Lynden Pindling, Prime Minister of The Bahamas, 8 November 1991, Commonwealth Secretariat archives, SGAN/09/025, 2.
51 Ibid., 3.
52 Joint Media Statement, F.W. de Klerk and Emeka Anyaoku, 7 November 1991, Union Buildings, Pretoria. Commonwealth Secretariat archives, SGAN/09/025.
53 Correspondence from Anyaoku to Pindling, 4.
54 Correspondence from Michael Manley to Emeka Anyaoku, 19 November 1991, Commonwealth Secretariat archives, SGAN/09/025.
55 Correspondence from Mohamad Mahathir to Emeka Anyaoku, 23 November 1991, Commonwealth Secretariat archives, SGAN/09/025.
56 Opening Statement by Nelson Mandela, First Plenary, CODESA 1, 20 December 1991, Commonwealth Secretariat archives, I-40/3–1.
57 Ibid.
58 The Commonwealth's Distinguished Observers were Revd. Canaan Banana (former President of Zimbabwe); Rt. Hon. Sir Geoffrey Howe (former Deputy Prime Minister, UK); Shri Dinesh Singh (former Minister of External Affairs, India); Tan Sri Ghazali Shafie (former Minister of Foreign Affairs, Malaysia); Hon, Mr Justice Telford Georges (Trinidad & Tobago, former Chief Justice of The Bahamas); and Rt.Hon. Sir Ninian Stephen (former Governor-General of Australia).
59 Report of the Commonwealth Group of Observers, *The Commonwealth at CODESA*, 20–21 December 1991 (London: Commonwealth Secretariat, 1992), Commonwealth Secretariat archives, SGAN/09/009, 9.
60 Joint Statement by International Observers to the First Meeting of CODESA, Johannesburg, 20–21 December 1991, Commonwealth Secretariat archives, SGAN/09/009 (CODESA1).
61 Record of a meeting between the Secretary-General and Nelson Mandela, 14 May 1992, Johannesburg, personal papers.
62 Douglas Anglin, "International monitoring of the transition to democracy in South Africa, 1992–1994," *African Affairs* 94:377 (1995): 521–2.
63 Stephen Ellis, "The historical significance of South Africa's third force," *Journal of Southern African Studies*, 24:2 (1998), 289.
64 The Waddington Report, "Report of the inquiry into the police response to, and investigation of, events in Boipatong on 17 June 1992," 20 July 1992, O'Malley archives, Accessed 12 October 2018, https://omalley.nelsonmandela.org/omalley/.
65 Ellis, "South Africa's third force," 286.
66 Aide-Memoire from Emeka Anyaoku to various interlocutors, "Proposed Commonwealth group to assist in arresting violence in South Africa," 3 July, Johannesburg, Commonwealth Secretariat archives, SGAN/09/054,1.
67 Anyaoku, *The Inside Story of the Modern Commonwealth*, 116.
68 Ibid., 116.
69 Ibid., 117.

70 Emmanuel Nwagboiwe and Chike Amaikwu (eds.), *Footprints of an Iconic Diplomat* (Abuja: Leverage Multi Global Concept Ltd, 2013), 93.
71 Anyaoku, *The Inside Story*, 120.
72 Anglin, "International monitoring of the transition," 523.
73 Brief for COMSA Observers, "Commonwealth observer mission to South Africa, October – December 1992," Commonwealth Secretariat archives, SGAN/09/054, 21.
74 UNSC/RES/772 (1992).
75 Report by Dr Boutros Boutros-Ghali to the UN Security Council, "Report of the Secretary-General on the question of South Africa," 22 December 1992, UN document S/25004, 281292, 11.
76 UNSC 772.
77 Commonwealth Secretariat, Report of the Commonwealth Observer Mission to South Africa (Phase 1: October 1992–January 1993), *Violence in South Africa* (London: Commonwealth Secretariat, 1993), 2–3.
78 Boutros-Ghali, Report to the UN Security Council, 12.
79 Simpson, *Political Violence: 1990*, 1.
80 Rupert Taylor and Mark Shaw, "The dying days of *apartheid*," in *South Africa in Transition* (London: Palgrave Macmillan, 1998) ed. David Howarth and Aletta Norval, 1998), 13.
81 Quoted in Commonwealth Secretariat, *Violence in South Africa*, 12.
82 Ibid., 13.
83 Graeme Simpson, Steve Mokwena and Lauren Segal, "Political violence: 1990," In University of Natal. Centre for Socio-Legal Studies, *South African Human Rights and Labour Law Yearbook* (Cape Town: Oxford University Press, 1990), 4.
84 Simpson, *Political Violence: 1990*, 1.
85 Commonwealth Secretariat, *Violence in South Africa*, 13.
86 Simpson, *Political Violence: 1990*, 2.
87 Ibid., 2–3.
88 Human Rights Commission, "Special focus: Violence in crossroads," UCT archives, BC 668, P4.10.
89 Kynoch, *Township Violence*, 197.
90 Gary Kynoch, "Reassessing transition violence: Voices from South Africa's township wars, 1990–4," *African Affairs* 112:447 (2013): 303.
91 Guelke, *South Africa in Transition*, 47.
92 Adrian Guelke, "Interpretations of political violence during transition," *Politikon: South African Journal of Political Studies* 27:2 (2000): 250.
93 Spence, *Change in South Africa*, 13.
94 Boutros-Ghali, Report to the UN Security Council, 7.
95 Commonwealth Secretariat, *Violence in South Africa*, 15.
96 Minty, "South Africa: From *apartheid* to democracy," 80–81.
97 Ibid., 80.
98 Boutros-Ghali, Report to UNSC, 11.
99 Commonwealth Secretariat, *Violence in South Africa*, 3.
100 European Community Observer Mission in South Africa, Confidential Report for the period October 1992–April 1993, Commonwealth Secretariat archives, SGAN/09/A18.2, 43.
101 Ibid., 40.
102 Commonwealth Secretariat, *Violence in South Africa*, 16–17.
103 ECOMSA, Confidential Report, Appendix K.
104 Personal observation by the author, temporarily assigned to COMSA over that period.
105 Anglin, "International monitoring of the transition," 535.
106 ECOMSA, Confidential Report, 2.
107 Ibid., 2.
108 National Peace Committee, *National Peace Accord* (Johannesburg: minit print arcadia, 1991), 3.
109 Commonwealth Secretariat, *Violence in South Africa*, 25.

110 Ibid., 26.
111 Ibid., 27.
112 Fred Khumalo, "Refugees are returning home," *City Press*, 13 December 1992.
113 Commonwealth Secretariat, *Violence in South Africa*, 27.
114 Ibid., 28–29.
115 Correspondence from Mark Butler to Emeka Anyaoku, 28 April 1993, Commonwealth Secretariat archives, SGAN/09/22.
116 Notes from a telephone conversation between Duncan Chappell and Commonwealth Secretariat staff, 1 May 1993, Commonwealth Secretariat archives, SGAN 09/22.
117 Correspondence from Beyers Naude to Emeka Anyaoku, 3 May 1993, Commonwealth Secretariat archives SGAN/09/22.
118 Annotation by Emeka Anyaoku to Anthony Siaguru on correspondence from Barry Munson, Toti Crisis and Upliftment Centre, Amanzimtoti, 5 December 1992, Commonwealth Secretariat archives, SGAN/09/002.
119 Memorandum, "COMSA budget estimates for period 15 January–15 April 1993," from Max Gaylard to Emeka Anyaoku, 15 January 1993, Commonwealth Secretariat archives, SGAN/09/22.
120 Obituary, "Clive Derby-Lewis," 5 November 2016, *The Times*, 82.
121 Ibid., 82.
122 Broadcast by Nelson Mandela, 13 April 1993, Accessed 18 November 2019, www.News24.com/NelsonMandela/speeches/FULL_TEXT_On_Chris_Hani_20110124.
123 Saul Dubow, *Apartheid 1948–1994*, 271.
124 Transcript of a press conference given by COMSA, 17 December 1992, Johannesburg, held in archives of the Department for International Relations and Cooperation (DIRCO), FOI request.
125 Statement by Department of Justice (P.A. Du Rand, Chief Liaison Officer), 22 December 1992 in response to COMSA statement, DIRCO archives, FOI request.
126 Editorial, "Upholding the law," *The Star*, 23 December 1992, DIRCO archives, FOI request.
127 Minty, "South Africa: From *apartheid* to democracy," 81.
128 Record of a telephone conversation between Emeka Anyaoku and Pik Botha, 24 November 1992, Johannesburg, Commonwealth Secretariat archives, SGAN/09/002.
129 Memorandum by COMSA (Colleen Lowe-Morna) to Commonwealth Secretariat, "Commonwealth assistance to the transition," 6 January 1994, Commonwealth Secretariat archives, SGAN/09/046, 1.
130 Memorandum by COMSA (C. Lowe-Morna) to Commonwealth Secretariat, "Update on assistance to the NPKF," 11 January 1994, Commonwealth Secretariat archives, SGAN/09/046, 2.
131 Correspondence from the Joint Executive Secretaries, TEC to Emeka Anyaoku, 19 January 1994, Commonwealth Secretariat archives, SGAN/09/46, 1.
132 Correspondence from Emeka Anyaoku to the Joint Executive Secretaries, TEC, 26 January 1994, Commonwealth Secretariat archives, SGAN/09/046, 1.
133 Anglin, "The life and death of South Africa's National Peacekeeping Force," *The Journal of Modern African Studies* 33:1 (1995): 33.
134 Press Release, "Commonwealth announces support to NPKF," 10 February 1994, Johannesburg, Commonwealth Secretariat archives, SGAN/09/046.
135 Memorandum from John Syson to Anthony Siaguru, "CPAG – Requirement for Commonwealth Secretariat Funding," 9 March 1994, Commonwealth Secretariat archives, SGAN/09/046.
136 Anglin, "The life and death of the NPKF," 33.
137 Gary Kynoch, *Township Violence and the End of Apartheid: War on the Reef* (Woodbridge U.K. & Rochester, NY: James Currey/Boydell & Brewer Ltd, 2018), 115.
138 Chris Louw, "Experts warned that NPKF wasn't ready," 22 April, *Weekly Mail & Guardian*, Commonwealth Secretariat archives, SGAN/09/046.

139 Colonel Cottam, CPAG, Report to Russell Marshal, COMSA, April 1994, Commonwealth Secretariat archives, SGAN/09/046.
140 Kynoch, *Township Violence and the End of Apartheid*, 117.
141 Cottam, Report to COMSA, 4.
142 Anglin, "The life and death of the NPKF," 52.
143 Cottam, Report to COMSA, 4.
144 David Ridley-Harris, "South African peacekeeping, 1994–2012," *Military History Journal*), 16: 1 (2013).
145 Annette Seegers, *The Military in the Making of Modern South Africa* (London and New York: I.B. Tauris & Co Ltd, 1996), 283.
146 Anglin, "The life and death of the NPKF," 50.
147 Srinivasan, "Principles and practice: Human Rights, the Harare Declaration and the Commonwealth Ministerial Action Group," 69–76.
148 Christopher Landsberg, *The Quiet Diplomacy of Liberation* (Johannesburg: Jacana Media, 2004), 224.

## References

Annette Seegers, *The Military in the Making of Modern South Africa* (London, New York: I.B. Tauris, Co Ltd, 1996).
Christopher Landsberg, *The Quiet Diplomacy of Liberation* (Johannesburg: Jacana Media, 2004).
Commonwealth Secretariat, *The Commonwealth at the Summit (Vol.2)*.
David Howarth and Aletta Norval (eds.), *South Africa in Transition* (London: Palgrave Macmillan, 1998).
David Welsh and Jack Spence, *Ending Apartheid* (Harlow, England: Longman Pearson, 2011).
Emeka Anyaoku, *The Inside Story of the Modern Commonwealth*. Op.Cit.
Emmanuel Nwagboiwe and Chike Amaikwu (eds.), *Footprints of an Iconic Diplomat* (Abuja: Leverage Multi Global Concept Ltd, 2013).
Gary Kynoch, *Township Violence and the End of Apartheid: War on the Reef* (Woodbridge U.K, Rochester, NY: James Currey/Boydell, Brewer Ltd, 2018).
James Mayall (ed.), *The Contemporary Commonwealth: An Assessment 1965–2009* (London, New York: Routledge, 2010).
J.E. Spence (ed.), *Change in South Africa* (London: RIIA, Pinter Publishers, 1994).
John Major, *John Major: The Autobiography* (London: HarperCollins Publishers, 1999).
Report of the Commonwealth Observer Mission to South Africa (Phase 1: October 1992-January 1993), *Violence in South Africa* (London: Commonwealth Secretariat, 1993).
Robin Renwick, *Unconventional Diplomacy in Southern Africa* (London: Palgrave Macmillan, 1997).
Saul Dubow, *Apartheid 1948–1994*, Op.Cit.
Sisifo Ndlovu (ed.), *The Road to Democracy (Vol.3, pt.1)* (Pretoria: SADET/UNISA Press, 2008).
W. David McIntyre, *A Guide to the Contemporary Commonwealth*, Op.Cit.

# 12 The 'Freedom Elections' and *Apartheid's* End

## 1 Introduction

As the car carrying the Commonwealth observers slowed at a junction out of Johannesburg, a passer-by spotted the blue and gold Commonwealth symbol and lettering emblazoned on the vehicle's side. "You bloody Commonwealth peacemongers," he cried: "You're wasting your time and ours."[1] The voice decrying "Commonwealth peacemongers," supposedly on a mission to nowhere, came from a middle-aged white male. His angry tone suggested a belief that any attempt to bridge the racial divide would be fruitless. His likely attachment to white supremacy, and hint of the disasters which would mark its passing, might have implied support for the *Volkstaat*. But only 42,400 of the 2,930,000 whites who voted in the 1994 elections supported the Freedom Front (FF) in that policy objective, around 2% of the electorate as a whole.[2] Most voters, of all communities and colours, supported a negotiated settlement and welcomed international observers, seeing their presence as reassuring and largely impartial.

Did the presence of international observers in South Africa by 1992 make it easier for South Africa's interim administration (the 'transitional structures') to invite foreign observers for the 1994 'freedom' elections? In turn, did that make it more likely that other international, national and regional bodies, and international faith and civil society organisations, would respond positively to that invitation and deploy effectively across the country? There is no doubt that, in preparing for the elections, "the challenges facing the IEC (Independent Electoral Commission) were formidable."[3] How did the Commonwealth, and other international observers, help in the successful conclusion of the elections where, in the words of Anyaoku, "a series of major obstacles melted away"?[4] Did the eventual outcome owe more to behind-the-scenes compromise and negotiation (including by turning a blind eye to electoral malpractice) than the foundational mythology of a 'miracle' election? Is David Welsh correct to accuse "sanctimonious foreign observers" of falling about themselves to accept the validity of an election marred by flaws they would never accept in their own countries?[5]

Having considered these questions, the chapter concludes by exploring South Africa's return to Commonwealth membership in 1994 after an absence of thirty-three years. South Africa's departure from the organisation in 1961 was seen by

10.4324/9781003208617-12

many of its citizens as a necessary part of its new republican identity and a final severance from its colonial past. That perception has become ingrained in a present-day narrative which both Black and white South Africans share in describing their journey to a non-racial and inclusive democracy. Minty has suggested that "for the people of South Africa, the Commonwealth never left them."[6] However, a return to membership of the Commonwealth had not been flagged as an early priority of the new ANC government, and yet it was among the first of its foreign policy decisions. Why was this so? Was this gratitude for the Commonwealth's support for the struggle or a whiff of sentiment and nostalgia at the breaking of a new dawn? Or did the new government, and its president in particular, see practical benefits to be had, and diplomatic influence to be gained, by rejoining the association? In that last respect, what practical contribution did the Commonwealth make to South Africa's reconstruction, not least in support of the new government's Reconstruction and Development Programme (RDP) after 1994?

## 2 Violence and the Election

The setting of an election date in June 1993 did not end political violence, but it did change its character. In May 1993, prior to Chris Hani's assassination, the COMSA had noted "a marked decrease in violence in the PWV area" prior to Hani's death, though the mission was unclear at that point as to whether levels of violence would continue to fall or would escalate. But COMSA felt that there was a new and strong consensus among political leaders that "negotiations should not be held hostage to violence."[7]

In a dramatic illustration of this imperative, the Multi-Party Negotiating Forum (MPNF), the successor to CODESA II, was temporarily halted by a physical assault on the venue of the talks, the World Trade Centre in Kempton Park. On 25 June, around 3,000 supporters of Eugene Terre'Blanche's Afrikaner Weerstandsbeweging (AWB) and the AVF used an armoured vehicle to smash their way into the Centre and temporarily halt the talks. The SAP was ineffectual in containing the assault, and there was considerable damage during the occupation but no fatalities or serious injuries. However, it was a reminder of the potency of the "white right" to disrupt the transitional process and threaten free and fair elections. By November, the MPNF had ratified the interim Constitution, a temporary IEC had been established, and a TEC was formed to provide a neutral administration for overseeing the period up to the elections. For some, this marked the culmination of a decisive ascendancy by the ANC over the NP, established in the aftermath of Hani's death.

These developments in turn had a considerable impact on the four international observer missions. While mitigating violence and monitoring the negotiations had been their initial focus, it had always been privately accepted that this would be superseded by "the ultimate purpose of promoting conditions conducive to free and fair elections."[8] In any case, COMSA had recognised from the outset that violence was rooted in the *apartheid* system. While the mission had no illusions that violence would cease with the election of a non-racial, democratic government, they nonetheless believed that a government which enjoyed the support of a majority of the population "is in a far better position to address the issue of violence than one which does not."⁹ However, it was by no means certain that South Africa would wish an international observer presence at the elections. After all, de Klerk had railed against foreign interference early in his tenure and had initially dismissed the idea of an international observer presence to address the violence. The ANC and others had also been sceptical, as indeed had the United Nations. Opinion only began to turn after the Boipatong massacre.

The presence of the international missions in South Africa after September 1992 certainly served to allay many fears. That said, COMSA in particular was publicly critical of aspects of government policy, and this was not universally welcomed. De Klerk in particular was conscious of the international community's previous hostility to his party and government and reminded Anyaoku that "[i]t was necessary for them to maintain a more impartial stance in relation to all the political forces in South Africa."¹⁰ Nevertheless, he expressed "appreciation for the cooperative and helpful approach of the international community" for the work it was doing.¹¹ A year later, he gave a guarded welcome to the United Nations to send international observers for the elections but "to observe not to monitor."¹² Many internationally considered this a distinction without a difference and used the two words interchangeably.¹³ Nevertheless, both the NP and the ANC made a functional distinction between the two, and this was reflected in the IEC Act. International Election Observers (IEOs) were therefore told that they "must not perform tasks which, under the relevant laws, are to be performed by voting officials of the IEC, such as monitors, etc."¹⁴ The precise functions of IEC monitors were set out in the relevant legislation.¹⁵ In practice, in the sometimes chaotic circumstances of the 1994 elections, this line between observers and monitors was also one which in practice was often blurred.

The Commonwealth summit in October 1993, the Limassol CHOGM, took a number of important steps. Firstly, leaders recognised that, with the setting of an election date and the formation of the TEC, the process of change in South Africa was now irreversible. Apart from the arms embargo, they therefore lifted all other sanctions. Secondly, they noted that COMSA "had made an important and widely acknowledged contribution towards helping stem the violence, reconcile communities, return refugees and initiate socio-economic reconstruction," and they decided that COMSA should remain until the elections.¹⁶ Its remit was to be widened to include preparatory electoral assistance.¹⁷ Thirdly, in view of the profound challenges still facing South Africa, they were of the view that "a sizeable international observer presence would be indispensable if confidence in the process were to be assured."¹⁸ Fourthly, apart from channelling technical assistance to a number of transitional agencies, the Heads declared that "they looked forward to welcoming a non-racial and democratic South Africa back into the Commonwealth at the earliest opportunity," should the new government so decide.¹⁹

Anyaoku later reported to leaders that:

> at the time of the April 1994 elections, 119 experts from 19 Commonwealth countries were providing technical support, including fifty electoral experts

*Figure 12.1* Nelson Mandela and Chief Anyaoku at Marlborough House, 1993. Commonwealth Secretariat.

seconded to the Independent Electoral Commission (IEC) and thirty-three military and police officers drawn from eight member countries, involved in helping train the National Peace-Keeping Force. The culmination was the largest ever Commonwealth Election Observer Group, led by Rt Hon Michael Manley of Jamaica.[20]

While the COGSA was the second-largest international observer group, numbering around 118 all told, with an impressive line-up of skills and experience within the group, it was dwarfed by UNOMSA. No less than sixty-seven Americans alone were part of UNOMSA, out of a total of 1,800 observers from one hundred participating states. At the same time, the civil rights campaigner Jesse Jackson led an official US observer team, supported by a $35 million US government grant.[21] The other intergovernmental organisations already working in South Africa, the OAU and the EU provided similar-sized observation teams to the Commonwealth.[22] In addition to IGOs and overseas national delegations, international observers also came from the NGO sector. The largest of these was the EMPSA, which was based in South Africa from 1992 to 1994 and recruited 443 participants to the programme during the period.[23] Additionally, there were numerous local observers, many from South Africa's 54,000 NGOs. A National Electoral Observer Network (NEON) was formed immediately prior to the elections. It was expected to deploy around 30,000 domestic observers and 2,000 international observers from sixty-seven foreign NGOs.[24] The official IEC monitors completed the picture.

## 3 The Freedom Elections

Timothy Sisk has written that "[t]he end of *apartheid* unfolded perfectly scripted for a conflict-weary world."[25] It may not have seemed like that at the time, but, one by one, the impossibilities standing in the way of a fair poll were steadily, almost miraculously, overcome. Despite a series of bombings at the start of the campaign, which in total claimed 21 lives and injured at least 173, the threat of right-wing violence disrupting the campaign receded.[26] The bravado of Terre'Blanche and the AWB had dissolved in the blood and dust of Bophuthatswana, and General Constand Viljoen had defused a serious paramilitary threat from his supporters by deciding to participate in the elections, heading the FF. The other principal source of violence, centred in KwaZulu-Natal (as it had now become), came from Chief Buthelezi's initial boycott of the elections, given his strong opposition to a unitary state. At the last moment, following a flurry of discussions and concessions, Buthelezi decided to register the IFP for the elections. The violence in KwaZulu-Natal fell away substantially, and Justice Kriegler later stated that not a single death could be attributed to election violence during the period of voting.[27]

However, despite an improving political climate, the remaining logistical challenges were immense. Adding the IFP name and emblem to millions of already printed and secure ballot papers (by means of a special sticker) was one issue. The absence of voter rolls was another. Eligibility to vote had to be proved by means of a suitable identity document which millions did not have, relying instead on the IEC issuing temporary voting cards; 3.5 million of these were given out, nearly half in the four days of polling.[28] If this expedient invited fraud and under-age voting, the procedures instituted for polling generally were highly complex. This included scanning the hands of would-be voters in case there was any sign of previously administered invisible ink; applying new ink to the finger to avoid double voting; and issuing each voter with two large scrolls of paper – one ballot covering the nineteen parties standing nationally, and the second for the twenty-six parties standing in the nine provincial elections.[29] For an electorate used to such complexities and polling staff experienced in such matters, the challenge might have been manageable. But most of the electorate of 22.5 million had never cast a vote in their lives; polling stations had never before been sited across large parts of the South Africa land mass; and many of the 30,000 extra polling staff had had the barest of training.

In the event, in the words of Anyaoku, these major obstacles "melted away" because they were met with "patience, good humour and flexibility."[30] The queues of voters stretched, people waited, and polling was extended by a day and a half to make up for stations that failed to open and for ballots and election material that did not arrive. It was not, therefore, that everything suddenly fell into place: it did not. "There were irregularities and cheating," but for many, including most Africans, "the election was a joyful catharsis and a symbolic affirmation of their newfound rights as citizens."[31] Nearly all wished the end, a peaceful deliverance from *apartheid*, and most were prepared to accept the practical and political compromises needed to achieve that goal. "We promised an adequate and respectable election," pronounced IEC Chair, Judge Kriegler, "not a 12-cylinder supercharged election."[32] Despite the deficiencies, it was, said Kriegler, "substantially free and

*Figure 12.2* Black and white voters queue in South Africa's first democratic elections, 1994. Commonwealth Secretariat.

fair."[33] This was echoed by de Klerk: "If we cannot have a 100 per cent perfect election, we must go for a 95 per cent perfect election."[34] The Canadian electoral expert, Ron Gould, who served as an IEC international commissioner, also spoke frankly: "We expect that in some cases the number [of votes] will not balance. We are not running a fast-food operation here."[35]

As expected, the ANC emerged triumphant, winning seven of nine provinces and 62% of the vote nationally with 252 seats. It fell short of the two-thirds majority needed to amend the interim constitution unilaterally, but such a course would have been unthinkable in any event. The NP, with 20% of the vote, won eighty-two seats in the National Assembly and took control of the provincial government in the Western Cape. The IFP, which polled poorly outside its base, secured 10.5% of the national vote, and forty-three seats. More importantly, the IFP were declared the winners in KwaZulu-Natal and qualified for a presence in the Government of National Unity. Nelson Mandela became South Africa's first Black President, with De Klerk and Thabo Mbeki as deputies and with Buthelezi holding the influential Home Affairs portfolio. In the eyes of some this may have been "a loveless marriage of convenience," but all recognised that it was a democratic imperative.[36] The FF, DP and the PAC polled poorly but managed to secure a foothold in the National Assembly. The principle of inclusivity, which had been so important to containing the violence and delivering the election, was therefore preserved. In that respect, the positive and decisive role of the police and the SADF proved vital, not only in the security field but in logistical support for the electoral process.[37]

Perhaps the most questionable element of what was in part a negotiated outcome was the results in KwaZulu-Natal. Reynolds suggests that the province had "the worst election irregularities and possibly the best case for the invalidation of an election."[38] A Commonwealth observer in KwaZulu-Natal, reflecting on his experiences, commented: "I would say the vast bulk of the incidents we encountered were generated by Inkatha and their supporters and which is why we who were there were frustrated by the 'handover' of the province to that party."[39] Nevertheless, given that there were significant irregularities across the country (including a possible 1 million illegal votes), to have invalidated the process only in Natal would have been difficult to justify, and the political ramifications would have been huge. On 6 May, immediately following the announcement of the results of the elections by Judge Kriegler, coupled with his stated conviction that polling was substantially free and fair, the four intergovernmental observer groups issued a joint statement. This began by saluting the fact that South Africans had turned out in enormous numbers to participate freely in the elections. Nonetheless, the missions pointed to "serious inadequacies in the control and accounting of sensitive electoral material," "irregularities" at the counting stage and "evidence of malfeasance." In that last respect, they urged that all formal complaints should be thoroughly investigated by the IEC, and the SAP and criminal investigations pursued. However, while taking into account these issues, they declared that the missions "share the collective view that the outcome of the elections reflects the will of the people of South Africa."[40] The Commonwealth's own report on the elections makes clear that it was not for the mission to apply the 'free and fair' test; only that the elections were "a free expression of will" and whether the results reflected "the wishes of the people."[41] COGSA's cautious conclusion was that the elections were "a credible democratic process which was substantially fair."[42] In the Commonwealth's case, certainly, Welsh's accusations against 'sanctimonious foreign observers' cannot be justified. COGSA did not pronounce the elections 'free and fair'. It did not ignore the abuses and malpractices it found but reported these fully and urged that they be properly investigated by due process. It made recommendations to the IEC for future elections to correct shortcomings, but it did not exceed its mandate by seeking to directly interfere with the electoral process. That said, the international observers, the IEC and the political parties all recognised a greater truth. As *The Star* put it, "[t]he big picture is majestic," whatever the multiple faults and failings. It continued: "Democracy, simply, was the winner. Its triumph was bigger than parties or policies or personalities."[43]

## 4 South Africa and Commonwealth Membership

The circumstances of South Africa's departure from the Commonwealth in 1961 were in part accidental. Were the vagaries of chance a similar factor in South Africa's return to membership in 1994? South Africa's exit thirty-three years before had been seen by many South Africans as a necessary stage in its post-colonial development. As the years passed and South Africa became enclosed in the cocoon of a pariah state, many of the old loyalties of English whites to a British Crown and an old Commonwealth also fell away. If the driver for a return to the Commonwealth was therefore largely from the ANC and the liberation forces, the evidence for this is not widely recognised. A return to Commonwealth membership had not been obviously flagged as an early priority of the new ANC-led government, and yet it was among the first of its foreign policy decisions, taking effect on 1 June 1994, less than a month after the formation of the government of national unity.

Geyser has argued that the background reasons for this decision were twofold: the disintegration of *apartheid* and the end of the Cold War. He commented: "It is a reality that Africa can no longer use the iniquities of *apartheid* to shelter it from exposure to its own inadequacies; and communism's collapse has bared the continent to a new economic realism."[44] Geyser pointed to Namibia's accession to the Commonwealth on independence in 1990 as a case in point, though the country was never a British colony. Writing in 1994, he suggested that Mozambique, Angola and Cameroon were among those other African countries who had put out soundings about possible membership.[45]

South Africa's return to the Commonwealth as a post-*apartheid* state was not a new topic. Ramphal has recalled raising the matter with Oliver Tambo not long before his death and Tambo's insistence that "black South Africa never left the Commonwealth."[46] It was also a thought never far from Anyaoku's mind, though he chose not to respond when in May 1993 the South African Ambassador raised the issue with him. Kent Durr, who had previously been an NP Minister and headed South Africa's sanctions-busting operations, told Anyaoku that the challenge "was for South Africa to continue to evolve to the point where it could confidently expect to be welcomed back into Commonwealth circles."[47] While Anyaoku may have been reticent at that point, prior to agreement on the election date, the formation of the TEC and the final lifting of Commonwealth sanctions, Durr was later to become a significant advocate for the issue in South Africa. In September 1993, he sent a paper to all South Africa's political leadership about South Africa and the Commonwealth. In it, he argued that reversing the effects of South Africa's long isolation would be a key priority so that the nation could be reintegrated into the international community and the global economy. Involvement in international organisations, including the Commonwealth, would assist in that task. The Commonwealth was "transcontinental, multiracial and multicultural."[48] He also saw it was becoming "a vehicle for serious dialogue on democracy and development."[49]

At the Cyprus CHOGM, in October 1993, South Africa's transition to democratic elections looked fragile with the far right and Buthelezi's IFP refusing to join the negotiating process or the 1994 elections. At one point, Anyaoku secretly toyed with the idea of inviting Chief Buthelezi to the summit "solely to provide Commonwealth leaders collectively an opportunity to put pressure in him to be constructive and helpful" but found the ANC reluctant.[50] Preparations were made for assisting the elections and for Commonwealth support for post-*apartheid* reconstruction and development. However, South Africa's return to membership was also on the minds of leaders. John Major of the UK was among a number expressing the hope that South Africa would rejoin. Major said he was sure that his colleagues would offer "the warmest of welcomes to a South African Head of Government at its next meeting, thereby bringing to an end a very long and very unhappy chapter in the Commonwealth's history."[51] Even Queen Elizabeth, the Head of the Commonwealth, intervened in the debate by privately telling leaders that the possibility of South Africa rejoining the Commonwealth "gives cause for hope and pleasure."[52]

The Commonwealth's formal offer came in the summit communiqué. Almost at the end of a long statement on different aspects of South Africa's transition, it declared:

> While it was for the new, democratically elected government in South Africa to decide on whether it should seek to return to the Commonwealth, Heads of Government looked forward to welcoming a non-racial and democratic South Africa back into the Commonwealth at the earliest possible opportunity.[53]

In the fraught and frantic months leading to the 1994 elections, it would be fanciful to suggest that the issue was high on anyone's agenda. Nevertheless, exchanges and public statements continued. On 19 January 1994, in an address to the South Africa Club in London, Anyaoku considered the whole question of South Africa's future relationship with the Commonwealth, repeating the invitation from Commonwealth leaders for the new non-racial government to rejoin the association. The following day Pik Botha confirmed that procedural steps were underway to facilitate South Africa's return to membership of the Commonwealth and other 'reputable' international organisations "at the earliest moment after the elections."[54] Botha added that this approach had the full support of the ANC, though he reiterated that the final decision would be for the new government.

Mandela was inaugurated as South Africa's first Black President on 10 May, and South Africa's return to the Commonwealth was announced shortly thereafter. Anyaoku records that it was one of the first decisions of Mandela's Cabinet.[55] What were the reasons behind this decision and why did the Government of National Unity embark on this policy so swiftly in its new life? Hyam and Henshaw comment that "pariah states have to find a point of re-entry into the international community."[56] Undoubtedly, after decades of isolation over most facets of public and professional life, connecting with the Commonwealth network offered a rapid means of re-integrating with the world. Clearly, this included rebuilding relations with the UK with its long-standing ties with South Africa and its still considerable number of UK passport holders among its citizens, as well as with other Western nations. But it was also about healing old enmities and building links where they might not have existed. For example, India had cut all ties with South Africa prior to 1948 and the formal inauguration of the *apartheid* policy. Other South-East Asian states, such as Malaysia, had come to independence at the time of South Africa's growing ostracism and had therefore looked elsewhere for its friendships and trade. Even in Africa, with 25% of Commonwealth members, use of the organisation had immediate advantages. Geyser quotes Anyaoku to demonstrate the mutual benefits which South African membership of a largely Commonwealth SADC would bring, making it "the engine of development there."[57]

Quite apart from the economic benefits, Hyam and Henshaw point to the diplomatic and political advantages of the Commonwealth as a North-South forum with its biennial summits of leaders from a highly diverse spectrum of countries. But they also reveal the hazards of analysing the Commonwealth through a bilateral UK-South Africa lens. They incorrectly ascribe to the British Government the hosting of the 1994 ceremony of welcome to the new South Africa in Westminster Abbey, rather than to the Commonwealth.[58] They then ask why the ANC should have taken up the renewed hand of friendship after a "formidable legacy of mistrust."[59] But that mistrust between the UK and the ANC, which accentuated markedly in the Thatcher years, was absent from the ANC-Commonwealth relationship. Abdul Minty, on behalf of the AAM, was a discreet attendee at every Commonwealth summit, except two, between 1960 and 1994.[60] Other ANC figures were regularly in the wings of CHOGM, especially as the Commonwealth's anti-*apartheid* programmes developed. In 1993, Thabo Mbeki quietly lobbied the Commonwealth Secretariat to include a reference in the summit's communiqué to respecting the "human rights and fundamental freedoms of all its people" within a new democratic South Africa. This was designed to assist the ANC in its delicate negotiations with General Viljoen, the CP and advocates of the *Volkstaat*.[61] The ANC, among others, had also been closely involved in Commonwealth initiatives, such as the 1986 EPG mission and negotiations, the sanctions campaign and the 1992–1994 deployment of Commonwealth observers. None of that could have happened without their tacit consent. Other practical assistance was also offered and taken up, including fellowships, education and training. Denis Goldberg, one of the Rivonia trialists and imprisoned with Mandela, was in 1991 nominated by the ANC to take part in an advanced administrative training course in India and Malaysia, organised by the Commonwealth Secretariat, something he later described as "a wonderful experience."[62]

In any case, Anyaoku had close links with South Africa's Black leadership. As Mbeki put it, "[w]e trusted him and considered him our representative in the Commonwealth, not just for South Africa as a country but for the reconstruction of Africa."[63] They also knew that the process of change would not end with the 1994 elections. The Commonwealth had an important role in support of South Africa's RDP, not so much in drawing upon its own modest financial resources but in leveraging funds from significant donors and assisting the coordination and absorption of assistance. Nor was Commonwealth membership solely intergovernmental: South Africa's thriving civil society and professional organisations would find ready counterparts in all corners of the Commonwealth.

Finally, Hyam and Henshaw rightly identify the value of Commonwealth sporting links, both for South Africa externally and, internally, as a source of cohesion and shared ethos. South Africa's return to international cricket took place in 1991 even while Mandela separately argued for the maintenance of international non-sporting sanctions. Similar steps followed in rugby, and, in 1992, South Africa participated in the Olympic and Paralympic games in Barcelona. South Africa's speedy resumption of Commonwealth membership in June 1994 was just in time for the rainbow nation's participation in the XVth Commonwealth Games, held in Victoria, Canada, in August.[64] South Africa came twelfth in the medal table. In all this, the ANC saw the power of sport as a way of mobilising the new nation around its rainbow identity and forging a shared purpose as it returned to competitive international sport.

Rejoining the Commonwealth may have seemed a reassuring step back into the past for many of South Africa's whites. In truth, however, it was the ANC which drove the process and which was most hard-headed about the modern nature of the Commonwealth and the practical benefits it could offer. As the ANC's Foreign Policy document had put it, "[t]he ANC therefore believes that South Africa's return to the Commonwealth will represent the symbolic ending of the country's isolation" and that it would be "central to the spirit of the new foreign policy."[65] The Commonwealth, of course, was only one of the sixteen multilateral organisations South Africa joined, or gained readmission to, by the end of 1994.[66] Pretoria's policy was therefore one of 'universality', explained by Deputy Foreign Minister Aziz Pahad as "being very nice to the rich and powerful, nice to the potentially rich and powerful, and kind to old friends who are neither."[67] The Commonwealth offered a route to countries in all three categories.

Nonetheless, South Africa's return to the Commonwealth in 1994 was to give Mandela a new role as a Commonwealth statesman. He was pivotal in the new internal mechanisms and rules adopted by the association in 1995 to implement the Harare Declaration in practical terms as an international human rights regime.[68] In this respect, the Commonwealth proved to be an innovator in fresh approaches to upholding and enforcing international norms.

## 5 Conclusion

The Commonwealth presence at the 1994 elections had its origins in the work of the four international observer missions, including the Commonwealth, which had been operating on the ground in South Africa since 1992. Their mandate came from the UN Security Council, and their task was to address the mounting violence which, quite apart from its substantial human cost, was causing the negotiation process to falter and trust between the various parties to disintegrate. Nevertheless, despite its potentially catastrophic effects, the violence was highly localised. This allowed international support to be concentrated where it was most needed. It also built confidence in South Africa about the role of international observers and made their involvement – as election observers – much more likely as polling day drew near.

However, in the circumstances of 'all-out' elections, held across the country, achieving meaningful coverage by international observers everywhere was much more problematic. Of course, given that the electoral work of the four intergovernmental observer groups was coordinated by the United Nations to provide an integrated operation on the ground, all assistance no doubt proved valuable in coping with South Africa's considerable geography. There were many civil society and local observers, and official monitors, who helped improve scrutiny. It was also the case that (as in any election) the most pressing issues were in the areas of extreme party competition rather than in most districts where one or other party was dominant. Indisputably, the 1994 elections were beset by shortcomings and irregularities. For that reason, COGSA avoided the trap of the 'free and fair' test, reported abuses and malpractice, and urged that they be properly addressed. But, along with many others, it recognised the elections as the authentic final stage of South Africa's liberation. In the words of Waldmeir, "it was the perfect end to the negotiated revolution – a negotiated election."[69]

Guelke argues persuasively that the international community had considerable influence over the final stages of negotiations and transition. This involved promoting accepted definitions of political violence and the respective legitimacy of the various parties, as well as pressing for majoritarian principles in the constitutional dispensation.[70] While it can be argued that the political parties were to some degree themselves the drivers of political violence, the presence of international observers, with leaders able to interact at the highest level with key South African figures, was a powerful restraint on any such actions. In the case of the Commonwealth, Anyaoku was regularly in contact with political leaders and, in turn, was sometimes asked to act as an intermediary. Similar capabilities were evident among COMSA, headed by Justice Amissah and Duncan Chappell, and with COGSA's chair and deputy chair, Jamaica's Michael Manley and New Zealand's Archbishop Sir Paul Reeves, who had similar levels of skill, experience and status which allowed their voices to be heard. International support and acceptability, during the crucial period of transition, mattered to South Africa, to its leading parties and, perhaps not least, to its joint Nobel Peace Prize Winners, Mandela and de Klerk. Spence refers to the willingness of Mandela and de Klerk "to use the resources of private, informal diplomacy," alongside "astute crisis management," regardless of what may have been their public antagonism.[71] External pressure, from governments and international organisations such as the Commonwealth, helped maintain the momentum of the negotiations in the face of a deteriorating South African economy and rising popular expectations. Ultimately, however, no amount of outside assistance could have helped a South Africa unable to seize this unique moment of national liberation. As it was, acts of decisive leadership came not only from the two principal protagonists, Mandela and de Klerk but also from figures as varied as Chief Buthelezi of the IFP and General Viljoen of the Freedom Front. It was a mood which was reflected and amplified many thousands of times by the patience and tenacity of the ordinary people of South Africa, at last on the threshold of their long-delayed freedom.

**Notes**

1 Peter Lyon, "South Africa's April 1994 elections in PVW and especially in the Vaal triangle," *The Round Table* 83: 331, (1994): 312.
2 Andrew Reynolds, "The results," In Reynolds, *Election '94: South Africa*, 185.

3 Welsh and Spence, *Ending Apartheid*, 138.
4 Anyaoku, "The Commonwealth, Mandela and the death of *apartheid*," 641.
5 R.W. Johnson, "How free? How fair," in *Launching Democracy in South Africa the First Open Election, April 1994*, R.W. Johnson and Lawrence Schlemmer (New Haven and London: Yale University Press, 1996), 323.
6 Minty, "South Africa and the Commonwealth," 59.
7 COMSA Press Release, "COMSA urges political tolerance," May 1993, Johannesburg, Commonwealth Secretariat archives, SGAN 09/16.
8 Anglin, "International monitoring of the transition," 526.
9 Commonwealth Secretariat, *Violence in South Africa*, 5.
10 Record of a meeting between Emeka Anyaoku and F.W. de Klerk, 13 November 1992 (Note taken by M.J. Gaylard, 24 November 1992), personal papers, 1.
11 Ibid., 4.
12 Anglin, "International monitoring of the transition," 526.
13 M. Abutudu, "Monitoring and observation of elections in Africa," Accessed 23 September 2019, www. www.elections.org.za>content>work.
14 IEC, "Manual for international observers: April 1994," 7 April 1994, Johannesburg, 38.
15 Ibid., 14.
16 Commonwealth Secretariat, *Final Communique, Commonwealth Heads of Government Meeting 1993*, 25 October 1993, Limassol, Accessed 6 March 2020, kttps://www.thecommonwealth.org/history-of-the-commonwealth/commonwealth-heads-government-meeting-limassol-cyprus-21–25-october-1993, 10.
17 Emeka Anyaoku, "Meeting the challenges of change," *Biennial Report of the Commonwealth Secretary-General 1993* (London: Commonwealth Secretariat, 1993, 6.
18 Ibid., 11.
19 Ibid., 12.
20 Emeka Anyaoku, "Development and good governance: Local action, global reach," *Biennial Report of the Commonwealth Secretary-General 1995* (London: Commonwealth Secretariat, 1995), 5.
21 Andrew Reynolds (Ed.), *Election '94 South Africa: The Campaigns, Results and Future Prospects* (London, James Currey, 1994), 153.
22 The European Union had come into being on 1 November 1993 under the Maastricht Treaty. Its mission at the elections was the European Union Election Unit in South Africa (EUNELSA).
23 World Council of Churches, *Report of EMPSA 1994*, Aluka digital library, http://psimg.jstor.org/fsi/img/pdf/t0/10.5555/al.sff.document.ydlwcc2170_final.pdf, Accessed 24 April 2022.
24 Commonwealth Secretariat, *Brief for Observers: Commonwealth Observer Group to the National and Provincial Elections in South Africa, 26–29 April 1994*, 7 April 1994 (London: Commonwealth Secretariat, 1994), 7.
25 Timothy Sisk, "A US perspective of South Africa's 1994 election," in Reynolds, *Election '94 South Africa*, 144.
26 Commonwealth Observer Group, *The End of Apartheid: The Report of the Commonwealth Observer Group to the South African Elections, 26–29 April 1994* (London: Commonwealth Secretariat, 1994), 44.
27 Commonwealth Observer Group, *The End of Apartheid*, 48.
28 Welsh and Spence, *Ending Apartheid*, 137.
29 IEC, "Manual for international observers," Appendix 2, 1–11.
30 Anyaoku, "The Commonwealth, Mandela and the death of *apartheid*," 641.
31 Welsh and Spence, *Ending Apartheid*, 138.
32 Reynolds, *Election '94 South Africa*, 179.
33 Interview with Justice Kriegler, 5 May 2014, *SABC Digital News*, Accessed 3 February 2020, www.youtube.com/watch?v=EZR_jlOG.yg.

34 Reynolds, *Election '94 South Africa*, 179.
35 Johnson, "How free? How fair," in *Launching Democracy*, 323.
36 Briefing, 20 May 1994, *Africa Confidential* 35 (10), 2.
37 Briefing, 6 May 1994, *Africa Confidential*, 35 (9), 1.
38 Reynolds, *Election '94 South Africa*, 210.
39 Email exchanges between Chris Bowman and the author, November 2019.
40 Press Release, "Final statement by the international observer missions on the South African elections," 6 May 1994, UNOMSA/PR/55, Commonwealth Secretariat archives, SGAN/09/019.
41 Commonwealth Secretariat, *The End of Apartheid*, 4.
42 Ibid., 71.
43 Editorial, "The power of process," 29 April 1994, *The Star*.
44 Ockert Geyser, "South Africa re-joins the Commonwealth," *The Round Table* 83:331 (1994): 324.
45 Both Mozambique and Cameroon became Commonwealth members in 1995, and Rwanda joined in 2009.
46 Ramphal, *Glimpses of a Global Life*, 461.
47 Record of discussion between Kent Durr and Emeka Anyaoku, Tuesday, 18 May 1993, Marlborough House, London, Commonwealth Secretariat archives, 40/3–1, 4.
48 Kent Durr, "South Africa and the Commonwealth – my point of view," A paper for South African leaders, Commonwealth Secretariat archives, SGAN/03/016, 4.
49 Ibid., 8.
50 Aide Memoire, prepared by the Political Affairs Division, 6 September 1993, Commonwealth Secretariat archives SGAN/03/016, 1.
51 Record of the Second Session, HGM (93), 21 October 1993, Commonwealth Secretariat archives, SGAN/03/016, 5–6.
52 Queen Elizabeth II, Private speech to Commonwealth Leaders, 21 October 1993, H.M.Y. Britannia, Commonwealth Secretariat archives, SGAN/03/016, 4.
53 Commonwealth Secretariat, *Communiqué, Commonwealth Heads of Government Meeting*, Limassol, Cyprus 1993, Accessed 28 September 2018, www.thecommonwealth.org/history-of-the-commonwealth/commonwealth-heads-government-meeting-limassol-cyprus-21-25-October-1993, 7.
54 Kent Durr, Speech: "South Africa's future relationship with the Commonwealth – a South African view," 7 March 1994, Commonwealth Trust, London, personal papers, 3.
55 Anyaoku, *The Inside Story*, 125.
56 Hyam and Henshaw, *The Lion and the Springbok*, 349.
57 Geyser, "South Africa re-joins the Commonwealth," 324.
58 Service Booklet, Westminster Abbey: "Service to welcome South Africa back into the Commonwealth," 20 July 1994, personal papers.
59 Hyam and Henshaw, *The Lion and the Springbok*, 347.
60 Minty, "South Africa and the Commonwealth," In *The Commonwealth in the 21st Century*, 57.
61 Aide Memoire, Moses Anafu to Emeka Anyaoku, 4 November 1993, "South Africa at the Cyprus CHOGM," Commonwealth Secretariat archives, SGAN/09/019.
62 Denis Goldberg, *The Mission: A Life for Freedom in South Africa* (Johannesburg: STE Publishers, 2010), 323.
63 Thabo Mbeki quoted in *Footprints of an Iconic Diplomat*, 92.
64 Durr, "South Africa's future relationship with the Commonwealth," 10.
65 Peter Vale and David Black, "The prodigal returns: The Commonwealth and South Africa. Past and future," Centre for Southern African Studies, University of Western Cape, unpublished article, personal papers, 13.
66 John Siko, *Inside South Africa's Foreign Policy: Diplomacy in Africa from Smuts to Mbeki* (London and New York: I.B. Tauris, 2014), 32.

67  Ibid., 33.
68  Don McKinnon, "Mandela and the Commonwealth: Identifying and Upholding Common Values," *The Round Table: The Commonwealth Journal of International Affairs* 106:6 (2017): 650–1.
69  Waldmeir, *Anatomy of a Miracle*, 262.
70  Guelke, *South Africa in Transition*, 151–153.
71  Spence, *Change in South Africa*, 8.

**References**

Adrian Guelke, *South Africa in Transition*. (London, NY: I.B. Tauris, 1999).
Andrew Reynolds (ed.), *Election '94 South Africa: The Campaigns, Results and Future Prospects* (London, James Currey, 1994).
COGSA, *The End of Apartheid: The Report of the Commonwealth Observer Group to the South African Elections, 26–29 April 1994* (London: Commonwealth Secretariat, 1994).
COMSA, *Violence in South Africa*, (London: Commonwealth Secretariat, 1993).
David Welsh and Jack Spence, *Ending Apartheid* (Harlow, England: Longman Pearson, 2011).
Denis Goldberg, *The Mission: a life for freedom in South Africa* (Johannesburg: STE Publishers, 2010).
Emeka Anyaoku, *Biennial Report of the Commonwealth Secretary-General 1993* (London: Commonwealth Secretariat, 1993).
Emeka Anyaoku, *Biennial Report of the Commonwealth Secretary-General 1995* (London: Commonwealth Secretariat, 1995).
Emeka Anyaoku, *The Inside Story of the Modern Commonwealth*, Op.Cit.
Greg Mills and John Stremlau, *The Commonwealth in the 21st Century* (Johannesburg, London: SAIIA/CPSU, 1999).
J.E. Spence (ed.), *Change in South Africa* (London: RIIA, Pinter Publishers, 1994).
John Siko, *Inside South Africa's Foreign Policy: Diplomacy in Africa from Smuts to Mbeki* (London, New York: I.B. Tauris, 2014).
Patti Waldmeir, *Anatomy of a Miracle*. (London: Penguin Books, 1998).
Ronald Hyam and Peter Henshaw, *The Lion and the Springbok: Britain and South Africa since the Boer War* (Cambridge: CUP, 2003).
R.W. Johnson and Lawrence Schlemmer (eds.), *Launching Democracy in South Africa: The First Open Election, April 1994* (New Haven and London: Yale University Press, 1996).
Shridath Ramphal, *Glimpses of a Global Life*, Op.Cit.

# 13 The Commonwealth Without a Cause? *Apartheid* and After

## Conclusion

In 2002 the South African Government instituted a national honour, *The Order of the Companions of O.R. Tambo*, to pay tribute to foreigners who had rendered exceptional service "to the efforts of the people of South Africa to define themselves as human beings," in the example set by Oliver Tambo.[1] Of its 110 current members, some 44 are Commonwealth citizens, many of them leading figures in the anti-*apartheid* struggle. In view of their 'outstanding contribution to the ending of *apartheid*', both Ramphal and Anyaoku have been inducted into the highest level of the Order, normally reserved for Heads of State.[2] Manley, Mulroney, Fraser, Rajiv Gandhi and Kaunda are among those also honoured. No other international organisation is recognised to the same degree.

No full account has yet been written of the Commonwealth's role in the ending of *apartheid*, but it is one which features strongly in the Commonwealth's own mythology. Although an official history is missing, with nothing more definitive added to the Commonwealth Secretariat's slim 1989 volume, there are numerous Commonwealth references confirming the campaign's totemic quality.[3] There are also the biographies of some of those most closely involved and summary accounts, as well as oral histories, though inevitably these do not offer a comprehensive view. Reference has already been made to South Africa's own initiative in documenting and assessing its recent past. Its account describes the Commonwealth's role as 'substantial' but does not include key elements of that history and does not attempt any overall assessment of the Commonwealth's role.[4]

More generally, aspects of the Commonwealth's involvement have been ignored, misrepresented or understated. On occasions, especially from a UK perspective, there is a tendency to enlist Commonwealth actions as a subordinate narrative of British policy and practice. Where a Commonwealth contribution is acknowledged, it can sometimes lead to an overall assessment that is dismissed as 'uneven' or 'insubstantial', although often without proper explanation.[5] In any case, analysing what part the Commonwealth played in the international campaign against *apartheid* raises a pre-existing question about the impact of external forces in helping bring about *apartheid's* demise. Set alongside the resistance of South Africans themselves, with numerous stories of forbearance, courage and self-sacrifice, forgiveness and redemption, it may appear a small thing indeed. Within South Africa itself, there has been a growth in recent years in 'struggle' literature, which shines a light on hitherto neglected aspects of mass resistance to *apartheid* and counteracts the tendency of some to ascribe decisive change solely to the actions of two men, Mandela and de Klerk.[6] This emphasis on the internal struggle chimes with a Marxist analysis of the failings of the post-*apartheid* state amid highly racialised economic and social inequalities.[7]

At the same time, there is a large body of historical writing, inside and outside South Africa, which acknowledges the international dimension in the anti-*apartheid* cause. It was an aspect of the struggle which was widely recognised at the time, has been honoured subsequently, and is now part of South Africa's public history. Guelke is among those who believes that the significance of international pressure and norms has been underplayed.[8] He considers that the influence of the international community was evident in "a myriad of different ways." Crucially, he sees the international commitment to democratic majoritarianism having a decisive impact on the transition process.[9]

This book does not attempt to untangle the multiplicity of forces which contributed to *apartheid's* ending, whether internal or external. Ultimately, it was the part that the people of South Africa, of all races, played in reaching a negotiated settlement that proved crucial. At the same time, this volume is underpinned by the conclusion that the international campaign against *apartheid*, whether of governments, international organisations or the global AAM, made an important contribution to its ending. It brought pressure to bear on the regime, it succoured and sustained the forces of opposition, and in various ways it supported and helped determine the course of the final settlement.

What therefore was the significance of the Commonwealth's contribution to that international campaign? Was it minimal for all or any of *apartheid's* ascendancy? Was it sustained and persistent, or sporadic and uneven, as some have suggested? What forms did it take and how can the Commonwealth's actions be measured to assess their impact and therefore their significance? In what ways did the Commonwealth's prolonged engagement with *apartheid* lead to changes within the association itself?

The result is an analysis which challenges several myths. The first of these is that the Commonwealth, in its modern guise, was an implacable opponent of *apartheid* from 1949 until that system's demise in 1994. The second myth was that the Commonwealth's overall opposition to *apartheid* throughout the period was insubstantial and variable, being "at best very marginal."[10]

As regards the first, it was the Sharpeville massacre in 1960 and the animated disagreements about *apartheid* that resulted at both the 1960 and 1961 Commonwealth Prime Ministers' Meetings which precipitated the action which eventually led to South Africa's exit from the Commonwealth. At this point, the Commonwealth was largely post-imperial in its leadership, structures and purposes. While individual member countries made clear their opposition to *apartheid* elsewhere, the association collectively remained mute. At the same time, there were two developments underway which were to prove transformative. Firstly, changes to the membership of the United Nations and the Commonwealth brought about what Donnelly describes as "a change in the structure of international power."[11] In the case of the United Nations, there was a significant increase in African membership, which altered the dynamics in the General Assembly. In the Commonwealth, an influx of new members resulted in what has been characterised by Ali Mazrui as "the Afro-Asian takeover" of the organisation with the 'new', developing Commonwealth membership in the ascendancy. The second of Donnelly's variables was an "international moral shock" profoundly affecting the prevailing international political culture.[12] Sharpeville, Stultz argues, was just such a shock. At the United Nations, Sharpeville hardened opinion against South Africa, shifted the UK and France away from their steady support for Pretoria, and undermined the argument that Article 2(7) of the Charter prevented the United Nations from acting on *apartheid*. A new arena of debate therefore opened with the involvement of the UN Security Council. Even so, the United Nations remained in 'declaratory mode' "the most elementary and weakest of international regime types."[13]

South Africa's departure from the Commonwealth in 1961 came as a result of the collective actions of Commonwealth leaders.[14] However, it was also the case that South Africa's Black opposition had joined forces with some Commonwealth governments and with the emerging AAM to campaign for the *apartheid* regime's exclusion from the association. While the uncertain signals from Commonwealth governments eventually resolved into a clear view of South Africa's exit, it was far from being an expulsion, as it is sometimes characterised. Nevertheless, the significance of the decision should not be underestimated, regardless of the hesitancy about its execution or the potentially grave consequences for the Commonwealth had it not so acted. In 1970, South Africa was expelled from the Olympic movement, having been barred from the Games since 1964. In 1974, it was prevented from participating in the UNGA. Even though in the short term South Africa's exit from the Commonwealth was received as a triumph for Afrikanerdom and arguably strengthened *apartheid's* dominance and its allegiance among white South Africans, it nonetheless represented the regime's first step into isolation and pariah status. It altered the terms of international debate and increased acceptance of the emerging global norm of racial equality. It saw the beginnings of a worldwide campaign against *apartheid* and, in the Commonwealth itself, hastened far-reaching changes to its governance and leadership.

It was also the case that the Commonwealth's preoccupation with the white settler regime in Rhodesia, after UDI in 1965, should be seen as an intrinsic part of the Commonwealth's wider campaign for racial justice in Southern Africa. The year 1965 also saw the birth of the Commonwealth Secretariat (and Foundation) and the appointment of the first Commonwealth Secretary-General, Arnold Smith. Despite profound differences with the British Government on Rhodesia, the Commonwealth's newly established decision-making bodies were able to develop a distinctive approach to the crisis, including in monitoring international sanctions, while accepting the UK's ultimate responsibility for the colony. As Secretary-General Smith put it, "[i]t was crucially important to prevent a sell-out and to hold the line in Rhodesia until the necessary international and domestic pressures could be developed to bring about majority rule."[15] Later, the Commonwealth had an important role in the ending of white rule in brokering a constitutional settlement and in the birth of Zimbabwe.

This was also true of the question of arm sales to the Republic. In 1971, the Commonwealth was plunged into crisis by the new UK government's announcement that it intended to resume arm sales to South Africa. While the Commonwealth could resort only to declaratory actions, its Singapore Declaration on Racial Prejudice nonetheless established an important set of principles which provided the normative framework for the Commonwealth's actions over *apartheid* for the next twenty years.[16] In practice, the UK's resumption of arm supplies was very limited, and within a few years a change of government had seen supply finally halted and the Simon's Town Agreement terminated. At the United Nations, the 1963 voluntary ban on arms sales was criticised as being "in practical fact non-existent."[17] It became mandatory in 1977.[18] While this enforcement action was the last of the sanctions against South Africa to be lifted, its effects were mixed.[19]

The Soweto students' revolt of 1976, with its graphic image of a dying 13-year-old Oscar Pietersen murdered by the South African Police, provided the world with another international moral shock. After what some have described as the golden age of *apartheid*, a new resistance was taking root in South Africa's townships. It came at a time when white colonial rule on *apartheid's* frontiers – in Mozambique, Angola and Rhodesia – was collapsing and ceding power to African nationalism. Under Secretary-General Ramphal the Commonwealth now assumed new agency in driving forward the sporting boycott. Ramphal had a reputation in the NAM as a rising star of the Third World. As he explained, "I came to the job as Foreign Minister of a country that was leading its region in support of these liberation movements."[20]

Faced with the threat of boycott of the 1978 Commonwealth Games, Ramphal knew that the Commonwealth would need to act at the 1977 London CHOGM. At the Gleneagles Retreat, Ramphal first developed a multilateral diplomatic method which was to bring a reluctant Muldoon on board and secure the unanimous adoption of the 1977 Gleneagles Agreement on *Apartheid* in Sport. In Donnelly's terms, the Agreement was declaratory, promotional and involved enforcement action, at least within the permissive remit of Commonwealth governance. It was an elaboration of the norm of racial equality set out in the Singapore Declaration. It was also a promotional accord insofar as it "welcomed the efforts of the UN to reach universally accepted approaches to the question of sporting contacts" and set out its own commitments, by each country individually, to the undertakings in the Agreement.[21]

Gleneagles undoubtedly made a significant contribution to internationalising measures against *apartheid* in sport. It gave fresh stimulus to the rise in popular anti-*apartheid* activism in the period and closed down another aspect of South Africa's relations with the wider world. The sporting boycott proved to be particularly keenly felt by South African whites, as South Africa retreated into near total isolation. At the same time, critics attacked Gleneagles for lacking teeth. As a result, there would be recurring issues of implementation (and interpretation) and bitter battles, with New Zealand in particular. In the process, Ramphal stretched to the limit the influence available to him in pressing for compliance and for the extra powers needed to enforce Gleneagles. In this he was largely successful. But, as the Commonwealth clashed with Thatcher over sanctions as well as sport, Ramphal could not prevent a disastrous boycott of the 1986 Commonwealth Games by most of its new Commonwealth members.

Two years after the adoption of the Gleneagles Agreement, Ramphal was to be deeply involved in the settlement reached at the 1979 Lusaka CHOGM on Rhodesia/Zimbabwe, the Lancaster House talks which followed, and Zimbabwe's transition to independence in 1980. As with the development of the Commonwealth's diplomatic methods over sport, new diplomatic mechanisms and techniques were honed as part of a distinctive Commonwealth contribution to Zimbabwe's birth.

Fresh energy was given to the Commonwealth's campaign against *apartheid* following peace in Zimbabwe. The Commonwealth Accord on Southern Africa set out a two-pronged strategy for the Commonwealth.[22] On the one hand, it resolved to further pressurise and isolate the South African Government by the adoption of economic sanctions. On the other, the association delayed further sanctions while it explored the path of mediation. This opened the way for the 1986 Commonwealth EPG Mission to South Africa with its ambitious remit to negotiate the end of *apartheid*. After extensive consultations, including with an imprisoned Mandela, the Commonwealth's "Possible Negotiating Concept" came near to acceptance, observed closely by sympathetic Government Ministers. Ultimately, hostile elements in the regime effectively aborted the mission with the SADF's surprise attack on three Commonwealth neighbours in May 1986.

The ostensible failure of the EPG's mission resulted in a critical report which became a Penguin bestseller and provided impetus to the widening campaign for economic sanctions.[23] The influence of the report was not only exhortatory: a Commonwealth demarche to key capitals led to the EPG's co-chairs being on hand to give specific advice to Congressional leaders in the United States, as they introduced anti-*apartheid* legislation. As well as the Commonwealth, the EU, the United States and Japan were among those adopting further sanctions. While the 1986 Special Commonwealth Summit in London marked a widening rift with Thatcher and the UK government over sanctions (marking the emergence of a 'binary' Commonwealth), Commonwealth leaders placed increasing emphasis on financial pressures and divestment. In late 1989, F.W. de Klerk replaced the ailing P.W. Botha, and the seeds of irreversible change began to germinate.

In the course of its mission, the EPG was granted unprecedented and unfettered access to all shades of South African political opinion, including to Mandela. No other international organisation had achieved anything of that kind before. It also managed to establish a basis of negotiation which won the support of the ANC, as well as Mandela, and came close to being accepted by the government. For the next four years, the leadership of white South Africa, picking up from where the Commonwealth left, engaged in a covert dialogue with the still-imprisoned Mandela, and other informal negotiating groups, and wrestled with the unresolved issue exposed by the EPG. If free dialogue could be established between the principal parties based on the suspension of violence, how could either side be prevented at a later stage from abandoning peaceful negotiations and pushing South Africa into uncontrolled violence? This was a fundamental question which hung over South Africa's transition from 1991 until it was finally answered in March 1994 with the 'freedom' elections which marked *apartheid's* end.

The EPG's engagement with *apartheid* was prolonged, substantial and politically significant and should be seen as part of a pattern of pre-negotiations, in particular with Mandela, now evident in the period from 1986 to 1989. The apparent failure of the EPG, and the disappearance of any immediate prospect of all-party negotiations, inevitably led to renewed pressure for enhanced sanctions. Clearly, the absence of the UK from further Commonwealth sanctions severely diminished their impact. However, the Commonwealth made a strong contribution to the international sanctions campaign. Its own sanctions were not insignificant; it helped to 'internationalise' sanctions, particularly in the United States, and it was a powerful advocate of financial sanctions, which proved highly effective. Taken together, the Commonwealth's twin-track approach of sanctions and negotiations came at an important moment.

Remarkably, the Commonwealth was able to lay out a new strategic path following the release of Nelson Mandela and the beginnings of fundamental change within South Africa. After the turbulence of the Thatcher years, the 1991 Harare summit marked a rapprochement which sought a new unity between the UK and other Commonwealth countries, based on the values adopted in the Harare Commonwealth Declaration. Anyaoku's mission to South Africa, in November 1991, began to give substance to the notion of renewed engagement. There were few in South Africa, apart from the PAC, who wanted the international community to have any role in the internal negotiating process itself.[24] However, it was inescapable that the principal parties to South Africa's negotiations would look to the international community from time to time. A case in point was the question of lifting sanctions. The ANC and others were strongly opposed to the early raising of sanctions because they saw their continued application as constituting an important pressure on the regime during negotiations. This was despite the 'pro-business' approach of Mandela since his release and the ANC's desire not to inherit a broken-backed economy. At the same time, caution over lifting sanctions was not apparent when it came to normalising sporting links and South Africa's participation in major sporting events.[25] This suited both the ANC and the NP with the end of the sporting boycott featuring prominently in the whites-only referendum, of March 1992, approving de Klerk's negotiation strategy.[26]

Anyaoku's early attempts to develop a role for the Commonwealth and other international organisations resulted in the presence of international observers at CODESA. But, in the face of alarming degrees of internal violence, and the negative impact this had on the faltering negotiation process, an acceptance of a wider international role began to emerge. If Anyaoku was not the only advocate of the deployment of international observers to address the violence, he undoubtedly played an important role in encouraging the United Nations to act, through the adoption of UNSC resolution 772/92.

What thereafter was the impact of the Commonwealth on the ground in South Africa during the transition period? This involved the three phases of COMSA's deployment between 1992 and 1994, including its role in mediation and dispute resolution in Kwa-Zulu/Natal under the provisions of the NPA. COMSA also investigated issues relating to violence and security, and the administration of justice. It ran schemes for the training of marshals and provided a substantial international military and police unit (CPAG) in the training of the ill-fated NPKP. As the elections approached, it provided electoral experts to assist the Electoral Commission. The organisation also deployed a Commonwealth Observer Mission to the elections (COGSA), the largest ever mounted by the Commonwealth, before or since.[27] After the elections, support was given to the new government's RDP with the Commonwealth joining the United Nations (and the South African Government) to co-sponsor an International Donor Conference on Human Resource Development (in the RDP) in Cape Town in October 1994. This emphasis was in line with many years of Commonwealth scholarships, fellowships and training for South African refugees. Under *apartheid*, whole generations of Black Africans were denied the right to education and skills training, with a gross imbalance in spending on Black education, compared with that invested in white education and training. For example, during *apartheid* research showed that South Africa had no Black engineers alongside over 26,000 white engineers; only 400 Black doctors against 25,600 white doctors; and 450 Black lawyers to 8,700 white lawyers.[28] The result was, said the Commonwealth, a "quiet, human tragedy."[29]

Apart from support for the RDP, a special programme of Commonwealth technical assistance was scheduled to last until June 1998, supported by special contributions, among others, from the UK and Australian governments. In all, around one hundred experts from nineteen Commonwealth countries have contributed advice and assistance through such programmes in the two years since 1995.[30] Notably, the Commonwealth's ability to rapidly mobilise quality technical assistance drew the approval of the United Nations.[31]

Purely quantitatively, in terms of expenditure and human resources, the United Nations' operations dwarfed those of the Commonwealth. But, compared to the modest size of the Secretariat's regular budget, expenditure on its anti-*apartheid* activities was considerable. COGSA, for example, had a core budget for the 1994 elections of £500,000 (at 1994 prices) though member governments also provided in-kind support, in addition to special budgetary contributions. COMSA, across its three phases of deployment, had a much smaller core budget with the burden of providing for the costs of the mission's individual observers spread across participating countries. The EPG initiative had a core budget of £1 m which did not include much of the personnel costs or the very considerable expenditure by the Canadian Government in providing a Challenger aircraft, with a full crew, fuel and associated costs, for shuttle travel across the Southern Africa region for weeks at a time. Together, this amounted to many millions of pounds. Even so, there was much more that could have been done, had the resources been available. As it was, COMSA's operations were threatened early in its life by a shortage of funds.[32] Wherever possible, the Commonwealth was able to secure special funding support

## The Commonwealth Without a Cause? Apartheid and After 247

not only from its membership but from external donors, including UN agencies, non-Commonwealth countries (such as Sweden, Norway and Japan) and trust funds.

In qualitative terms, the Commonwealth asserts that despite its smaller financial and human resources, it was able to 'punch above its weight'. There is supporting evidence for this, both in the qualifications, skills and standing of serving personnel and in the preparedness of the Commonwealth to push its mandate to the limit.[33] This was true of mediation and also in analysing shortcomings and promoting policy advice, sometimes to the public irritation of the regime. Crucially, field staff within South Africa were in close and regular contact with the Secretary-General and his office and would trigger interventions from Ramphal or Anyaoku where this could be useful or had been requested by one of the parties to negotiations. For example, COMSA's operations in KwaZulu-Natal highlighted the urgent need for a peace summit between Mandela and Buthelezi (with the aim of bringing the IFP into the political process), and Anyaoku's help was sought in this task.[34]

What overall assessment can be made of the distinctiveness and significance of the Commonwealth's collective contribution to the international campaign against *apartheid*? One response is to draw upon Donnelly's categories of international action. These have merit in helping refine the areas of Commonwealth pressure and offering some measure of impact. The key Commonwealth interventions were concerned with, firstly, isolating *apartheid* (in withdrawing Commonwealth membership from South Africa, pressing for an effective arms embargo, leading the sporting boycott of *apartheid*, helping end the viability of Rhodesia as a white-settler state, and encouraging economic and financial sanctions). These were all types of *enforcement* action. Secondly, in the later stages of the relationship with South Africa, the Commonwealth approach was collaborative and *implementing* (in terms of the EPG initiative and negotiations, the mediatory role during the transition, as well as local examples of conflict resolution). From 1960, the Commonwealth also accompanied its actions by *declaratory* statements and declarations, as well as *promotional* activity, including its work with civil society and the global AAM. Although apparently 'weaker' actions, these last two steps helped develop and spread international norms that were particularly influential in South Africa's transition phase.

Of course, none of this is necessarily evidence that any of these actions on their own were effective in bringing about change, but, collectively, their impact proved significant. There are contrasting views on the effectiveness of isolation and the various forms of international pressure, including economic and financial sanctions, which bore down on the regime. In many ways, South Africa was successful in dealing with punitive measures. It was able to circumvent the arms embargo and build its own arms industry. It countered the oil embargo by buying on the black market. But these countermeasures were achieved at a very considerable price, as van Vuuren has demonstrated.[35] South Africa could afford to take such extraordinary steps when its economy was buoyant with a current account surplus, substantial inward investment and ready access to international credit. When that was no longer the case, when 'forward defence' beyond South Africa's borders was failing, when containing township violence threatened internal stability and when 'reforming *apartheid*' had reached its limits, then white rule was no longer sustainable.[36] It was therefore the combination of circumstances, rather than any particular action in itself, which proved decisive.

A critical underlying theme was the issue of violence. From 1975, the Commonwealth (with the exception of Britain) made clear its support for the liberation forces, and therefore armed struggle, in Rhodesia and thereafter in South Africa itself. Some Commonwealth countries, particularly in the FLS, provided those forces with bases and material support, often to the significant detriment of the host state concerned. The unresolved issue of violence in the end unravelled the promise of the EPG mission, and violence could so nearly have destroyed South Africa's transition process.[37] Ultimately, aware of the new realities of a post-cold war world, white South Africans looked into the abyss of interracial conflict. Even if victory was possible (in the short term at least), a negotiated transfer of power was now far more likely to preserve white wealth and privilege than a destructive internecine war.[38]

The Commonwealth was not therefore neutral on the question of violence or its root cause – *apartheid*. But it twice proved able, in 1985–1986 and 1991–1994, to use its by then developed status as an international organisation representing a broad range of countries to offer itself to South Africa as interlocutor and facilitator. This was not only because of the leadership qualities of its Secretaries-General and the diplomatic method they used, but it was also crucially dependent on the leadership evident in member countries across the Commonwealth, sometimes in Presidents and Prime Ministers but also among campaigners, politicians and writers.

In the case of the UK and its relationship with the rest of the association, the Commonwealth remained caught in its symbiotic embrace: a country sometimes difficult to live with and impossible to live without. At the same time, that close relationship with the UK also carried influence which was arguably considerably greater than, for example, that of Francophone Africa in its relationship with the national interests and policies of France.[39] By working on the ambiguities of Britain's South African policies, the Commonwealth was on the frontier of the battle over *apartheid*. But, once those differences were past, the UK helped remake the Commonwealth as a rule- and values-based association with an adopted Charter, common institutions and established conventions.

After the 1994 elections the UN Security Council commended the 'vital role' played by the United Nations, the Commonwealth, the OAU and the EU in helping bring about a democratic, non-racial South Africa.[40] Did South Africa also recognise as significant the Commonwealth contribution to the ending of *apartheid*? Many said so at the time, and South Africa's speedy resumption of Commonwealth membership is a testament to the organisation's global connections and its usefulness as an anti-*apartheid* ally. In May 2020 in South Africa's parliament, President Cyril Ramaphosa was urged by Vuyo Zungula, leader of the African Transformation Movement, to pull South Africa out of the Commonwealth because of its colonial origins. Ramaphosa replied that his government had no intention of removing

*Figure 13.1* The Queen, the Prince of Wales, Chief Emeka Anyaoku, Mrs Bunmi Anyaoku and Thabo Mbeki, Deputy President of South Africa, at a Marlborough House reception to mark South Africa's return to Commonwealth membership, 1994. Commonwealth Secretariat.

South Africa from the Commonwealth and emphasised that the country took its membership seriously. He then added: "When South Africa re-joined the Commonwealth in 1994, shortly after its first democratic elections, the South African Government recognised the Commonwealth's contribution to the global campaign to end *apartheid*."[41]

As one of those in the vanguard of the ANC at the point of liberation, Ramaphosa had special reason to recall his links with the Commonwealth and the value of the international campaign. It was a role in helping end *apartheid* which was substantial, sustained and significant. That contribution was not defined in terms of volume of resources or scale of actions. Its substance and significance arose from the combination of institutional flexibility and creative multipolar leadership, working on the internal fault lines of conflicted interest. In 1986, on the issue of sanctions, the organisation could no longer sustain its unity and, for the period of the 'binary Commonwealth' broke free of its mutual interdependence. While this may have been necessary for both the UK and the majority of the Commonwealth at that time, neither benefitted in the longer term, and the Commonwealth came together again in 1990. As a result, as it returned to grappling with contradiction, the Commonwealth was again able to be both pathfinder and interlocutor on the pathway to South Africa's freedom. In turn, South Africa, now at last restored to its totality in liberty, was able to address the existential question posed by Olive Schreiner in

1923: "How, of our divided peoples, can a great, healthy harmonious and desirable nation be formed?"[42]

In the prologue to this volume, the underlying theme of race was identified as defining the Commonwealth over the first five decades of its modern existence. If it was to shed its post-imperial patterns of dominance, prejudice and racial exclusion, this new Commonwealth, as an emerging multicultural association, had to find a fresh unity based on racial and political equality. While the issue of racial justice in Southern Africa – whether in Rhodesia or South Africa – was not the only challenge facing the Commonwealth in that period, it became an external measure, and a litmus test, of the sincerity and commitment of each of its member nations to the principles of racial and political equality. From the beginning of the Rhodesian white settler rebellion in 1965 to the lifting of international sanctions on South Africa and the final ending of *apartheid* in 1994, the Commonwealth was repeatedly rocked by actions and allegations across the fault line of race.

Some have suggested that with independence for Zimbabwe and the creation of a non-racial and democratic South Africa, the Commonwealth has lost its central purpose and the source of its unity. This, Mayall argues, has created a 'strategic vacuum' which the Commonwealth has yet to fill.[43]

Even so, such a view would discount the considerable steps the Commonwealth took in the 1990s to remake the organisation as a values-based organisation, committed to the principles set out in the 1991 Harare Commonwealth Declaration. This was to lead to a new emphasis on democracy, good governance and human rights alongside the association's long-lasting commitment to sustainable economic and social development. The Commonwealth established new programmes in support of democracy-building, including providing electoral experts to help prepare for elections (over such matters as constituency delimitations, voter registration and the setting up of independent electoral bodies) and despatching election observer groups which could be present at the polls themselves and help evaluate how far the elections met agreed international norms. Indeed, since 1980, the Commonwealth has sent around 180 observer missions to more than a thousand elections in forty member countries.[44] As important, this post-Harare initiative was accompanied by a proactive and energetic good office's role by the new Secretary-General, Chief Anyaoku, in seeking to persuade leaders to submit to regular, multi-party elections. As Anyaoku had put it, the Commonwealth had long been accused of double standards, of "proclaiming the democratic idea and upholding human rights in southern Africa while at the same time turning a blind eye to failings and abuses in our own ranks."[45] In 1991, attending his first CHOGM as Commonwealth Secretary-General, Anyaoku was keenly aware that of the Commonwealth's then forty-two member countries, some nine were one-party states or military regimes. By the end of Anyaoku's final term, in 2000, there were none in that category, though there were member countries whose democratic systems were questionable, notably Brunei Darussalem and Swaziland (now eSwatini) who could best be described as absolute monarchies.

This far closer attention to how far individual member countries were willing and able to uphold the association's fundamental values was accompanied, in 1995, by the establishment of an enforcement mechanism, the Commonwealth Ministerial Action Group (CMAG). This representative grouping of Commonwealth Foreign Ministers was charged with investigating persistent and flagrant contraventions of the organisation's shared values. Its starting point was the Abacha military regime in Nigeria whose treatment and execution of Ken Saro-Wiwa and eight Ogoni activists had sparked international outrage and condemnation.[46]

The story of this new emphasis on democratic values and human rights, and its effect on the Commonwealth and its membership, is too substantial for the closing lines of this book. Suffice it to say, that in this respect also the Commonwealth proved a pathfinder in developing ways in which international norms could be sustained in the face of the failure of an individual member country to comply. Equally, in 1999, as Mandela stepped down from South Africa's Presidency at the conclusion of his term of office, the Commonwealth was in a few short years facing a crisis in Southern Africa. Once again, Zimbabwe and Robert Mugabe were centre stage. This time calls for racial justice (through land expropriation) were met by a counter-response asserting democratic values and human rights. By the end of 2002, accused of abusing Harare principles, Zimbabwe was to leave the organisation it joined with such fanfare at its creation in 1980.

It might yet return.

**Notes**

1 The Presidency, Republic of South Africa, *National Orders Booklet 2008*, Accessed 3 March 2020, http://www.thepresidency.gov.za/content/national-orders-booklet-2007, 8.
2 Anyaoku, "The Commonwealth, Mandela and the Death of *Apartheid*," 644.
3 Emeka Anyaoku, "Development and Good Governance: Local Action, Global Reach," *Secretary-General's Biennial Report, 1995* (London: Commonwealth Secretariat, 1995), 2.
4 Houston, "Introduction," *The Road to Democracy in South Africa*, 1–40.
5 Deryck Schreuder, "The Commonwealth and Peacemaking in South Africa," In *Peace, Politics and Violence in the New South Africa*, ed. Norman Hetherington (London: Hans Zell Publishers, 1992), 75.
6 Simon Jenkins, *Talk to a meeting of the Round Table*, 17 January 2020, London, Personal notes of Stuart Mole.
7 Kirk Helliker and Peter Vale, "Radical thinking in South Africa's age of retreat," *Journal of Asian and African Studies*) 47:4 (2012): 338–9.
8 Guelke, *South Africa in Transition*, 135.
9 Ibid., 153.
10 Chris Saunders, "Britain, the Commonwealth, and the question of the release of Nelson Mandela in the 1980s," *The Round Table: The Commonwealth Journal of International Affairs* 106: 6 (2017): 659.
11 Donnelly, "International human rights: A regime analysis," 614.
12 Ibid., 636.
13 Stultz, "Evolution of the United Nations anti-*apartheid* regime," 2.
14 Commonwealth Secretariat, *The Commonwealth at the Summit (Vol.1)*, 67.
15 Smith, *Stitches in Time*, 75.
16 Commonwealth Secretariat, *The Commonwealth at the Summit (Vol.1)*, 156.
17 Sean Gervasi, "The breakdown of the arms embargo against South Africa," Testimony before Sub-Committee on Africa, US House of Representatives, 14 July 1977, *A Journal of Opinion* 7: 4 (1977): 27.

18. UNSC Resolution 418, November 1977, Accessed 6 January 2020, www.undocs.org/S/RES/418 (1977).
19. UNSC Resolution 919, May 1994, Accessed 6 January 2020, www.undocs.org/S/RES/919 (1994).
20. Shridath Ramphal, interviewed by Sue Onslow, 23 November 2013, *Commonwealth Oral History Project*, London, Accessed 20 October 2017, www.sas-space.sas.ac.uk/5900/1/Shridath%20Ramphal%20Transcript%201.
21. Commonwealth Secretariat, *The Commonwealth at the Summit* (Vol.1), 199.
22. Ibid., 267–269.
23. Commonwealth Group of Eminent Persons, *Mission to South Africa*, 140–141.
24. Correspondence from Emeka Anyaoku to Lynden Pindling, Prime Minister of the Bahamas, 8 November 1991, Commonwealth Secretariat archives, SGAN/09/025, 2.
25. In 1992, South Africa participated in the Cricket World Cup in Melbourne, Australia (22 February–25 March) and the Summer Olympics in Barcelona, Spain (25 July–9 August).
26. Guelke, *South Africa in Transition*, 140–1.
27. Letter from Anthony Goodenough, FCO, to Emeka Anyaoku, commenting on the 1994 elections and the "Commonwealth's special expertise and experience in election monitoring," 2 June 1994, Commonwealth Secretariat archives, SGAN/09/019, 1.
28. Commonwealth Secretariat, *Report of the Commonwealth Secretary-General 1991* (London: Commonwealth Secretariat, 1991), COMSEC/CPAD/RSG 1991, 27.
29. Ibid.
30. Commonwealth Secretariat, *Report of the Commonwealth Secretary-General 1995* (London: Commonwealth Secretariat, 1995), COMSEC/CPAD/RSG 1995, 25.
31. Memorandum from John Syson to Emeka Anyaoku, "UNOMSA's tribute to Commonwealth technical assistance programme," 28 June 1994, Commonwealth Secretariat archives, SGAN/09/019, 1.
32. Letter from Emeka Anyaoku to Paul Keating, Prime Minister of Australia, 10 December 1992, Commonwealth Secretariat archives, SGAN/09/002, 2.
33. Confidential Report, "European Community Observer Mission in South Africa, October 1992–April 1993," Commonwealth Secretariat archives, A18.2, 2.
34. Record of a telephone conversation between Emeka Anyaoku and Pik Botha, 24 November 1992, Commonwealth Secretariat archives, SGAN/09/002, 2.
35. van Vuuren, *Apartheid, Guns and Money*, 103.
36. Hermann Giliomee, "Intra-Afrikaner conflicts in the transition from *apartheid* 1961–1991," In *Peace, Politics and Violence*, 190.
37. Mandela, *Long Walk to Freedom*, 726.
38. Joan Wardrop, "The state, politics and violence 1989–91," In *Peace, Politics and Violence*, 68.
39. Anirudha Gupta, "Arms, African States and the Commonwealth," *Economic and Political Weekly* 6: 14 (1971): 749.
40. UNSC Resolution 930, 27 June 1994, Accessed 3 March 2018, www.undocs.org/S/RES/930 (1994).
41. Bongani Nkosi, "South Africa has no intention of pulling out of the Commonwealth – Ramaphosa." *The Star*, 20 May 2020, Accessed 4 August 2020, www.iol.co.za/the-star/news/south-africa-has-no-intention-of-pulling-out-of-the-commonwealth-ramaphosa-48z13043.
42. Olive Schreiner, *Thoughts on South Africa* (London: T. Fisher Unwin Ltd, 1923), 63.
43. James Mayall, "Introduction," In *The Contemporary Commonwealth*, 8.
44. Patricia Scotland, *Opening Remarks*, Launch of "40 years of Commonwealth election observation," online seminar series, 15 September 2021.
45. Emeka Anyaoku, "Through the past, glimpses of the future," *The Commonwealth Yearbook 2009* (London: Nexus Strategic Partnerships, 2009).

46 Stuart Mole, "From Smith to Sharma: The role of the Secretary-General," In *The Contemporary Commonwealth: An Assessment 1965–2009* (Abingdon & NY: Routledge, 2010), 51.

## References

Adrian Guelke, *South Africa in Transition*, Op.Cit.
Arnold Smith, *Stitches in Time*, Op.Cit.
Commonwealth Group of Eminent Persons, *Mission to South Africa*, Op.Cit.
Commonwealth Secretariat, *The Commonwealth at the Summit (Vol.1 & 2)*, Op.Cit.
Dirk Willem te Velde, *The Commonwealth Yearbook 2009* (London: Nexus Strategic Partnerships, 2009).
Emeka Anyaoku, *Secretary-General's Biennial Report 1995* (London: Commonwealth Secretariat, 1995).
Hennie van Vuuren, *Apartheid, Guns and Money: A Tale of Profit*, Op.Cit.
James Mayall (ed.), *The Contemporary Commonwealth: An Assessment 1965–2009* (Abingdon, NY: Routledge, 2010).
Mandela, *Long Walk to Freedom*, Op.Cit.
Norman Hetherington (ed.), *Peace, Politics and Violence in the New South Africa* (London: Hans Zell Publishers, 1992).
Olive Schreiner, *Thoughts on South Africa* (London: T. Fisher Unwin Ltd, 1923).
Sisipho Ndlovu (ed.), *The Road to Democracy in South Africa*, Op.Cit.

# Appendix

## Commonwealth Member Countries 1945–1995

*Commonwealth and United Nations' membership*

| Country | Commonwealth Member | UN Member | Constitutional Status |
|---|---|---|---|
| UK | 1931 | 1945 | Monarchy/Realm[1] |
| Canada | 1931 | 1945 | Monarchy/Realm |
| Australia | 1931 | 1945 | Monarchy/Realm |
| Ireland | 1931–1949[2] | 1945 | Monarchy/Rep.1949 |
| Newfoundland | 1931–1949[3] | – | Monarchy/(Realm) |
| New Zealand | 1931 | 1945 | Monarchy/Realm[4] |
| South Africa | 1931–1961, 1994– | 1945 | Monarchy/Rep.1961 |
| India | 1947 | 1945[5] | Monarchy/Rep.1950 |
| Pakistan | 1947–1972, 1989– | 1947 | Monarchy/Rep.1956 |
| Ceylon/Sri Lanka | 1948 | 1955 | Monarchy/Rep.1972 |
| Ghana | 1957 | 1957 | Monarchy/Rep.1960 |
| Malaya/Malaysia | 1957 | 1957 | Malaysian Monarchy |
| Nigeria | 1960 | 1960 | Monarchy/Rep.1963 |
| Cyprus | 1961 | 1960 | Republic |
| Sierra Leone | 1961 | 1961 | Monarchy/Rep.1971 |
| Tanganyika/ Tanzania 1964 | 1961 | 1961 | Monarchy/Rep.1962 |
| Jamaica | 1962 | 1962 | Monarchy/Realm |
| Trinidad & Tobago | 1962 | 1962 | Monarchy/Rep.1976 |
| Uganda | 1962 | 1962 | Monarchy/Rep.1963 |
| Kenya | 1963 | 1963 | Monarchy/Rep.1964 |
| Zanzibar/ Tanzania | 1963 | 1963 | Sultanate/Rep.1964 |
| Malawi | 1964 | 1964 | Monarchy/Rep.1966 |
| Malta | 1964 | 1964 | Monarchy/Rep.1974 |
| Zambia | 1964 | 1964 | Republic |
| The Gambia | 1965–2013, 2018– | 1965 | Monarchy/Rep.1970 |
| Singapore | 1965 | 1965 | Republic |
| Guyana | 1966 | 1966 | Monarchy/Rep.1970 |
| Botswana | 1966 | 1966 | Republic |
| Lesotho | 1966 | 1966 | Lesotho monarchy |

*Appendix: Commonwealth Member Countries 1945–1995*

| Country | Commonwealth Member | UN Member | Constitutional Status |
|---|---|---|---|
| Barbados | 1966 | 1966 | Monarchy/Rep.2021 |
| Mauritius | 1968 | 1968 | Monarchy/Rep.1992 |
| Swaziland/ eSwatini | 1968 | 1968 | Swazi monarchy |
| Nauru | 1968 | 1999 | Republic |
| Tonga | 1970 | 1999 | Tonga monarchy |
| Western Samoa/ Samoa | 1970 (ind.1962) | 1976 | Samoa Head of State |
| Fiji | 1970–1987, 1997– | 1970 | Monarchy/Rep.1987 |
| Bangladesh | 1972 | 1974 | Republic |
| Bahamas | 1973 | 1973 | Monarchy/Realm |
| Grenada | 1974 | 1974 | Monarchy/Realm |
| Papua New Guinea | 1975 | 1975 | Monarchy/Realm |
| Seychelles | 1976 | 1976 | Republic |
| Solomon Islands | 1978 | 1978 | Monarchy/Realm |
| Tuvalu | 1978 | 2000 | Monarchy/Realm |
| Dominica | 1978 | 1978 | Republic |
| St Lucia | 1979 | 1979 | Monarchy/Realm |
| Kiribati | 1979 | 1999 | Republic |
| St Vincent and the Grenadines | 1979 | 1980 | Monarchy/Realm |
| Zimbabwe | 1980–2003 | 1980 | Republic |
| Vanuatu | 1980 | 1981 | Republic |
| Belize | 1981 | 1981 | Monarchy/Realm |
| Antigua and Barbuda | 1981 | 1981 | Monarchy/Realm |
| Maldives (ind.1965) | 1982–2016, 2020– | 1965 | Republic |
| St Kitts and Nevis | 1983 | 1983 | Monarchy/Realm |
| Brunei Darussalam | 1984 | 1984 | Brunei Sultanate |
| Namibia | 1990 | 1990 | Republic |
| Cameroon (ind.1961) | 1995 | 1960 | Republic |
| Mozambique (ind.1975) | 1995 | 1975 | Republic |

**Notes**

1 There are currently fifteen Commonwealth realms (including the UK) with King Charles III as their monarch and head of state.
2 Ireland ceased to be a Commonwealth Dominion on 18 April 1949 with the coming into force of the Republic of Ireland Act 1948. However, the Irish Government effectively withdrew from participation in Commonwealth affairs with the end of the Irish Free State in 1937.
3 Newfoundland, an original Commonwealth Dominion, voluntarily suspended self-government in 1934, accepting rule by a British-appointed Commission of Government

until 1949 when it chose confederation with Canada. It was not independently represented at Commonwealth meetings between 1945 and 1949.
4 India joined the United Nations at its foundation in 1945 under the British Raj. Pakistan joined the UN in 1947 with the creation of an independent Pakistan.
5 The original formation of the Commonwealth is usually dated to the Statute of Westminster (1931) though some prefer the adoption of the Balfour Declaration in 1926 or the year in which each of the founding members attained Dominion status and self-determination within the Commonwealth.

# Index

Act of Union (1910) 31, 37, 42, 51
Afghanistan, Soviet invasion (1979) 112
"Africa-Freedom in Our Lifetime" 2
African hostility to apartheid, Verwoerd reaction 59–60
African National Congress (ANC) 38; Anyaoku, influence 203; apartheid resistance 40; archive initiative 8; ban 51; electoral process 230–231; leadership, exile 152; march against violence (1990) *207*; Ramushwana, support 217; reactions to Chris Hani slaying, violence/l 215; refugees, return (1992 appeal) *214*; SDUs, conflict 217; support for EPG 244; unbanning 195, 202
African Resistance Movement (ARM) 63
African Transformation Movement 248–249
Africa Year (1960) 57
Afrikanerdom, triumph 242
Afrikaner Party, parliamentary seats (1948 election) 35
Afrikaner Volksfront (AVF) 208; assault on multiparty talks 226
Afrikaner Weerstandsbeweging (AWB): attack on World Trade Centre 226; failure in Bophuthatswana 229
Afro-Asian takeover 72, 242
Agreed Memorandum on the Commonwealth Secretariat (1965) 79, 102
Al-Jinnah, Muhammad 21–22
All Blacks rugby tour of South Africa (1970), mixed-race team involvement (South Africa acceptance) 104; 1976 Tour, international implications 105
*amakhosi* (chiefs), KwaZulu-Natal, exclusion from peace accord 213

Amery, Julian 153
Amin, Hafizullah 114
Amin, Idi human rights in Uganda 105
Amissah, Austin 209, 215
Anafu, Moses 144, 213, *214*
Anderson, David 21
anti-apartheid: activists, exit/exile 63–64; struggle, support 11
Anti-Apartheid Movement (AAM): AAM/Commonwealth relationships 6; formation 94; global AAM, emergency 50; global AAM, growth 13; reaction to EPG report, vindication of AAM approach 187; South Africa Bill renewal, protest/lobby 65; STST, tension 99
Anyaoku, Bunmi (Marlborough House reception, 1994) *249*
Anyaoku, Emeka 151; accusation of double-standards 250; Commonwealth influence 236; Commonwealth mission departs 204; COMSA 247; diplomatic initiative (EPG) 160–161; 'Freedom Elections' 225, 227, 228; Future of COMSA 214–5; honour 240; Major and Harare CHOGM (1991) 200; Mandela (Marlborough House, 1993) *228*; Marlborough House reception (1994) *149*; PW Botha meeting 204; Rhodesia crisis meeting(UN) 82; Secretary-General-length of tenure 5; South Africa's return to Commonwealth 232, 233, 234; special mission and transition 196–197; Special Mission to South Africa 202; Training NPKF 216; transition 245
Anyone But Mugabe (ABM) 140
apartheid: anti-apartheid activists, exit/exile 63; apartheid's end, transition problems 195; approach to study 1; 'blind eye',

258  *Index*

refusal 2–3; boycotting, sport 94; British Government, equivocal approach 53; campaign, 'virtual crusade' (Ramphal) 156; cessation 195, 225; change in, Commonwealth reluctance to debate 52; Commonwealth debate 60; compromises, inclusive elections (1994) 229–230; description 183; disintegration 232; dismantling, Commonwealth declaration on required steps 158–159; doctrine, implementation 35; ending apartheid, de Klerk) 195; ending, Commonwealth desire 48; ending, negotiation 150; EPG engagement 245; EPG report 183–184; evidence/archives 4–10; factors in ending 241; intensification of segregation (HNP desire) 38; Nationalist doctrine 38–39; oppressive system, codification 35; post-apartheid South Africa 240; post-apartheid South Africa, sport 125; reforming apartheid limits 248; resistance 39–42; rise 31; sanctions, internationalisation 187–190; short-term strengthening 242; Smuts, culpability 36–39; South Africa, relationship 12–14; sport, Gleneagles Agreement (1977) 99, 101–106; 'stain', removal (Ramphal) remarks) 2–3; state, Afrikaner ideological construct 36–37; total apartheid, policy 38; transition out of apartheid 3
Apartheid Museum, Johannesburg, Commonwealth information 9
Appleyard, Len 1
Arlott, John 98–99
Armstrong, Robert 119, 200
Ashford, Nicholas 180
Asquith, Herbert 37
Astor, David 183
Attlee, Clement 24–25
Azanian People's Organisation (AZAPO) 206

Baines, Gary 8–9, 13–14
Balewa, Abubakar Tafawa 60, 83
Ballinger, Margaret 60, 62, 63, 64
Bandung Conference (1955) 56–57
Barber, Anthony, Lord 160; efforts (EPG existence) 181; EPG report, signing 184
Barnard, Niel 173
Barrow, Nita 161, 165
Bevin, Ernie 20
binary Commonwealth: rift, deepening 188–189; UK and Commonwealth, symbiotic embrace 249–250

Bisho massacre 209
Black Africa/apartheid, growing tensionswith impact of, decolonisation 52
Black majority rule, basis 136–137
Bodleian Library, Anti-Apartheid/African collections (research usage) 6
Boer War 12
Boer Wars, white population conflict 37
Boesak, Allan 42, 161, 165, 204
Boipatong massacre (1992) 197
Botha, P.W.: black market oil purchases 190; EPG visit give credibility to government 152; replacement 244; South African acceptance of EPG 159; Thatcher intervention on EPG access 163; Thatcher leverage 155–156; Thatcher meeting 122; Thatcher meeting, controversy 156
Botha, Pik 166; Anyaoku meeting 204; South African Commonwealth return 233; support 163
Boutros-Ghali, Boutros 208, 211
Boycott Movement: formation 100; UK Labour, Liberal and trade union support 61
Brisbane Games *see* Commonwealth Games
Britain, double-dealing (India reaction) 32
British, loss of Commonwealth prefix 27
British Admiralty, race controversy over goodwill visit 53
British Commonwealth Association, proposed formation 96
British Crown, English whites (loyalty) 232
British Dominions: associated status, preference 24; prominence 20
British Empire, colour bar (usage) 37
British General Elections: 1966 102; 1970 85; 1974 39, 89; 1979 112–113
British Government, Rhodesia crisis, "Five Principles" 81
British Lions Tour (1980) 114–115, 155
British Victorian sports, introduction 95–96
Brockway, Fenner 61, 100
Brook, Norman 23
Brunei Darussalem, questionable democratic system 50
Budd, Zola 122; passport of convenience, AAM condemnation 122
Buthelezi, Mangosuthu Mandela view 166–167; Anyaoku meeting (Ulundi) 204–205; election boycott 229; election results, government post 230; involvement in negotiations/elections 232; leadership 236; Mandela

Index 259

saw Buthelezi as 'freedom fighter' 170–171; Mandela/Buthelezi, possible peace summit 213; peace summit 247; sidelined 202; Winnie Mandela perception 169
Butler, Mark 214
Byatt, Robin 144

Caetano, Marcelo 133
Callaghan, Jim: 1979 General Election (UK), loss 113; Cricket Council, withdrawal of South African invitation 102; Gleneagles Agreement 106; Gleneagles Retreat (1977) *107*
Cape Coloured, parentage of Basil D'Oliveira 98
Cape Town, St George's Cathedral 9, Princess Elizabeth 1947 radio broadcast *34*
Carnation Revolution, Portugal (1974) 133
Carrington, Peter, Lord 78; British Government concessions (Lusaka 1979 CHOGM) 137; divide and rule approach, opposition 139–140; influence 135, 137; Ramphal meeting 113; thinking, change 134
Castle, Barbara 61
Central African Federation (CAF): disintegration 74; emergence 53–54
Centre for the Study of Violence and Reconciliation (CSVR) 210
Chagla, M.C. (1962 Marlborough House arrival) *22*
Chalker, Lynda 6
Chappell, Duncan 214
Chikane, Frank 42
Chitnis, Lord 134
Chona, Mark 85, 88
Churchill, Winston 18, 19
civil liberties: apartheid government assault 39; Suzman protest 39
Coetsee, Kobie 166, 170, 173
Coetzee, J.M. 58
Cohen, Robin 190
Cold War: cessation 232; impact 56–57
Cole, Tony 189
colonial policy, self-government within Commonwealth 3
colour bar, usage 37
Committee on Assistance for Training for Training for Rhodesian Africans 84
common allegiance, redefinition 24
Common Market negotiations 76
Commonwealth: apartheid role 10–12; approach, strengths/weaknesses 123–124;

Asiatic countries (membership), admission (consequences) 24; binary Commonwealth, mutual interdependence 249–250; binary Commonwealth, rift (deepening) 188–189; collapse of EPG mission 180–181; Commonwealth disagreements on lifting sanctions, Commonwealth reform, overcoming 197–201; Commonwealth election observers(1980), Zimbabwee 140; Commonwealth Secretariat, proposal to establish 77–80; countries, two-tier ranking (consideration) 53–54; 'disintegration of Commonwealth' (Verwoerd) 60; election technical support 227–228; Empire, disguise (perception) 60; evidence/archives 4–10; future, Harare CHOGM meeting (importance) 200; governments, recognitions 132–133; human rights programme, changes 203; "Imperial" Commonwealth, decline 18; India membership, retention (question) 23; law officers, 1966 Smith meeting *79*; leaders, King George VI (1949 meeting) *26*; leaders, Queen Elizabeth II (1962 meeting) *73*; liberals, isolation (increase) 63–64; liberals, racial policies (unacceptability) 64; member countries (1945–1995) 254–255; membership, change 103; membership, formal offer 233; membership, Verwoerd reapplication 72–73; membership, Verwoerd wish to retain 56–57; Nassau division on sanctions 157–158; neighbours, SADF attack 244; New Commonwealth, creation 72; peaceful dialogue, promotion 203; post-war changes 42–43; post-war Commonwealth 19–24; Pretoria perception 203; Prime Ministers, meeting (London) 54–56; principle of non-interference in internal affairs 56; private family character 5–6; Rhodesian issue/meetings (1966) 83; Secretary-General, biennial reports 11; self-government, goal 23; South Africa exit 48, 242; South Africa exit, aftermath 60–65; South Africa membership 231–235; South Africa membership, resumption 248–249; South Africa return (debate), Queen Elizabeth (intervention) 233; South Africa sport, relationship 99–106; special mission (1991) but resistance to mediation or monitoring 203; sporting links, value 234–235; Stultz/Donnelly framework 88; transition and election role 248–249;

## 260  Index

two-tier Commonwealth, presence 24; unity and role of the Crown 25; unity, Crown (bonding role) 25; Zimbabwe, relations 153–157
Commonwealth Accord on Southern Africa 158–159
Commonwealth Committee of Foreign Ministers on Southern Africa (CFMSA): establishment 189; Mandela sanctions plea 198
Commonwealth Committee on Southern Africa, establishment 138
Commonwealth Eminent Persons Group (1986) *162*; access, securing 161–164; all-party negotiations, initiative (disaster) 180; birth 158–161; co-operation, rejection (implications) 163; diversity, deployment 161–164; EPG mission to South Africa 164–165; existence, Lord Barber (efforts) 181; initiative 190, 246–247; Mandela comments 183; Marlborough House meeting 180–181; mission 3, 11, 126, 150–152, 244; mission, aims 159; mission, promise (unravelling) 248; Moberly assessment 162; negotiation initiative 158–161; political dialogue, pursuit 184; proposals 171–172; rejection, possibility 163; report 182–185, 187; session *182*; South Africa, interaction 163–164; South Africa, negotiated solution (relationship) 172–173; South African mission 3, 11, 126, 150
Commonwealth Finance Ministers' Meeting (FMM) (1981) 117; hosting, problem 120
Commonwealth Games 95; XVth (1994) 235; Brisbane (1982) boycott pressures 112, 117, 118; Edinburgh (1986) 119, 121, 122, 184; Edmonton (1978) 105, 106
Commonwealth Games Federation (CGF): General Assembly, Code of Conduct 121; Ordia communication 116–117
Commonwealth Heads of Government Meetings (CHOGMs) 6, 85; biennial cycle 88; Cyprus (1993) 232; Harare meeting (1991) 196–197, 199–200, 203; Kuala Lumpur 1989 meeting 199–200; Limassol (1993) 227; London (1977) 104, 105, 243; London Review Meeting (1986) 185–187, *186*; Lusaka (1979) 133–138, 244; Lusaka (1979), Muzorewa/Patriotic Front (attendance) 137; Marlborough House meeting 78;

Melbourne 118; Nassau Summit (1985), sanctions 157–158, 180, 184; Singapore (1971) 86–89; summit, impact (1977) 105; watershed 157–158
Commonwealth Ministerial Action Group (CMAG), establishment 251
Commonwealth Monitoring Force (CMF) 133
Commonwealth Observer Group (COG): deployment 133; monitoring 141
Commonwealth Observer Group to South Africa (COGSA) 219, 228, 231, 236, 246
Commonwealth Observer Mission to South Africa (COMSA) 197, 209; COMSA phases of deployment 246–247; contribution 227; sustaining financial supportlems) 215
Commonwealth of Nations, India membership (declaration/affirmation) 25
Commonwealth Peacekeeping Assistance Group (CPAG): assembly 216–218; provision 246
Commonwealth Prime Ministers' Conference: 1960 59; 1961 59–60; 1965 81
Commonwealth Prime Ministers' Meeting: 1948/1949 24–25; 1960/1961, disagreements 241–242; 1966 83, *101*; Lagos 1966 83; London 1966 85
Commonwealth Relations Office (CRO) 79
Commonwealth Secretariat Act (1966) 5
Communism, Commonwealth membership political defence 58
Conference of Independent African States (1961) 59
Congress of South African Trade Unions (COSATU) initiative 8
Congress of the People, attendance 40
Conservative Government (UK), election(1970) 86
Conservative Party, election manifesto 86
Constitutional Conference: agreement chances 137; proposal 202
constructive engagement, Huddleston condemnation 156
Contact Group of Western nations 150
Convention for a Democratic South Africa (CODESA): CODESA II 207–208; opening (1991) 205–207; welcoming *206*
Council of Europe 107
Cowley, Annette 122
Craft, Hugh 27, 151, 152–153; picture *182*
Craven, Danie 125

Crossroads township, clashes 9
Crown, symbol of free association 25
Cuito Cuanavale (battle) 9
Curtin, John 18

Dabengwa, Dumiso 144
Dadoo, Yusuf 57, 61
Dayal, Rajeshwar 133
de Beer, Zach 58, 204
Debt Ceiling Act (USA), anti-apartheid amendment 188
debt relief, Commonwealth initiative 199
Decker, Mary collision, Olympics (1984)) 122
Declaration of Intent, All-Party negotiations 207
de-colonisation, dangers of too slow and too rapid progress 20
De Gaulle, Charles 76, 85
de Klerk, F.W.: Anyaoku proposals 205; apartheid, cessation 195; initiatives, praise 197; international dimension 241; Mandela greetings, exchange *196*; Mandela, clash 206; National Intelligence Agency material destruction authorisation 8; negotiation strategy 245
de Klerk, Willie 173
democracy: South African view 203; Westminster model 201
democracy-building, technical programmes of support 250
Democratic Party (DP) 204; electoral foothold 230–231
Department of International Relations and Cooperation material, research usage 8
Derby-Lewis, Clive (assassin) 215
Desai, Morarji (1962 Marlborough House arrival) *22*
detention without trial (Suzman protest) 39
Devlin Report, condemnation of 'police state' 74
de Zulueta, Philip 75
Diederichs, Nicolaas 38
Diefenbaker, John 73, 75
Doctrine of Lesser Risk 20
D'Oliviera, Basil 98–99, 122
domestic racial discrimination, globalised concern 11
Dominions, terminology (changes) 26–27
Donges, T.E. (South Africa sport racial policies) 97
Donnelly, Jack 4
Douglas-Home, Alec (Lord Home) 86; Rhodesia sovereignty requirements 80

Drew, George 75
Dubow, Saul 13, 54, 151
Duke and Duchess of Marlborough, land lease for building Marlborough House 72
Duncan, Patrick 54
Durr, Kent 232

Ecumenical Monitoring Programme in South Africa (EMPSA) 214, 228
Edmonton Games (1978) *see* Commonwealth Games
Eglin, Colin 39
El-Alamein, battle, Allied victory 31
Eloff, Sarel 95
Eminent Persons Group (EPG) (COMGEP) *see* Commonwealth Eminent Persons Group
English alibi 37, 39
English Test and County Cricket Board, swift action on rebel tour 122
eSwatini, questionable democratic system 250
European Community (EC) Foreign Ministers 160
European Community Observer Mission in South Africa (ECOMSA) 209
European Economic Community (EEC): Britain, application 72; negotiations, Macmillan Cabinet paper 76; UK/Britain: application 75–77
European Union (EU), election role 248–249
Evatt, Herbert (UN Charter Preamble drafting) 4

Fagan Commission, proposed relaxation of Black African migration restrictions 38
Falkland Islands, recapture 82
Fergusson, Ewen 161
Fifth Brigade *see* 'Gukurahundi' Fifth Brigade
financial sanctions, description 198–199
First, Ruth 61
First Boer Wars, white population conflict 37
First-Past-The-Post electoral system 35
Fisher, Nigel 20, 73, 76
Five Principles, Rhodesia (British Government) 81
Follows, Denis 115–116
Foreign and Commonwealth Office (FCO) 116, 135, 138, 143; sources 151
Fraser, Malcolm 103, 116, 135, 154; EPG co-chair 161; *EPG in session 182*;

EPG role, meeting with ANC 167; Howe claim of support 181; personal relationships 164
Fraser, Peter 18, 24
Freedom Charter: adoption 40; disagreements 57
Freedom Elections 225, 229–231; black/white voters, queuing (1994) *230*; violence, impact on negotiations 226–228
Freedom Front (FF) 236; electoral foothold 230; support 225
Freedom of information (FOI) request 8
Frontline States (FLS), impact in ending apartheid 1, 154, 248

Gallipoli, campaign 19
Gandhi, Indira 103
Gandhi, Mahatma 33
Gatting, Mike 124–125
Geldenhuys, Deon (framework usage) 151
Ghana, Commonwealth membership 56
Gilmour, Ian 142
Gleneagles Agreement (1977) 4, 94–95, 99, 100–106; adoption, impact 244; boycott, Thatcher relaxation 116–117; British Government/Muldoon interpretation 119; challenges 112–126; contributions 243–244; difficulties 114; implementation, problems 112; prelude 105; relaxation, difficulty 119; third party boycotts 124; UK government approach 138
Gleneagles Retreat (1977) *107*
global AAM: Commonwealth relationship 145; emergence 50; growth 13, 243
Goldberg, Denis 234
Gold Coast 56
Goldstone Commission 212
Gow, Ian 120
Graaff, De Villiers 58–59, 61
Gracey, Douglas 21–22
Greenhill, Lord 20
Grenada, US invasion (1983) 155
Griffiths, Jim 43
Group Areas Act 9
Group of Eminent Persons *see* COMGEP
Guelke, Adrian 151, 172, 210
'Gukurahundi' Fifth Brigade terror (Zimbabwe) 143–145
Gurney, Christabel 151–152

Hague, William 21
Haig, Glen 115

Hain, Peter 98, 107, 112, 125
Hall, Catherine 6
Hall, John, peace accord (leadership) 212–213
Halt All Racial Tours (HART) 119, 120
Hani, Chris (assassination) 215, 226
Hanlon, Joseph 189
Hanslope Park, colonial files (discovery) 21
Harare CHOGM meeting *see* Commonwealth Heads of Government Meetings
Harare Commonwealth Declaration (1991) 4, 200, 201, 245, 250
Harare principles, abuse (accusations) 251
Harris, John 63
Harris, Verne 8
Hawke, Bob 155, 185, 187, 189; EPG report comment 183
Hayden, Bill 187
Heads of Government 6; avoid provoking Thatcher 154–155; Elephant Hills Retreat 200; EPG mission, special review meeting 164, 181; ideas of shared Commonwealth leadership 2; Lusaka 136; meeting, Kuala Lumpur (1989) 199–200; Ramphal, channel of communication 138–139; relationship 124; special mission (1991) 202
Heads-Only Retreat, innovation 103–104
Healey, Denis 89
Heath, Ted Victory in General Election (1970): aftermath 88–89; meeting with Arnold Smith 88; Singapore CHOGM (1971), Queen, arms to South Africa, (1971 Kuan Yew meeting) *87*
Hendricks, Krom 96
Herenigde Nasionale Party (HNP): native policy, racial appeal 35; decisive victory, 1948 elections 35; segregation, intensification/into apartheid 38
*herrenvolk* mentality, rejection by Black Africans 35
Heseltine, Michael 144
Heunis, J. 170
High-Level Group (HLAG) of Ten Heads of Government, formation 199–200
Hlengwa, Inkosi Mhlabunzima Wellington *214*
*HMS Illustrious* (goodwill visit) 53
Hofmeyr, Jan 31, 36, 39, 51
Hola scandal (1959) 21
Holmes, John 20

Home, Lord 60
Hoskyns, John 162
Howe, Geoffrey: CODESA distinguished observers 206n58; European Council demarche 182; no EPG conclusion, claim 180–181; Prime Minister, substitution for at review meeting (1986) 186; Thatcher EPG Chair nomination 159–160
Huddleston, Trevor 40–41, 98, 150; AAM president 187; constructive engagement condemnation 156; farewells 100
Huggins, Godfrey 18
Human misery/deprivation, apartheid South Africa, EPG report 183–184
human rights programme, changes (Commonwealth) 203
Humphrey, John Peters (UDHR draft creation) 4
Hurd, Douglas 155

"Imperial" Commonwealth, decline 18
Imperial Cricket Conference (ICC), formation 96
in-country deployments, Commonwealth observers 197
Independent Electoral Commission (IEC): challenges 225; formal complaints investigation 231; impact 228; recommendations 231
India: Commonwealth of Nations, India membership 25; constitution, adoption 23; independence, perception 35; independent Commonwealth dominion, acceptance 24; national sovereignty 25–26; republicanism 25
India, possible Commonwealth secession 23
Indians (South African population) treatment, UNGA vote 3–4
Indo-Pakistan conflict (1947) 21
Inkatha Freedom Party (IFP) 204; electoral wins 230–231; impact 229
Institute for a Democratic Alternative (IDASA) 172
Institute of Commonwealth Studies 152; collections, research usage 6–7
Institute of Race Relations 62
International Committee of the Red Cross, humanitarian visits 166
international community, pariah state re-entry (Commonwealth membership) 233

International Convention against Apartheid in sport, ratification 125
International Court of Justice (ICJ), African countries (legal challenge) 33
International cricket, Black-white split 124
International Cricket Council 101
International Declaration Against Apartheid in Sport (UN), adoption 120–121
International Donor Conference on Human Resource Development, co-sponsorship 246
International Election Observers (IEOs), legal definition of role) 227
international observers, criticisms 211–212
International Olympic Committee 101
International Rugby Football Board 101
International Table Tennis Federation (ITTF), white South Africa expulsion 97
Ivey, James 113, 116

Jagger Library, collections (research) 8
Johannesburg Drill Hall, Treason Trial protestors (1956) *41*
Jordan, Clive 182
Jordan, Pallo 167

*karma*, washing out past evil (Nehru) 26
Kashmir: 1947 war and divisibility of Crown 21–22; issue, raising at UN 32–33
Katlehong, political violence 210
Kaunda, Kenneth 85, 103, 139, 165, 185; Lusaka CHOGM (1979) *136*
Kennedy, Edward 188
Kenya, Mau Mau insurgency 21
Kenyatta, Jomo 103
Khama, Seretse 103; British Government banishment 53
King, W.L. Mackenzie 18
King David Hotel, Jerusalem, bombing 20–21
King George VI: Cape Town arrival, South Africa tour 33; Commonwealth leaders, meeting (1949) *26*; first Head of Commonwealth, Dominions at war 21–22; South Africa's Commonwealth membership and recognition of Queen as Head 56
King Moshoeshoe, appeal for support for his people 158
Kinnock, Neil 180–181
Kirk, Norman 105

Klotz, Audie 11–12
Krogh, Desmond 190
Kuala Lumpur CHOGM meeting *see* Commonwealth Heads of Government Meetings
KwaZulu-Natal: 1994 elections, negotiated outcome 231; conflict resolution 9; violence 209–210, 229

Labour Party (UK), defeat in 1970 election 85
Laidlaw, Chris 104, 120
Lambeth Borough Council 199
Lancaster House Agreement (1979) 138–140, 144–145
Lange, David 158
Lee, Kuan Yew Singapore CHOGM (1971): Gleneagles group 106; Heath meeting 87; new Commonwealth leadership 103
Legum, Colin 118
Liberal Party (South Africa) 61; pacifism/constitutionalism 63
liberals, cultural differences on racial policies among whites) 64
Lilliesleaf Farm, remembrance of resistance 9
Local Dispute Resolution Committees (LRDCs), contact 212–213
London Agreement (1949) 24–27
London Declaration (1949) 1; adoption 27; Malan acceptance 52–53
London Review Meeting (1986) 185–187, *186*
Louw, Eric 50, 54; informal debate on racial policies 56
Luce, Lord 141–142
Lusaka *see* Commonwealth Heads of Government Meetings
Lusaka Accord, implementation 138
Lyford Cay, leader retreat 158

Macleod, Iain 20
Macmillan, Harold 60; Makarios, welcoming *55*; South Africa's racial policies and Commonwealth 52; UK's application to European Community 75–77; "Wind of Change" speech 51
Maharaj, Mac 167
Maharaja of Jammu and Kashmir 18
Mahathir, Mohamad 158, 205
Major, John 100, 189, 199, 233
majoritarian voting systems, usage 123–124

Makarios, Archbishop 60; Macmillan welcome *55*
Makiwane, Tennyson 61
Malan, Daniel F. 1, 35, 52; London Declaration acceptance 52; popular vote and seats (1948 election) 36
Malawi (Nyasaland), emergence 74
Malaysia, independence 233
Malecela, John 161; Winnie Mandela meeting *168*
Malhoutra, Moni 6, 182
Mandela, Nelson 35, 151; Anyaoku (Marlborough House, 1993) *228*; arrest 40; Buthelezi, peace summit (need) 247; Buthelezi, peace summit, proposed 213; Castle, meeting 61; de Klerk, clash 206; de Klerk, greetings (exchange) *196*; election to presidency (1994) 230–231; EPG comments 183; freedom, Botha offer 166; Harare meeting 201; impact on decisive change 241; influence with ANC leadership 171; leadership in campaign against South Africa in Commonwealth 50; London visit (1962) *62*; Pollsmoor prison access 142; Pollsmoor prison, meeting with EPG 166; "possible negotiating concept" 165–171; post-prison UK press conference 6–7; presidency, end of term 251; prison records, access 8; release 156, 195, 197; Robben Island 166; Youth League president 40
Mandela, Winnie 168–169; Malecela meeting *168*
Manley, Michael 103, 106, 124, 205
Marlborough House: Commonwealth Secretariat archive, political accountability 4–5; fine rooms 79–80
Marshall, Peter 26
Marylebone Cricket Club (MCC), team tour announcement 98
Masire, Quett 157, 165
Matabeleland (Zimbabwe), massacres (reports) 143–144
Mau Mau insurgency 21
Maxwell, Robert 184–185
May, Alex 75, 77
Mazrui, Ali 242
Mbeki, Thabo 6, 11, 125, 167, 173, 204; Marlborough House reception (1994) *249*; seeking ANC support on sanctions 198
McFarlane, Neil 120
McIntyre, David 74, 150, 189

Index 265

McKinnon, Don, New Zealand Foreign Minister (perspective) 10–11
Mells House talks 172–173
memorialisation, impact 9
memory wars 9, 13–14
Menzies, Robert 27, 60, 76
Meyer, Rolf 173
Milner, Alfred, white unity (winning over the Dutch 1897 statement) 37
mini-United Nations, danger of Commonwealth becoming 88
Minto, John 119
Minty, Abdul 61, 88, 211
miscegenation, problem (*Die Transvaler* perspective) 97
Mitchell, C.R. 151
Mitchell, Douglas (white supremacist) 58–59
mixed sport, South African ban 97
Mkwetu, Clarence 208
Moberly, Patrick (EPG mission assessment) 162
Montreal Olympics (1976) 101
Mortimer, John 183
Moscow Declaration 18
Moscow Olympics boycott 142–143; Thatcher boycott, Muldoon support 116; Western support 112
Moshoeshoe *see* King Moshoeshoe
Mountbatten, Lord, Indian force dispatch authorisation 22
Mshayazafe Hostel, assault 217
Mugabe, Robert 185; British miscalculation 142; exclusion of Mugabe from talks 142; Harare principles abuse, Zimbabwe exit 251; Lancaster House Constitutional talks (1979) *139*; Thatcher regular contact 144–145; ZANU-PF election victory(1980) 133
Muldoon, Robert: criticism in discouraging sporting contact 119–120; 1975 general election 105; anti-apartheid protest 119; electoral base, dog-whistle issue 119; Moscow boycott support 116; Muldoon letter to Ramphal 107–108
Mulroney, Brian 185
Multi-Party Negotiating Forum (MPNF), physical assault 226
Munro, Hector 115, 119
Murray, Gilbert 19
Muzenda, Simon (Lancaster House Constitutional 1979 talks *139*
Muzorewa, Abel 140; international legitimacy 137; leadership of nationalist delegation, Kingstom CHOGM (1975) 132; Muzorewa's mandate 134; neutralising lMuzorewa obbying 135; no recognition, Lord Carrington (influence) 135; possible coalition with Nkomo 142; recognition of internal settlement (Thatcher instinct) 113; Smith-Muzorewa government, recognition delay 134

Nassau Accord 164; adoption 180
Nassau Summit *see* Commonwealth Heads of Government Meetings
Natal, detachment (possibility) 58–59
Natal Indian Congress, boycott 33
Natal violence 211
National Archives, usage 7
National Committee of Liberation 63
National Electoral Observer Network (NEON), formation 228
National Intelligence Agency material, destruction (de Klerk authorisation) 8
National Intelligence Service (NIS) 173
Nationalists: doctrine, apartheid (cornerstone) 38–39; British High Commission view of referendum result 59; isolation, Commonwealth exit 65
National Party congress, Botha address 156
National Peace Accord (NPA) 204, 209, 213; adoption 202
National Peace Committee 212
National Peacekeeping Force (NPKF) 216–218; training 228, 246
national self-determination, decolonisation struggles 201
National Socialism, sympathies 12
nations, polyphonic contribution 19–20
Native Representation Council, establishment/abolishment 38
Natives (Urban Areas) Act (1923) 38
Naude, Beyers 42, 214
Negotiating Concept, viability 167
Nehru, Jawaharlal 103; Attle seeking constitutional link 25; India, independence and full Commonwealth membership through Headship 25; India, seeking to retain Commonwealth membership as republic 23; Marlborough House arrival (1962) *22*
Nel, N.M. 203
Nelson Mandela Foundation, archive (research) 8
New Commonwealth, creation 72
New Commonwealth: South Africa, interaction 201–207

266  *Index*

New Zealand: challenges to existing sporting links with South Africa 104; Gleneagles Agreement (1977), problems of implementation 112–126; Ramphal intervention 105; SA sporting contacts, New Zealand embarrassment 105
New Zealand Rugby Union (NZRU), Springboks invitation 117
Nhlanhla, Joe 167
NIBMAR (No Independence Before Majority African Rule) 83, 85
Nixon, Richard M. 10
Nkobi, Thomas 167
Nkomo, Joshua 140, 142; British hope of Muzorewa alliance 142; Lancaster House Constitutional 1979 talks *139*
Nkrumah, Kwame 75, 103; sanctions 157; Support for a Commonwealth Secretariat 77
No Independence Before Majority African Rule (NIBMAR) 83, 85
Non-Aligned Movement (NAM), anti-apartheid struggle support 11
non-interference, principle 52
non-whites: majority excluded from referendum, campaign against republic) 50; political rights, reduction 38
Northern Rhodesia: Afrikaner infiltration 43; Southern Rhodesia/Nyasaland, combination 74
Nyerere, Julius 103; Tanzania Commonwealthwithdrawal threat 87

Obasanjo, Olusegun 139, 164; EPG co-chair 161
Olympic Games (Montreal 1976) 105
Olympic Movement, South Africa suspension 97
Onslow, Sue 144
Open Secrets, FOI requests (usage) 8
Operation Neptune, allied war preparation 18
Orange Free State 96
*Order of the Companions of O.R. Tambo, The,* (honour) 240
Ordia, Abraham 115, 116
Organisation of African Unity (OAU) 154, 197; anti-apartheid struggle support 11; Council of Ministers, declaration adoption 121; election role 248–249; impact 1
Organisation of African Unity Observer Mission in South Africa (OAU-OMSA) 212

Orr-Ewing, Ian 53
Ovenden, Keith 189

Paget, Reg 53
Pahad, Aziz 6, 235
Pan-Africanist Congress (PAC): ban 51, 54; cessation 195; electoral foothold 230–231; formation 57, 206
Pandit, Vijaya Lakshmi 32
Park Station, Johannesburg, time bomb (placement) 63
Parsons, Anthony 160
pass laws, African demonstration *13*
Patriotic Front: Lancaster House Constitutional 1979 talks *139*; Lusaka 1979 CHOGM attendance 137
Patriotic Front of Zimbabwe (PF), inclusion 133
Paxman, Jeremy 144
Payne, Anthony 105
Peace Conference of Paris, British Dominions (influence) 20
Peace of Vereeniging (1902) 37
peace structures, establishment 212–213
people-to-people sanctions 198
Permanent Under-Secretary (PUS), Foreign Office advice 65
Pietersen, Oscar, Soweto student, (South African Police killing) 243
Pillay, Vella 61
Pindling, Lynden 185
Pollock, Graeme 99
Pollsmoor prison, EPG access to Mandela 152
Pollsmoor prison, Mandela meetings with EPG 166–167, 169–171
Pope, Jeremy 120, 121
Portugal, coup d'état *see* Carnation revolution
"Possible Negotiating Concept" 151, 152, 169–171, 201–202, 244
"possible negotiating concept" (Mandela) 165–171
post-apartheid South Africa 240
post-apartheid South Africa, resumption of international sport 125
post-war Commonwealth 19–24
prejudice/fear, HNP appeal 35–36
Pretoria, shift of support after Sharpeville 242
Pretoria-Witwatersrand-Vaal (PWV), violence 211
Prince of Wales, Marlborough House reception (1994) *249*

Princess Elizabeth: 1947 Cape Town radio broadcast *34*; Cape Town arrival 33
Princess Margaret, Cape Town arrival 33
Privy Council, appeal 54
Progressive Party: Commonwealth membership threatened by racial policies 58; formation 63; impact 39

Queen Anne, land lease for Marlborough House 72
Queen Elizabeth: Cape Town arrival 33; royal warrant (1959) 72; Silver Jubilee (1977) 103; South African return, debate (intervention by Head) 233
Queen Elizabeth II: Commonwealth leaders (1962 meeting) *73*; Marlborough House reception (1994) *249*; South Africa recognition of Head 56

race discrimination, South African association 58
races, separation under apartheid 39
racial discrimination: Black African and church resistance 40–42; against Black Africans 37; Commonwealth and South Africa 48; against Indians 32; racism: opposition 106; Suzman protest 39
Rahman, Tunku Abdul 54
Rahman, Ziaur (1979 Lusaka CHOGM) 136
rainbow society 164
Ramaphosa, Cyril 173, 204, 208, 248–249; Commonwealth links 249–250
Ramphal, Shridath "Sonny" 151; Alongside Commonwealth Eminent Persons Group *162*; apartheid, stain (removal) 2–3; CHOGM 1977 meeting, perspective 104; Commonwealth Secretary-General, length of tenure 5; congratulations on EPG mission and report 183; election as SG (1975) 103; Gleneagles Agreement (1977), impact 95; interview 104; Muldoon communication 107–108; negotiations, joint chairmanship of EPG 161; Rhodesia problem 100–101; Secretaries-General interference, perspective 145; speeches/ correspondence/memoirs, availability 7, 10; tenure ends, succeeded by Anyaoku 199; ZIPRA ceasefire, Lusaka CHOGM negotiation 135
Ramsammy, Sam 97, 106, 120
Ramushwana, Gabriel, National Peace-Keeping Force (ANC supporter) 217
Rand, value (fall) 190

Reagan, Ronald (constructive engagement): joint policy 152–153; policy, condemnation 187
Reagan, Ronald (South Africa policy problem) 188
Reconciliation and Development Committees, establishment 213
Reconstruction and Development Programme (RDP): provisions, impact 246; support 226, 234
Reddy, Enuga 154, 195
Reeve, Anthony 203
Reeves, Archbishop Ambrose 41–42
Reeves, Archbishop Sir Paul, (New Zealand) 236
referendum: campaign, Verwoerd entry 50; republican status question 51–60
RENAMO, South African collusion (evidence) 156
Renwick, Robin 173, 190, 199
Representation of Natives Act (1936) 38
Republic Bill, parliamentary debate 58
Reunited National Party (HNP), native policy (racial appeal) 35
Rhodes, Cecil 96
Rhodesia: crisis 10; guerrilla activity 133; independence, terms for British Parliament decision 80; problem of racism (Ramphal) 100–101; rebellion 11, 72, 80–85; Southern Rhodesians (neighbours), linking (prevention) 43; Southern/Northern Rhodesia, Afrikaner infiltration 43; sovereignty (granting), Douglas-Home requirements 80; white settler regime, Commonwealth preoccupation 242–243; white settler rule, cessation 12; white-settler state, viability (cessation) 247; Wilson government, policy 83
Richards, Trevor 120–121
Robben Island, Mandela move to Pollsmoor 166
Robben Island Museum, tapestry of memory 9
Row, Raman Subba 114
Royal Commonwealth Society (RCS) Collections, research usage 6
Royal Tour (1947), South Africa, impact 33–36, 54
Rugby Football Union (RFU) 115
Rugby World Cup, South Africa exclusion 126
rule of law: apartheid government assault 39; Suzman protest 39

Sachs, Albie (assassination survival) 6–7
Salim, Salim 113–114
Sampson, Anthony 13, 183
sanctions, implementation/impact (monitoring) 84
sanctions, internationalisation 187–190
Sanctions campaign 180
Sanctions Committee, establishment 84–85
Sandys, Duncan 89
Schreiner, Olive 249–250
Scott, Archbishop Ted 161, 165, 166, 167
Scott, Michael 40
Second All-African People's Conference (AAPC), meeting (1960) 57
Second Boer Wars: impact 95; white population conflict 37
Second Chimurenga (liberation war) 133
Secretary-General: biennial reports 11; 'dynamic personality' requirement 78; interference, Ramphal perspective 145; SA visit, usefulness 203; shared ideas in Commonwealth leadership 2
security forces, children protest *123*
segregated sport, opponents 94
segregation, Smuts attitude 36–39
Self-Defence Units (SDUs), ANC 217
Shamuyarira, Nathan 198
Sharpeville 48; lessons 51; violence 212; massacre (1960) 3, 32, 51–60, 241
Siege of Mafeking 95
Simon's Town Agreement 86, 89
Singapore Declaration of Commonwealth Principles (1971) 88, 106, 4, 201, 243
Singh, Hari 18
Singh, Sardar Swaran 161, 165; Wilson meeting (1966) *101*
Sisulu, Walter 40
Skinner, Rob 13
Slovo, Gillian/Jo 61
Smith, Arnold 82, 242; Commonwealth law officers 1966 meeting *79*; Downing Street, Heath (change of tone) 86; health, problem 132; length of Commonwealth tenure 5; memoir 10; memoirs, sport boycott reference 100; speeches/ correspondence/memoirs, availability 7; warning to UK over Rhodesia 84
Smuts, Jan Christian 19; apartheid, relationship 36–39; death 36; defeat 12; government, opposition 35; leadership, risk 35; popular vote 36; racism 39; reputation, Royal Tour (1947) impact 33–36; segregation, relationship 36–39;

UN Charter Preamble drafting 4; United Nations, relationship 31–33
Snyman, J.P, siege of Mafeking (sanctity of Sabbath) 95
Sobukwe, Robert 57
social mixing, (*Die Transvaler* opinion 97
Sophiatown, forced removals (opposition) 41
South Africa: African governance, unacceptability 43; aftermath 60–65; all-party negotiations,impact of violence 245; anti-apartheid activists, exit/ exile 63–64; apartheid, negotiation 150; apartheid, relationship 12–14; arms, supply 72, 85–89; arms sales, resumption (UK government announcement) 243; bloodbath, UK government fear 184; borders, forward defence 247–248; Britain, interaction (dilemma) 42–43; Commonwealth Eminent Persons Group (1986) mission 164–165; Commonwealth Eminent Persons Group (1986), interaction 163–164; constitutional settlement, Commonwealth role 202; Defiance Campaign, Freedom Charter 40; economy, control 198; "effective sanctions" 180–181; elections (1948) 35–36; elections (1994), malfeasance (evidence) 231; Eminent Persons Group (COMGEP) mission 3, 11, 126, 150–152, 244; exit (Commonwealth) 48; history, liberal interpretations 12; human misery/deprivation, creation 183–184; Indian population treatment, UNGA vote 3–4; internal politics, strengthening Afrikaner control 50–51; internal unrest, increase 57; international council expulsions 48; international missions, presence (impact) 227; international observers, presence (impact) 225; international sport teams, all-white makeup (requirement) 97; International Table Tennis Federation (ITTF), white South African body expulsion 97; isolation/ ostracism, increase 62; long-term credits, deprivation 190; majority rule, obtaining 243; membership (Commonwealth) 231–235; mission 150; mixed sport, ban 97; negotiated solution, EPG (relationship) 172–173; New Commonwealth, interaction 201–207; new investment ban, lifting

197; no desire for external mediation 219; official memory, sanitisation 8; opinion (change), Sharpeville massacre (impact) 242; peaceful dialogue, promotion 203; political dialogue, process (problems) 202; political forces, impartial stance 227; political reform, engagement (failure) 184; race/sport, relationship 95–99; racial segregation, enforcement 23; racial situation, Louw (discussions) 56; raid, Thatcher condemnation 180; regime, obduracy/intransigence 183; republic, Nationalist arguments 57–58; republican status, question (referendum) 51–60; SA departure from Commonwealth, Duke of Devonshire comment 65; sanctions, internationalisation 187–190; security forces, children protest *123*; sovereignty, infringement 207; sport, Commonwealth (relationship) 99–106; sport, introduction 95–99; sport, mixed-race team (acceptance) 104–105; sport, racial policies 97; sporting boycott 107; tourism promotion, ban (lifting) 197; UK government, pandering to SA pressure 53; UNSC voluntary arms embargo 86; violence, combatting 207–216; violence, deaths 209–210; violence, impact 226–228

South Africa Bill, renewal (AAM protest/lobby) 65

South Africa Government: defeat, impossibility 167; negotiations 169; State of Emergency declaration 51

South African Armed Forces, UK (link) 64

South African Communist Party (SACP): activists, impact 61; apartheid resistance 40

South African Congress Alliance, Freedom Charter principles 40

South African cricket tour to England (1970), cancellation 102–103

South African Defence Force (SADF): attacks on Botswana, Zambia and Zimbabwe 171–172, 202, 244; impact of raid 180–181

South African Democracy Education Trust 11

South African Football Association, English FA reaffiliation 96

South African History Archive (SAHA) initiatives 8

South African Institute of Race Relations 62

South African Native National Congress (SANNC), rights of Black Africans) 40

South African Non-Racial Olympic Committee (SAN-ROC) 106; formation 97

South African Sports Association (SASA), establishment 97

Southern African Development Community (SADC) 153–154; South African membership benefits 234

Southern African Development Coordination Conference (SADCC), formation 153–154

Southern Africa, racial justice (issue) 250

Southern Rhodesia: Afrikaner infiltration 43; crisis, development 76–77; neighbours, linking (prevention) 43; Northern Rhodesia/Nyasaland, combination 74; reversion 141

South West Africa (Absence of African political autonomy) 32

South-West Africa, mandated territory (incorporation) 31–32, 43

Soviet imperialism, tide (halting) 153

Soweto Student revolt (1976) 13–14, 105

Soweto, violence 210

Sparks, Alistair 151

Special Mission to South Africa (1991): Anyaoku proposal to Heads 202; Commonwealth reengagement 245; visit to South Africa 203–205

sport: Gleneagles Agreement (1977) 99, 101–106; international sport teams, all-white makeup (requirement) 97; mixed sport, South African ban 97; mixed-race team, South Africa agreement 104; mixing, problems 97; race, relationship 95–99; "subversive" Black sportsmen, South Africa passport refusal 97; whites/non-whites, separate organisations 97

Sport Action Committees, formation 125

Springboks: global event 119; protests 117–118; rugby tour (1969) 101–102

Stals, Chris 190

Standerton parliamentary seat, Smuts defeat (1948) 36

"standstill" Bill (UK), UK-South Africa relations (Commonwealth exit) 64–65

"Stooge tour" accusation, South African Barbarians (1979) 113

Stop the Seventy Tour (STST) 94, 113; AAM, tensions about direct action 99
Stuart, James 167
Stultz, Newell 3–4
Supreme Council for Sport in Africa (SCSA) 113, 115
Suzman, Helen 39, 63, 187
*Swart gevaar* (black peril), containment 35
Swaziland, absolute monarchy, questionable democratic system 250
Swinton, Lord (South Africa statement) 43

Talboys, Brian 117
Tambo, Adelaide 204, 232
Tambo, Oliver 6, 36, 40, 61, 165–166, 167, 168 204, 232; national honour 240
Tanzania, Commonwealth withdrawal, Nyerere threat 87
Ten Heads of Government, High-Level Group (HLAG) formation 199–200
Terre' Blanche, Eugene 226, 229
Test and County Cricket Board (TCCB) 114
Thakur, Vineet 32
Thatcher, Margaret 185; apartheid boycott involvement 116; Botha meeting 122–123, 163; Botha meeting, controversy 156; Botha support 163; election (1979) 108; Howe nomination 159–160; internal settlement commitment 134; leadership on Gleneagles, problem 119–120; Lusaka 1979 CHOGM *136*; Mugabe, meeting 144–145; opposition to sanctions 150; position, undermining "constructive engagement" 152–153; power, loss 199; private archive, research usage 7; Ramphal meeting 113; sanctions, lifting 197; signals 150; triumph 113; turbulence 245; Zimbabwe involvement/ impact 132
Thokoza, political violence 210
Tobruk, (Libyan campaign) fall 31
Tonga High Commission, recruitment of Tongans (unofficial tour) 125
total apartheid', key policy elements 38
Transitional Executive Council (TEC) 216; formation 227
transnational thinking, impact 6
Transvaal Indian Congress 38
Trelford, Donald 144
Trend, Burke 77–78

Trent Bridge, Test match 102
Treurnicht, Andries 204
Triomf (Sophiatown designation) 41
Trudeau, Pierre 88, 106
Truman, Harry S. 19
Truth and Reconciliation Commission (TRC) process 12–13
Tutu, Archbishop Desmond 42; catastrophe warning 180; international monitoring 207; picture *181*; sanctions 172
two-tier Commonwealth, presence 24

Uganda, human rights issues 105
Umbumbulu, conflict resolution 213
UN Charter Preamble, drafting 4
Unilateral Declaration of Independence (UDI) 80–81; military intervention, British Government failure 82
United Cricket Board of South Africa, application (ICC support) 126
United Democratic Front (UDF) 167; initiative 8
United Kingdom (UK): assistance to Zimbabwe 185–186; prophylactic action 144–145; South African Armed Forces, link 64; Zimbabwe, relations 153–157
United Nations (UN): Panel of Eminent Persons on the Role of Transnational Corporations in South Africa 154; Smuts, relationship 31–33
United Nations General Assembly (UNGA) 31; trusteeship agreement proposal 32
United Nations Observer Mission in South Africa (UNOMSA) 209, 211; impact 228
United Nations Organisations, prominence of British Dominions 20
United Nations Security Council (UNSC): expansion 20; resolution 134 (1960), UK support (absence) 32; resolution 772 208–209; resolution 772/92 245; selective mandatory sanctions vote 81; voluntary arms embargo 86
United Party (UP): 1948 elections, Royal Tour (impact) 33–36; opposition 35
Universal Declaration of Human Rights, first draft (John Peters Humphrey) 4
University of Cape Town, collections (research) 8
University of the Free State archives, examination 173
University of Witwatersrand, collections (research) 8

Unkhonto We Sizwe (MK) cadres, impact 9
"Upholding the Law" editorial 215

Vance, Cyrus 208
van Rensburg, Patrick 61
Van Vuuren, Hennie 8, 14, 247
*verkrampte* (conservative)/*verligte* (liberal), divide 64
Verwoerd, Hendrik: attempted assassination 54; ideologue 49; Macmillan speech, impact 44; objectives 49; premiership, succession 52; referendum campaign entry 50; referendum triumph 49–50; republic and survival of white man 64; South Africa reception 48
Viljoen, Constand 208; negotiations 234
Viljoen, Gerrit 204
Vimy Ridge (battle) 19
violence: combatting 207–216; suspension 245
*Volkstaat:* advocates, negotiations 234; support, implication 225
Voortrekker Monument, remembering the past 9
Vorster, John 98

Waldheim, Kurt 114
Walker, Patrick Gordon 43
Walus, Janusz (assassin) 215
Wandesforde-Smith, Geoffrey 12
"The Way Ahead" proposals 77
Webster, Charles (UN Charter Preamble drafting) 4
Westland WASP helicopters, replacement/sale 86, 89
white Boer republic, vote 57
white Dominion 42
white hegemony, Verwoerd appeal in referendum debate 58
white opposition, diminished support 64
white racial supremacy, application in sport 96–97
whites, sporting contact and post-apartheid possibilities 125
Whitlam, Gough 103

Whyte, Quentin, loss of Commonwealth (identity) 62–63
Wilf Isaacs XI, protests 99
William Cullen Library, collections (research) 8
Williams, Eric 77
Williams, Ruth 53
Wilson, Harold 85; anti-apartheid credentials demonstrations, Springboks Rugby (1969) 101; election defeat (1970) 85; parliamentary majority, fragility (1965) 82–83; Singh meeting (1966) 82–83
Wilson, Mary (Singh 1966 meeting) *101*
"Wind of Change" speech (Macmillan) 51
Worger, William 12
World Cup, Men's Football (1966) 102
World Trade Centre (Kempton Park), assault 226
Wren, Christopher (Marlborough House) 72, 80

Yar'Adua, Shehu Musa 106

Zambia (Northern Rhodesia), independent nation 74
Zimbabwe: birth 141–143; Commonwealth election observers, white voter meeting (1980) *141*; 'Gukurahundi' Fifth Brigade, killings/ 143–145; independence 153; Matabeleland, massacres (reports) 143–144; nationalist forces, rivalry 143; settlement (1979–1980) 112; Thatcher, impact 132; UK relations, 'constructive engagement' 153
Zimbabwe African National Union (ZANU) 132
Zimbabwe African National Union-Patriotic Front (ZANU-PF) 142
Zimbabwe African People's Union (ZAPU) 132, 143
Zimbabwe People's Revolutionary Army (ZIPRA), ceasefire 135
Zuma, Jacob 9, 204
Zungula, Vuyo 248–249